THE WAR FOR LATE NIGHT

ALSO BY BILL CARTER

The Late Shift: Letterman, Leno, and the Network Battle for the Night

Desperate Networks

THE WAR FOR
LATE NIGHT

WHEN LENO WENT EARLY
AND TELEVISION WENT CRAZY

BILL CARTER

VIKING

VIKING

Published by the Penguin Group

Penguin Group (USA) Inc., 375 Hudson Street, New York, New York 10014, U.S.A.
• Penguin Group (Canada), 90 Eglinton Avenue East, Suite 700, Toronto, Ontario,
Canada M4P 2Y3 (a division of Pearson Penguin Canada Inc.) • Penguin Books Ltd,
80 Strand, London WC2R 0RL, England • Penguin Ireland, 25 St. Stephen's Green,
Dublin 2, Ireland (a division of Penguin Books Ltd) • Penguin Books Australia Ltd,
250 Camberwell Road, Camberwell, Victoria 3124, Australia (a division of Pearson
Australia Group Pty Ltd) • Penguin Books India Pvt Ltd, 11 Community Centre,
Panchsheel Park, New Delhi – 110 017, India • Penguin Group (NZ), 67 Apollo Drive,
Rosedale, North Shore 0632, New Zealand (a division of Pearson New Zealand Ltd) •
Penguin Books (South Africa) (Pty) Ltd, 24 Sturdee Avenue, Rosebank, Johannesburg
2196, South Africa

Penguin Books Ltd, Registered Offices:
80 Strand, London WC2R 0RL, England

First published in 2010 by Viking Penguin,
a member of Penguin Group (USA) Inc.

10 9 8 7 6 5 4 3 2 1

Page 406 constitutes an extension of this copyright page.

LIBRARY OF CONGRESS CATALOGING IN PUBLICATION DATA
Carter, Bill, date.
The war for late night : when Leno went early and television went crazy / Bill Carter.
p. cm.
Includes index.
ISBN 978-0-670-02208-3
1. Tonight show (Television program) 2. Television talk shows—United States—
History—21st century. 3. Leno, Jay. I. Title.
PN1992.77.T63C375 2010
791.45'6—dc22   2010034988

Printed in the United States of America
Set in Palatino LT Std
Designed by Daniel Lagin

For all the Carters and everyone else who shared the love at Fourth Street and Breezy—and especially in memory of Mom (Grams), who served it up to all of us in such abundance

Jeff Zucker, Jimmy Fallon, and Jay Leno

Jeff Ross, Conan O'Brien, and Mike Sweeney

David Letterman

Jeff Gaspin

Gavin Polone

President Barack Obama, Jay Leno, and Debbie Vickers

James Dixon and Jon Stewart

Craig Ferguson

Marc Graboff

Jeff Zucker and Dick Ebersol

Rick Rosen

Jimmy Kimmel spoofing Jay Leno

CONTENTS

THE WAR FOR LATE NIGHT

CHAPTER ONE

COMEDY TONIGHT

B y eight thirty on the evening of May 19, 2009, a stream of cabs and limos was snaking slowly down West Forty-third Street, pulling up one by one to the doors of the venerable, somewhat shabby Town Hall. The theater was a fabled Broadway-district house, and everyone from Richard Strauss and Sergei Rachmaninoff to Louis Armstrong and Bob Dylan had played there long ago to sold-out audiences. The newly dark sky over Manhattan was clear but the temperature cool for a mid-May evening—only fifty-seven degrees.

The arriving crowd didn't want to linger in the night air anyway, preferring to get inside as quickly as possible, if only to avoid the haranguing voices from members of the National Association of Broadcast Employees and Technicians, who were arrayed in force across the street in an effort to shame the management of their employer, NBC, into offering them a new contract.

Most of the milling guests were specifically in the city on this night because it was the middle of "upfront week"—a long-standing television industry rite of spring during which the broadcast networks trot out their newly selected programs for the fall in hopes of luring cash commitments from advertisers. The gathering swarm outside the theater, arriving in packs of five and six, was mostly under thirty-five and was much better dressed and significantly whiter than the average American population. If they barely paid attention to the noise of the demonstration—or the large inflated rat looming over the proceedings—it was because they had no vested interest in the protesters' cause. Largely buyers from ad agencies, honchos from the big Hollywood production studios, or executives from NBC's affiliated television stations—the broadcast stations owned by other companies that carried NBC's programs—they had turned up at Town Hall to see a night of entertainment—and to get a first look at what NBC had been telling the world was the "new paradigm" for the television industry:

Jay Leno at ten o'clock.

The network had put together the event on short notice, announcing it only a month earlier as NBC's Comedy Showcase—a night devoted to the great tradition of NBC comedy, as exemplified by shows like *Seinfeld*, *The Office*, and *Saturday Night Live*. In truth, it was all about grabbing some attention during upfront week for what Alan Wurtzel, the head of research for NBC, had labeled "clearly the highest priority for the network" going into the fall television season: the new, five-night-a-week *Jay Leno Show*.

The evening was built around an appearance by Jay, the perennial late-night leader, now in his final weeks as host of *The Tonight Show*, doing his thing: classic, joke-intensive stand-up. The organizers had blocked it out so that Leno would walk out onstage precisely at ten p.m.—his symbolic debut at that hour.

The time element was one reason the evening's show was set to start relatively late—nine p.m.—for a Broadway performance. The other was NBC's belated entry into upfront week. The network was actually squeezing itself into a day that was technically the property of ABC, and it had to be sure to allow enough time for its advertising clients to take in the ABC presentation, which started at four, and get a little dinner before heading back to midtown for some laughs. (NBC also had to assuage any fears at ABC that it was going to pull people away from its competitor's event.)

According to the long-established pecking order of upfront week, Tuesday was slated for ABC's presentation, which was routinely staged at Lincoln Center uptown. CBS owned Wednesday, with Carnegie Hall the somewhat incongruously grand setting. Fox, the newest of the networks, was usually relegated to Thursday and whatever venue that network could scrounge up. In recent years, Fox had turned to the less than ideal City Center after some infelicitous, though memorable, forays to other locations—such as the flight deck of the aircraft carrier *Intrepid* (hard to get to, hard to navigate around, and hard to hear anything inside the cavernous tent that Fox had erected) and the 69th Regiment Armory, which had established a new low for upfronts in 2006 by being hothouse humid, leaky roofed (it was teeming outside) and redolent of urine. (On top of that, one Fox executive had turned up onstage so drunk that he couldn't pronounce the word "Tostitos.")

Monday, by tradition, belonged to NBC, which had the supreme advantage of having its 30 Rock headquarters located right across Fiftieth Street from the pinnacle of Manhattan showbiz arenas, Radio City Music Hall. But the hall went vacant that year because NBC had abdicated its leadoff position in the upfront lineup. That allowed Fox to grab Monday for itself and thereby make a statement: The network was taking its bows first, a post it could legitimately claim it deserved, having clawed its way to the top in the ratings competition that counted most in the TV business—the battle for eyeballs owned by viewers between the ages of eighteen and forty-nine.

In truth, NBC had abandoned the field a year before, when, in another declaration of paradigm upheaval, it had pronounced the upfront era dead, with much the same revolutionary zeal it had when it introduced an even earlier paradigm-buster called TV 2.0, which posited that the eight p.m. hour was no longer a place for high-priced scripted comedies and dramas but should ideally be filled only with low-cost reality fare. As had been the case with the TV 2.0 plan—which had faded quickly into television press-release history—the decision to kill off the upfronts was less a matter of paradigms than piles of dimes. Jeff Zucker, NBC's chief executive, who announced each successive paradigm shift with the same resolute fervor, had targeted the upfront as a financially extravagant relic of a past era when broadcasters were flush with cash, and no longer relevant at a time when networks were squeezing program budgets for pennies and slashing staffs with broadswords. (NBC was only six months removed from an announcement of five hundred layoffs.)

It was in December 2007, in the midst of a disruptive writers' strike, that Zucker had pulled the plug on the traditional upfront, "in light of the current business environment," as he put it. He dismissed the elaborate presentations—which usually featured stars walking out onstage and making inane scripted comments about shows they knew little about because they had only acted in a pilot by that point—as a chore and a bore that induced people to show up only because of the lavish parties that followed them. "It's a show that everyone wants over as soon as possible," Zucker proclaimed. "People always say: Can't we get to the party sooner?"

NBC, a network that had once taken in as much as $800 million a year in profits, was now exsanguinating red ink after years of disastrous prime-time ratings. Under the increasingly green eye-shaded vision of its corporate managers at General Electric, it had done away with both the presentation and the profligate party in 2008, initiating instead something it cutely labeled the "infront." This consisted of a scaled-down series of presentations to ad buyers—with no fancy after-party. Advertisers would get a chance to offer their own input after an earlier-than-usual look at NBC's proposed shows, though many would be based only on scripts or sketchy outlines, because NBC also wanted to cut out expensive pilots.

In 2008 NBC staged the infront more than a month before its competitors' week of upfronts. But in 2009, after another year of dismal results with new programs, the network decided to schedule the process closer to upfront week, holding it in New York on May 4, only two weeks prior. Zucker had added the Comedy Showcase event (again, minus the party) after deciding NBC needed to be a presence during the upfront, what with all those buyers, affiliate managers, and studio heads in town. "It's another way to reinforce our brand," NBC's entertainment division chief Ben Silverman said.

Zucker turned to a man he trusted—and loved like a brother—to put together his comedy night, or as several NBC executives had taken to calling it, the "chuckle-front." Michael Bass had opened doors for Zucker when both men were at Harvard, and later at NBC; the two had been roommates for a time in New York; both had been producers at NBC's *Today* show. (Zucker, as all of television knew, ignited his career there as executive producer during the strongest era in *Today*'s history.) After a stint running the CBS morning show Bass had returned to the NBC fold, at Zucker's invitation, to take charge of special events—like hastily arranged comedy nights.

Bass assembled the Town Hall event from familiar NBC parts: He called on Rainn Wilson from *The Office*, Tracy Morgan from *30 Rock*, and Seth Meyers and Amy Poehler from *Saturday Night Live*, all for brief appearances. Bass had prevailed on one of the network's greatest stars,

Jerry Seinfeld, to drop by as an unannounced guest to toss five minutes of surefire stand-up into the mix.

But the headliners were not in doubt. NBC was eager to show off its new weeknight comedy triumvirate: Conan O'Brien, the incoming host of *The Tonight Show*; Jimmy Fallon, Conan's successor as host of the 12:35 a.m. *Late Night* franchise; and of course, Jay Leno, the centerpiece of the showcase—and the network's future.

To emcee the festivities, Bass reached out to one of NBC's most reliable go-to guys, a man who had done so well fronting formal dinners and other special occasions that his name had actually been kicked around in some quarters as a player talented and funny enough to be a potential late-night host himself. This, even though he still filled a rather important day job for the network: anchoring *NBC Nightly News*.

Brian Williams didn't mind being part of an NBC Comedy Showcase because he had no problem proving he was funny in front of crowds. He had already scored a coup hosting *Saturday Night Live*, to widespread praise. Williams had agreed to take that leap only after much concern about whether being in goofy comedy sketches might undermine his credibility as the face of NBC News. By all accounts, it had actually helped his image with viewers, some of whom had previously read his body language on newscasts to mean that he was overly stiff and sober. That hurdle cleared, Williams was now free to let his comedy freak flag fly with abandon, which he did during guest spots in late night, with Leno, O'Brien, David Letterman on CBS, and especially Jon Stewart on cable's Comedy Central.

When Michael Bass, after clearing the request with Zucker, approached Williams about serving as onstage host for the Comedy Showcase, Brian had the impression the producer was a bundle of nerves, which he took to mean this event was clearly of high importance to Jeff Zucker. Bass warned Williams that this was going to be a different role than playing tuxedoed toastmaster at the Waldorf.

Bass didn't much doubt what answer he would get. Like everyone else at NBC, he had observed how much Williams enjoyed invading the world of comedy.

"I'll do as good a job for you as I possibly can," Williams assured him with anchorman earnestness.

So Williams was backstage hanging with the comedy crowd as the ticketholders filed in to Town Hall, taking their limited-legroom seats inside the eighty-eight-year-old theater while being warmed up by the infectious beat of the Roots, the smoking-hot house band for the Fallon show. The comics themselves were squeezed into an uncomfortable, dimly lit twenty-by-twenty space equipped with some cold drinks, snacks, and a large video screen. The star power was considerable, but even with the formidable Seinfeld on hand, most of those backstage knew who would be playing the top cats on this night: Jay and Conan.

Both Leno and O'Brien had flown in from LA—separately—for this gig, and neither was especially enthused about it. Conan was exactly thirteen days away from his opening night as *Tonight* host and would have preferred to keep focused on his increasingly intense preparations, which had only recently included the first of four practice shows in his newly constructed studio. But he had put the trip east to good use. With access to the jet NBC had chartered, Conan and his team had touched down in a couple of locations—including Wrigley Field in Chicago—that they planned to use in the elaborate opening of Conan's *Tonight Show*: Conan running across the country through various highly American locales. Leno, for his part, didn't particularly see the need to have to throw a repeat on the air—Jay had always despised going into repeats, for any reason—just so he could cross the continent and do stand-up in front of a group he expected would be largely the same crowd he had worked only three months earlier, when he had been the featured entertainment at a different NBC party. The network had thrown one in February for its affiliate board and some big ad clients prior to its coverage of the Super Bowl, in Tampa, Florida. Conan had been present at that gathering as well, and though he had not performed, he and his entourage had the same reaction as the rest of the audience that evening. As Conan's executive producer and closest adviser, Jeff Ross, put it, "Jay killed; he did twenty minutes and he destroyed."

Pressed to come east for this new comedy event, the reluctant Leno asked Bass, "Is this the affiliates again?" He was told that this would be a significantly different group, though, yes, some affiliates would again be present. From his conversation with Bass, Leno took away the fundamental message: "It's a night of stand-ups; I want you to do your stand-up act." So after finishing his *Tonight Show* taping on Monday night, Jay had gotten up before dawn the next morning, drove to the Burbank airport, and jumped on a private jet for New York—to be, as he saw it, the closing act on a "night of stand-ups."

As Jay arrived backstage, he was greeted warmly by the assembled comedy talent, including O'Brien, who said a quick hello; the two late-night stars had already seen each other briefly at four that afternoon at rehearsal. One of the other performers was a bit surprised by Jay's somewhat ragged appearance: "He looked kind of fat, with his hair out of control." When the makeup artist hired for the night approached Jay and asked if he wanted some work done before he went on, he declined. The performer, who had seen the *Tonight* host work in clubs many times before, was equally concerned by Jay's demeanor. "It was striking that he was just sort of showing up and hadn't bothered to put a comb through his hair," the showcase participant said, adding, "In his defense, he had just flown across the country."

In fact, Jay had been in Manhattan for just a few hours by that point. Arriving at Teterboro Airport in New Jersey at about 3:30, Jay had rushed into town for his first appointment. NBC had brought him to a meet and greet with some of the affiliate board managers in the afternoon. Jay had no issue with that assignment, because he appreciated the importance of the affiliated stations as much as or more than any other star—or even executive—at NBC. His committed courtship of the station guys had been a key factor, after all, in his campaign to land the *Tonight* job back in the early nineties, when he won the fierce competition with David Letterman to succeed that show's comedy colossus, Johnny Carson.

Jay had long held an almost Willy Loman–like belief in the power of the personal sales pitch. "Clean shirt, handshake" was one of his mantras for the process. "You come in, shake hands, meet the local news team. It's just serving the customers—basic Dale Carnegie stuff."

Leno knew some of the customers were uneasy about NBC's ten p.m. gambit. He had already worked to douse a brushfire sparked when Ed Ansin, the owner of WHDH—NBC's affiliated station in Boston (Jay's home city, no less)—announced in April that he simply wasn't going to run the new Leno show at ten p.m., supplanting it with an hour-long local newscast. "We don't think the Leno show is going to be effective in prime time," Ansin said. "It will be detrimental to our eleven o'clock news. It will be very adverse to our finances."

NBC had every reason to fear such a move could lead to further

defections from local stations fed up with the network's abysmal performance in prime time for much of the previous decade, and so it had moved
a howitzer into position in response: NBC threatened to yank *all* the network's programs from the Boston station if it dared take that step with the
Leno show. Jay himself stepped up, calling Ansin personally and telling
him, "I'll do what I always do: I'll do local promos, whatever it takes." The
promise—and the howitzer—did the trick. Ansin backed down.

Conan, meanwhile, had passed much of the three months between the
end of his run on *Late Night* in February and his arrival in Los Angeles
to start work on *The Tonight Show* hopscotching the country making nice
with affiliated stations, doing the same glad-handing of news anchors
and smiling through the same promotional copy urging viewers to watch
Phil and Denise on Channel 13 or Frank and Diane on Channel 5 that Jay
had made de rigueur for *Tonight* hosts. In January Conan spent a morning in Detroit, visiting an auto show with reporters from WDIV, and an
afternoon in Chicago, cutting promos with the anchors for WMAQ. "This
is old-school television," O'Brien told the *Chicago Tribune*. "You actually go
into America and you talk to these people who put your television show
on. I really find it fascinating." By May, after visiting about fifty cities,
exhausting had all but replaced fascinating. When he arrived in New York
on May 18, O'Brien had been off television for the longest period of time
since he had started on *Late Night* in 1993, but he had had little time for
relaxation. He concluded that between the preparation for the new show
and the affiliate tour, "It may be the hardest I've ever worked."

But at least O'Brien's day in New York would not be taxing: He was
doing only the Town Hall gig. NBC, meanwhile, was wringing all it could
out of Jay's drop-in to the city. Besides the affiliate meetings, Jay had been
asked to spend an hour or so with another constituency of likely ten p.m.
skeptics: the press. At about six that evening, a phalanx of NBC publicity
executives, accompanied by many of the network generals, including Jeff
Zucker, ushered Jay into a suite at Hotel Mela, where a group of about a
dozen reporters was waiting for him.

Jay arrived looking relaxed and in good spirits, if a little puffy faced,
dispensing his usual greeting—"Hello, everybody"—to the room and
offering shout-outs to several of the reporters by name. He sprawled his
blocky frame into an armchair chair behind a coffee table, settling in for
the session with no discernible signs of concern—not even when the first

question carried an implied shot about NBC's decision to try him out at ten.

Stephen Battaglio, a reporter for *TV Guide*, wanted to know if Jay had heard what one of his late-night rivals, Jimmy Kimmel of ABC, had said in his comedy monologue at the ABC upfront that afternoon. Jay hadn't, so Battaglio explained it to him. Kimmel had referenced his fear, before NBC announced the ten p.m. plan, that ABC was going to lure Leno away, place him at 11:35 p.m., and knock Kimmel back from his perch in the midnight hour to a start time of 12:35 a.m. " 'But NBC said we will not let Jay go to ABC,' " Battaglio quoted the ABC star, " 'even if we have to destroy our network to keep him.' "

As the reporters laughed, Jay rolled with it. "As long as it's funny!" he bellowed in his best punch line voice. "That's the rule."

Most of the subsequent questions covered the obvious territory:

What would the new show be like? Jay offered few details because he hadn't started planning it yet.

Why did he believe this idea might work? "I thought: There's no comedy at ten o'clock. Maybe we'll try that," Leno said, with his characteristic no-big-deal insouciance, as if he were discussing a dinner order rather than a career change. And, as usual, how much of that detachment was real and how much was calculated was impossible for anyone in the room to read.

How could he compete against expensive dramas like *CSI: Miami* on CBS and *Private Practice* on ABC? "Hopefully when they're in reruns, we'll catch them," Jay said, turning to familiar ground: a car metaphor. "We may not get them in the straights. We'll catch them in the corners."

Didn't he worry about tarnishing his legacy as the longtime winner on *Tonight*? "I'm not much of a legacy guy," he said, tossing a scoff. "I hosted the *Tonight* show for seventeen years. It's like the America's Cup. I didn't screw it up. I passed it off to the next guy—whew! Everything else now is gravy. If this is a success—wonderful. If it's a huge bomb . . . Well, I hope not." Jay's tone rang more with confidence than mere hope.

What about the notion that staying at NBC and moving to ten amounted to stealing Conan's thunder? "No, I don't think so," Jay said, quickly locating his familiar Conan take. "Conan is terrific. We've been friends for a long time. This will be a smooth transition."

Then Jay, who at various times in his career had enjoyed performing the role of analyst of other comics' acts, became expansive on the subject of Conan. "He's a very funny guy. Conan is all about the material, and that's what I like about him. When he started, obviously the critics went after him a little bit. He always had a solid writing and comedy foundation. He just needed to learn how to perform a little bit better." Those first few months, Jay continued, "Conan was a little awkward. But if you thought he was awkward, he still had good jokes. We'd go, 'That was a funny joke. He didn't tell it quite right.' But he's learned to become a master at it and, obviously, that's why he's doing the show."

He also weighed in on the early critical reaction to Conan's 12:35 successor. "I watched the reviews of Jimmy Fallon after one night," Jay said. "Give the kid six months; give him a year. Conan—give it a year." Mindful of his own early ratings drubbings at the hands of Letterman, he added, "I mean, Dave was beating me for the first eighteen months or so."

What about that little frisson of tension with the Boston station? Was there any reason to worry whether other affiliates might bail on him? "I talk to the affiliates," Jay said. "You know, there is no NBC. There's only the affiliates. They're the customers. NBC is just a bunker in Burbank somewhere, and you have all these affiliates. They buy your product. And if your franchisees are unhappy, they close your restaurant. Simple as that."

At this point, Jeff Zucker, who had been leaning against a wall of the suite, taking it all in, stepped forward. He was having none of any suggestion that NBC's backing of Jay was anything but unstinting. He turned to a reporter who had persisted with a line of questioning about how long the network would hang on if Jay's initial ratings were lackluster. "We're completely committed to this," Zucker said quietly, adding, "This question comes from a very anachronistic way of looking at it. This is going to be judged on a fifty-two-week basis, not on a first-month basis."

"There's a poker player!" a suddenly energized Leno jumped in, pointing to Zucker. "Right there! You know, if it's not working, kick my ass out! Thank you! I know how it works."

By no means did Jay see that as a likely outcome, however. He explained how his ten p.m. show would be much cheaper to produce than those hour-long dramas on the other networks—he could do his show for one-fifth of the cost, he promised. And all he really needed to do was improve the ratings for the ten p.m. time period over the lame shows NBC had been programming at that hour—like *Lipstick Jungle*—to be judged an immediate success. "And then you build from that," he concluded.

Besides, Leno noted, "You have something of a proven product here. Logically it stands to reason you'll do better at ten than you did at eleven thirty."

In both his words and his air of assurance, Jay was making it clear that he saw this latest transition in much the same way he regarded every move he had made in his career. At bottom, it was all about doing something he had worked on his whole life and now had complete confidence in: telling audiences—in clubs, on TV—jokes. Lots and lots of jokes.

"It's like people always say to me: What happens if you go to a club and you just bomb? Well, you know, after a while you don't bomb anymore. You do better than you might have done, or you do a little worse. But you don't go out there and just bomb."

Just before Brian Williams stepped onstage at precisely nine p.m., he glanced at the big video monitor in the ersatz greenroom backstage, which showed the Roots pounding through their last warm-up number and the faces of the crowd, now settled into their seats. As he looked around, Williams noticed that in this room full of comics, few ever raised their eyes to the screen. Their demeanor reminded him of athletes at sports events, like Olympic skiers closing their eyes and mentally running through the course before being set loose onto the snow—a cross between that and jittery thoroughbred horses right before being loaded into the starting gate for the derby.

Williams, freshly turned fifty but still youthful looking with his close-cropped hair and lean frame, walked out and greeted the crowd, promising them a fun night with the great lineup that NBC had assembled. He mentioned the big names, leaving out Seinfeld, who was the evening's surprise. Then he got right to business. One of the men this night was all about, he announced, was the guy about to take his place beside the names of Allen, Paar, Carson, and Leno on the shortest of short lists in television's pantheon, the next great host of *The Tonight Show*: Conan O'Brien.

With his long-legged, loping stride, O'Brien took center stage to warm, enthusiastic applause. Conan, now forty-six years old (like Letterman, Leno, and Seinfeld, his birthday was in April), fit and relaxed in an unbuttoned blue suit, his pompadour of red hair adding even a couple more inches to his six-foot-four height, loomed high above the fans clapping for him in the orchestra seats. After a few thank-yous and a little salute to the Roots—"an amazing band"—Conan settled into his routine, beginning almost conversationally:

"As you know, folks, I've been very busy out in Los Angeles preparing for the June first premiere of *The Tonight Show*. I have just thirteen days left," he said, his voice starting to rise, adding a note of mock exasperation. "I don't have a second to spare. But I definitely wanted to fly across the country and be here tonight for one very important reason. . . ." He took a beat, maybe half a second, setting the fuse.

"I wanted the chance—just *once*—to go on before Jay Leno!"

The laughter rolled down from the balcony and through the orchestra, hitting a crescendo before igniting spontaneous applause. It was a full ten-second laugh, one born of the audience's awareness of just what the ten p.m. relocation of Leno meant for O'Brien. It was a joke crafted with precision for the occasion—and it killed.

"It feels *real* good," Conan said, extending the joke. Then he shifted into his ultra-high-pitched mock Jay voice for a little coda: "He went, 'Uh, what's he talking about?' " And Conan was rewarded with a rebound laugh almost as long as the original.

O'Brien let that settle before moving on. "It's great to be here, ladies and gentlemen, seriously. I am so proud to work at NBC, one of the world's oldest and most respected"—pause—"nonprofit organizations." (Another appreciative laugh.) "Of course the theme of tonight's event is the history of comedy on NBC. So once we get to 1998, feel free to take off." The lower register of the laughs that greeted this shot included a chorus of *ooohs* at O'Brien's brazen evocation of his network's futility since that year.

Feigning nervousness after launching that grenade, Conan scanned the front rows. "Where's Zucker?" he asked, knowing exactly where the smiling NBC boss was sitting. "Oh, this is going well," Conan said, shifting into his Ernst Stavro Blofeld impression, with pinched-in face, beady eyes, and, of course, imaginary cat in his lap. "Petting the white cat," Conan said in his evil genius voice. "Get him off! Get him off! He's being mean to me!"

In total command of the audience, Conan did about an eight-minute-long monologue, with steady laughs throughout. He had hit only notes that would resonate most effectively with this particular audience—and it paid off for him. He was bathed in applause as he wrapped up. Then NBC allowed him to serve as the introducer of the night's "surprise guest," a man Conan described as "one of the pillars" of the NBC comedy tradition, as well as "one of the best things ever to happen to NBC."

That was Jerry Seinfeld, of course, and the audience was appropriately surprised—and thrilled—to see him. Jerry, looking sharp if slightly older (he had just turned fifty-five) than in his sitcom days, with a thinner thatch of hair and a couple of extra pounds, delivered his five sparkling minutes in a routine about the peccadilloes of married life. The centerpiece was his version of marital discussions that take on the flavor of "a game show where you're always in the lightning round," trying to work your way through testy categories like "Movies I Think We Saw Together." Seinfeld arranged the beats of the laughs like an orchestra conductor: a little more, a little less, big finish, thank you very much.

The other booked acts had a few highs and lows, with Meyers and Poehler scoring with a version of "Weekend Update" from *SNL* that mocked NBC's prime-time machinations. Williams then returned to the stage to set up the next of the evening's highlights: the latest of NBC's late-night stars, Jimmy Fallon.

Fallon had been on the air since March, displaying typically rocky rookie moments but quickly making his mark by hitting the sweet spot for the *Late Night* audience: the college crowd, which Fallon was expanding by reaching out through his blog and his Twitter account.

He shambled out in his aw-shucks manner, his suit looking maybe one size too big, underscoring how much younger—he was thirty-four—he was than most of the others who'd appeared onstage. Fallon got a quick laugh with a throwaway line directed at Williams: "Thank you, thank you very much—Anderson Cooper, everybody." Since he had his house band at hand, Fallon was able to lead the Roots into one of the signature bits from his nascent show, "Slow Jammin' the News"—only, given the occasion, Jimmy made it a slow jam of the NBC schedule.

If that routine played a little arcane for this particular audience's taste, Fallon had something more surefire prepared, a bit he had actually performed at an earlier dinner.

Grabbing his acoustic guitar, Jimmy explained he was going to do something he did regularly on the *Late Night* show: lure a member out of the audience to come up onstage, where he would make up a song about him or her on the spot.

"Any volunteers?" Fallon asked, looking down into the front rows. "You, sir? You want to get up?"

Jeff Zucker, in his impeccably tailored suit, the fringe of hair around his bald pate buzzed close, clambered onstage, playing his part of looking reluctant.

"What is your name, sir?" Fallon asked, all innocence amid the laughs.

"Zucker" came the reply, accompanied by an "as if" look.

"What do you do, sir?" Fallon asked, pretending to write the information on a card.

"I'm with NBC."

"And . . . straight or gay?"

After getting the predictable boisterous laugh, Fallon began strumming chords and launched into his song:

Going to sing you a song about a friend I know.
He has no time for a late TV show.
He ain't tall, completely bald,
My friend, Zucker.
He says his last name's pronounced Zooker.
He's a crazy mother-fooker.
He's the man who makes decisions.
He ain't got 20/20 vision (he wears glasses),
My man, Zucker!

He's the guy calls all the shots.
What if he married Courteney Cox?
They'd be so in love with each other,
She'd be Courteney Cox Zucker!

After the biggest laugh of the night since Conan's Leno joke, Fallon squeezed in his last notes:

And . . . And, I just got fired!

It was a wow finish for a performance that made the impression NBC was seeking. Fallon demonstrated compellingly that he was both funny and appealing; as a replacement at 12:35 for Conan, he just might do.

Backstage many of the comics who had finished their spots lingered to watch their compatriots, but mainly, it seemed to one of the stars that evening, out of "a palpable curiosity about how Leno would perform." Conan, however, had long since departed. He had been happy to get on the bill early so he could hit the road fast, back to the small jet waiting at Teterboro to fly him back to Los Angeles.

Jerry Seinfeld had remained, and he had a small concern that he thought about mentioning to somebody in charge. Jerry hadn't had any problem connecting with the crowd during his crisp five-minute stint, but he was a bit uncomfortable out there nonetheless. What disturbed him was that throughout his spot—and the entire evening, really—the house lights had been kept all the way up, making the audience totally visible to the performers onstage. For a seasoned professional stand-up like Seinfeld, this was "one of the poison darts of comedy." For Jerry the ideal setup was light on the comic, audience in the dark, preferably laughing. To Seinfeld, this oversight meant that somebody had been incompetent. But in the theater that night, he didn't raise the issue.

Leno, still waiting backstage, had noticed the lighting situation as well but had concluded that it was because NBC was taping the event. Indeed, NBC was taping much of the show and wanted lights to capture reaction shots. Jay had expressly asked that his performance not be taped. That didn't mean the lighting would be adjusted, however. What Jay knew from his own endless stand-up gigs was that if lights were shining on an audience, they tended to become self-conscious—and a lot less likely to laugh.

Whatever running time had been planned, the combination of extended laughs and just general banter and interaction onstage had by now pushed the hour past ten thirty—more than half an hour into Jay time. No one had really noticed except for Leno himself, who, as was his custom, was carefully attuned to the rhythms of audience members.

Jay was well aware that this crowd had already been to one upfront in the late afternoon. Others had come from work, having knocked off at around six to get dinner. That meant it was well past the time they usually headed for home. And they had already been sitting in this theater for over an hour and a half.

Bass had asked Jay to do about fifteen minutes, the longest spot of the night. Jay had said he would do between ten and fifteen minutes. For Jay, doing fifteen minutes was like Bruce Springsteen dashing off a commercial jingle. He routinely dished out hours' worth of stand-up in his appearances in Vegas. Tonight it was only a matter of which fifteen minutes he chose. For an industry audience, like the one he had performed for at the Super Bowl, he was surely going to rely heavily on his topical-humor file.

As he waited to go on, Jay still looked a bit askew to at least one of his fellow cast members, who wondered what was up with his hair. To this observer "it looked like a Leno-fro." Jay himself continued to believe that this was one booking that just didn't make much sense, no matter how he broke it down. But he had a job to do, and if he believed in anything, he believed in the virtue of an honest day's work.

Jay was off and running from the moment Williams finished the introduction. As he crossed the stage, mic in one hand, Jay began furiously running his other hand through his impressive shock of luxuriantly thick, now mostly gray hair. Just to let the audience know he was cognizant that he was arriving onstage later than planned, he opened with a cheery notice: "We are almost a tenth through the evening!"

Maybe the awareness that the hour was late pushed him to pick up his pace, but from the moment he started talking, Jay seemed in hyperdrive, pacing from one side of the stage to the other, fluffing his hair, spraying jokes like a water cannon firing into the crowd.

"Well, good to see everybody. As you know, President Obama, first hundred days, pretty exciting. It's been a fascinating year. To see a black man born to a white woman—see, that's the decision Michael Jackson made . . ."

Boom: next one. "Of course, Hillary and Barack, now best friends. Not always that way. Remember, seven to eight months ago they met in Unity, New Hampshire. To show unity, they met in Unity, New Hampshire. Bill could not be there." Pause. "I believe he was in Intercourse, Pennsylvania."

Passable laughs to kick the act off, though they didn't last long. Jay marched on double-time to Sarah Palin and Joe Biden, targets of choice from recent monologues on *The Tonight Show*, followed by one about the decision to close the prison camp in Guantánamo Bay. "See, that's when you know the economy's in bad shape. When even the terrorists are losing their homes!" The jokes were coming so quickly that it was hard for the audience to laugh at one and catch the start of another. Jay was also moving, moving, traipsing around the stage, bending at the waist, leaning forward into the mic, which had the effect of swallowing up some of his words. In the orchestra seats a few NBC executives exchanged glances.

Jay now moved on to airline jokes, drunk pilots. "Imagine the pilot comes on and you hear him say, 'My name is Bob; I'm an alcoholic!' Well, thank you, Bob!" He punched the last line, raising his voice a decibel to sell the joke harder, one of his best-honed techniques. Jay could always modulate his voice to underscore a line and almost force a laugh. He had learned the skill long ago in the clubs, and his peers considered him a master at it.

But longtime Jay observers in the audience and among the comics backstage sensed something amiss. It was all coming too frantically; Jay seemed to be rushing, stepping on his own laughs. One top NBC official noticed with some alarm that Jay's brow was coated with sweat, and he looked heavier than many New York–based executives remembered him. And the hand constantly thrusting through his hair . . . It all seemed slightly manic, not at all like the Jay of the dependable nightly monologue on TV.

Lorne Michaels, thirty-five years into his run of steering *Saturday Night Live*, had seen every kind of comedy performance. Gauging Jay from his seat in the orchestra, Michaels thought the comic was "really, really angry" about something, and was determined to satisfy whatever was expected of him—only "at double speed. Like, I want to get out of here. I know I have to do it. So I'll give full value—the whole of the act will be in, but it will be in half the time a normal audience would be seeing it."

Jay wasn't displaying any overt signs of anger, but Michaels believed he was too professional to ever allow himself to let that out in public. "He can't be an angry guy, just can't do it. He can feel it, he can be it—he just can't act it." Michaels could only guess the source of Leno's displeasure. "They made him come in, they made him do it. He had to sing for his supper, he had to audition again, and it was just all in a hostile room."

It wasn't as though his jokes weren't winning laughs; it was just that the laughs seemed so perfunctory, not natural and prolonged. For many who had seen Leno kill—virtually without fail—in many previous venues, this was more than surprising. One longtime NBC executive found himself "stunned" by the performance.

"White collar crime is up—and that's just in the church!"

It began to occur to the other comics in the lineup that Jay was having trouble finding a theme that would connect with this audience—and several concluded that the reason was obvious: The jokes had nothing to do with the event everyone was attending. Prompted in advance by Bass that this was what NBC wanted, all the other comics—other than Seinfeld, who at least connected his set about marriage to his upcoming NBC reality series, *The Marriage Ref*—had come prepared with material that related to NBC's bold plan for ten p.m., or the changes in late night, or NBC's desperate need for hits from the latest crop of new series. Jay was relying on his standard act.

"It was a sloppy, dated set of jokes," one of the other performers said. "As if frozen in time." Of course no one at NBC had asked Jay what areas and topics his routine would cover. He was the biggest star on the network; he knew comedy better than any of them. They had every reason to trust his judgment on what would be funny.

Jay dredged up Idaho senator Larry Craig and his infamous bathroom escapade, which had taken place in June 2007—two years earlier.

Jay moved on to the Icelandic singer Björk and her memorable swan dress—which she had worn at the 2001 Oscars. The joke was that she had donated it to Hurricane Katrina victims. "How would you like to be the one that actually got that dress?" Jay asked. Katrina had hit New Orleans in 2005.

About fifteen minutes into Jay's monologue, Marc Graboff, the cochairman (with Ben Silverman) of NBC Entertainment, heard his BlackBerry ping. He peeked down at it and saw a text message from his friend Lloyd Braun, the onetime top programmer at ABC, now an NBC-based producer: "Jay not funny."

Many members of the audience had also attended the ABC upfront in the afternoon, when that network took a major risk and showed an entire sitcom pilot to the crowd. The show was *Modern Family,* and ABC's gamble paid off, generating gales of laughs and establishing itself as a likely instant hit. Jimmy Kimmel had also almost brought down the house during the ABC event with his searingly funny monologue about the fraudulent dance that took place every year during upfront week.

One of the comics backstage observed that not too many minutes into Jay's performance, clusters throughout the audience "started to use their BlackBerrys. All those faces on all those ad agency people—they were bathed in the light of their BlackBerry screens."

For NBC's executives, who supported and liked Leno, this was more than unfortunate. It was borderline mean—but they considered the whole episode completely unnecessary. "It was just a misread," one of Leno's main NBC supporters in the audience said. "Jay didn't read the crowd right."

By now even Jeff Zucker, Jay's most prominent supporter, was squirming in his seat. The whole idea of the show had been for Jay to do a kick-ass set at the end of the evening and send everyone out into the night juiced about having comedy of that quality available five times a week at ten p.m. Yet even Zucker could not deny what he was seeing and hearing: Jay was doing terribly. He was going on too long and his material wasn't current. In Zucker's theater-chair psychoanalysis, Jay's floundering that night had everything to do with two factors: New York and David Letterman. Zucker believed that Jay had long ago concluded that New York was Letterman's city. It was, after all, where Dave did his show. Dave, who after all these years, most of them in second place, still haunted Jay in many ways. Dave, who had become something close to the voice of the city after the 9/11 attacks, when no late-night host would dare go back on the air until after Letterman had addressed the tragedy and reopened television to the possibility of being funny again.

Jay would travel just about anywhere to perform, but he avoided booking dates in New York—not at Carnegie Hall, where he had played early in his career; not at the Garden. NBC had tried for years to convince him to come to New York for the upfronts or other events, but he had always declined.

Though New York's comic sensibility was widely acknowledged to be significantly different from what came out of LA—and certainly Vegas—Zucker didn't believe Leno's reluctance to play Manhattan had anything to do with his comic sensibility being wrong for the city. (Though he himself was from Miami, Jeff had lived and worked his entire career in New York—and *he* certainly appreciated Jay's comedy style.) No, Zucker simply thought Jay hated New York, the idea of New York, Dave's town. Somehow, psychologically, New York had become screwed up for Jay.

But now he was in New York and still trying. Jay, widely acknowledged as the most skilled stand-up of his generation—even Letterman, in interviews early in his career and late, agreed with that assessment—sensed things weren't going well. He dug deep, searching for a comic vein that might offer some riches, something down in the vast store of material recorded in his brain, anything that might ignite the audience, and then maybe he could find his rhythm and turn it around, as he had so many times before.

He tried earthquakes in LA. One joke got a solid laugh for being sharp and smart: "When Bush was in the White House, all the black people were out of work. Now the black guy is in the White House . . . hmmm." But then he tried talking about his wife's cat—and cats in general. Jay hammered away for six minutes on cats, scoring only glancingly when he stopped to ask a woman in the audience if she had any cats. "Three," she said. "Three cats!" Jay replied and, dropping his voice, added, "Single woman?"

At around that time, some twenty minutes in, the squeak of chair seats lifting could be heard in isolated locations around the theater. In the aisles figures with ducked heads began darting up toward the exit. People were walking out on Jay Leno.

If he noticed this display of rudeness—and with all the house lights on, it was hard to miss—Jay didn't show it, nor did it slow him down in the least. Instead he tacked toward absurd side-effect warnings on drug labels, including one for restless leg syndrome and another that threatened "explosive diarrhea and possible sexual dysfunction," which he used as the perfect setup to explore how this could affect someone's love life. "For some reason women are not attracted to men with explosive diarrhea."

Another ping from Graboff's BlackBerry. Braun again: "Make him stop!"

At twenty-seven minutes the chair squeaks were spreading and the stream of exiting guests had grown steadily, with the evacuees looking less embarrassed as they fled. Jay turned to a tried-and-true source of laughs for him: "How fat are we getting!"

Down in the front row, Zucker had one thought: *Is this gonna end?*

Finally, thirty-two minutes into his monologue, Jay looked around and said, "Well, let's see, what else can we talk about?" He added to this awkward transition by observing, "I guess I've answered all the questions about the new show!" Then, looking down at the audience again, he asked, "Does anybody have any questions?"

A woman not far from the stage had one that no one else in the theater could hear because she wasn't mic'd. Jay's answer was also muffled, though it drew enough of a laugh from the spectators in the first few rows for Jay to close the proceedings. He offered a big-voiced thanks and good night to the crowd, bowing briefly to applause that sounded respectful, even warm. He had been at it for more than half an hour, working it and sweating, and he was, after all, the guy in America's bedroom for the past seventeen years. Jay waved and exited, stage left.

After returning briefly to thank everyone for coming, Brian Williams felt he had to say something about Leno's performance: "Jay, Bea Arthur called; she needs her hair back." It drew what sounded to Williams like "a relief laugh—the kind of laugh you get in church when you're allowed to laugh at the sermon."

Out in the lobby, moving among the departing crowd, NBC executives exchanged looks of chagrin. No one knew what exactly had happened. Jay had always been Mr. Reliable—not only in politicking for his show with affiliate managers and admen, but also in joke delivery. This night he had swung big—and missed.

Marc Graboff, cornered by a couple of reporters, didn't dodge the obvious. "Jay was just off," he said. "He didn't read the audience and had the weakest act of the night."

Jay himself wasted no time in jumping into a car and heading for Teterboro, where his plane was also waiting. He was still disturbed by the house lights, how alienated the audience had seemed with the lights on them. Even though this upfront—like all others—was dominated by ad buyers, not affiliate managers, Jay was still convinced that many of the people in the audience that night were from the same crowd he had performed for at the Florida event. And the earlier acts had stretched the evening out, leaving him to appear so late that people were eager to get home on a work night. It had turned into a disaster pretty much all the way around.

But Jay was too much a pro to make excuses for himself. He knew the night had not gone well, but he did not view it as a setback. There would be other nights—there were always other nights.

Some of the comics stayed backstage while the crowd left, more than one of them somewhat aghast. Most would have agreed with Jay's assessment at the mini press conference that evening that comics of his rank and experience never really bombed anymore, but what had they just witnessed happen out there? Some were flabbergasted that Jay had seemed to violate a fundamental comedy prohibition in his wrap-up by admitting that he had no more jokes and then asking the audience if they had any questions. That was the stuff of lectures, not comedy acts.

The worst thing his struggling performance had done was to expose the most vulnerable side of Jay Leno—the alleged lack of edge and hipness in his comedy—to withering appraisal from his detractors. Many of those detractors happened to be denizens of that place that so unnerved him: New York. Even among some of the comedy talent at NBC, there was an undercurrent of latent disrespect toward Leno. Now it slithered to the surface.

One showcase cast member blamed Jay for undoing what had been an entertaining and successful night. Others offered comments about how dated the material seemed to be. The most vocal Jay critic took the nastiest tack, wondering out loud if the audience had just been "served the same shit Jay feeds to the free-buffet crowd in Branson, Missouri."

Early the next morning—even cooler, with a sprinkle of rain, which was CBS's problem now—Jeff Zucker arrived at 30 Rock, not overly disturbed by the disappointment of Leno's performance. On the whole the night had gone extremely well. Conan and Fallon were outstanding. The other acts scored. People got a lot of laughs from NBC's impromptu chuckle-front. An aberrant off performance by Jay was not going to have any significant impact on either the expectations for *The Jay Leno Show* or the willingness of advertisers to buy time in it. It was unfortunate that Jay had misfired, but it was hardly a crisis; nothing to do about it but shrug it off.

Still, the view from the fifty-second floor, high above Rockefeller Plaza, where NBC had its suite of senior executive offices, was almost always awe-inspiring. Way up there, literally among the clouds on that overcast morning, it may not have been easy to hear what another NBC staff member who had seen the show called "the cautiously hushed buzz" about Jay. That buzz was "decidedly caustic toward Leno," the staff member said.

As various employees discussed the evening, they realized they were for the first time expressing real fears about what might happen in the ten p.m. hour in the fall. The network had so much invested in this guy, five hours of prime time a week, which meant that he had arguably more riding on his shoulders than any individual had in the history of television. It seemed, to some at least, that Jay Leno had come to New York for an event of clear, vital importance, in a theater packed with buyers, the very people who would decide the financial future of this show, and the entire network, and, in essence, he had "phoned it in."

Some of the staff members were surprised when one of those executives from the fifty-second floor aerie visited the lower reaches of the company later in the day and—in an eruption of honesty—admitted differing with the groupthink going on at the highest levels.

"Last night was supposed to *sell* the network," the executive told several distressed colleagues. "Not *hurt* the network."

CHAPTER TWO

SELL-BY DATE

On a mid-March afternoon in 2004, Jeff Zucker found himself facing a meeting with real trepidation—and he was not by nature a trepid man.

By that point in his career Zucker had made the convoluted daily machine of the *Today* show run as smoothly as a Swiss fire drill; he had produced with distinction the endless election night of November 2000 for NBC News; he had navigated his way—not unbloodied, but certainly unbowed—through the piranha-filled waters of Hollywood during a three-year stint running NBC's entertainment division; and he had beaten cancer—twice.

So what was so unnerving about having to walk down to Jay Leno's dressing room at NBC's headquarters in Burbank, California, and hand him a closing notice for his long run as host of *The Tonight Show*? Maybe it was knowing that Leno could not possibly have seen this coming, not with his ratings still dominant in late night, not with his compulsion to do this job—and only this job, as long as there was breath still in his lungs—undiminished in the slightest. Or maybe it was the private conversation he'd had with Jay's executive producer, Debbie Vickers, two days earlier.

In her office at *Tonight*, Zucker had run the scenario by Debbie, a kindred spirit because of their shared experience producing the two most famed franchise programs in television history, *Today* and *Tonight*. Zucker's affinity with Debbie, built over the course of many one-on-one chats about the challenges and miseries of dealing with daily deadlines and the care and feeding of talent, had led him to trust her as one of his few real confidantes during his fractious sojourn running NBC's West Coast operations. It only made sense to run the plan by Debbie—sound as rock, smart, dependable, patient, levelheaded Debbie—before taking it to Jay.

When he sat down with her in her *Tonight* office, his presence didn't raise an eyebrow. Zucker almost always stopped in to see Debbie during his trips west; everyone knew how simpatico they were. Vickers had no reason to expect anything but another casual chat that March day, unless it involved some sort of confirmation that the network had agreed to another extension for Jay. That move was pro forma about eighteen months out from whatever the end date was on the current Leno deal, which was about where they were now. Vickers had every reason to believe things were moving along as normal.

Jeff Zucker, however, had other business to conduct. After some pleasantries he got directly to the point of his visit. He presented his proposal to Vickers in a "what if" sort of way: "What would you think if we extend Jay's contract now, but at the same time we make it clear this will be his last contract for *The Tonight Show?*"

A petite redhead in her fifties with a work-hard, stay-humble producing style and a thoroughly winning personality, Vickers had worked for Jay Leno since the beginning of his *Tonight Show* tenure in 1992 (and for Johnny Carson before that). After witnessing Jay survive his crisis-filled first eighteen months on the show, then having helped steady him, refashion him, and guide his ascension to late-night supremacy, she was able to read the feelings, intentions, and moods of the often impenetrable Leno better than anyone else on the show—or the planet (not counting Jay's wife, Mavis, at least). Zucker's proposition, though, needed no penetrating insight.

"I don't think that's gonna work," Vickers told him, thoroughly taken aback by what she was hearing. The idea that NBC was even considering such a move—let alone now running it by her—left Vickers incredulous: Had the network been mounting this plan over the course of weeks? Months? While everybody at the show had been blithely working away? All she could picture was an image of a husband having an affair while his wife remained clueless.

"Jay's not gonna go for this," Vickers told Zucker flatly. If anyone knew how unremittingly committed Jay Leno was to *The Tonight Show*, now and forever, it was Debbie Vickers. "I mean, it's ridiculous."

Ridiculous or not, two days later Zucker steeled himself to go face-to-face with Jay himself in his private dressing room. The plan that he had in his (rhetorical) pocket, in fact, involved no "what if" scenario at all: NBC had already decided its course of action over several months of consideration and talks in New York and LA. What Debbie Vickers didn't know, and what Jay Leno wouldn't know either (but it probably would not take long to guess), was that NBC had for weeks been quietly back-channeling its plan for the future of *The Tonight Show* with the representatives of its other late-night star, Conan O'Brien. And prior to this sit-down with Leno, both sides had already come to an agreement.

Conan O'Brien, after a rigidly specified waiting period, was going to become the fifth permanent host of *The Tonight Show*—and the fourth, Jay Leno, was going to go gently (NBC hoped) into that good late night.

The plan hadn't begun on a specific date, nor was there an operation geared to make it happen according to a specific timetable. It happened because NBC wanted to protect its late-night empire—the one part of its entertainment operation that still claimed unchallenged leadership, with Jay at 11:35, Conan at 12:35, and *Saturday Night Live* on the weekend. It happened because with prime-time revenues plummeting, NBC more than ever needed the profits it still collected from late night—even though they had diminished from several hundred million dollars a year at their height to a more modest, but still essential, number. In 2004, *Tonight* by itself was set to generate a little under $150 million in profits on revenues of about $230 million.

Mostly, though, it happened because some executives at NBC had a sense of history and were determined to learn from the past, not repeat it.

In the 1990s, as Johnny Carson ended his long, unassailable reign over the only domain that mattered after prime time, NBC had ongoing deals with the two top names in late night in Leno and Letterman, but owned only one *Tonight Show* chair for one of them to occupy when the music stopped. The network had tried mightily—if ham-handedly—to keep both stars, but the plan blew up. Dave exited in grand opera style for CBS and created the first truly substantial competing franchise to *Tonight*, proving for the first time that late-night television—and the profits that came with it—could exist beyond *The Tonight Show*.

Now NBC had the late-night champ again in Jay and, thankfully, only one obvious next-generation successor: Conan. The only problem was the age disparity this time was not so stark. In 2004, Jay would turn fifty-four and Conan forty-one, whereas when Johnny retired, he had been old enough to be Jay's (or Dave's) father. Jay clearly had plenty of game left in him, but Conan had by now reached the professional juncture where Letterman had been when he pressed to move up from the lounge (12:35) to the main room (11:35). Though younger than Dave had been (forty-six) when he chafed under NBC's decision to pass him over for Jay, Conan had hosted *Late Night* (the show Letterman had created) for exactly as long as Letterman had—eleven years.

And suitors had already come knocking. Three years earlier Fox had mounted an extended, comprehensive campaign to land Conan, a talent who Fox executives believed was a sweet match for their image of themselves and their programming style—young, hip, somewhat subversive. The wooing had been managed from the very top: Peter Chernin, the chief executive of the Fox entertainment empire—and one of Hollywood's genuine power brokers—had authorized the pursuit of Conan. But it was kicked off with a contact based in the personal connection between Gail Berman, the talented Fox network entertainment president, and Jeff Ross, Conan's executive producer and closest adviser. Both now in their forties, the two had become friendly as kids trying to break into the New York theater and music worlds twenty years earlier. Shortly after Berman assumed the Fox network job in 2001, she invited Ross to her office and planted the seed:

"What do you think about coming over to Fox? Not right now, but sometime—you should think about it. When your contract is up."

Ross certainly appreciated the interest but didn't think too much about it until the calls from Chernin started. Chernin systematically hit all the legs of the Conan support system—his manager, Gavin Polone; his new group of agents from the Endeavor agency, led by Rick Rosen; and Ross— as well as Conan himself. Chernin's arguments on behalf of Fox were, as the experienced and savvy Rosen saw them, "incredibly compelling."

The timing wasn't bad, either. By 2001, the latest of O'Brien's deals had a little more than a year to run, and NBC was—as it had too often done with Conan—"dicking around a bit" with the negotiations, in the words of one of Conan's team. The executive then in charge of NBC's West Coast division, Scott Sassa, offered Conan a raise, but only of about 10 percent. O'Brien was, at the time, on the low end of the late-night pay scale, earning about $3 million a year—a fraction of what Leno and especially Letterman (with a salary of upwards of $25 million) were taking in. Conan had come into his own in the preceding years; he was featured on magazine covers and became a darling on college campuses in America. But NBC still didn't seem to be taking him seriously where it counted—at the pay window.

Fox entered this scene with verve—and a big offer. Chernin took Conan and Ross to several dinners. Between courses, he laid out Fox's plan for a Conan late-night show: It would start at eleven, getting the jump on both Jay and Dave; it would receive precisely targeted promotion on youth-oriented shows like *Family Guy* and *The Simpsons* and on Fox's NFL games on Sundays; Conan would become the signature star of the network.

While O'Brien was flattered and hugely impressed with Chernin on a personal basis, he and his team had concerns about Fox—not so much the network itself, but its lineup of stations and the hour-long newscasts those stations ran from ten to eleven p.m. Those newscasts had a different audience makeup from Fox in prime time—older, less affluent—and they would be serving as the direct lead-in to Conan at eleven. But that was not the only hang-up. Could Fox also deliver on station clearances—in other words, how many stations would actually jump in to carry a Conan show? Did too many of them have deals with syndicators for reruns of sitcoms like *Seinfeld*? Would they be willing to drop those for Conan? Could Conan compete on equal footing with the big boys, Jay and Dave?

The Conan team commissioned a consulting firm to look into the clearance issue specifically. The report was encouraging: Fox did have the right in its affiliate deals to push through the clearances across the entire network.

For the hired guns in charge of Conan's career, the resolution of the clearance issue meant the Fox offer had to be taken very seriously, especially after Chernin laid down his marker. His opening offer to Conan was $21 million a year—*seven times* his NBC salary, a figure so impressive that the agents didn't even consider a counteroffer. Chernin also argued persuasively that Conan's hanging around waiting for Jay Leno to leave the stage was only an invitation to long-term disappointment, and potentially a path toward undermining a promising career.

"Jay's not going anywhere," Chernin told them decisively. "And if you wait for *The Tonight Show*, it won't be worth what it is today."

Jeff Ross heard Chernin's impressive spin, contrasted it with the half-hearted stroking they were getting from NBC, and he felt the wind shifting hard in Fox's direction. That concerned him, because he knew one thing better than the money guys working for Conan. His guy had the bug, the congenital disease that had afflicted virtually every comic of the baby-boom generation—and, yes, that still included O'Brien, born in 1963: a craving to do the job Johnny Carson had defined so indelibly, to host *The Tonight Show.*

Conan didn't speak about it in public—his young fans, who didn't know Carson from carpeting, would have been baffled by it—but Conan had the dream, the same one that had inspired and infected Letterman and Leno. As a serious student of the history of American television, and a devotee of its classic programs, he could not help himself. He was in thrall to the dream: He wanted *The Tonight Show.* He wanted to be the guy at the head of the franchise, the show that, when he was twelve, he had watched with his dad, taking in the things Carson said and did that his father laughed at and enjoyed so much late at night in their home in Brookline, Massachusetts. That shared memory had a powerful pull on Conan.

Ross himself could not deny the seductive appeal inherent in being the guy who produced *The Tonight Show* every night; for a late-night producer, that was still the mountaintop, as well.

And both men had such links to NBC that tearing themselves away, just as Conan was steering into the fast lane of his career, would be personally wrenching. Bob Wright, the NBC chairman, had built a true connection to Conan, who sparked to Wright's genuine interest and human touch. Lorne Michaels, the impresario of *Saturday Night Live,* was showbusiness godfather to both of them; he had plucked the unknown O'Brien and installed him in the *Late Night* chair, and he had opened the door to a big-time television career for Ross.

Then there was Zucker. Though O'Brien and Zucker had a Harvard connection that bonded them, the real relationship that mattered on a personal basis was between Ross and Zucker. Their friendship—again initiated by the shared challenges of producing daily television—had set down deep roots. The two men were frequent golf partners; more than that, they were just plain buddies.

Still, none of that was going to matter if NBC placed something puny on the table against the magnitude of what Fox was promising. Ross set out to make sure Zucker was aware of the danger NBC was in. He told Zucker he had heard that Zucker's nominal West Coast boss, Sassa, had been assuring people at the network that they need not worry about Conan defecting because Fox could not clear enough stations to give the show a realistic chance.

"We gotta get this deal made," Ross told Zucker, "because they're fucking around with Conan and they're gonna push him to Fox."

"They can't clear Fox anyway," Zucker replied, having heard much the same intelligence as Sassa.

"Yeah they can," Ross shot back. "I know they can." And he laid out the research from the consultant.

Zucker took that information away with him, and NBC soon came back with a more realistic offer, extending Conan through the end of 2005 and bumping up his salary to $8.25 million a year. Although that was still only about a third of the Fox money, the NBC side was convinced it could risk the lowball offer, because it was dealing from strength: namely, the accumulated history of the network's preeminence in late night—and of course, the ultimate prize, the gold standard, *The Tonight Show*, still dangling in the distance.

For Conan's professional advisers, it wasn't nearly enough. The Endeavor agency had no formal titles, but its acknowledged leader was Ari Emanuel. Ari, already establishing himself as one of Hollywood's most aggressive, energized, and plugged-in talent reps, pushed for the Fox deal. So did his Endeavor colleague Rick Rosen, though as Conan's more day-to-day agent, and already growing close to him personally, Rosen wanted to be sure to read and serve his client's intentions as best he could. As for Gavin Polone, Conan's manager, he was about 80 percent of the way to "We gotta do this with Fox."

The NBC side was well aware of how things stacked up. As Marc Graboff, the business affairs boss, analyzed it, the Endeavor team—and Polone—would surely be lured by the big dollar signs coming from Fox. If Conan defected to Fox, Endeavor would also be in position to claim the package. (A "package" is when an agency brings together several of the creative elements of a given project and receives a healthy fee for its efforts. One of Endeavor's biggest rivals, the Creative Artists Agency, had held the package—and commensurate fat annual fee—on the Letterman show for almost a decade.) The NBC executives guessed that Endeavor must be "salivating at the opportunity to package Conan," especially because the alternative, staying with NBC, offered no such shot. *The Tonight Show* was unpackageable—it was a franchise rooted so deep that no agency could enhance it by packaging other elements beyond the host. Conan's professional representatives were up front with NBC about their intentions: They were advocating that Conan take the $21 million and a better overall deal at Fox over the measly $8 million NBC had put on the table.

Still, NBC was unworried. However ardently the management side was promoting the Fox offer, Conan and Jeff Ross had been equally candid about their reluctance to leave. Ross had heard his star's analysis of the situation clearly, and personally he agreed: It wasn't time. "I've only been at this for eight years," Conan told Ross, adding, "You know what? This company has been good to me."

O'Brien had studied the tangled 1990s business with Letterman closely and taken note of how wrenching it had been for Dave to be separated from the body of work he had created during his eleven years at NBC. Conan had a passion to stay connected to his own body of work, work he felt he had "poured my bone marrow into," work he was intensely proud of.

When the decision finally came, it was Conan alone who met with Peter Chernin. After telling him how impressed and overwhelmed he had been by the offer, and how appreciative he was for the time and effort Chernin had personally put into the courtship, he had to give an answer that Chernin was not going to like: "I'm not going to do it."

Chernin and the rest of the Fox team, while disappointed, could not have been completely surprised by the outcome. They had reasonably calculated that their gambit might have come a little early in the game, but at least they were now in good position for whenever the late-night wheel spun again. Nor had Conan's advisers, avid as they were for the Fox deal, been undone when Conan had told them his feelings.

"I'm still young," Conan explained to Rosen and the others. "I'm not forty yet. I still have one more contract to see if they'll give me *The Tonight*

Show. So we can make one more deal with NBC, and then at the end of that they have to give me the show."

Polone, as hard-assed as any talent manager could possibly be, nevertheless grasped that the essence of his client was his accommodating nature—and his straightforward decency. Conan was not only not cagy but was totally transparent and upfront, qualities that were no advantage in a negotiation. With Zucker and Wright, Conan felt he was dealing with friends as well as bosses. From Conan's point of view, everything coming from NBC's direction was positive. Polone himself would never have had such faith, but he recognized that people had different ways of looking at life. A dedicated single man, Polone concluded that it would be impossible for him to convince a happily married man that it was better to be single—in the same way it was impossible for him to convince Conan not to want *The Tonight Show.* "We all have those things," Polone concluded.

In January 2002, Bob Wright and his wife, Suzanne, were among the guests at Conan's wedding to Liza Powel in Seattle. A month later Conan signed a new deal to stay on *Late Night* through 2005, a term that guaranteed he would host the show longer than Letterman, its legendary progenitor, had. The deal added a few goodies: Conan got some guarantees of program commitments for prime-time series that his production company might create.

Much more significant was the other commitment he landed. The new deal included an explicit Prince of Wales clause: If anything happened to Jay Leno—illness, accident, sudden desire to give up show business—Conan would step in as *Tonight* host. The official line of succession was now codified.

It was an issue of great importance to O'Brien that, whatever happened in the future with *The Tonight Show,* no one would ever accuse his side of using any kind of ugly muscle tactics to wedge out Leno so that he could slide into his place. Everyone in late night remembered the campaign that Jay's former manager, Helen Kushnick, had waged to win the job for her client, which included planting some nasty stories about NBC wanting Carson out. Jay came to be ashamed of those tactics, and after he split with Kushnick, did his best to apologize abjectly to Johnny, insisting that he had not been a party to those moves, and if he had known about them he would have repudiated them.

In contrast to the always chilly relations between the Carson and Leno camps, Jay and Conan seemed to go out of their way to be cordial to each other—on the air and off. Every quote each of them gave during the years after Conan agreed to remain at NBC was respectful, without ever quite approaching affection. Both men used the "friends" word, but in the way that professional colleagues do, not true intimates. Jay invited Conan onto his show as a guest, and Conan always nailed his shot. Jay once made a crack about Conan's coming in to measure the drapes, but that was no more provocative than Carson had been in the early eighties, dropping Letterman's name in jokes about his being the presumptive heir: "If I quit, what would the succession be? Would it be Letterman, Bush, Haig? Or would it be Letterman, Bush, Tip O'Neill, and then Haig?"

Beneath that warm surface current, however, frigid waters swirled— at least on one coastline. Some of the Conan brigades continued to vent their frustration on occasion about having to still ride in the caboose, when it ought to have been as clear to NBC as it was to the press and most of the entertainment world that their guy was the comer, the fresh act in late night.

If the Conan side did offer any credit at all to Leno for his continuing success during their honest moments, it was begrudging and tinged with flecks of outright disdain. As one important member of the Conan team put it: "He's there for all those huge years of prime-time ratings for NBC, and he's not doing anything to innovate, not doing anything interesting."

Some on Jay's staff suspected their host didn't really "get" Conan or his quirky, non-joke-centric humor. But Jay never expressed that opinion openly; in fact, he never said much about Conan at all. As always, he concentrated on his show, with most of the emphasis on his monologue, which one writer on the show estimated absorbed 80 percent of Jay's daily attention.

In September of 2002 Conan sent out the most resounding message yet about his growing strength as a performer when he stepped onto a huge stage in prime time as host of that year's Emmy Awards. Award shows had proved more risk than opportunity for late-night hosts over the years. The most memorable case involved Letterman, when in 1995, at the pinnacle of his fame, he accepted—against his better judgment—an offer to host the Oscars; though he hardly bombed, he misfired enough to embarrass himself into telling the world for years he'd ruined the evening for everybody.

Still, O'Brien went into the Emmys feeling he had something to prove. "When I went in front of that Emmy crowd," he said later, "it was like they had marked my height when I was about four years old. Then it's ten years later and six-foot-four Conan walks in, and they're shocked. Because their frame of reference is always Letterman or Leno. I don't think young people were shocked at all."

Conan opened with a taped segment of him waking up at the house of Ozzy Osbourne's family, then the stars of the hottest reality show on television. Realizing he was late for the awards event, he rushed out only to stumble onto the set of *The Price Is Right* instead. The bit scored huge laughs. Later he made killer use of the award-show fetish for finding annoying ways to play long-winded accepters off the stage, warning the nominees that he would cut them off by playing an acoustic version of the worst parts of Jethro Tull's "Aqualung." Which he proceeded to do, bringing down the house.

O'Brien had been right: That evening he shocked anyone at the Emmys who thought late night still meant only Leno and Letterman. The host assignment proved to be a critical smash, a star-emerging performance for the TV historical record.

A year later, in September 2003, NBC cleared out two hours of prime time for Conan's tenth-anniversary special. (Notably, Leno had always declined the network's offers to mount big anniversary specials for him, with the comment "Ugh, no!") Staged at the Beacon Theatre on Manhattan's Upper West Side, the special was a litmus test for the erupting passion for Conan among fans under thirty years old. They lined the streets outside the theater for hours, chanting Conan's name and buying Conan merchandise from enterprising street vendors. One college-age guy wore a white T-shirt emblazoned with the message: "I took Conan for my Confirmation name!"

Up in the balcony, waiting for the show to begin and watching the raucous crowd file in, the whole Conan entourage was assembled: Rosen, Polone, and Emanuel, among others. In the row in front of the paid help, Liza O'Brien sat unobtrusively among her husband's fans. The talk was of how crazy Conan mania seemed to be getting. One of the group shook his head in wonderment: "How on earth can NBC not give him the show? Jay's used up. That old, stale stuff he does . . . Can't they see what's happening?"

For some of them, even Jay's sustaining success in the ratings was suspect. NBC had long since come down from its heights of prime-time dominance, to a point where CBS frequently trounced it in the ten p.m. hour that led into late night—and still Letterman almost never topped Leno in the numbers. But the Conan supporters questioned Jay's record, wondering whether it was Jay himself who was really attracting viewers or the reflexive habit of those viewers to tune in to *The Tonight Show.*

In one of the harshest assessments, a member of the Conan team dismissed Jay's performance utterly: "He's there, and for some of those years, if you had a cinder block in that time slot it would have done a great rating." And for good measure: "What do you want *The Tonight Show* to be? Please go find me the person under forty-five who's like, 'I've gotta leave this party early 'cause I gotta go see my Leno.' What the fuck are we doing here?"

Early in 2004, with the issue of Conan's long-term future unresolved, Jeff Ross got a call from Rick Rosen. Rosen asked him to set up a quiet place for lunch in New York with an executive named Andrea Wong, who was in charge of reality shows and late night for ABC.

This was the first time the letters ABC had appeared on the horizon, though Ross knew that nothing serious in terms of a new negotiation for his star could even begin until well into the following year. Still, having another network interested couldn't hurt.

Ross was aware that ABC's entertainment executives had been agitating internally for several years, looking for an opening into late night. The network's long-venerated news program *Nightline* had seemed to be heading for the end of its run, with its anchor, Ted Koppel, less involved, and the show's original premise—live interviews on the news of the day—overtaken by cable news programs. In 2002 ABC's entertainment division had pulled an end run around the news division, secretly seeking to replace *Nightline* by courting Letterman with promises and birthday cakes as the CBS late-night star's contract neared an end. The talks had gotten serious by the time *The New York Times* broke the story of the negotiations, and the news division, poleaxed, released an anguished cry of betrayal. Although ABC didn't back off, Letterman soon did, thanking ABC for its interest but re-signing with CBS after some timely last-minute concessions by that network's boss, Leslie Moonves.

ABC responded by reaffirming its commitment to news in the eleven thirty time slot—even as it continued to chase entertainment talent. After making a run at Jon Stewart, hoping he might be induced to break away from his cable hit *The Daily Show*, ABC pursued a guy they thought represented a broader, more down-to-earth appeal, Jimmy Kimmel. Jimmy, best known at that point for the raunchy *Man Show* on Comedy Central and witty appearances on the NFL coverage on Fox, jumped at the network opportunity. In early 2004, he had been on the air for less than a year in the 12:05 time period, serving as the follow-up act to *Nightline*.

Conan was obviously not moving anywhere that wasn't going to slot him at 11:35 (or 11:00 in the case of Fox). So when Andrea Wong asked for a meeting, Jeff Ross had every reason to conclude that *Nightline* wasn't in the clear yet.

The pair lunched at the Café des Artistes, something of an alternate (and much more upscale) ABC cafeteria on West Sixty-seventh Street, not far from the network's Manhattan headquarters. Ross found Wong, a willowy Asian-American woman in her mid-thirties, personally appealing and impressively smart. (She might have been the only network entertainment executive in history with an electrical engineering degree from MIT.) He wasn't sure she fully comprehended the late-night television "thing," but then again, Ross didn't think many television executives really got late night, with the exception of the guy Ross dealt with most often, the one with real history in the genre, NBC's Rick Ludwin.

Conan's advisers were unsure how serious this initial ABC approach really might be until, soon after the meeting with Wong, Ross got a call from Bob Iger, then number two at ABC's parent, the Disney Company (and previously an ABC executive, including president of entertainment). Jeff knew Iger a bit from socializing in New York in earlier days, so they were comfortable with each other. Iger's message was simple and direct: "This is for real."

When Ross reported on the Iger call to Conan's career team, he learned that ABC was not the only network sniffing around. Fox had reentered the picture, making it clear in messages from executives to the Endeavor boys that they were keenly interested in another run at Conan.

Ari Emanuel knew exactly what to do with all this valuable information.

At NBC, the era of good feelings about late night was short-lived—as all the executives involved knew it would be. The peace achieved by hanging on to O'Brien for four more years couldn't last, because the fundamental equation had not changed: Two still did not go into one. At some point the issue of when Conan would get his shot at *The Tonight Show*—or wouldn't—had to be faced.

Still, there was time to find some solution, and everyone at NBC knew that they could not afford a replay of the events of the nineties. The message was clear: Keep the consistently winning Jay as long as possible while also preventing Conan from taking his increasingly impressive talent elsewhere. Rick Ludwin, NBC's top late-night executive for more than two decades, had no doubts about these marching orders, or where they originated: "down from the top." In numerous meetings early in the 2000s, Bob Wright, CEO of NBC, had asked the question directly: "How do we keep Conan O'Brien at this network?"

Everyone knew where Wright stood with regard to Conan: He loved the guy. Bob had jumped on the Conan train early, at a time when other NBC executives still saw more awkwardness than brilliance in the young comedian, and he had never wavered. He had established a relationship with Conan that some NBC colleagues saw as a kind of professional paternity. "Bob would do that with certain people—become a father figure," said one of Wright's closest associates at the network. "He certainly did with Conan."

Suzanne Wright, who also embraced the role of matriarch of the network, adored Conan and Liza. Conan had had his ups and downs with various sections of NBC's management over the years, but of Bob Wright he said, "I would walk over broken glass for that man."

But neither that warm relationship nor his long history with Zucker was going to be enough to keep O'Brien at NBC indefinitely. The earlier late-night slot of 11:35 beckoned, as Conan began freely to acknowledge. "I think it's natural to at some point want to move earlier," he said. "I think I've proved I can do a show that I don't think has to exist at twelve thirty."

Starting in late 2003, Zucker and Ludwin, along with Marc Graboff, who as the executive in charge of business affairs dealt with the issues of money and deal making, held a series of discussions about what they saw as "the next cycle"—the coming choice between Leno and O'Brien, if they were going to be forced to make one. Zucker would often report on calls he had started receiving from Ari Emanuel about Conan. It was hardly unusual for Emanuel to phone Zucker—or any of the other major players in television—with ideas for his clients. That was his job, after all. He spoke more often with Zucker, though, because he genuinely liked the NBC boss, their relationship consisting of good-natured hostility. Ari, then in his early forties, steely eyed, built like a middleweight and rising fast up the power-agent rankings to a point where he was able to slug with anyone in Hollywood, would make demands, or promises. Jeff would resist or insist. They would yell a bit, tell each other to go fuck themselves, and then hang up laughing (usually). A couple of days later they would repeat the process.

Ari had decided he would keep Zucker in the loop constantly about the precise nature of the danger Jeff faced regarding the future of Conan O'Brien. As Ari saw the process, he was "making sure he knew he would lose Conan if he didn't get the *Tonight* slot." If Bob Iger checked in about Conan, Ari let Zucker know about it. "If we set a Peter Chernin meeting or a Les Moonves meeting," Emanuel filled Zucker in on the time and place. (Moonves had cast out a little fishing line on behalf of CBS during his squabble with Letterman over the ABC approach in 2002, which Conan had instantly rejected out of respect for Dave. But Emanuel still counted Les—who everyone knew drove Zucker crazier than anyone else in the business—among the interested parties for Conan's services.) Ari was sending these little messages to Zucker "just to utz him—make him realize that if he fucked this up there would be other places for Conan to go."

To Zucker, all of this amounted to standard practice from his buddy Ari. The calls came in; Ari was threatening him with something or other; that meant what—it was Tuesday? Zucker was neither surprised nor overly irritated. He knew how he was supposed to interpret these calls on behalf of Conan: "They wanted assurance that they were gonna get *The Tonight Show* or else they were gonna leave."

In truth, NBC didn't need much utzing. Internally, there was little resistance to Ari's nudging. Some way was eventually going to be found to keep Conan in house.

The first real movement came from Jay's direction, though. He was a creature of habit so ingrained that he was rarely seen offstage in anything but the same denim work shirt, faded jeans, and $14.99 pair of black Payless SafeTStep work shoes. These, Jay explained, he bought "by the crate" because they were "impervious to oil and gas"—a feature important to him because of all the time he spent working on the fleet of vehicles in his automotive shop in a converted hangar at the Burbank airport. As he did with all his other habits, Jay had such a regular timetable for rolling over his *Tonight* contract that Marc Graboff could all but put the next negotiation on his calendar the day a previous deal was concluded.

And the Jay negotiations were, without question, the easiest Graboff had ever conducted. It had been that way ever since Jay had fired Helen Kushnick and sworn off all representation for his future television career. That decision played to some as foolishness, arrogance, or parsimony on an epic scale: To try to manage a career involving so many millions without a formal agent or manager seemed ludicrous. But it was a source of pride for Jay, one more example—to himself if no one else—that deep down he was an unpretentious working man. An insanely well-paid one, certainly, but still a guy with a boss and a job and a salary.

But beyond its symbolism, or whatever else the antiagent stance meant to Jay, there was a compelling logic to his position. What did he need an agent or manager (or their bills) for at this point in his career? He had no plans to do anything on television other than what he was already doing. What other job was a manager going to win for him? Helen had secured the *Tonight* position for him; now she was gone. (After splitting from Jay in 1993, Helen passed away from cancer three years later at only fifty-one.) He still had the job.

Alan Berger, a well-liked agent from CAA, represented Jay up until the late nineties, but only for his stand-up appearances. As a favor to Jay, however, Berger took the formal meetings with NBC about extending Jay's deal, along with Jay's lawyer, Ken Ziffren. One late-nineties instance stood out to Berger as representative of all of these "negotiations."

Berger and Ziffren had sat down to lunch in Beverly Hills with John Agoglia, Graboff's predecessor as head of business affairs for NBC and one of Jay's stalwart backers in the bitter battle with Letterman in 1993. As they gathered in the restaurant, the three men greeted each other warmly, schmoozing for a while about kids and families and things that were going on in their lives. Then Agoglia said abruptly, "OK, boys, let's do business." Berger and Ziffren grabbed a napkin and quickly wrote a figure on it—Jay was asking for a small bump, up to about $14 million a year at that point. Agoglia took one look at the napkin, stuck it in his pocket, and said, "Deal—now let's order."

The NBC money, as Jay always professed, had little impact on his daily life because he never spent a penny of it. He banked it all—either in his own accounts or in the small charitable foundation he had established. It again seemed bizarre to colleagues and most everyone else who heard of this idiosyncratic practice. The man was formidably rich but was sticking earnings under a mattress somewhere? Obviously Jay, who lived in a lovely Beverly Hills home, didn't hurt for cash; Mavis had everything she could ever want and more; and Jay bought every vintage car and motorcycle that caught his fancy. But money for those things came out of the pile he earned on the side, performing up to 160 nights a year around the country at venues ranging from the big Vegas showrooms to outdoor chicken festivals in Fresno in 104-degree heat.

By rights—and again, by any sense of fairness that a hard-nosed agent would have hammered NBC with—Leno should long ago have been outearning Letterman, whom he was not only outrating virtually every night of the year but also outworking by several weeks of shows a year. But Dave still pocketed millions more a year than Jay—a fact Jay never complained about, but actually trumpeted, usually trying to make a joke out of it: "My thing is, I always make a couple of bucks less than whoever the top guy is. You can't eat the whole pie; you'll get fat, choke, and die."

At least some part of Jay's attitude was due to the lingering fallout from the ugliness over Helen's actions, which still affected him deeply. He would tell people he never wanted an agent or manager again, someone who might get overly pushy and poison his relationships. "I've heard how the executives talk and how they treat the stars that make what they perceive as unruly demands. And then suddenly it's 'Didn't we used to get a promo at nine fifteen?' Things go away, and you die a slow death."

NBC knew that any typically aggressive agent would have insisted upon at least one dollar more than whatever Letterman was making (which peaked at about $31 million a year), but Graboff had a ready reply to any such demand: Jay was the guy sitting in the chair at *The Tonight Show*, the institution. Dave was the guy who had to set off on his own and create a franchise. Graboff had stored up a few more reasons why NBC could deny Leno Letterman-level money, but it never became a factor. "Jay never asked," Graboff said.

And so it came to pass, like clockwork, just as Graboff expected it, that in December 2003, a little more than three years into Jay's ongoing five-year deal, Ken Ziffren was on the line for a brief conversation about

NBC's most prominent talent. "We got less than two years left; Jay wants to extend."

The expected formula called for a redo for the remaining time, with a small raise for Jay, and then three more years added on. That arrangement would commit NBC to Leno through the end of 2008. Graboff told Ziffren agreeably, "Let me talk to Jeff and Rick, and let me get back to you."

There was no reason for Ziffren and Leno to have expected that their standard move to extend would set in motion anything other than the usual add-on years. But the request rolled the Mouse Trap ball out onto the first ramp of the still unfinished contraption that was NBC's plan to secure its late-night future. When Graboff called Rick Ludwin and let him know the call about lengthening Jay's contract had come, Rick didn't need to do much math to work out the salient problem.

"This is going to extend beyond Conan's contract," Ludwin pointed out. He knew that by coincidence, not design, Conan's contract was all but coterminous with Jay's, lasting only a few months more. That had been an accident, because it wasn't really advantageous to NBC to have both stars free to leave at more or less the same time if some arrangement could not be worked out. Now, Ludwin said, underscoring the point, if NBC simply agreed to Jay's terms as it usually did, the network would have Jay locked into the show without having Conan locked in as well.

Graboff knew all this, of course, just as he knew that Fox had made a galloping run at O'Brien in 2001 and likely was at the ready to sprint after him again. He also knew that Conan's people had been braying at Zucker's door about using him or losing him. It was time for the definitive meeting about late night.

Because the big decision had already been tacitly made, the actual discussion—which involved Zucker, Ludwin, Graboff, and NBC's new top program executive, Kevin Reilly—went largely without drama. Graboff got the message clearly: "If we have to promise Conan *The Tonight Show*, we will."

The only issue was how to accomplish this. Could they simply shut down Jay at the end of this deal, given that he was still cruising along in first place, throwing off dollars as he went? Did that make any sense? But then again, how long could they realistically ask Conan to wait before his hyperactive sled-dog team mushed him out the door to another destination?

Zucker made the final call on establishing the strategy. He told Graboff how he would handle it. They would go to Jay with a message: "Yes, we'll extend your deal. But this is your last contract. Time to hand over the keys."

Before they took that step, however, they had to be sure that Conan and his Wild Bunch would agree to cool their heels. That assignment fell to Graboff, who knew just the right person to call.

Jeff Ross had called nobody and pressured no one. He didn't utz his friend Jeff Zucker in any way. Golf was golf; *The Tonight Show* did not come up over five-foot putts. It was important to Ross, the straightest of straight shooters, that Conan not be cast as anything even approaching the heavy in his pursuit of the *Tonight* assignment. Strong-arming wasn't Conan's style—and it certainly wasn't Ross's.

That was one of many reasons why Jeff Ross belonged to one of the tiniest clubs in show business: the league of the universally well liked. The Conan staff, the NBC management, the publicists, the other producers in the late-night brotherhood (and sisterhood, counting Debbie Vickers, who had nothing but affection and respect for her counterpart in New York)—nobody seemed to have a bad word to say about Jeff Ross, no matter how heated the circumstances. Instead, they used words like "solid," "reliable," "flexible," "shrewd," and "menschy." Thin and wiry, dark hair cropped close, Ross, still in his forties, usually wore an inscrutable expression behind his John Lennon wire-frames, one that might have signaled dour, serious, or disinterested, but almost always indicated only that he was keeping his emotions—and everything else—under control. Conan often joked—sometimes in the middle of on-air monologues—about Ross's Zen-like mien, imitating Ross in a mock mumble, "Yeah, it was OK; sorta funny; could have been better." But he greatly valued what Ross had to say, because Jeff gave it to him straight. He lifted Conan when he needed lifting—which could be often, given O'Brien's depressive tendencies and penchant for beating himself up—and he brought Conan back to earth when his ego started to soar. "Sometimes I would kill for a yes-man," Conan said in an interview about his producer. "Jeff is completely honest with me. We argue, but Jeff doesn't trade in compliments, doesn't waste time stroking my ego." Everyone around the show—and connected with Conan's career—understood the critical role Ross played over the sixteen years they had put *Late Night* on the air together. He was the trusted counselor and more; he was the true-blue comrade.

In early February, when Jeff Ross got the unexpected call from Marc Graboff on the subject of what was then going on with Leno and his proposed contract extension, he took it as a completely unsolicited move by NBC to reach out to the Conan side.

Graboff made it clear that this was a back-channel conversation, not an official contact, network to talent. He had a simple question: Would Conan wait four years in exchange for a guarantee that he would ascend at that point to *The Tonight Show*?

The question being unofficial, Ross felt comfortable giving an unofficial response: "Look, the obvious answer is yes." But of course he would take the question—quietly—to Conan.

As the two warriors who had shed the most blood building Conan's television career from almost literally nothing, Ross and O'Brien shared an understanding that the rest of their team could never quite be part of. The agents Conan had hired were among the most impressive Jeff Ross had ever dealt with—and besides that, he was fond of them, especially Rick Rosen, who had become a confidant and friend outside the business. Ross knew they were dedicated to his guy and pushed to get the best for him. But they were still in a different business, and a different city, three thousand miles away. They were not in the offices at 30 Rock, sitting there every day with Conan, dragging him off the floor during the postmortems when he felt he'd botched a guest interview or a comedy bit. They did not really know what it took to make a show every day out of piles of written comedy notions and yellow cards with guests' names stuck to a wall. And so, to Ross, the agents did not totally get it—not what Conan was all about as a performer, and not what *The Tonight Show* meant to him. For agents, in general, money seemed to be too much the prime factor in considering a client's future, and a decision like the one they were now facing simply could not be based upon financial considerations alone. Waiting four more years to get to 11:35, when Fox and ABC were beating down doors with money and blandishments, might sound preposterous given how hot Conan was post-Emmys and post–anniversary show.

But Jeff Ross knew his guy, so the conversation about the news delivered by Graboff was going to be just between them. Ross would be telling Conan something he had longed to hear—NBC had a plan to give him

The Tonight Show—but it was coming with a delay that Conan likely did not expect. So in his usual low-key style, Ross laid it out: NBC is talking about maybe extending Leno until 2008, and then guaranteeing you the gig . . . if you're willing to wait. O'Brien's nimble mind could make all the requisite leaps in an instant. This solution had an elegance to it: Jay would be accorded all honors due him with a lengthy farewell tour of duty; Conan would be rewarded for loyal service to the network. Was there any doubt? Conan said, "I'll do it."

Then the two compatriots had a little laugh together about how the call to propose this notion had come in from Graboff. They both knew who was really behind the deal.

As for the delay involved, while it seemed easy to Conan to say he would wait, at the same time it struck him: Who in show business waited that long for anything? It was absurd, maybe the most ridiculous request in the world. But it was also kind of comical. By the time he got to host *The Tonight Show*, he could well be riding onto the stage wearing a jetpack.

Still, he had no real reservations. Conan knew that if he refused and went to another network, and then at some indefinite point in the future Jay really did step down and someone else was named to host *The Tonight Show*, it would have haunted him forever. He needed to take this deal. He had to say yes.

It was mid-February 2004, and Conan O'Brien had the assurance he had been looking for: NBC was committing to him as the next host of *The Tonight Show*. But he could hardly unleash a celebration. Jay Leno didn't know a thing about the deal. Nothing could be made public for a still-undetermined amount of time. But that didn't mean Conan couldn't share the happy news with a *few* people.

The secret was closely held; just the intimates Conan trusted. His wife, of course; and Jeff Ross. And a select few others.

On February 19, just days after learning the news, Conan, stepping up for his network as usual, participated in a gala event at the Waldorf-Astoria: The Museum of Television and Radio held a dinner to honor Tom Brokaw on his impending retirement as the anchor of *NBC Nightly News*. O'Brien enjoyed a warm friendship with Brokaw and happily signed on as one of the hosts for the affair.

As the celebrity-fest was drawing to a close, O'Brien and Ross quietly invited Marc Liepis, the longtime NBC publicist assigned to their show, who had also attended the dinner, to join them for a nightcap. It was a signal of their great affection for Marc, an engaging, sweet soul of a guy as well as a dedicated Conan loyalist, much more of the show than of the network. The three men, still in their tuxes, repaired uptown to the famous Bemelmans Bar in the Carlyle Hotel, trundling in out of the February cold, lightly dusted with snow, like iconic characters in a sophisticated thirties movie of Manhattan nightlife.

They settled into one of the mocha-colored leather banquettes under the gold-leaf ceiling, across from the black granite bar with the famous murals by Ludwig Bemelmans arrayed behind it, and ordered a round of martinis. Unrecognized in the discreetly dim lighting, Conan stretched out his crane-like legs and leaned back to relax. The white-jacketed waiter arrived with the drinks. Piano music played softly under the conversation. Conan casually told Marc that he and Jeff had some news. But it was something Marc had to keep to himself—for a while.

"I'm getting *The Tonight Show*," Conan said, just a trace of how-about-that in his expression. Liepis, eyes widening, popped to attention: What did he mean he was getting *The Tonight Show*?

Conan explained the approach from NBC, the promise that Jay would be asked to step away after a last long-term deal, and his own commitment to NBC that he would wait his turn in exchange for the assurance that the show would be his. He also emphasized that Jay didn't know about it yet.

Liepis was astonished—and overjoyed. He had long been a believer in Conan's talent, and more than that, he just liked the guy, his integrity, his decency. Liepis had trouble believing Jay Leno would ever consider walking away from *The Tonight Show*. But if Conan was satisfied it was happening, he was satisfied. He was also flattered to his shoes to be included in the intimate circle that shared this gratifying moment.

Marc and Jeff Ross toasted Conan. All three of them understood how far Conan had come; they didn't have to mention it. But it clearly colored the satisfaction evident in Conan's face.

Of course, they agreed, they would need to be hypervigilant about keeping the secret. A slip, even around the office, could put the whole arrangement at risk. They decided they needed some code, some word or phrase the three of them could turn to if they needed to communicate about the still-private plan.

Conan had an idea: Instead of saying "Tonight," they would say "Anderson Cooper 360" every time they wanted to refer to the show in question. Cooper's nightly newscast with that title had recently begun its run on CNN. They toasted Anderson Cooper as well.

Back at NBC, Graboff had his back-channel answer. He next set a meeting with Rick Rosen in his office at Endeavor to go over the terms. Sitting on Rick's couch, Graboff spelled them out: Conan would extend his own deal for the 12:35 show through to the end of the new agreement they were drawing up with Jay. The separate, specific deal for a new contract for *The Tonight Show* would be drawn up later, after they were sure Jay had signed on. Conan's representatives would no longer engage with Fox or ABC or anyone else who came knocking about Conan's future. As far as money went, well, Conan would have to stay at his 12:35 salary until he moved up, and then he would get "a little bump." After all, the *Late Night* show didn't attract anywhere near the revenue *The Tonight Show* did, so NBC could hardly afford to pay Conan some extravagant sum just for agreeing to stick around in the job he already had. Rosen emphatically countered with the argument that this was another four years of Conan's taking something like one-third the salary he could have been making elsewhere. But of course he would take the offer to his client.

When Conan heard the financial terms, he realized he was almost certainly in a position to play hardball with NBC. "Look," he could say, "I'm going to stay at twelve thirty, but it's going to cost you." But he informed his team that he wasn't prepared to do even that. He realized he had to give things up—it was part of his nature: "Fuck me. I'm Catholic."

This was the deal Jeff Zucker had painstakingly put together as he gathered himself for the daunting encounter with Jay that March afternoon in 2004 in Burbank. For support and expertise in late-night issues—and because he knew how much Jay respected him—Zucker brought along Rick Ludwin.

Ludwin had been an integral part of the planning for this moment. Of all the executives at NBC, he had the only ongoing, straight-line connection to both Jay and Conan. Ludwin's position throughout had been clear to everyone else in the talks: He supported Jay now and always but he believed the future was Conan. Ludwin was as soft-spoken, unpretentious, and unassuming in his mid-fifties as he had been over his two-decade tenure as NBC's late-night specialist. Still square shouldered and soft featured behind his professorial glasses, still frequently in uniform—blue blazer, gray slacks—Ludwin had the requisite reverence for NBC's late-night tradition. He saw *The Tonight Show* as a constant in the lives of Americans—"as comforting as your own living room," as he viewed it. Even the strongest shows in prime time came and went, Ludwin would argue, but *The Tonight Show* kept on rolling, more than half a century on, "like Ol' Man River."

The hosts, Ludwin accepted as an article of faith, became part of people's families in a peculiar way—viewers took it personally when something happened involving one of these guys, even if they hadn't watched the show in a while. Ludwin had long expressed his philosophy about the job of hosting *The Tonight Show*: It was a rental. "You get the keys to *The Tonight Show* when it's number one and you're expected to hand it off when it's number one. But you only have it for a certain amount of time. Someone was there before you got there. Someone's going to be there after you leave, and it's your obligation to maintain it until the next person takes over." As Ludwin saw it, Jay had fulfilled his obligation with distinction. And it could be expected he would continue to meet the network's expectations until the end of this next contract, leaving at number one. But then, it was time.

One of the other reasons Zucker was reluctant to sit down with Jay that afternoon was that they were meeting him in the private sitting room, the place where Jay would hold occasional postmortems about the show with his writers, the place Zucker called "the dungeon." Just outside his dressing room, deep in the bowels of the Burbank studio, it had the quality of a dank, well-worn rec room in a frat house. Pizza boxes with a few congealed slices left might be taking up floor space. Bowls of salsa or graying guacamole along with some stray chips might be on the coffee table, along with half-finished bottles of soft drinks. Zucker, who had been there only on a few previous occasions, thought it was disgusting. Jay found it relaxing and homey.

After the usual greetings, Zucker and Ludwin sat on one of the lumpy couches opposite Jay. Debbie Vickers had decided not to tip Jay off as to the purpose of the meeting—it was NBC's call; let their guys take the heat—and if Jay had any expectation of what he was about to hear, he didn't betray it.

Zucker began by saying that he had come to talk about the contract extension, and the news on that front was good. But he also had some other news. The network was going to extend Jay's deal just as Ziffren had proposed, Zucker explained, so it would add up again to five years total—the bulk of the two remaining years and three more, taking Jay to the end of 2008.

But the network had decided that at that point it would be time to make a move. They were going to give the show to Conan.

In the best of times and the worst of times, Jay Leno wore a mask of impassivity. That's all the two NBC executives saw now. Inside, however, Jay was as stunned as if he'd been hit with a Taser shot.

Zucker immediately emphasized how long they wanted to keep Jay on the show, almost five years from that point, an eternity in television time. Ludwin added the obvious: The network didn't want to lose Conan.

Jay said, solemnly, "I don't want to lose Conan, either."

There was history behind that concession. The realists about how show business works didn't have a problem with any of Jay's tactics during the contentiousness over replacing Carson. That included one close associate of Letterman's who, years after the tumult, said, "It's what you do in this business. You gun for the job." In some circles of the television industry, however, Jay's tactics during the succession battle had gained him a reputation as a Machiavellian schemer who had played dirty and screwed a guy he really *did* think of as a friend—Letterman—out of a job that was by rights owed to Dave first.

That was also the opinion frequently expressed in the press—and by Letterman, who, in his increasing mentions of Jay on the air (sometimes accompanied by a squeaky-voiced Jay impression), often did so in the context of NBC's having rejected him in favor of Jay. Almost every year at Passover the Letterman joke was the same: "Passover is a Jewish feast—it's also what happened to me at NBC."

Zucker and Ludwin had intended to reference the concern that Leno surely didn't want to get caught up in another PR bloodbath, and how this solution would preclude all that. But Jay himself quickly spoke up: "I know I don't want everybody to go through what Letterman and I did. I don't want to go through all that nonsense again."

Zucker found himself appreciating again Jay's solid professionalism. He was throwing no tantrums; he was expressing no antipathy toward NBC, or Conan, or anyone else, for that matter. Ludwin felt the same. Jay seemed to understand the situation completely and was showing support for the idea. Of course Ludwin realized there could be a difference between how a person reacted and how he felt inside.

Inside Leno was in pain. This was a guy who in fourth grade had been hit on the head with a hammer by a kid who thought anyone with a head that big must surely have a skull made of granite. Bleeding, Leno assured the class he was fine—though it hurt like hell. He got a big laugh, which made the pain pass more quickly.

Beyond the crushing disappointment of hearing this news—which to Leno sounded awfully like he was being fired—his other dominant feeling was befuddlement. Why was this happening now? What sense did it make, with him still so strongly in first place?

But he didn't raise those questions; he was in good-soldier mode. So instead he asked about the particular details: Why, if they were really saying he was going to have five more years on *Tonight*, did the deal run only through the end of 2008? That sounded more like four years, not five.

The explanation was mundane: That was the extension Jay, through Ziffren, had asked for. But maybe they could make it the full five years and extend it to the end of 2009. Maybe.

Leno knew they would have to get Conan's side to agree to that. But he also had another question: Would it be possible for NBC to announce his extension first, totally separate from any formal declaration of the deal to install Conan? That way there could be a period of time when it was still only about Jay's getting more years on *Tonight* and not that he was being readied for the exit.

The NBC executives saw the reasonableness of this request, and they agreed to it. NBC would announce that Jay was signing a new deal as the host. Months later—say, six months—they would make public that Conan was getting the show in 2008 or 2009.

As he left the dungeon, Jeff Zucker felt relieved and satisfied. His trepidation had been misplaced; Jay had taken the news just fine. In Zucker's

gut this felt like the right move. By the time this deal was over, he calculated, Jay would be almost sixty and would have been on *The Tonight Show*
since 1993. Those stats made an impression on Zucker: Close to sixty and
seventeen years on the air sounded like the appropriate time for a change.
All they had to do now was smooth a few things over with the Conanites,
including that little extra year Jay was asking for. And all sides would
have to agree to keep secret for six months that Jay's extension carried a
big asterisk, one that led to a footnote saying, "And no more." Normally
Zucker would expect that it might be asking a lot of Ari and the boys to
remain silent about big news like this for so important a client. But NBC
would make that part of the agreement. It wouldn't become official until
Jay had his six months of grace.

Jay, meanwhile, climbed out of the dungeon and made his way upstairs
to Debbie Vickers's office to let her know that he felt as if he had just been
fired—and to tell her, "The only reason they are doing this is because they
made a deal with someone else."

On March 30, 2004, NBC announced it had reached an agreement with
Jay Leno to remain as host of *The Tonight Show* until the end of 2009. In an
interview, Jay observed, "It seemed pretty simple. NBC came to me and
said, 'We'd like to sign you for about five more years,' and I said, 'Fine.'"
He had only one specific comment about the terms. "I'm still not making
Dave money."

Zucker said the deal had been negotiated "strictly between me and
Jay" and added, "We decided to do it now because Jay is now the perennial leader in late night and he only shows signs of getting stronger." At
the time, late in the 2004–2005 television season, Jay, with an average of
6.2 million viewers, had been posting increases in both his overall ratings
and his lead over Letterman, who was averaging about 4.4 million.

NBC made no comment about Conan O'Brien that day, but of course
the speculation was all over the press. What did it mean for Conan, whose
deal was to end on December 31, 2005, now that Jay was locked in until
the end of the decade?

Conan and his professional posse went along with the charade, acced-
ing to the terms that had been agreed upon. After all, there was always the
chance that the thing could blow up again, at least until Conan formally
signed a contract that contained the phrase "*Tonight Show*." That may have

been why they didn't shrink from flimflamming the situation a bit. Less than a week after the Leno announcement, in an extensive profile, Conan, speaking of his future, said, "A big question is looming. It's the elephant in the room that no one is talking about: What's next?"

He also pointed out, "No one at NBC has said, 'Here's what we're going to do. Here's the offer.' It's hard to figure these things out in a vacuum."

Gavin Polone laid it on even thicker. "I was a little surprised by what NBC did with Jay," Polone remarked in his own interview, overtly expressing surprise about how NBC had made this long commitment without first locking in Conan. "Conan has a lot of great choices ahead of him. NBC has probably only a lot of anxiety ahead of them."

And even though all outside contacts had been shut down per the arrangement with NBC, Polone went on to describe those alleged choices: "I think Fox has to offer. I believe CBS might have to offer. And ABC obviously has to offer. You might have three companies that need new jetliners at the same time, and we'll be the only company actually building a jet. Other people may be building washing machines. But why go to a company offering washing machines when you need a jet?"

All of Conan's people made their uncertainly about the future sound real, since it was either that or dodge the questions entirely. If they said nothing, Jay would get six months solo on the PR stage, which might make it look as if Conan had gone cold and the quest for an 11:35 slot had become moribund. So they fudged and dissembled.

Speaking about the deal that NBC had announced with Leno, Conan said, "It's hard for me emotionally to say, 'How can Leno deserve to be there, when I deserve to be there?' I don't feel that in my bones." But he also stepped back, trying to distinguish his own position from that of his representatives. "My agents can say that—and they do. But I have no control over them. They're Rottweilers that I bought. Their job is to attack. My job is to say, 'Dear me.' But I don't expect things that are unrealistic."

As for Jay's longevity, Conan played the game, making it sound as if he had no reason to expect his *Tonight* commitment wasn't open-ended. "Jay may decide he wants to do the show until 2025," Conan joked. "Jay could say, 'My brain will be in a jar and we'll wheel it out and I'll do the monologue.' "

But at the same time he took pains to express fondness for the man who at that point seemed—outside of the small circle involved in the deal, in any case—still to be in Conan's way. "I like Jay and I wouldn't want to do anything with NBC that I wouldn't be able to tell Jay I was doing," Conan said. He was being entirely sincere. That had never been his intention and would never be his intention. "I do not want to manipulate my way into this job."

Of course, even with every issue of potential contention apparently settled—in private—the situation was worth another innocent joke: "Let's just hope it gets ugly, and then we'll all have fun," Conan said.

On the morning of September 27, 2004, almost six months to the day after the formal announcement of the Leno extension, Conan O'Brien stepped into the NBC executive offices on the fifty-second floor of 30 Rock, picked up a pen, and signed his name to the document that promised to make him the next host of television's most storied entertainment show: NBC's *Tonight Show*. He returned to his *Late Night* offices, gathered his staff, and broke the news, beaming through the sustained applause.

At about ten a.m. in Burbank, Jay had his own staff meeting. Betraying no hint of reservation, he revealed that word was about to break in New York that he would be leaving the show at the end of 2009, with Conan taking over. The *Tonight* staff reacted with some shock, but Jay assured them 2009 was a long way off and they all had plenty of work to do in the meantime.

Soon after Jay made his announcement, NBC pushed the button on its prepared press release. It was official: Conan would be Leno's (and Carson's) successor in 2009, following the expiration of Jay's contract. The only quote in the release was a crafted statement from Jay: "When I signed my new contract, I felt that the timing was right to plan for my successor, and there is no one more qualified than Conan. Plus, I promised my wife, Mavis, I would take her out for dinner before I turned sixty."

NBC deliberately shunned answering any press questions, wanting to allow the first public comment to come from Jay on that night's show. Nothing emerged from the O'Brien camp, either—not even a pro forma statement from Conan—again permitting Jay to take the lead. This concession was not made out of deference to Jay's status as late-night's leading star, however, but rather was linked to the fulfillment of one of the demands that had come from Conan's representatives during the negotiations over the details of the *Tonight Show* contract.

One deal point that Conan's reps had insisted on was that NBC announce the deal publicly. The network would have much preferred to make the arrangements quietly, and then leave them in place for a couple of years before going public. To Graboff, Zucker, and the other NBC executives, it seemed far too soon to be creating a lame-duck situation, which they knew was going to happen the second the world heard a guaranteed succession was in place. But the network team had little choice. Even if they resisted and pushed to keep the agreement secret for some substantial period of time, they guessed it would be only a matter of days before somebody on the Conan side—most likely Gavin Polone—would plant a story saying O'Brien was staying at NBC because he had been given *The Tonight Show*. So NBC assented to full disclosure—and Jay presumed he should be the vehicle for that disclosure, a position Zucker supported. Zucker concluded that Ari and his group believed it was essential to put NBC on record as issuing an official notice that this was really happening—a gesture they would call proof of good intentions. And nothing could be more official than Jay himself announcing his departure on national television.

There had been one other demand from the Conan side, tied to their desire for some guarantee of good faith from NBC. It was all well and good to be told Conan was getting *The Tonight Show* in five years, but as even one senior NBC executive conceded, "You can't trust network executives; they go back on their word." The Endeavor agents were hardly going to take at face value NBC's assurances that they would go through with the deal, no matter what the coming five years would bring. They required a bit more value.

What was needed, Ari and his team concluded, was a penalty payment so crushing, so overwhelming, that nothing would ever induce NBC to put itself in the position of having to pay it. They consequently asked for $80 million. After the usual haggling, both sides settled on $45 million. Conan's agents plugged in various bells and whistles, accompanied by recitations about how Conan could have taken another offer to go to a different network, and how he was staying only because NBC was promising this show, and if he didn't get it, the damage was surely worth $45 million—plus his attorney's fees after he sued.

Simplified, the terms meant that if NBC decided to renege on Conan for any reason—other than Conan's refusal to work or some transgression of moral turpitude—the network would be compelled to sign a check of truly imposing magnitude. It was even bigger than Dave money.

That night, with a larger audience than usual watching—it included, after all, everyone who had been involved in this protracted deal, including Conan's lawyers, who would be checking to make sure that whatever Jay said satisfied the stipulations—Jay stepped up to his assignment.

Looking sharp in a fresh haircut, Jay sat at his desk after the first commercial and, displaying something that looked like enthusiasm, laid out the tale. Like Conan and his backers, Jay clearly dissembled on the details, making it sound as if the two NBC decisions—extending Jay, anointing Conan—had been agreed to at different points in time. He certainly implied that he had agreed with the notion that his doing the show past 2009, when he would turn fifty-nine, was untenable, because "there was really only one person who could have done this into his sixties, and that was Johnny Carson—and, I think it's fair to say, I'm no Johnny Carson."

Leno acknowledged that Conan was funny and "the hottest late-night guy out there." What was unquestionably true was the rationale for the move that Jay explained, which was the same one he had expressed to Zucker and Ludwin: He didn't want Conan to go anywhere else. Jay cited the animosity between him and Letterman that had marked the previous turnover in the job and regretted that "good friendships were permanently damaged. And I don't want to see anybody ever have to go through that again."

Leno ended his statement by linking the move to NBC's late-night doctrine of temporary stewardship. "'Cause this, you know, this show is like a dynasty," Leno said. "You hold it, and then you hand it off to the next person. And I don't want to see all the fighting and all the 'Who's better?' and nasty things back and forth in the press. So right now, here it is—Conan, it's yours! See you in five years, buddy!"

CHAPTER THREE

THE CONAN OF IT ALL

On a brisk evening in September 1981, hanging around his cluttered room in Holworthy Hall, an eighteen-year-old Harvard freshman from suburban Brookline—near enough to Cambridge that he could have been a commuter—had no special plans.

He had spent his first weeks wandering the impressive and imposing campus, trying on different hats, looking for a place where he might fit in. Fitting in had always been an issue for the spindly young man, who had reached six foot four but at that date weighed just 150 pounds. He was also a startlingly red figure, a mass of coppery hair and matching freckles that would have screamed Irish even if his name hadn't been O'Brien.

Having served the previous year as editor of the school paper at Brookline High, Conan had already tried on one hat, dropping into what was called a "comp meeting" at the *Harvard Crimson*, the deadly serious, tradition-steeped daily that beckoned to those among the student elite with a calling for journalism, social commentary, and perhaps even literary pursuits. O'Brien fell somewhere within that territory, having formed a vague picture of himself working in the future as a serious writer of short fiction. Still, the *Crimson* meeting hadn't felt right; he emerged thinking, *This isn't me; this isn't it.*

In the days since, he had wandered around the campus pondering which other Harvard headwear he might try on, without much success.

Like most everything else he had experienced in his early life, this Harvard thing was starting to feel as though it was going to be a slow build.

Then one of his suitemates, John O'Connor, poked his head in the door and asked, "You wanna go to the *Lampoon* meeting?"

Conan knew the name but not much else about the *Harvard Lampoon*. He had never even read its more popular commercial offshoot, the *National Lampoon*, in his life. In his ongoing hat survey, the *Lampoon* hadn't figured in at all. But he had no special plans. "Well, I'll come along with you," he said.

At the meeting, held in the *Lampoon* "Castle"—every Harvard publication had its own pretensions—prospective contributors were given the rundown: They had to write three audition pieces. If they made the cut with those, they would have to write three more. That's all it took: six funny pieces, and you were in.

Conan's reaction was not immediate enthusiasm, but writing something purely out of his head—rather than having to, say, gather facts for a piece in the *Crimson*—appealed to the nascent creative side of the O'Brien brain. So that night he sat down and wrote his first piece. It was quickly approved, so he wrote another. That, too, got enthusiastic approval. The third got him hired and also put him on the fast track to becoming the only freshman on what they called the "lit board" of the magazine.

For O'Brien, the experience was a rush. For the first time in his life, he was doing something that came easily to him and that people apparently valued. Suddenly a group of people who seemed like actual adults—twenty-two-year-olds—respected him, wanted to publish things that sprang from his imagination. And then he started hearing about former *Lampoon* writers who had written sketches on *Saturday Night Live*. That was another revelation: People got *paid* for doing this kind of thing? You could make a career out of this?

The following year O'Brien was elected "president" (anywhere else, editor) of the magazine, an unusual honor for a sophomore. That led to the even more unusual honor of holding the position for two years. (It was only the second time in the magazine's then-century-old history that that had occurred, and the first to hold that distinction was Robert Benchley.) His funny credentials assured, Conan began, at editorial meetings, to unleash his highly energized, spontaneous, almost Dadaist comedy, hurling himself around the room, doing almost anything to make his colleagues laugh—which they did, a lot.

His pals began to tell him he should save some of this material for when he had his show. His *show*—that sounded right. An inveterate doodler, he had already created the self-caricature—outline of features, dots for freckles, big swoosh of hair—that would later become his signature. When he passed the information kiosks that dotted the Harvard campus, he would quickly sketch the little Conan head and have it saying some nonsense words like "Jub, Jub." When people would ask him what he was doing, he would say, "It's a promotion—for my show."

It was all talk. When offered his first real on-campus performing gig—a chance to emcee the annual concert of the Radcliffe Pitches, an a cappella group that traditionally invited the *Lampoon* president to do the opening jokes for its show—Conan had to choke down raw panic before saying, with manufactured panache, "Yes, I'll do it!"

He went out and bought blue index cards and started writing jokes. He acquired a white yachting cap and a big cigar. And—even paler than usual from the surging fear—he set off for his stage debut. As he sat upstairs in the big Sanders Theatre, going over his cards, praying he knew what would make these people laugh, Conan could hear the crowd below, thump-thump-thumping their feet in anticipation. He realized he had arrived at the most frightening moment of his life and found himself frozen in his chair.

A stagehand finally came to nudge him: "You gotta get out there." So Conan O'Brien sucked in some air, stuck on his yachting cap, picked up his cigar, and galumphed those big legs out onto the stage.

He got laughs—genuine, honest laughs. The sound wafted up from the audience and enveloped him, embraced him, cocoonlike—or maybe like the ring of smoke in an opium den. O'Brien had never used drugs and never would. But this? This was the same thing; this was cocaine.

The week of graduation, the *Crimson*—now edited by a kid named Zucker—ran a series of profiles of some of the departing seniors. Conan had his own framed and hung in his boyhood room back in Brookline (where it would remain, always). It identified O'Brien—even with his American lit and history double major, and his thesis on "literary progeria" in the works of Flannery O'Connor and William Faulkner—as the "preeminent jokester" of the class of '85. The profile ended with a quote from Conan, answering the question "What do you want to be doing twenty years from now?"

"I want to be hosting my own show," O'Brien replied, "and hawking my own line of designer jeans."

Conan Christopher O'Brien was born in Brookline, Massachusetts, on April 18, 1963, third in a brood of six, the children of Thomas O'Brien and Ruth Reardon O'Brien—a family so deeply Irish they might as well have lived in a bog.

But they didn't; they lived in a big, rambling, comfortable home in a lovely neighborhood, a product of conspicuous professional success. Dad was a prominent physician, a specialist in immunology, who eventually would wind up teaching at Harvard Medical School. If anything, Mom's record of achievement was even more impressive. A scholarship student at Vassar, she graduated from Yale Law School (after turning down Harvard Law), worked on the creation of the Peace Corps for the Kennedy administration, put aside her legal career to raise her children, and returned to law and became only the second female partner at the well-regarded Boston firm of Ropes & Gray.

Their third son did not spring from the womb funny—nor academically driven, despite the parental example. Though well loved in his supremely functional and warm family, Conan felt awkward and out of place for much of his childhood. He started out with a deep distaste for school, until he saw it as a route to recognition for achievement. Then he applied himself toward excelling with a steely purpose. Too gangly to be an athlete, unwilling to turn himself into a bookish nerd, and not confident enough yet to exhibit publicly the wiseass within, he was a kid without a natural constituency through most of his precollege years.

His sense of humor was initially more defense mechanism than personal statement, and it certainly did not seem an avenue to show business for the young O'Brien. But then, what did a kid in Massachusetts, with two professional parents, know about getting into show business? "You might as well say I'm going to Mars" was how it seemed to Conan. But he loved the *idea* of show business. He loved comedy, loved to make his family and the other kids laugh. He loved comedy movies, watching them obsessively, especially the classics featuring the Marx Brothers or W. C. Fields. He took note of everything about comedy—pratfalls, verbal byplay, pure wit.

The young Conan thought the way you became an entertainer was by learning the basics—like, for example . . . tap dancing. How could you be in show business without being able to tap dance? His doting—but likely confused—parents found a protégé of Bill "Bojangles" Robinson, and Conan diligently took tap lessons for several years, the distinctly odd kid out, one white face among a group of inner-city black youths.

When that ended—as it had to, once the realization set in that vaudeville was dead—Conan channeled most of his deep reservoir of energy into shining in school. He became a grinder, especially in high school, when Harvard loomed as his goal. (The role of class clown had zero appeal; Conan always maintained that "the class clown is killed in a motel shoot-out.") He focused on schoolwork with an intensity that few of his contemporaries could match. His mother noticed and started to believe her son was a person who would never take things lightly. Conan wanted Harvard because no one in his preposterously high-achieving family had ever gone there. But mainly he wanted Harvard because that was where all the smartest people went, and this was a smart young man who wanted to get someplace.

High school was the last time Conan was unsure where he was ultimately headed, but it helped get him on the road. He did, inevitably, give the class speech as valedictorian—and, yes, he got some laughs.

Being funny onstage may have been something of a drug, but from the day he left Harvard, heading for LA and a career, O'Brien recognized that one form of comedy did not fit his particular specifications—or vice versa.

He knew he wasn't a stand-up. He had a different kind of mind, one that truly sparked only when touched to another. He was interactive— he was funny with people, and he made other people funny. Stand-up seemed a different art form, one he respected, but did not want to practice.

The notion of improv, however, intrigued him. He knew little about it, had never taken a class, or even seen it performed. But it *sounded* like him. So when he and his best *Lampoon* writing buddy, Greg Daniels, landed in LA in the summer of 1985, already hired as writers for the HBO sketch comedy series *Not Necessarily the News*, Conan spent part of his first day at the Sunset Gower Studios trying to wheedle his way into a class given by the improv troupe the Groundlings.

Crushed to learn that all the classes were filled, Conan said he had to do something, so they recommended a woman named Cynthia Seghetti, who taught at the Coronet Theatre. When Conan turned up there, he realized it was extremely informal, the kind of class where you stuck ten bucks in a jar when you left. The students, such as they were, seemed engaged in various exercises. One was "space work"—doing things like pretending to lift an imaginary heavy desk. Conan went at this assignment with his customary 100 percent conviction—so much so that an attractive tall blond girl came up and complimented him on his commitment to the exercise. Her name was Lisa Kudrow, and a long, sometimes romantic, always warm relationship was born.

The group performed improv in places like the basement of the Scientology Center, where it was almost impossible to get audiences because people were afraid of being shanghaied on their way in. There was no money in it, but money wasn't the point; O'Brien was already making a fine salary for an LA newcomer, thanks to his HBO job. But in off hours he was also accepting oddball assignments like industrial videos, driving two hours out into the San Fernando Valley in his 1977 Isuzu Opel, applying his own makeup during the drive. Often he played the know-it-all salesman whose technique drove the customers away. He would make up patter on the spot—something else he discovered he had a talent for. The level of gratification in this sort of acting was as slight as the pay, but it was an opportunity to perform.

Mainly, he was writing. The *Not Necessarily the News* job soon led to another gig: O'Brien and Daniels, already making an impression, were hired by a new late-night show concocted for the Fox network and touted as being the first real alternative to the staid talk-show format. *The Wilton North Report*—a bizarre amalgam of fake news and silly gags—lasted less than two months. O'Brien figured it was good experience doing "service on a ship that sank." Plus he occasionally got to warm up the (sparse) crowd.

But Conan knew in his gut the show he really wanted to write for—the show that had so captured him with its comic sensibility that he cringed with regret when it was impossible for him to catch it every night when he was in college. Everything about what David Letterman was doing on his NBC *Late Night* show spoke to the creative core of Conan O'Brien, and he was spurred by the possibility that he could someday write for Dave and find ways to satisfy his jones to perform at the same time. His inspiration in that regard was Chris Elliott, the young Letterman writer who had become a regular performer on the show, creating off-the-wall characters, most memorably "The Guy Under the Seats," in which he played a nutjob who lived beneath the seats of Letterman's studio.

Conan finally put together a packet—a collection of comedy pieces based on what the show was then doing, including monologue jokes, material written for established sketches, and some the writer would invent—sent in his submission, and waited for the good news.

The wait was considerable, because writing openings on Letterman's show were rare and, with a sizzling-hot show on their hands, the staff was flooded with submissions. But Conan's packet eventually made its way to the top of the pile, and when the first opening in a long stretch came up, he learned he was in contention for the spot with just two other guys. One was a kid named Rob Burnett, who had been on the Letterman staff for a while as an intern, receptionist, and anything else he was asked to do; the other was an advertising copywriter from Oklahoma named Boyd Hale.

The show went with Hale. Steve O'Donnell, the already legendary head writer for Dave—who had succeeded the equally legendary Merrill Markoe, Dave's first head writer and also once his longtime girlfriend—called Conan with the bad news. O'Donnell, himself a *Lampoon* alum, told Conan, "Dave doesn't want to go with another Harvard guy."

The news devastated O'Brien—he had been *that* close to working for his idol. The disappointment lingered for some time, although it would be mitigated somewhat years later when Dave, after being reminded during an interview that Conan had almost been a writer for him, replied wistfully, "Well, our loss."

Within months of that setback, however, he and Greg Daniels made it past another of television's toughest cuts and were hired as staff writers for *Saturday Night Live*.

The show, by then just into its second decade and with Lorne Michaels back in charge after his self-imposed interregnum, had been the incubator for a generation of comedy talent, in both performers and writers. Landing there in 1987, with a new cast (Phil Hartman, Dana Carvey, Jon Lovitz) about to explode, Conan thrived, though the fit always felt imperfect to him. Something about what Letterman did, the everydayness of it, simply appealed more to him. At the same time, breaking through as a performer on *SNL* given the existing lineup posed a forbidding challenge. Conan wasn't a mimic on the level of Carvey; he couldn't create and lose himself in characters the way the phenomenal Hartman did. Conan knew that whatever part he might play in a sketch, his sheer Conan-ness would burn through.

What his *SNL* stint did accomplish was to expose his burgeoning writing skills to a critical group of contacts. Lorne Michaels, chiefly, made note of the new kid's remarkable facility to write any kind of comedy and marked him as someone to keep his eye on. Conan was also slaying long-time *SNL* presences like Jim Downey and Al Franken with his spontaneous bursts of silliness. And he found a kindred spirit in Robert Smigel, a young writer with swagger who had been among the few to survive a staff purge by Michaels at the end of the 1986 season.

When a writers' strike hit the TV business early in 1988, shutting down production on *SNL*, Smigel and another staff member, Bob Odenkirk, decided to try creating a stage show of sketches too outrageous (they thought) to ever make it onto television. They had witnessed some of O'Brien's wilder moments in the writers' room and perceived someone like themselves: a performer caged inside a writer and not so quietly thrashing in the effort to get out.

Smigel and Odenkirk, who had made their first comedy bones at the Players Workshop in Chicago, asked Conan to join them in a show they were putting together that they would mount in Chicago that summer. It sounded to him like a fantastic adventure, and Conan jumped on board.

The income from this exercise figured to be so minuscule that Conan asked his new partners if they knew of some way he could save on housing expenses. Odenkirk, as it happened, had a friend with an apartment that might have an empty room, and a call secured the space. Jeff Garlin, then twenty-six and himself just trying to break in as a stand-up, had rented a place in his native Chicago within steps of the home of his favorite team, the Cubs. All he had to offer was a tiny room with no window and barely big enough to squeeze in the futon Conan was going to use as a bed. O'Brien took one look and concluded, "Not even by prison camp standards is that a room." But it was cheap, and he didn't expect to spend a lot of time there anyway.

Most of his time was going to be consumed first with putting together and then with staging the review, which they had decided to call "The Happy Happy Good Show." They rented out the Victory Gardens Theater on North Lincoln Avenue and got ready to rock and roll.

Conan had written a few sketches with Daniels. In one he played a character called "Kennedy Baby" and simply rolled on the ground in a diaper, saying "a dep, a dep, dep," and other gibberish in a Kennedy accent. For another character, "Spoon Eye," he came out holding a spoon over his right eye and in supercilious fashion would ask for questions from the audience. Whatever anyone asked of Spoon Eye, from politics to the weather, the answer would always contain the word "spoon."

The biggest hit of the "Happy Happy Good Show"—and there weren't many, because even the performers thought the show was only erratically funny—was a sketch Smigel had created called "Chicago Superfans." Later a legendary *SNL* sketch, it featured a mustachioed character named Bill Swerski and his deeply Ch-caeh-go-accented mates celebrating coach Mike Ditka and "Da Bearss" with copious quaffs of lager and mounds of Polish sausage.

That summer of 1988 in Chicago was torrid at record-setting levels. Conan's little windowless cell had no air-conditioning. He would return from the theater and enter the hot box like Colonel Nicholson getting into the corrugated torture oven next to the River Kwai. He would collapse onto his now permanently sweat-soaked futon, but not before he and Garlin spent some quality time together deconstructing their lives and careers, with Conan frequently setting off on one of his unfettered comedy rolls. Garlin would sometimes wake O'Brien in the middle of the night because he wanted to hear again something that Conan had said that destroyed him earlier in the evening.

But nothing killed Garlin quite like one regular bit he and Conan cooked up that sweltering summer. Joan Rivers had just flamed out in her effort to start up a late-night show for Fox, and the talk in the comedy business was about possible replacement shows and all the different names people were kicking around as candidates. Without any kind of forethought, sitting around the apartment, O'Brien and Garlin fell into a byplay that quickly took the shape of a new talk-show entry, one they called, for no apparent reason, "Wild Blue Yonder."

Conan played the host—but not as himself. Instead he pulled up his deadly impression of the onetime *Star Trek* actor George Takei. In this conceit, Takei had somehow landed the new Fox talk show. And every night he had the same guest: Jeff Garlin. They created an ersatz set with host base behind a coffee table and guest on the couch. Almost every night they would fall into doing the show. Conan as George Takei would ask Garlin about his act and touring: How was that going? Garlin would go along for a time, but eventually he would come around to asking Takei about those residuals from *Star Trek*: And how were they coming along? After first trying to be dismissive, or to change the subject, Conan's Takei would start to become agitated and then bitter about how he'd been cheated on his residuals. And the interchange would get out of hand, with Takei ever more furious.

The bit slayed Garlin. He marveled at Conan's ability to wind the Takei character up ever tighter. All summer they went back to "Wild Blue Yonder"—always only for themselves. It did not make Garlin picture Conan as a future talk show host—maybe because he was always George Takei. But he was blown away by Conan's comedy mind.

When the summer ended, Conan dragged the disgusting futon out of his steam room and threw it away. On his last night in Chicago, though, he had to have George Takei sit down one last time with Jeff Garlin.

Again, Takei tried to explore the homey details of Garlin's emerging show-biz career, but as soon as Jeff went to the indignity of those missing residuals, it proved too much for George Takei. He howled to the moon and committed seppuku on the spot.

"And that was the end of 'Wild Blue Yonder,'" Garlin said.

The cast took "The Happy Happy Good Show" for a two-week run in Los Angeles, hoping it might burnish their comedy reputations a little. It didn't, but it was by chance seen by a young agent for ICM named Gavin Polone. He enjoyed it and was particularly impressed by the tall redheaded guy.

In mid-August, after five months and seven days, the writers' strike ended, and everyone from the stage show returned to New York and the new season of *Saturday Night Live*. Conan settled back into his writing assignments, relishing the times that he got little on-camera shots on the show, like "handsome guy in the background."

Conan had idiosyncrasies unusual even for *SNL*. Though he loved to be in the writers' room kicking around ideas, when he got down to the actual word-on-page process, he would sometimes like to wander off with Greg Daniels—the way they used to at Harvard when they had to study for an exam. At *SNL* they took to drifting through the floors and halls of 30 Rock, looking for the best place to get inspired and write. At some point this led them to the sixth floor and the entrance to Studio 6A.

To their amazement, there was no guard there, nothing to stop them from drifting in and checking out the place where it all took place every evening. The Letterman studio, which always shocked fans when they turned up in the audience because it was so much smaller than it looked on TV, was as quiet as a church late at night when O'Brien and Daniels moseyed in. Dave's desk had a plastic covering over it, but it didn't stop Conan from stepping up and planting himself in the chair, Dave's chair, facing out into the empty seats of his audience, while Daniels, the undemonstrative partner in the pair, would find a seat down in the first row. There they would sit, Conan behind the desk, conducting a writing session like Dave conducted an interview.

It wasn't as if he were a kid in a "look at me" moment, sitting behind the wheel of Dad's car in the garage. Nor was it a sign of any innate audacity; if someone had walked in, he would undoubtedly have been embarrassed and fled the scene. But sitting there, in the dim light, at *that* desk, looking out into *that* studio, the sensation, the aspect, felt right to Conan. He found himself thinking, *What this guy is doing, this is the kind of thing I could do. It wouldn't be the same way he does it. I'm not a precision instrument like David Letterman. But when I am having fun and I'm in the moment, there's nothing else like it. . . . If only I could figure out a way . . .*

In 1991, having established himself as one of the hottest writers on the show, Conan told Lorne Michaels he was quitting *Saturday Night Live*. While the decision didn't make sense—he had no other job—all Conan could think of was salmon swimming upstream. They don't know why they're doing it; they just have to do it. The vaguest of feelings was telling him he had to leave *SNL*, had to get out of New York for a time and do—whatever.

Michaels had a keen feel for the psychology of talent, and he recognized that indefinable urge in talent to move on even when nothing specific was impelling them to do so. Still, he implored Conan to stay; he loved the guy's writing. Conan didn't offer any ultimatums, such as insisting that he be added to the cast, because he still knew that was not right for him. What was right, he still couldn't say. But he parted with Michaels on excellent terms and pondered his next move. He had some money because he rarely spent any, so he decided to hit the road.

Not long after word got out that he had left *SNL*, Conan got a call from Al Jean. Like many young comedy types, O'Brien had been bowled over by the early years of *The Simpsons* on Fox. He was keenly aware of Jean not only as a famed *Lampoon* alum, but also as one of the top *Simpsons* writers. Jean, who had just taken over as show runner, was, in turn, well aware of Conan's reputation on *SNL* and invited him to take one of the rare slots that had opened up on the writing staff. Not having done that kind of formal scriptwriting before, Conan temporized for a moment, but this was *The Simpsons*, after all, and he had to give it a shot.

Soon fans of the show, who were acute observers of even its smallest details (trained, as they had been, to look for the most subtle sight gags and throwaway lines), began to notice that some of the episodes they were enjoying most bore a writer's credit with the odd name of Conan O'Brien. Conan soon had gained a reputation as a spinner of gold, never more so than in his script for "Marge vs. the Monorail," an elaborate gag-filled quasi-takeoff on *The Music Man*, always cited by fans and critics as one of the classic episodes in the show's long history.

Thanks to his impressive work on *The Simpsons*, Conan's name circulated around Hollywood studios as potentially the next great creator of sitcoms. His manager (and Greg Daniels's) at the time, Howard Klein, called to tell him that the Fox production studio Twentieth Television was beating down his door to sign Conan to an overall deal as a writer. (Studios secured hot writers by committing them to deals in which they would be paid simply to sit in a room and develop ideas for shows.) Conan suggested that he and Klein meet to discuss the offer.

In the meantime, hanging out with Lisa Kudrow, who was beginning to land parts in shows like *Mad About You*, Conan only felt the tug to perform ever stronger. He found himself getting edgy, angry even, at the prospect of restricting himself to writing. Kudrow suggested they might do some kind of Nichols and May improv act together, but then the Groundlings called with an offer to bring a bunch of alums together for a special show, people who had been associated with the troupe in some way. Conan qualified because he had finally taken some classes with them and at one point had been on track to get into the company. He enthusiastically signed on.

The show was impromptu and nerve-racking, because he had never really performed improv on a big stage before. But Conan loved it extravagantly. That night "the nickel dropped" for him. He realized he would rather make no money at all doing this than make several hundred thousand a year working as a *Simpsons* writer.

When O'Brien had his meeting with Howard Klein, he decided to reveal to his manager what he had really been thinking about for a long time. "I really don't think I want to sign myself up to a long-term thing as a sitcom writer," Conan told him. "I think I need to start performing."

It seemed to Conan that the mere mention of that word caused Klein's face to fog over. And after some hemming and hawing, he would come back again with: "But, anyway, at Fox, we can get this fantastic deal . . ."

Conan liked Howard Klein, respected his work—but he fired him.

He started having a vague feeling that his life was changing, and he needed to be ready when the next door opened. So he asked a string of high-profile agents if they wanted to step up and explain why they might want to represent him. The agents all but lined up to pitch him their credentials. At the various meetings, Conan let them all know what he was intending: He wanted to shift to performing.

When Gavin Polone arrived for his appointment, he knew Conan would remember him from parties involving writers from *The Simpsons*, because many of them were Polone's clients. He was now at United Talent (having been fired from ICM, the first of many contentious business separations in Polone's career). But he had another ace to play.

Conan made his usual points about wanting to find a way to tap his urge to perform. Polone responded that he could totally understand that, because when Conan and his *SNL* friends had brought "The Happy Happy Good Show" to LA several years earlier, he had made a point of seeing the act. And he had liked it; he had especially liked Smigel and the redheaded guy. Of *course* you should be a performer, Polone told Conan. Maybe they could build a sitcom where he would write *and* star in it. Gavin was hired.

Still writing on *The Simpsons*, Conan spent his free time fighting off anxiety and frustration—and depression. He had always been prone to falling into an occasional slough of despond, sometimes even when things were going relatively well. Now he was picturing himself on an access road running parallel to the freeway, riding along mile after mile, looking for a ramp to get on but never seeing one. He knew he was close, so close, but he had no idea how to get onto that main highway.

Not that there weren't distractions to alter his mood. It was 1993, and he couldn't help but follow the tumult going on over at NBC in late night. NBC had picked Leno over Letterman as Carson's *Tonight Show* successor—unaccountably, to an unabashed Letterman fan like Conan. Now, in the subsequent uproar, Dave was leaving for CBS and NBC seemed to have no clue how they were going to replace him.

By sheer coincidence Conan's younger sister Jane had landed a job at the William Morris Agency. This put her in position to see confidential e-mails, and in the midst of the Letterman-Leno fracas, one that crossed her desk caught her eye: NBC was about to make a deal with Lorne Michaels that would give him control over the choice of the new host of the *Late Night* show. (NBC had to announce *something* the day Letterman was exiting; while it still had no host, it could at least tell the world that the talent maestro Michaels was on the case.) Knowing how much Lorne had respected Conan during his time on *SNL*, Jane called her brother to tip him off and assure him: This was meant to be; this is your slot.

Conan waited. He couldn't realistically pitch himself to NBC as the replacement for David Letterman. Who the hell would take *that* seriously?

It was Lorne who did the calling, a couple of days later. Conan would compare his overture to being on the street when a meteor hits. But this wasn't the crash at his feet; it was only the flash in the distance. The job Lorne pitched hard to Conan was as the creative brain behind the new *Late Night* show, a position that would place him somewhere between head writer and producer. Not the executive producer, responsible for the daily running of the show—Lorne had somebody else in mind for that. He wanted Conan to put his wildly inventive mind to work on the comic sensibility of the show.

Without a doubt this was an attractive offer: to put your own creative stamp on a big-time network show; to be, in essence, the Merrill Markoe of the new show, the brains behind the operation. Even so, Conan didn't jump at the suggestion, but told Lorne about his plan to be a performer. They noodled around with a few ideas. There was the semibaked suggestion that if Conan took this job for a while, maybe he'd be in line to host the 1:35 a.m. show *Later*, which the top NBC sportscaster Bob Costas had put on the late-night map. Costas might be leaving to go back full-time to sports, Michaels intimated.

Conan hedged: Lorne needed to talk to his agent.

Polone, the new agent, didn't have to concern himself with sounding ludicrous. He was representing a client. He flat out told Lorne to forget the producer thing: "Conan should star in the show." He wasn't, in fact, entirely serious. In the back of his mind he was thinking about the 1:35 show. That was Polone's real plan—insist on the 12:35 job in order to get the 1:35 job. Like everyone else, he expected NBC to go after Garry Shandling for the Letterman job. Who in his right mind was going to suggest Conan over Shandling? Polone was now doing precisely that, but nobody could ever accuse him of being in his right mind where a client was concerned.

The issue never really came to a head, because before Polone could push any harder Conan weighed back in. As he had pondered it, in between *Simpsons* writing sessions, Lorne's idea grew less and less appealing. Finally, kicking it around in his head one night, Conan had a violent reaction to the whole notion. He decided he just had to get out of this.

Conan called Lorne in New York to tell him thanks, but "I can't do it."

Michaels did not hide his disappointment. He had been counting on Conan; that was one thing about this acid-inducing situation that he had been depending on getting off his plate with minimum trouble. The conversation became a bit unpleasant, the first time Conan had ever had that kind of interaction with Lorne. But when they hung up, Conan all but fell back in his chair, overcome with relief. His only thought was: *I'm out of it. I'm done.*

Lorne Michaels, never fazed when a live show looked as if it was about to implode, was hardly going to be ruffled by not having an easy answer to the question of who was going to succeed David Letterman. He did have a strong conviction that his choice needed to be new and fresh: No one was going to be able to stand up as a match with Letterman, so why try anyone familiar? At least a new name might start out under the radar and get a chance to grow. And young was essential, because the only way to break a new name in late night was to grab the same crowd that had made Letterman a star—college kids.

Even with Conan out of the picture, Lorne believed he had one element solved that would give him some degree of confidence. He would turn the daily control of the show over to Jeff Ross, a producer he had groomed for years for just this kind of assignment. Ross, who started as a road manager for Diana Ross (a job that included managing her famous stormy-weather concert in Central Park in 1983), segued into television when Michaels invited him to produce a series for a Canadian sketch comedy troupe, the Kids in the Hall, in 1989.

Ross wound up working on multiple projects for Michaels, including another Central Park concert, this one starring Lorne's close friend Paul Simon. Ross had just come off a root canal of an assignment, producing a special with the comedian Dennis Miller—known for being difficult to work with—when Michaels proposed that Jeff become the executive producer of the *Late Night* show Lorne was assembling for NBC.

Ross knew he should be flattered—and he was—because this was obviously a potential career-making assignment. But he admitted to Lorne, "I don't know if I want to do it." He knew he couldn't simply reject an offer like this, but the prospect of building a show that was supposed to follow a groundbreaking, industry-changing icon like David Letterman struck Ross as overwhelmingly daunting.

Lorne assumed Jeff would simply come around, and when he next approached Ross, it was in LA. "Are you going to produce this show for me?" Michaels asked.

Ross told him he was still thinking about it, but it would depend on who the host was.

Michaels looked incredulous. "What do you mean it depends on the host?"

Ross, recalling his recent experience with Miller, knew he didn't want to live through that on a full-time basis. He repeated his concern. He needed to know who the host was going to be before he could commit.

OK, Michaels told him, it just so happened that that very night he was going over to the Improv club on Melrose to watch a showcase of comics auditioning for the *Late Night* chair. He invited Ross to come along.

The entire NBC Entertainment hierarchy was arrayed at the club, with Don Ohlmeyer and Warren Littlefield the two men in charge, thanks to their roles as the top executives at NBC Entertainment. Ross knew next to no one, so he sat quietly observing the long roster of comics. Most he had never encountered before, some he had seen perform, and a few he—and everybody else—would come to be familiar with over time. The group included veteran stand-ups, like Allan Havey, Paul Provenza, and Michael McKean (well known as a onetime member of Spinal Tap), as well as some lesser-known but accomplished comics, like Rick Reynolds, along with newcomers, like a roundish guy in thick-framed black glasses named Drew Carey and a witty, compactly built guy with long hair named Jon Stewart.

After the long show ended, the NBC group crossed the street to a restaurant for a postmortem. Nobody's name seemed to be rising to the surface in the discussion, which hardly surprised Ross. How could it? They were all sitting there thinking the same thing: *Not bad, but he's sure not Letterman*. Ross judiciously kept silent, but as the group was leaving, Lorne approached him. "There's a meeting tomorrow in Littlefield's office; I want you to come."

The request struck Ross as slightly surreal. He hadn't accepted the job, they had no host, and no one had any idea where they were going to find one. But now he was going to sit in on a meeting with the NBC bosses at the network's Burbank headquarters.

When he showed up the next morning he was accepted without question as "Lorne's guy." Again Ross said nothing as the execs began batting around names; again nobody was compelling. Lorne wasn't crazy about the idea of a pure stand-up as host, in any case—they always seemed to want to score, and that approach didn't work when talking to guests. For his part, Ross kind of liked Stewart; he had previously worked with him at a New York Comedy Festival and was impressed by his quick comic mind. But nobody solicited his opinion.

Then, out of nowhere, somebody asked about Conan O'Brien: Was he going to run the writing for the show? Michaels explained that Conan had decided he didn't want to do it. He had his mind set on turning himself into a performer.

That seemed to stop the conversation dead. After a pause, Lorne had another thought: "Hey, maybe Conan can host it."

Few in the room had a clue who this Conan guy was. But Warren Littlefield did; he knew him from his *SNL* background and from his reputation as the hot writer from *The Simpsons*. It didn't seem to strike Warren as all that crazy an idea. "Well, should we test him, maybe?" Littlefield asked.

For reasons Ross could not fathom, Lorne turned to him and said, "Well, can we test him?"

The first thought that popped into Ross's head was, *What the fuck do I know?* But what he replied was: "Yeah. Sure, we can test him."

Conan got the call in his office at *The Simpsons*. It was Lorne, in that hypercalm voice of his: "We haven't found anyone yet. Would you consider doing a tryout?"

Fear? Yes, for sure. Disbelief? Naturally, but there was no time for either. "Yes, of course," Conan said. "What's the harm in trying?"

What Conan had also been feeling was something eerie; he had been feeling it for months, since before he had parted with Howard Klein. Something was coming for him. Maybe it was an oncoming train—or maybe a ticket on that train. But it sure felt like something was coming.

When he got home that evening to the apartment he was renting on Wetherly Drive at the edge of Beverly Hills, Conan tried to make sense of what might be happening. Before he could get too far, his phone rang. It was Michaels again.

"Whatever this audition is going to be, you need to meet with Jeff Ross," Michaels told him. "Jeff's going to produce it. You guys should arrange to get together and talk it out." Conan agreed, took Ross's number, and called as soon as they hung up.

He introduced himself to Ross, who had obviously been waiting for the contact. "Where are you?" Conan asked. Ross told him he was staying at the Four Seasons—a very short walk from his apartment on Wetherly. "I'll come over and meet you in the lobby," Conan said.

When he arrived, he called Ross, who said he'd be right down. As he waited Conan looked around and noticed that directly past the concierge's post in the lobby was a small officelike room with a faux fireplace. It also had a desk. Without hesitating, he slid into the chair behind it.

When Ross entered the lobby a few seconds later, he quickly spotted the guy he was looking for: really tall, really red. Ross walked over and held out his hand. "I'm Jeff."

Conan extended his arms wide over the desk, slapped both hands down on top of it, and said, "Whaddya think?"

"Well," said Ross, looking at this guy behind a desk in a hotel lobby pretending to be on television and wondering just how crazy this was going to get. "I, uh . . . I—I . . . guess?"

Conan had only a couple of weeks to get ready. He worked on writing a little monologue, but had to cover a few more bases. Not only did he own no suits, but he didn't even own a sports coat. He contacted Lisa Kudrow, his one female confidante at that point in his life, and they went jacket shopping. They picked out a pale linen sports coat—a little casual, yes, but that was what they were going for. What they weren't going for would only become apparent on the air—a pale coat on a pale face was not a good look.

Polone weighed in with some help. The actress Mimi Rogers was a friend; she agreed to act as a first guest. Larry Charles, one of the top *Seinfeld* writers, was a Polone client; he helped get Jason Alexander as a second guest. NBC carved out some time in Jay's studio at *The Tonight Show*. Ross took care of the details, and though the process was rushed, it would do as a reasonable facsimile of a late-night show.

On the evening of April 13, 1993, Conan arrived at the *Tonight* studio, possibly among the few present who could compare what was about to take place to a Pirandello play—though almost all of them surely appreciated that it was all a little absurd. Ross fell easily into the flow of production, but he more than anyone else recognized just how bizarre the situation was. This kid nobody knew was going to sit on the set of *The Tonight Show* and try to justify NBC's picking him to replace David Letterman. It was totally nuts.

Conan was not suffused with fear—this was nothing like Harvard and the Radcliffe Pitches. It was too crazy to get wound up about. Sure, it loomed like the ramp onto that dreamscape freeway, but the circumstances of how it had come together were so bizarre. Why get overwrought about something that wasn't actually real?

Robert Smigel had checked in to help with a few of the jokes. The *Tonight Show* researchers had dug up information Conan could use in talking to Rogers and Alexander. All he had to do was walk out and pretend he knew what he was doing.

Conan waited for that night's taping of *The Tonight Show* to end. As he hung out in the hallway backstage, Jay came by after closing the show. Spotting the tall guy in the ill-fitting coat—he had obviously been clued in to what NBC was up to—he stopped briefly and said, "Oh, Conan," in his earnestly pleasant way. "Oh, hey!" Jay's greeting seemed to echo in the air like a distant train whistle as he went by.

After the seats were cleared the audition audience was brought in, many of them NBC types, others guests of either Conan or Polone. A few minutes before he was to go on, someone told Conan he had a call in the control room. It was Lorne, back in New York. He would be watching on the satellite feed.

"So listen," Lorne was saying in his apparently half-distracted way, lowering the flame on Conan's kettle, making sure he didn't get to a boil. "You know, nothing is probably going to come of this thing tonight. . . ."

Conan interrupted him. "Lorne, listen. It's going to be great. I'm sure of it." The line had been unplanned, but it was the truth. He wasn't sure exactly why he had said it, but he was sure of one thing, something that probably nobody out there in that audience would have believed: He was not scared shitless.

And then he was onstage, standing on his mark, acting like a real entertainer. He looked more sheepish than anything else, a point he underscored with his jokes, which mainly had to do with trying to explain precisely how he came to be standing there that night. "This is the result of a drunken wager between Lorne Michaels and Don Ohlmeyer," he said. With his arms swinging loosely and his indifferent posture, he didn't look like a guy accustomed to standing up and telling jokes—but he didn't look bad, either. Something close to charm managed to filter through the awkwardness.

His quasi-monologue finished, O'Brien made the crossover to sit in Jay's chair behind Jay's desk. He read the prepared introduction, and Mimi Rogers stepped out, looking a bit as though she was worried that she had stumbled into a *Candid Camera* bit. But she quickly turned giggly and seemed to warm up to the kid behind the desk.

At one point, after Conan asked about her modeling career, Rogers started to explain what hard work modeling was—much harder than people thought. Conan responded with his best unscripted line: "No. People always say being a model is hard. Turning a big crank, that's hard"—and he mimicked great effort with a crank (not unlike trying to lift an invisible desk). He scored—with Rogers, who laughed effusively, and also with the little audience in the studio.

During an ersatz commercial break Jeff Ross approached from where he had been standing off camera and leaned in to straighten Conan's tie a bit. "How'm I doing?" Conan started to ask. But before he could finish the question Ross held up a piece of paper. On it was written, "You're killing." Then he walked away.

Conan chuffed up, having concluded, *At least I've won* him *over.*

As he left the studio that night, Conan felt he had done well, surely better than anyone expected. As he replayed the audition, he started to feel real joy—euphoria, even. He let himself dream: *Shit, I think something's going to happen now.*

Over the next week, however, the inside word was that NBC was hard after Shandling. For his part, Lorne was still positive. "Bob Wright really loved your tape," he told Conan. Conan asked, "Who's Bob Wright?" Then one morning a *Simpsons* colleague walked into his office and casually asked, "Hey, have you seen *Variety* today?"

Conan rushed out to the newsstand on Fairfax Avenue. The headline was on the front page: "Talks of Conan for *Late Night* at NBC." It was the first time he had seen his name in print since the *Crimson*. He imagined people all over Hollywood asking, "Conan who?" and "What's a Conan? Sounds like a joke name."

That same day the call came in: Get to Ohlmeyer's office for a meeting. So he sped over to Burbank, where he faced another gathering of NBC princes. Ohlmeyer, who seemed intrigued by O'Brien, led the meeting, seconded by Littlefield, who seemed openly skeptical. "The Wrights really loved your tape," Ohlmeyer said. (Conan wondered: *There's more than one?*)

"Here's the thing," Littlefield chimed in. "The tape's OK, but what kind of show would you do?"

Conan had not really prepared a formal treatise on this subject, but he had, after all, been thinking through every aspect of having his own show since about the time he gave up tap.

He leaned forward in his chair and, as though possessed by a demon, let fly:

"Letterman's done irony. He did the anti–talk show. This show has to have a different quality. I think the time is right for silliness. Dave's got that dignity and that personal space. My thing is, I don't really do that. I do silliness. We're going to do things like have plants in the audience—not unprofessional performers like Dave uses, but real performers who will actually commit. If someone stands up in the audience and pretends to be a gold miner, they'll be an actor playing a gold miner. The show will have a little bit of a *Pee-wee's Playhouse* feel to it. We'll have puppets; I think we'll try to use animation. We're gonna have fake guests. We'll bump a guest every night, an actor who will pretend to be really passive-aggressive and pissed about being bumped over and over."

Conan sensed that Ohlmeyer had sparked to some of the ideas— especially the fake guests. Littlefield remained impassive.

O'Brien left the meeting feeling even more confident than he had after the test show—it had the flavor of a second audition, or maybe an oral exam in college. That evening he spoke with his sister Jane. "I think I may have just talked myself into that job."

The NBC executives did like what he had to say. There was a fresh-ness about him that was appealing. But come the fall, they were facing the biggest challenge the network's late-night empire had ever taken on: David Letterman on CBS. If *Tonight* took a hit, certainly *Late Night* would as well. More than $70 million in ad revenue was tied up with that show. The fallback position was to sign Conan as backup to Costas for the *Later* show—the plan that Polone seemed to be promoting in the first place.

At that point NBC made a full-out run at Shandling, with a financial offer that had grown to nearly $5 million a year. Shandling pondered for about a week. Finally, on April 26, with Ohlmeyer fed up and opposed to spending that much anyway, Shandling let NBC know his decision: no.

Jeff Ross, back in New York, had no idea what was going on. The try-out had convinced him that he and Conan could work together well, so he had committed to Lorne. But things had gone quiet. On the twenty-sixth, he came back from lunch and saw a stack of messages waiting. He knew at once: "Oh my god, he got it!"

Later the same day in LA, Conan was at a table read of another *Simpsons* episode. The phone rang as the session ended, and the person who answered said, "Conan, it's for you." He picked it up and heard Gavin Polone say, "You got twelve thirty." This time Conan was not euphoric, the cold calculation of what this meant starting to sink in. It was the be-careful-what-you-wish-for moment. Polone said Ohlmeyer would be calling in five minutes.

Conan was far enough away from his bungalow office that he needed to sprint across the lot to get there. He was slightly out of breath when he grabbed the ringing phone and heard the news officially from the top NBC West Coast executive.

The life change began instantaneously. That night, Ohlmeyer told him, Conan would do a walk-on with Jay to be introduced to the nation. A few days later they would fly him east, and he would meet the press in New York.

Back at the *Tonight* studio that night, Jay brought him on with appropriate fanfare and not a little curiosity. Conan, in a new (dark) blazer over jeans, looked mildly stunned by the latest developments in his life, though he made the point—several times—that he was thrilled.

Over at CBS Letterman addressed the news on his show. He called Conan "the new guy" and said, "I don't know him. I heard he's a nice boy. The only thing I heard about him is he killed a guy once." He made the subject of that night's Top Ten List tips he could offer the new host. Based on his own contentious relations with NBC management (and its parent company) as well as several famous incidents Dave had had with a stalker, these included: "GE executives are pinheads," "NBC executives are boneheads," and "Don't panic if you find a strange woman in your house."

Desperate for any information on the new guy, reporters contacted anyone who had worked with O'Brien. Most of his former colleagues had the same reaction: really funny guy, does wild, spontaneous things for no apparent reason. Matt Groening, the cartoonist who created *The Simpsons*, said Conan made perfect sense as the choice for a talk-show job: "He can keep a room of seething, self-hating, resentful comedy writers laughing for minutes on end. He does a lot of shtick and runs around the room. It first makes you laugh, then gets annoying, then exasperating, and then comes full circle and makes you fall out of your chair."

NBC didn't even have a photograph of him that could be sent out with its press release, as Conan had never bothered to take a head shot—the principal calling card for any would-be performer. Every story wound up being illustrated with the same picture, lifted off the air: Conan with a goofy smile on his face towering over Leno on the *Tonight* stage. Conan found himself suspecting he was coming off like the Chauncey Gardiner character Peter Sellers played in the movie *Being There*. He pictured the CIA going though his suits in his LA apartment, ordering people to "pull the file on Conan O'Brien! There is no file? Pull the tape! There is no tape?"

NBC scheduled his press debut at the Rainbow Room in 30 Rock for a week later, on May 3. That day Conan proved he had some mettle. When he entered the building, he stepped into an elevator and was immediately confronted by a reporter from the *New York Post,* who taunted, "I counted how many laughs Letterman got in his press conference leaving the show and I'm gonna count how many you get!" Far from throwing Conan, the encounter relaxed him. It was when things were calm that he leaned toward depression or panic. When his back was against the wall, he seemed to do things he didn't know he could do.

The press was charmed. Far from shrinking in the spotlight, Conan seemed to grow in it. He acknowledged being a "complete unknown." He sparred with John Melendez, "Stuttering John" from Howard Stern's radio show, exposing the silly disguise he was wearing. Conan seemed boyish, clever, fast with his wit, and fully appreciative of the absurdity of the position he was in. To buck him up, Lorne told him that day of an observation one of his fellow *SNL* writers, Bonnie Turner, had offered: "All I know is that guy will charm the shit out of any crowd."

For Conan O'Brien nothing would ever quite match the thrill of that first time—his introduction to the American television audience on September 13, 1993. The first look anyone got of him was a pretaped cold opening—a segment run before the credits—in which young Conan strolled cheerfully through Manhattan, greeted by vendors, cabbies, and passers-by, all of whom had the same helpful message: "Lot of pressure—you better not screw this up." When he arrived at the NBC building, he ran into the news anchor Tom Brokaw, who was sterner, and more specific: "You better be as good as Letterman—or else."

Finally alone in his dressing room, showing no ill effects and whistling merrily, Conan pulled out a chair, stepped up on it, and in the same cheerful way swung a noose around his neck. In perhaps an inadvertent callback to the night of the Radcliffe Pitches, a stagehand knocked on the door to say it was time to go on. "Right now?" Conan asked meekly and then climbed down with a shrug, ready to step out onstage.

That introduction stamped him as an entertainer with obvious charm and pluck, and it was those qualities that dominated the early comments about the show. In *The New York Times* John O'Connor assessed the opening night as better than anyone could have expected, observing, "There's a fine lunacy here that bears watching." Others interpreted that lunacy as an indication that Conan was jumpy, tense, and ungainly. But in truth, he had not been overly anxious that first night. What looked like nerves was actually excitement. A charge had been lit under him; he was exploding with the thrill of knowing: Yes! This is it!

Of course it was near impossible not to start out rooting for a guy who seemed to have been pulled off the subway and handed a television show. Conan's other early advantage was his relatively low profile in what had become a barroom brawl between the leading men in late night. Letterman stormed onto the air on CBS—as NBC suspected he would—and was already battering a reeling Leno. A bit later in September, Chevy Chase's much anticipated new effort on Fox hit the air, but it was accompanied more by a thud than an explosion. A disaster that made for easy skeet-shooting for the critics, it helped keep the spotlight away from the new show on NBC.

Conan had the predictable growing pains—the learning curve was proving expectedly steep. But it occurred to him that even on the nights when the show seemed to be spinning out of his control—or else lying there like a beached tuna—something happened, one little moment, a witty remark or a shtick he tried with the camera—and the promise flashed through. To make Conan more comfortable they had installed one of the show's new writers, Andy Richter, as a sidekick. It came about organically. The two of them had hit it off screwing around before the test shows. Jeff Ross saw that and guessed having somebody on set who Conan could "fuck around with" would help steady his jittery host. What they were all trying to do was different, even breakthrough, and some nights they did push it too far. "We were cocky," Smigel said. "We really set out to do weird stuff. We just wanted to blow people away with how different the show was." To Ross the whole show seemed to be "flying by the seat of our pants."

In October, after only five weeks on the air, the Chevy Chase show was canceled. One of the writers broke the news to Conan, with a note of glee in his voice: They had already outlasted one of the big guys. Conan didn't see it that way. "Oh, shit," he said. "They're going to reload."

The mocking fusillade did begin soon after—not in a concentrated way, but more with a random shot here and there. The most persistent assault was coming from a high-profile voice. Tom Shales, the TV critic of

The Washington Post, who had gained a reputation as the wittiest (if sometimes most purposefully astringent) assessor of the medium, with a special interest in the late-night arena, had already fired a few salvos toward Conan. He was one critic who had hated the opening night, having labeled Conan "a living collage of nervous habits—he giggles and titters, jiggles about and fiddles with his cuffs. He has dark, beady eyes like a rabbit."

But five weeks later, Shales had poured a new store of powder into his cannon, and Conan was about to walk headfirst into the line of fire.

Looking to capitalize on the demise of Chevy Chase, NBC had set up a round of interviews for Conan, with Charlie Rose of PBS and a host of morning-drive radio DJs, which he would do from a studio in a single marathon session. Blissfully unaware of what had been printed that morning in Washington, he arrived for the round of publicity and discovered that every one of the questioners had seen Shales's latest commentary about the show, and every one of them opted to read selections from it.

Such as: "Chevy Chase has done the honorable thing. Now Conan O'Brien should follow him off the cliff. . . . Let the host resume his previous identity: Conan O'Blivion. Hey you, Conan O'Brien! Get the heck off TV."

The piece also managed to brand Andy Richter a "nitwit sidekick" and declared the show "as lifeless and messy as a road kill." Shales suggested that Conan was "out of his head if he thinks the show is working" and had a firm recommendation for NBC: "Cancel O'Brien now."

All Conan could do was pretend to find some humor in this drubbing, making as many self-deprecating jokes as possible. For hours worth of interviews the pummeling went on. When it was over, O'Brien walked outside in the rain to a waiting car. It was a weekday; he had a show to do. He slouched into 30 Rock, and in the *Late Night* offices the staff watched him slink past, afraid to say anything. O'Brien, the man who could fly high on comic inspiration, was also capable of the deepest of lows when he spiraled all the way down. He walked into his office, passed his assistant, and closed the inner door behind him. He made his way behind his desk, stood there for a second, then bent, went to his knees, and crawled down under it.

He rolled on his back and just lay there until after a while he heard the door creak open a crack. The door closed, and a few minutes later—Conan still hadn't moved—it opened again. He recognized the shoes: Ross.

"Are you OK?" Jeff asked, masking the concern with a little touch of playful rue.

"I'm gonna be fine," the voice from under the desk said. "I just need to be under here for a little bit and just lie here."

For the most part, all of them—Michaels, Polone, Ross—tried to shield Conan. Not from the press; that was impossible. What they worried about was his getting wind of the building dissatisfaction at the network. The numbers weren't very good—not awful yet, but clearly a concern. Worse was the network's assessment of the show. The executives wasted few chances in ripping it in private conversations; Conan was getting no better. The comedy was more weird than funny. He didn't listen to the guests in the interviews. And Andy . . . He was like an affront to the concept of entertainment. Polone got a call from Warren Littlefield excoriating the show and Conan. "And get that fat, fucking dildo off the couch!" he demanded. Most everybody on the show loved Andy; so, apparently, did the studio audiences. But Polone had little ammunition to fire back. The ratings showed no growth, and the critics were annihilating Conan.

For that, O'Brien could not fully blame them. He could feel the show coming together in little ways, but he knew it wasn't there yet—or even close. How could he blame anyone, viewers or critics, who had been accustomed to seeing someone like Letterman at that hour? It struck him that the comparison might be one his dad would have made about the great Red Sox star of his generation: "Ted Williams has departed the field. But here to replace him, ladies and gentlemen, number seventeen and a half, Chip Whitley!" Conan pictured a kid running out onto the field in a diaper and saying in a high-pitched voice: "Hi, everybody! Gee, I'm gonna miss Mr. Williams too, but don't you worry!" And then the kid would pop out.

The flaws were everywhere. The comedy might miss, and then the distraction would spill over into the guest interviews. About four months in, his old Chicago pal Jeff Garlin called with some advice. "I don't know what anybody is telling you. You're doing a great job. You're funny. But in the interviews you're just not listening to a word anybody says. You really need to get into listening."

It was midway through the first year that Ross heard the serious rumblings begin. Affiliates were unhappy; what if they started to preempt? NBC had already hired a young hotshot named Greg Kinnear to succeed Costas as host of *Later*. Word was filtering out about how much the network loved the guy—and why the hell hadn't they given *him* the 12:35 show in the first place?

In the spring of 1994 Conan was due for a twenty-six-week pickup—Conan had a one-year deal but the show had an original commitment of only twenty-six weeks. Polone dutifully called John Agoglia, the deal guy for NBC, who told him they were picking up Conan for the next six months. Polone said that was great, but the contract required he get the extension in writing.

"I can't give it to you in writing right now," Agoglia told him. "We're having some affiliate problems. But don't worry about it; you're picked up." He said he merely needed another month before committing the deal to writing.

"Well, if we're picked up, what's the difference?" Polone said. "You're just giving me a piece of paper. I'm not sending it to *The New York Times*."

Agoglia hedged again, assuring Polone that he needn't worry about it. But Polone did, becoming suspicious that everything with NBC was not what it seemed. The Kinnear talk only made him more uncomfortable, but he had no juice to use against the network. They would simply have to wait for the paperwork.

As spring turned to early summer, Conan remained on the air, but without a document that made his renewal official. Polone went off to Cancun on vacation, but on Friday of his week away he decided to call in to NBC; the time on the extension was up, and all was still quiet at the network.

"Yeah, we got a problem," Agoglia finally admitted to Polone. "We're going to be picking him up week to week."

"Week to week!" Polone exploded. "You told me we were picked up for the twenty-six weeks. You lied to me!"

Agoglia, all business, never thrown by high emotion, shrugged that off. "What are you gonna do?"

Polone called in to New York and broke the news to Ross, who didn't share it with Conan until after the show that night, honoring a fundamental rule of good show business: Don't rattle your star before a performance. None of them could believe NBC was pulling this. Week-to-week renewals? No one had ever heard of such a thing. O'Brien, Ross, and Smigel met in Ross's office after the show and put the speakerphone on the floor. The three of them—partly to hear better, partly just worn down from another week of shows and more disrespect from NBC—sprawled themselves on the rug surrounding the phone as they put in a call to Cancun.

Ross argued that Polone had to make a counter to NBC right away. "If they aren't going to give us the six-month pickup, we can't give them week to week. The blood's in the water then. Everyone will take it that we're being canceled." How many people—writers, segment producers, publicists for the guests, anyone—would stick with a show that was on a weekly deathwatch? "We gotta get them to go up to thirteen-week renewals," Ross insisted.

That was the plea that Gavin made to Don Ohlmeyer, appealing to Don's sense of fairness. Polone had always been impressed that Ohlmeyer, who started in the business as a sports producer (most famously of *Monday Night Football* in its heyday), was not a typical network executive. "In the entertainment industry," as Polone assessed it, "you very rarely sit down with someone and have a bacon cheeseburger and then light up a smoke afterward. You're on a different planet when that happens."

Ohlmeyer listened to Polone's plea and granted a reprieve. NBC would extend Conan in thirteen-week increments. At the same time, he set some ratings targets Conan would have to reach. Instead of a vote of no confidence, they now had a vote of minuscule confidence.

To Ross, NBC's moves felt cheesy—and personally shitty. Conan was making so little by late-night host standards—only about $1 million—that it would have been a minimal risk to NBC to extend him the full six months and pay him off if he didn't cut it. To make them grovel like this had an edge of purposeful nastiness to it.

Now it was a matter of Conan's putting in the hard work and somehow finding some magic—along with a dose of good luck—as he churned out shows night after night. Whether Conan had studied a little Samuel Johnson in a British Lit class at Harvard and knew the famous quote or not, he was certainly living it:

"Depend on it sir: When a man knows he is to be hanged in a fortnight, it concentrates his mind wonderfully."

Ross had good enough contacts inside the network to know that if Greg Kinnear decided he wanted a long-term career as a late-night star, they were toast. Then he heard Kinnear was reluctant. Maybe he wouldn't do a test for a 12:35-style show; maybe he wanted to be a movie star instead. It could all be posturing, but whatever it was, it seemed to be buying them some time.

The ratings demand set by Ohlmeyer was the looming noose. Get there or they were done. Conan pictured himself as a farmer who had been told, "If it doesn't rain within a month, we're taking your farm." So what was the farmer supposed to do? "Work hard and pray for rain."

The drought went on, through late 1994 and into 1995. But good things were happening elsewhere, namely in Kinnear's movie career. He won the third lead in a Harrison Ford movie, *Sabrina*, leaving NBC without another obvious option in late night. And there was luck on another front. Letterman, who in his CBS deal controlled the 12:35 time period as well, passed on choosing a young comer for the slot and decided on one of his personal favorites, Tom Snyder.

As good—and often unpredictable—as Snyder was as an interviewer, he was no comic. And he was twenty-seven years older than Conan O'Brien. Dave might have opened the trapdoor still trembling under Conan's feet by selecting someone like Jon Stewart, who would have challenged him for young viewers. Instead he gave Conan free access to them. The under-forty-year-olds who watched Jay or Dave had little reason to watch Snyder. More and more of them tried out Conan—and if they did, they at least started to see some truly original and often bizarre comedy ideas.

Conan had a guy come on as "the Lenny Bruce of China," a beat comic who told jokes in Chinese accompanied by a translator. Conan was given advice in a "Devil-Bear" sketch, which placed the devil on one shoulder and a bear (for no good reason) on the other, giving him useless opinions. Fulfilling another of his early promises to Ohlmeyer was "Polly, the NBC Peacock," a puppet version of the NBC logo, who came on and trashed shows on the other networks in especially vituperative terms. And Conan found increasingly offbeat ways to involve just barely not-obscure show-biz vets like Nipsey Russell and Abe Vigoda.

A hint of favorable buzz began in mid-1995, but NBC wasn't listening to the buzzing. Conan stayed in place, but he was still rolling over the absurd thirteen-week renewals.

And then, suddenly, it rained.

On June 18, 1996, Tom Shales officially recanted. With a headline that read, "So I Was Wrong," Shales switched sides with a vengeance. Acknowledging that "some critics, present company included, were excessively mean," Shales declared that O'Brien had gone through "one of the most amazing transformations in television history." He quoted Letterman's recently fired executive producer, Robert Morton, saying that Conan was doing "the most innovative comedy in television," and cited numerous recent O'Brien bits that had scored. In perhaps the most startling turnaround, Shales even revised his "nitwit sidekick" appraisal of Andy Richter, saying Andy now was a "key to the success of the show."

The conclusion of Shales's reassessment could not have resonated more plangently in the heart of a lifelong Dave worshipper. "Conan O'Brien is more than just an adequate Letterman substitute," he wrote. "He's his own secret ingredient, and his show an inspired absurdist romp."

Forever after, Conan would cite that piece as the moment that heralded the turnaround. By September he was on the cover of *Rolling Stone*, and then the cover of *Entertainment Weekly*. Ratings were climbing, to Ohlmeyer's designated level and then well past. Among the young-adult audiences he began to soar, doubling the ratings Snyder was attracting in that group. Multiyear pickups—with actual raises for Conan and his staff—were on the way.

Warren Littlefield called and impressed Ross with how manfully he stepped up. "Guys, I want to apologize," Warren told them. "I was wrong."

The lesson seemed clear to Conan and his support group: When the network and the rest of the outside world step in to push you around, tell them what is best for them to hear, but don't flinch. Just shut them out. They don't get it, they never really would, and they don't belong with those who do get it.

As Jeff Ross worked it out, "We learned at that point: You just ignore everybody and do your own show. Do the polite thing—and then you ignore them."

CHAPTER FOUR

LANDSCAPE AT
LATE NIGHT

I n the days after Jay Leno's September 27, 2004, announcement that he
would be leaving *The Tonight Show* in five years' time, Debbie Vickers
knew the most important part of her job would be to calm her star
down. Jay's mood, always so unruffled by almost any real-life development, was darker than she could ever remember seeing it. She understood. NBC's decision to designate Conan O'Brien the official future of
The Tonight Show had left Jay incredulous—and reeling. Within days of
his announcement—on the air, no less—Jay was overcome with what one
colleague labeled "postpurchase anxiety."

One NBC executive, only slightly an acquaintance of Leno's, passed
him in the hall just three days after the official word had gone out. Upon
greeting him with a "Hey, Jay, how're you doing?" the executive was met
with a punch line response:

"I'm fine for a guy who's gonna be out of work! Put out to seed!"

It didn't help when guests came on the show and naturally made
reference to the big recent news, almost always expressing shock that
Jay, of all people, the man who considered vacations—or time off of any
kind—even less appealing than green vegetables (which he never ate),
had agreed to turn in his talk-show badge.

"Yeah, I'm retiring," Jay would say, in a half-mocking, half-pained
way. And then he would quickly change the subject. How could he discuss it? He didn't really understand it.

Nor did other people. Around Hollywood, many in the industry found themselves mystified by NBC's move, which just seemed inexplicably bizarre. Who in show business made calls five years in advance about *anything*? The status quo changed every five minutes. One agent with clients connected to late-night said, "Who the fuck let this happen? This guy is so proud that he doesn't have an agent. Let me tell you something, any agent with a heartbeat would have told NBC, 'Go fuck yourselves. This guy is winning. He's going nowhere.' Who makes a move like this?"

Another executive with long connections to late-night programming observed, "I thought they were out of their minds. Conan had to say yes if he had that drive that most comics have regarding *The Tonight Show*. I also thought it might explode in his face that he was gunning for Jay's job. Jay's politeness toward Conan seemed thin to me. But you don't take someone who's doing very well in the ratings off the air—I'm sorry. What is the life expectancy of an executive like Jeff Zucker? Five years? Seven? So he's really worried what the company is going to be like in five years? Hell, he'd be lucky to be in that position in five years."

One outside—but familiar—voice checked in almost immediately with both Debbie and Jay. Don Ohlmeyer, now five years out of his leadership position over the network's entertainment division, had developed close working relationships with both the *Tonight* star and producer during his time at NBC's Burbank headquarters. While he no longer had authority over any decisions at NBC, Ohlmeyer certainly had opinions.

He got to Debbie first—and she had no doubt about where he stood. He was furious.

Ohlmeyer put NBC's decision in some historical television context. In the mid-eighties a top programmer at ABC named Lew Erlicht had gained everlasting fame (or infamy) for having turned down a proposal from a couple of producers named Marcy Carsey and Tom Werner for a new sitcom starring Bill Cosby. (Later, Erlicht became the subject of one of the most lasting and likely apocryphal stories in TV lore. Supposedly he was approached in the street years afterward by a homeless guy looking for a handout and said, "Hey, don't give me *your* sob story; I'm the guy who passed on *The Cosby Show*.") "I think this is a bigger mistake than Lew Erlicht passing on *Cosby*," Ohlmeyer declared. "Why do they want to force out the guy with the first or second most profitable show on the network?"

And the way the situation had been handled made Ohlmeyer livid.

Compelling Jay to announce the Conan deal on his own show, he believed, was the most demeaning thing he had ever seen done in the television business. Ohlmeyer had a characteristically colorful metaphor for it: "It's one thing to stick a knife in a guy's heart. It's another thing to stick it up his ass and *then* stick it in his heart."

Ohlmeyer did not even believe NBC's motivation had any credibility. He suggested that the supposedly imminent offer for Conan from Fox was a fantasy—just Ari Emanuel conning gullible executives. In that view he had some supporters inside NBC, including one major one: Dick Ebersol, the president of NBC Sports and longtime close friend of Don's from their early days as protégés of the great ABC sports impresario Roone Arledge.

Though Ebersol was by this point serving as mentor to Jeff Zucker, Zucker had not consulted him on the Jay move, but Dick didn't like it. Don, crazed about the decision, called Dick to kick it around. Ebersol's sense was that Conan and Jeff Ross, whom he knew to be savvy guys, would surely perceive Fox as the wrong place for them. And he wished Zucker had asked him or somebody else—like maybe Lorne Michaels—about the decision.

Ohlmeyer also called Jay directly, basically to tell him, lovingly, that he was an idiot—that he should never have accepted this affront from NBC. He was dominant in late night; nobody should be telling him when to leave the stage.

However much Jay appreciated the sentiments, it still seemed to him that resistance would have been futile—"You serve at the pleasure of the king," as he put it—not to mention out of character.

Jay's public image had always been that of the blue-collar, work-hard, don't-expect-much regular guy, so that had to be his for-the-record stance in the wake of NBC's move. When the topic was raised, he would say things like "There's nothing worse than whining in show business," which he frequently compared to the lowest form of commercial enterprise: "You don't fall in love with a hooker."

Love was a prevailing theme of these shrugged-off remarks, and he mockingly equated NBC's decision with being dumped romantically. "I've never been one of those guys, when the girl says, 'I don't think we should see each other anymore,' who says"—and here the vocal pitch would reach a falsetto of mock anguish—"'Why? Why not? What can I do?' No"—with his voice returning to its usual register—"I don't do that. It's 'OK, babe, I'm gone.'"

The relationship metaphor had not popped into Jay's head by chance. Even in his private conversations with Debbie Vickers and others, Leno came off sounding a bit like the jilted lover. He'd been loyal; he'd been true. And yet NBC had picked somebody else. Jay was, by his own description, "brokenhearted." He sat in his dungeon thinking, *We could not have been doing better. We were the only show making money after eight o'clock at night. It doesn't make any sense.*

It made sense to Jeff Zucker. With Fox breathing down his neck, Zucker—who fully believed that the offer from Fox was real because his trusted friend Jeff Ross had told him so and Ross was no spinner of self-interest-based yarns—seemed to have little choice. If he wanted to preserve his late-night lineup intact for as long as possible, he had to summon up enticement for Conan while locking in Jay. This plan had done it—and, in the bargain, avoided a replay of the Leno-Letterman train wreck. So Zucker was more than pleased with how efficiently it had all gone down.

But the strategy of "don't lose Conan" also bred detractors. A veteran producer of entertainment series said, "Conan wasn't Letterman. That was the difference. I don't know if anybody looked at Conan and said: That's the next host of *The Tonight Show*. He was hot, but, you know, the host of *The Tonight Show*? It was shocking."

So shocking that from the moment of the announcement this producer had doubts about whether Conan should count on it happening. "I wondered that. A lot of people did. I never thought Jay Leno would give up the chair so easily. Jay Leno is a wolf in sheep's clothing. A big bad wolf."

Up in the Burbank offices of *The Tonight Show*, that was not the animal Debbie Vickers was seeing. She was looking at a guy who felt like a lame duck—and a wounded one.

Jay was also angry—though he tried to keep that submerged. When Kevin Reilly, the new president of entertainment for NBC, came by asking if Jay wanted to talk about any of this, Leno suspected Reilly had been dispatched by the NBC hierarchy to massage his bruised ego. "Hey, I don't want a therapist," Jay told him.

Vickers felt caught in the middle, serving as mediator between Jay and NBC. On the one hand, she got the network's point, in theory at least. But she thoroughly understood Jay's reaction. Why not wait until he at least showed signs of fading before stepping up to erase him?

Debbie also knew shows had to get produced every night, no matter what was going on inside Jay's head—and heart. So day after day she did what she could to keep Leno from going to a bad place. And when he questioned again why all this had happened, she would tell him, "Jay, look. It's about transitions."

Jeff Zucker had always emphasized the importance of the transition process at NBC and took pride in how he handled each one. When he ran the *Today* show, he steered the onetime dominant anchor of the morning, Bryant Gumbel, to the sidelines, replacing him with Matt Lauer, who became even more dominant. More prominently, he helped smooth the reset in an area long afflicted with contentious changes of ownership: the evening news anchor chair. Brian Williams bloodlessly took over for Tom Brokaw on the *NBC Nightly News* in December 2004, with Tom still ruling in the ratings.

The success of those decisions reinforced Zucker's philosophy on big changeovers: You didn't wait until the incumbent leader had slid into second place; you made your moves when he was on top. *The Tonight Show* should be no different.

By 2005, transitions were much on Zucker's mind, because he had every reason to expect he himself would be part of one. The long and hugely successful tenure of Bob Wright as chief executive of NBC Universal—Wright had skillfully orchestrated NBC's acquisition of Universal in 2003—was winding down. Zucker, now president of the NBC Universal Television Group, clearly sat in the successor seat. This, despite a record in his previous posting as chief of the entertainment division that even friends labeled mixed and detractors labeled mucked. While it was true that with Zucker at the helm NBC's prime-time fortunes collapsed after a long run at the top, his defenders cited his efforts to shore up what had already been a sinking sand castle of programs when he arrived in Burbank in December of 2000. Still, by his own acknowledgment, Zucker had not won any congeniality awards in Hollywood while he was there. With his journalism background he simply didn't take to the place, its pretensions, its posturing, its moguls, its agents, or its style; and Hollywood returned the sentiments. Still, Zucker retained the respect and support of the only mogul that counted, Jeff Immelt, the chairman of GE, NBC's corporate boss.

The network entered 2005, however, beset by a precipitous downturn in its prime-time ratings and profits. Having tumbled from first place to last in the space of one season, NBC's take in that year's annual upfront ad sales, which determine the bulk of revenues for each network, would plunge by a staggering $1 billion.

Fortunately its portfolio of cable networks was proving to be a cash fountain, and increasingly Zucker would point to them as the future—and even the present—of the company. Even with prime time in free fall, the big profit areas of morning and late night seemed secure because of the steps Zucker had taken to facilitate the big transitions. If the *Tonight* transfer of power worked as well as the *Today* one had, NBC would maintain ratings dominance even as a new face replaced the old. This strategy would also likely please GE, famous for its corporate personnel policy that demanded successors always be identified.

As one of the midlevel executives under Zucker explained, "Jeff tends not to project very far into the future and he likes to be a can-do guy. He looked at late night and asked, 'What's a win-win scenario where I can put this off, but on paper it looks very smooth and I'm going to keep everybody locked in?' GE loves transitions, so this was going to be a very big thing on the scorecard."

Another West Coast executive, unsurprised by Zucker's heavy emphasis on transitions and lines of succession, described his policy as "Jeff always likes to carry a spare."

But moving executives in and out of position was one thing; playing chess with the future of performers was a completely different game. According to one experienced developer of entertainment programming, "Jeff got everyone signed on—it will be a baton handoff. On paper that sounds great, and it sounds very GE-like. Except there are human beings involved, and human beings who are talent, who never, ever go the way you want them to go."

Zucker, confident of his abilities in most areas of management, was especially convinced of his skill in talent relations. Throughout his history at *Today*, he exhibited a deft hand at massaging the egos of big players like Gumbel and Katie Couric (who didn't much like each other) and later Matt Lauer. All of the stars of *Today* grew close to him, trusted him, relied on his counsel and advice. In Hollywood Jeff believed he had connected equally successfully with important NBC stars, like the cast of *Friends*.

But as he climbed he seemed to tip toward talent himself, at least as some saw it. One NBC executive heard Zucker complain about how his contract situation had been handled, compared to what the network had done for Lorne Michaels in his latest *Saturday Night Live* deal. "I don't think Jeff got it," the executive said, "that Lorne is talent."

The executive, who liked Zucker generally, suggested that Jeff and other top leaders across the entertainment industry shared a common genetic trait: "They have narcissistic personalities. Almost every conversation will eventually be about them. But maybe that's what it takes to be in jobs like that."

The personal quality most often cited by Zucker supporters and detractors alike was his high intelligence. But as much as that impressed many, it gave others more reason to question how effective he had actually been as CEO. The knock was that he didn't delegate well, mainly because he always seemed certain he could do the job as well or better himself.

"Sometimes it's a curse to be too smart and think you can do too much," said an NBC executive who worked closely with Zucker for a time.

The area that clearly needed the most attention at NBC was its crumbling entertainment division in LA. When Zucker left Hollywood in 2003 to return to New York and his new corporate assignment, he had hired Kevin Reilly to rebuild the foundation of the prime-time lineup. But it wasn't as though Reilly had free rein. "Jeff ran every scheduling meeting," said one of the lower-level development executives. "Kevin didn't handle Jeff well, and Jeff didn't handle Kevin well."

Reilly and others in the entertainment division felt ping-ponged at times by Zucker's rapidly changing assessments of shows, trends, the business in general. His strongest leadership quality, his total sense of confidence, had a downside in what staff members came to identify as "Zucklamations." As one longtime NBC executive—and Zucker backer—acknowledged, "Jeff does have a thing for proclamations and pronouncements."

These could deal with smallish details, like the breakdown of a show's format "It was like with the show *Las Vegas*," said the development executive, citing an NBC drama of this era that starred James Caan. "According to Jeff, that could be 85 percent self-contained and 15 percent serialized." At other times the proclamations could affect weightier issues. At one point, several NBC executives recalled, Zucker decided that no single-camera comedy—shows like *Scrubs* or *30 Rock*, which were shot on film like little movies with no laugh track—could ever be a hit. NBC should therefore lean toward three-camera comedies—shows like *Two and a Half Men* and *Friends*, shot on tape like little plays in front of studio audiences whose laughter accompanies the jokes.

That decision almost cost NBC the one new breakout comedy of Zucker's tenure, *The Office*, which Jeff did not initially embrace. After its first six episodes aired to minimal impact in the ratings, Zucker pushed for the show to be canceled, announcing during an NBC program strategy meeting, according to an executive who was there, "The audience has spoken—it's outright rejection." But Kevin Reilly liked the series a lot—as did Bob Wright (and even Jeff Immelt). The show hung on, and then took off, at which point Zucker, too, finally came around.

In private conversations with colleagues and friends, Zucker would occasionally open up about the economic squeeze he was feeling from GE. What was clear from staff meetings was that he was under constant pressure to "make the quarter," as he would put it. Somehow NBC's balance sheet needed to tip upward for each three-month period, which led to budget-tightening measures aimed at tiding the network over for a quarter, but they only seemed to increase the problem in the following quarter. As one entertainment division executive explained, "It always involved cutting. 'Maybe if we start this pilot later we can make the quarter. We gotta make the quarter.' It seemed we were always shoving problems off to the next quarter."

In early 2005 one major financial decision in particular was generating significant fallout for the entertainment division. Ebersol had put NBC in position to grab the prime-time NFL package, and move it from Monday to Sunday night, where it would steer clear of interrupting NBC's lucrative late-night lineup. But Ebersol gave it to Immelt straight: The deal, if the network could step up to it, would provide a huge, dependable audience that could be introduced to NBC's other shows, but it would mean a $150 million loss on the books every year.

Immelt told Ebersol that wasn't tolerable. But Dick said he had a way to account for $100 million of the annual loss. He explained that he had worked it out with Zucker that the entertainment division would give up $100 million a year out of its program development budget. The rationale:

With twenty weeks worth of four-hour-long football coverage every Sunday in the fall, NBC would not need nearly as much money to develop shows for the rest of the week.

Immelt agreed to accept the deal (and the loss of $50 million) as long as the entertainment division was audited every year to make sure it was cutting that $100 million from its budget. Although Zucker was thrilled to get a Sunday night of guaranteed huge ratings every week, some of his West Coast executives worried about how starved they were going to be for development funds, especially at a time when NBC desperately needed to find hits to drag itself out of the ratings basement.

But by then Zucker was convinced that NBC wasn't really a network-based company anyway. With a portfolio of assets that included the USA Network, Bravo, MSNBC, and CNBC, Zucker pushed for a new emphasis. "We're a cable company," he began to proclaim, with more and more frequency—and to more and more dismay among those trying to revive that network business. Or star in it.

Jay Leno certainly fit that description. To him only the network business really mattered. The game that ultimately counted was the daily comparison between network late-night shows. He knew he was number one; then came the other guys. Few if any other late-night hosts broke down the numbers—and every other clue to potential adjustments they might provide—the way Leno did. He knew what percentage of his audience stayed only for the monologue, when exactly they left, how many people he retained for each of the bits in act two (the comedy act after the monologue). He broke it all down to the minute.

"He's a real student of this stuff," said one of the principals at a competing show, who marveled at the detailed analysis Leno could offer for every one of the network late-night shows. "He loves the game. He really understands the ratings. He knows the lead-ins and how they affect his audience."

Leno found it amazing that he was considered some kind of oddball or sellout for paying attention to the minutiae of the ratings. He had spoken to at least a half dozen hosts of late-night shows that had failed since he'd won the job in 1992, and invariably they told him the same thing: "We just do our shows. We don't look at the ratings. We don't even want to know."

To Jay that attitude meant you might be able to develop a niche audience, but there was no way you were going to grow to be widely popular.

For years Leno brushed off the plaints coming from the camp of his main competitor, David Letterman, about how Dave was losing chiefly because he suffered under the handicap of dreadful lead-in ratings from CBS's woeful lineup of shows at ten p.m., while Jay was able to bask in the reflected glory of ten p.m. NBC blockbusters like *ER* and *Law & Order*. But as NBC's prime-time fortunes melted away in mid-decade, and CBS came on with a rush thanks to powerhouse ten p.m. shows like *CSI: Miami*, Leno pressed on, undiminished and (virtually) undefeated. The arguments for Dave's secret superiority became muted.

Soon the comparisons delivered by the Letterman camp took a different tack, such as "Dave is a four-star French restaurant; Jay is McDonald's." What Jay knew about McDonald's was he liked to eat there occasionally, and that many more billions of meals were served there than at Le Bernardin. He would even make the analogy himself, describing his comedy as "good food at reasonable prices."

Still, Letterman mattered to Jay. Like no one else on television, no one else in show business, no one else even in his life, Letterman mattered. The two comics had been linked since their earliest days as stand-ups in LA; they also broke into television at about the same time, with Letterman opening the way for Jay to emerge into public consciousness by having him as the most frequent guest on his *Late Night* show.

And of course they came together like estranged princes in a Shakespeare history play, each seeking to succeed the departing king. When NBC anointed Leno the host of *The Tonight Show* in 1992, it first played as a usurpation, as Letterman had for far longer been the presumptive heir. Later, when NBC came close to ousting Jay in favor of Dave, it turned into a Restoration drama—but only in one act. Leno survived, and rewrote the ending, but only at the cost of seeing his rival installed in the castle next door. And there they sat for sixteen years, separated by the narrowest of channels. Dave's realm enjoyed a brief giddy reign before the size and strength of Jay's historic empire of the night gradually overwhelmed him, leaving him permanently the lesser power.

By 2005 the outcome was routine: Jay supreme; Dave suppressed. Mercurial and moody in the best of times, a perpetually frustrated Letterman tipped often toward maddening to both his always admiring but usually cowed staff and to any executives at CBS who came into contact with him. Apart from the big boss, Leslie Moonves, whom Dave grew to respect and would sometimes chat with playfully by phone on the air, network inter-action tended to be minimal. Little good usually came of any request or suggestion from CBS. Letterman never deigned to try to enhance his posi-tion by making some effort to help out affiliates or cater to advertisers—no upfront appearances for him—and he certainly had no interest at all in speaking to the press, even when advantageous moments for publicity arose. Virtually every interview request was declined, unless there was an element of duty involved—paying back guests like Ted Koppel at *Nightline*, Regis Philbin on his morning show, or Oprah Winfrey on her afternoon show. To even innocuous appeals for his reaction to some development, significant or trivial, Letterman would tell his press representatives, "What I have to say I say on the show."

His tenth-year anniversary at CBS? No acknowledgement in the press. His twentieth anniversary as a late-night host—perfect fodder for some high-profile attention—received none. Emmy Awards won five years in a row, from 1998 to 2002? Dave didn't show up to accept any of them and gave no interviews to express his feelings about them. The end of a famous feud with Oprah (she had resented his jokes about her) was marked by Dave's publicly escorting her to the theater on Broadway next door to his own, where the musical she had produced, *The Color Purple*, was opening. While the stunt lifted the ratings for one glorious night, Dave had done no publicity to build up the numbers that night and he let the much covered moment with Oprah pass without taking any further steps to capitalize upon it.

Sometimes his reluctance was based on his commendable com-mitment never to play the shameless showbiz shill in situations either intensely private or highly sensitive. So, talking only on the air about the life-threatening heart condition that led to serious bypass surgery in 2000—or even the bout with shingles in 2003 that induced him to call in guest hosts for the first time—became a matter of his personal integrity. And of course, Dave handled the most trying episode of his career—becoming the first entertainment voice to address the horror of the 9/11 attacks on New York and the nation—with such sensitivity and grace that he needed to do nothing else to add to his legend.

By some sort of tacit agreement, everyone else in late night acknowl-edged that Dave needed to speak out first on the tragedy. On September 17 he brought his show back. Talking extemporaneously and from the heart, fighting his emotions all the way, Dave, in an eight-minute mono-logue from his desk, tried to put the reaction to the attack in some context. He praised New York's mayor, Rudy Giuliani, and the city's police and fire departments. He observed, "There is only one thing required of any of us and that is to be courageous, because courage, as you may know, defines all other human behavior. I believe, because I've done a little of this myself, pretending to be courageous is just as good as the real thing." He ended with a salute to the city, saying that if anyone didn't believe it before, they "could absolutely believe it now: New York City . . . is the greatest city in the world."

Letterman won unanimous praise for that show and the ones that fol-lowed, when he seemingly found just the right moments to weave some wit and comedy into the ongoing gloom. One NBC executive—speaking privately, because his opinion would hardly please the network's own star—paid Dave the ultimate compliment: "Everybody looked to Dave for the way to do this. If there's a Johnny out there, it's Dave."

That was a comparison Dave himself would surely have disavowed; but it truly was only valid on the cultural level, not the ratings one. Johnny qualified as the all-time winner. Leno ranked as the current one.

Jeff Zucker tried to underline that point in red. "There is no more late-night war," he declared in 2003. There was only a victor and a vanquished—and NBC had the victor, no matter what Dave's support-ers in the media may have tried to argue. "I think the Letterman show appears more tired," Zucker suggested, not caring if he drew a penalty for taunting. "I think it's hard for the national media to accept the fact that Jay is so dominant. The national media has always been more drawn to the dark, brooding cynicism of Dave, rather than the populist wit of Jay."

How deep in Dave's craw did comments like that stick? It was impos-sible to discern from the man himself, silent as always, except when he would let loose on the air with an occasional shot at Jay or NBC. (Every spring brought the Passover joke.) But Letterman did have someone to serve as his public mouthpiece: his executive producer, Rob Burnett. Long the most outspoken Letterman defender, Burnett, in the face of Jay's con-tinuing ratings superiority, returned fire from a subjective foxhole. "There are two parts of the so-called late-night war," Burnett said. "One is: Who's the best? That part of the war is over. Dave won."

Of course, that pronouncement was not going to stop people from keeping score. The stats had a different message: Jay was winning not only in the ratings but in financial terms as well. According to a cost analysis by the Nielsen ratings company, *The Tonight Show* in 2003 was able to charge about $65,000 for each thirty-second commercial; for the *Late Show* the price was about $53,000. Over the course of a year, that would add up to an advantage of tens of millions of dollars for NBC.

Letterman, brooding up in his offices above Broadway, could not escape the box scores and balance sheets. Predisposed to kick himself unmercifully for even the slightest mistake or failing he perceived in himself, he punished staff members who disappointed him in less volatile ways, most often by stopping talking to them entirely. Few were ever fired—one exception had been his longtime executive producer Robert Morton, whom Dave dispatched in 1996 with unusual churlishness, declaring him to have been a "diseased limb"—but Dave's silent treatment could go on for months, sometimes years. Even top producers, once put on ice, found themselves showing up for work but having nothing to do except continue to be paid.

For his part, Leno never looked away from what Dave was doing. Partly, colleagues said, it was because Jay remained fascinated by Dave, his unpredictable nature, his whipsaw wit. But another part of Leno grew more and more astonished that Dave not only never seemed to pay a price for not making every effort to win, but was outright disdainful of the things Jay did routinely in his pursuit of quantifiable success.

He couldn't believe the attitude behind comments from the Letterman camp like one from Rob Burnett: "Jay runs *The Tonight Show* like a political campaign. If he thinks something will attract more viewers, he'll do it. Jay sees that Arnold Schwarzenegger is hot, so he introduces Arnold at a political rally. He sees that wrestling is hot, so he wrestles for the WWF. Maybe Jay earned himself a few more viewers for doing those things, but you have to ask yourself: Who would you rather be? Jay or Dave?"

Arrogance in the face of endless losing? In private moments, Jay could not help noting that Dave didn't do that well anymore and wondering:. *Where does all this power come from?*

But he knew the answer. Whenever Jay broke down the differing courses their careers had taken, Jay always acknowledged Dave's great strength—on television. "I'm a comedian," Leno said, analyzing their relative assets. "I'm not a talk-show host. I think Dave as a broadcaster is as good as there has ever been. I would say Dave is the better broadcaster and I am the better stand-up comedian." He felt they had learned from each other. From Dave, Jay had learned to be a wordsmith. From Jay, Dave had learned how to be a performer and be aggressive and "hit the mic hard."

But faced with the change proposed by NBC in 2004, Dave didn't factor much in how Leno parsed out his future. As he surveyed the changing late-night landscape around him, he considered the possible threats to his preeminence if he chose to dig in his heels and decline NBC's proposed five-year plan. Say no, Leno reasoned, and he would be going up against Conan on Fox or ABC. "It's not so much Conan—well, it's Conan and it's everything I've worked for in my career," Jay said. "Conan would go to ABC, and then I would be fighting a war on two fronts. Dave . . . who knows what Dave was going to do? And whether Jon Stewart would step in for Dave, and then you're fighting . . . *two* younger guys."

Jon Stewart? Nobody else seemed to be including him in the coming network late-night equation. NBC had not imagined any scenario that would have CBS turning to Stewart to replace Letterman, creating more viable competition for that younger audience they expected Conan to attract. But Jay had been a regular viewer of Jon Stewart dating back to a late-night show Jon had starred in on MTV. It seemed to Jay then that Stewart was reaching every possible person in his chosen demographic group (young, smart, hip) but no one else. It was obvious, though, that the guy was really funny. "You know, you never know," Jay assessed. "Things come along; you never know what's going to knock you out of the box."

As Jay peered over the horizon of his potential future, he saw a possibility that few others did: the cable guy who was coming into his own.

Jon Stewart had been buzzing around the late-night airfield for years, usually landing on some auxiliary runway before taking off again in search of a better heading. He had tried out for the *Late Night* opening post-Dave with the rest of the stand-up community at NBC's showcase in early 1993 when he was thirty. Later the same year he successfully pitched MTV a thirty-minute late-night talk show. It only lasted a year but generated enough attention that Paramount stepped up and offered to syndicate it in an hour-long version. That, too, lasted less than a year.

David Letterman, however, had noticed his show and saw a break-out host in the making. Dave's production company, Worldwide Pants, offered Jon what was known as a holding deal: He would get paid; they would get access to Stewart's clearly emerging talent. (And, conveniently, for a couple of years Jon would be off the market, just in case NBC fell out of love with Conan again and went looking for other late-night talent.) Surely somewhere a door would open a crack during this stint under Letterman's aegis, and Jon would finally get a real chance to break through.

And so he did—but only tangentially thanks to Worldwide Pants. Jon actually got little out of his association with Dave's company, apart from the occasional invitation to guest host Tom Snyder's *The Late Late Show*. Given his availability to the Letterman camp, Stewart ought to have been teed up and ready to go when CBS, finally alarmed by Snyder's sliding ratings and aging audience, sought a change. But when the Pants people went back into the host selection business, they passed over Jon Stewart again and decided instead that Craig Kilborn would be a better choice.

Kilborn, tall, blond, and jocky—he had played basketball at Montana State and made his name in television as an anchor on ESPN's *SportsCenter*—was coming off a checkered run as the first anchor of the faux newscast on Comedy Central, *The Daily Show*. Created by two sharp, funny women, Lizz Winstead and Madeleine Smithberg, *TDS* quickly established itself as a clever nightly center for topical satire. Kilborn had won some fans with his wiseacre style, but he irritated an almost equal number. The show was a genuine hit by cable standards, though, and Kilborn might have settled in for a long run. But about a year in, he gave an interview to *Esquire* magazine in which he apparently wanted to underscore his masculinity, telling the reporter, "To be honest, Lizz does find me very attractive. If I wanted her to blow me, she would."

Kilborn was suspended. Although he apologized, claiming he meant it as a joke, Winstead wasn't amused—nor were many other women. The show had that hit thing going for it, however, and Comedy Central's management thought better of letting Kilborn go. Only a year later, the Worldwide Pants organization sought him out to replace Snyder, though internally some members of Letterman's company were appalled by the choice. Whatever his virtues as an on-air presenter—and Kilborn had a legitimate facility as a broadcaster—he didn't seem to have a fraction of Stewart's comedy talent or pure wit. And that magazine interview did not speak well of his judgment.

But Rob Burnett, the executive in charge of the Pants production unit, had his reasons for choosing Kilborn, which mainly had to do with Stewart's being much like Dave and Kilborn's being totally unlike Dave. (That was hardly surprising, given that Stewart was another young comic heavily influenced by Letterman.) On the face of it, having a talent with the potential to be the next Dave might seem like a recommendation. Burnett, however, viewed it as a problem. It would require, for one thing, that the show hire another stable of writers similar to the ones who worked for Dave, and to Burnett that seemed a tall order. When the Pants organization made the decision, Kilborn was also arguably better known than Stewart, which may have factored into the thinking. Another suggestion was offered by outsiders: Dave didn't really want a guy playing immediately after him who might generate talk about succession. The quick-witted Stewart might have been good enough to do that; the preening Kilborn—some critics suggested it looked like he was doing the show in front of a mirror rather than a camera—was not likely to be any threat to Dave's hegemony at CBS.

So another late-night opening suddenly closed for Jon Stewart. But his friends at the Letterman show had at the same time vacated another late-night chair. Did Jon want the job Craig Kilborn apparently thought was second rate enough to move out of the first chance he got? Stewart had by this point signed a movie deal with Miramax, and while he did get a few cracks in films (most notably a campy horror comedy from Robert Rodriguez called *The Faculty*), the experience was enough for him to conclude he belonged on television.

In 1999 Stewart accepted the anchor job on *The Daily Show* that Kilborn had abandoned—with just one week to prepare for his first appearance. It wasn't network; it wasn't after Letterman; it was even kind of sloppy seconds. But it was a nightly comedy show, with a bent toward news. Jon Stewart knew he was a news junkie, but more than anything else, he knew he was a comic.

Comic came after busboy, waiter, bartender, mosquito sorter, and construction worker, among other temporary roles. Jon Stewart was not preordained to be funny onstage the way Jay Leno had been as a boy in Boston. Stewart grew up in Lawrenceville, New Jersey, near Trenton. He was Jonathan Stuart Leibowitz then, second child of an elementary school teacher mother and physics professor father. The family broke up when Jon was nine, and later jokes left listeners with the impression that Jon did not easily forgive his father. (As late as 2002, Jon told interviewers that his father had never seen him perform.)

Jon was smart and athletic, ending up at William and Mary, where he played left wing on the soccer team. His only real entertainment background to that point was some horn playing in the high school band. At loose ends after graduation, he fell into a succession of odd—and odder—jobs, highlighted by one that made a real impression: as a puppeteer for children with disabilities. That tapped at least obliquely into the latent streak of humor submerged in Stewart, and the experience inspired him to set out to try stand-up.

It was a long and brutal initiation. Stewart spent close to a year working up the material—and courage—to appear at New York's Bitter End club. When he finally did, he barely got through half the act before the flop sweat from the profound bombing he was delivering drove him from the stage—and almost out of the business. He stuck with it because at that point he wasn't sure what else to do with his life.

For two years he worked during the day as a bartender at a Mexican restaurant in Manhattan, earning just enough to live on so that he could show up every night at the Comedy Cellar and go on as the last act. Every weeknight, somewhere near two a.m., Jon Stewart performed before the drunk and the lonely of the New York metropolitan area. "I sucked for two straight years," Jon would later tell aspiring comics, partly as advice and partly as storm warning.

But slowly, incrementally, it came to him. Performing as Jon Stewart—he would later take the formal legal steps to abandon the name Leibowitz—he put on comedy muscle. His material got sharper, smarter. He landed some writing jobs, finally scoring a crucial gig hosting Comedy Central's *Short-Attention Span Theater*. At around the same time, a young agent from William Morris, James Dixon, saw Jon performing stand-up. Sensing enormous appeal and potential in the obviously super-bright young comic, he signed him up. Much good—for both of them—would come from that initial connection.

Throughout the quick demise of his MTV and syndicated shows, his passage in and out of dalliance with the movies, and his unrequited affair with David Letterman's production company, Stewart built his reputation with consistently impressive work. Everybody who worked with Jon came away thinking they had just encountered a driven, creative, and, yes, appropriately neurotic future star. All it would take was the right launch module.

The Daily Show was precisely the rocket he required. Stewart's sensibility—and his insight that the show's comedy should have a harder edge about the folly of both those in the news and the people in the media who were covering them—transformed *TDS* first to more smart than silly, and then from awfully smart to damn brilliant. By 2000 it was celebrated enough to start grabbing Emmy nominations and ultimately collecting awards.

At the prime-time Emmy Awards ceremony in Los Angeles on September 19, 2004, Conan O'Brien sat with his group in the audience, close by Lorne Michaels, who, since he still retained an executive producer credit on *Late Night*, would take home a prize if Conan's show won for best comedy or variety show. Michaels was also present because his meal ticket, *Saturday Night Live*, had been nominated in the same category.

Almost every season both shows would share the nominations with Letterman, perhaps Bill Maher's HBO series, and inevitably with *The Daily Show*. Inside Conan's camp the frustration mounted: starting in 2003 Jon Stewart's show racked up wins every year in that category as well as the best-writing award, a streak that would continue right through 2009. As much as Conan and his group tried to shrug off Stewart's success—topical and political humor always impressed awards types, they reasoned—it quietly drove them all nuts. They had all worked so hard, come up with so much distinctively original material, but they never got a shot to be recognized—because Jon Stewart was always there.

Michaels, who was losing every year as well with *SNL*, was more philosophical about Stewart's winning streak. With his insight into Conan's darker side, he knew this level of frustration with Stewart's Emmy dominance could not be productive for the melancholic Irish comic. So, just as the telecast began, Lorne thought he should offer a helpful observation.

"Look around this room," he said to Conan. "Do you see anyone who looks like you in this room? You know, there are a lot of very small Jews in the room."

Lorne himself fit that description, though perhaps not as precisely as Stewart. But the joke was meant to let Conan know both that he shouldn't take the Emmy voting too seriously and that Jon Stewart was no fluke. He was going to be around as a formidable player in late night.

Leno had a similar impression, which was why he feared a double-pronged assault from O'Brien and Stewart. Leno refused to acknowledge any Emmy envy, however. He was never nominated anymore, which he put down to a typically perverse Hollywood dismissal of the merely popular. Jay would take numbers over trophies anytime. He had made that bargain with himself long before.

When Jay Leno was the most frequent—and popular—guest on David Letterman's *Late Night* show in the 1980s, he eagerly embraced the role he had then carved out for himself: Mr. Cutting-Edge Comic. Letterman fans loved him for his ferociously funny harangues on the absurdities of life. Dave would simply set him up with "So what's bothering you this time, Jay?" and Leno would be off, ranting about this idiocy (airline flights, bad movies) or that (corporate greed).

It gave him a profile in the business, which is what he wanted. But it wasn't all he wanted. That level of success might make him money and attract favorable critical notices, but Jay was after the ultimate comedy career, and the models there were not Letterman or Richard Pryor or Sam Kinison. Jay consciously set out to have the career that a Bill Cosby or a Johnny Carson or—even more aptly—a Bob Hope had had. He wanted to be a comic for *every* audience.

That meant jettisoning Mr. Cutting Edge and slipping into Mr. Regular Guy. That persona was a snugger fit for Leno, anyway. He often joked about being "a great believer in low self-esteem," but he came by the quality honestly.

One constant figure played a central role in Jay's act, and in most of his stories about the formation of his character and views on life: his mom. Mainly Jay made merry references to his mother's habitual embarrassment and emotional stringency, qualities he summoned up when discussing why he never wanted the title of his show to be the "Tonight Show Starring Jay Leno" as it had been with Carson, but instead insisted on the

"Tonight Show *with* Jay Leno." "Why would you want to call attention to yourself like that?" Jay would say, imitating his mother's pinched Scottish accent. Of course, while the disavowal of "starring" also played well with that everyman image he sought to cultivate, the frequent citation of his mother's cringing discomfort with his fame came from a deeper place.

James Douglas Muir Leno grew up in Andover, Massachusetts, feeling like a townie in a village dominated by its illustrious prep school, Phillips Academy. His exposure to that elite world gave Leno insight into what he concluded was the fundamental prep school mentality: class superiority. Jay himself was a child totally outside the WASP culture. His father, Angelo, son of Italian immigrants, was a popular insurance salesman for Prudential, and the family took pride—"That's our company!"—when those "piece of the rock" commercials would play on television during shows of the fifties like *Victory at Sea*. His mother, Cathryn Muir, had survived a difficult childhood. She was sent to America from Scotland at age eleven to live with an older sister, because her mother had abandoned the family for a younger man and her father couldn't afford to take care of all his children at home. Her formal education never extended past second grade. As Jay saw it, the experience had left her with an air of sadness that permeated her life.

Jay was born when Cathryn was forty-one, and his only sibling—a brother, Patrick—was ten years older. Jay acknowledged that he had never been close to Patrick, which had in part to do with their age difference, but also with the fact that Patrick was remarkably gifted academically. He was one of the top students in New England in high school and won an ROTC scholarship to Yale. After graduation he became an army officer, serving in Vietnam, and then it was on to law school. For a woman who never had a chance to get beyond second grade in elementary school, this outstanding, high-achieving son was naturally a source of huge pride.

At the same time that she basked in the glory of Patrick's intellectual accomplishments, Cathryn Leno found herself often trudging off to school in Andover to hear about the latest embarrassing tribulation her younger son had brought upon the family. Teachers discussed Jay's lack of attention and his apparent interest only in cutting up and amusing his classmates. The highlight of this experience, as Jay wove the tale (and fair context demands a note that Jay can be a world-class fabulist in the service of a humorous story), took place with a guidance counselor in high school, Mr. Neal, who decided that Cathryn had to be brought in for a conference. Jay always claimed he "overheard" the subsequent conversation: "Mrs. Leno, have you thought of taking Jamie out of school? He works at McDonald's now and he seems to like that. Maybe he would do better at something like that. You know, education's not for everyone, Mrs. Leno."

As Jay remembered it, his mother was furious, telling Mr. Neal she had never heard of a guidance counselor suggesting a child be taken out of school. "Well, he's disruptive," the counselor complained. And then his mother took a stand, saying she was not doing anything of the sort and Jamie would stay in school to get his high school diploma.

Whether actually diagnosed or not, Jay made reference to his school difficulties by explaining, "I'm a little dyslexic." His mother's reaction to this was what Jay came to call her mantra: "You know you're going to have to work a lot harder than the other kids to get the same things they have." Leno seared that advice into his psyche. If he wasn't as gifted as other kids—later, other comics—he would hit them where they might be weak: their work ethic. Leno especially loved to tell one story about his early days as *Tonight Show* host. He was at his post at home, as usual, writing jokes for the next day's monologue, when he turned on the TV and saw a competitor. (Jay didn't mention the name because he had resolved his differences with the rival, and good relations carried enormous weight with Jay, but it was pretty obviously Arsenio Hall.) "There he was sitting at the Lakers game," Jay recalled. "And I thought, 'Got ya! I'll have a monologue tomorrow night and you won't.' And you know what? He didn't."

For Jay, the job always seemed to be as much about the self-abnegation involved in the effort as the effort itself: "It just seems like common sense. If you go to a party, or go out drinking, I win. It doesn't seem that hard to understand. I'm amazed at people who can't get that." (Jay swore that he had never consumed an alcoholic beverage in his life. Of course he never took drugs, either, and, he said, he steered clear of caffeine as well.) How much of this attitude was a function of his relationship with his mother was always difficult to guess for those close to Jay, because Leno rarely exposed his emotions. But Jay brought his mom up often, on stage and off, and usually in the context of how repressed she was.

Like in his story about Carnegie Hall. As his career was taking off, thanks to his many breakthrough appearances on Letterman (sixty, he estimated at this point), Jay was booked in the hallowed New York concert venue. At first, he said, his mother found this simply astonishing. "Why are you going to be in Carnegie Hall?" he quoted her. "She thought it was a mistake."

But of course he wanted his parents at such a prestigious show, and he got them excellent tickets in the third row back, right in the center. Behind them was a row of seven or eight college-age guys. "These guys knew all the bits from watching Letterman," Jay said. "So whenever I started something they recognized, these guys would go *woo, woo* and start to laugh and applaud." Jay threw himself as usual into the bit but could not help noticing from the stage that his mother was turning around in her seat.

"She starts to go, 'Shush! Shush!' She's trying to shush them."

Appalled, Jay stopped his act to speak out to his mother. "Mom! You don't shush people." He realized it was another example of his mother being somehow humiliated and embarrassed by the attention he was getting. It made her completely uncomfortable.

Her discomfort seemed amplified when the contrast between her sons grew wider. Patrick's life took unexpected turns, all unhappy in various ways—his marriage, his career. Jay, meanwhile, thrived. He started making solid money as a comic at a remarkably young age and was able to buy a house before all the other young comics in the LA scene at the time. He got on television. He was, of all things, booked into Carnegie Hall.

And then, *The Tonight Show* beckoned. It should have been a glorious accomplishment to share with his family, but it didn't quite go that way. Jay sensed that Patrick had issues accepting his kid brother's success. And his mother seemed to resist expressing a lot of joy about it as well. Jay, making millions, could afford to give his parents anything, but that became a sensitive area. Sometimes Jay would return home to Andover with an expensive gift for his mother—a piece of costly jewelry, for example. Jay would present it to his mother, who would quickly get fluttery and say, "Don't tell your brother you bought this," and then would run and hide the gift away.

Jay would explain all this and say he understood it; his brother had to feel cheated in certain ways. Patrick was stuck with the Scottish traits in the family; Jay inherited the Italian. (That's where the good teeth and fantastic head of hair came from.) Patrick became a worrier, stressed over everything in his life. It only swelled the cloud of sadness that hung over his mother.

Jay's confidants—and they were few—could only draw inferences from the snippets of his background that he dropped here and there. Jay never spoke of his mother without evident deep affection. Still, if some suspected that Jay had missed out on a full, externally expressed measure of motherly love, leaving him with a hole in his heart that he could never fill, and even refused to address, he was certainly no candidate for therapy. Jay disdained any kind of psychological mumbo jumbo, and not just because as a comic he was supposed to make fun of people's foibles. Leno was not inner directed because he was primarily joke directed. He stripped away almost any other interest—other than his vehicles, which he worked on avidly, filling just about every waking hour when he wasn't writing or telling jokes. He certainly didn't chase women. His marriage to Mavis did not strike colleagues as gooily romantic (they didn't seem to spend much time together), but it was, by every indication, solid and comfortable to both. Jay, in establishing his mainstream bona fides, would always point out, "I'm still on my first wife."

He and Mavis had never had children. They rarely vacationed together, mainly because Jay abhorred the very idea of vacation. During weeks off he booked himself into Vegas or some high-paying corporate retreat, while Mavis often traveled the world. Jay loved to tell a story of an ill-advised decision to take a booking in Hawaii, with an extra day scheduled afterward to relax on the beach. A morning on the beach led him to wonder if his watch had become filled with sand, because it indicated that only an hour had gone by when surely he had been out there all day. He was on a plane back to LA before noon. Jay also famously asked NBC to consider hiring a separate staff of writers and producers for the six-to-eight-week period that the show was scheduled to be dark so he could work all fifty-two weeks of the year while the rest of the regular staff got a break. (NBC politely declined.)

His aversion to going anywhere except places where he could tell jokes led to his making pronouncements that even his closest associates acknowledged sounded bizarre. "You start taking vacations and you go, 'Uh-oh, what if I like this?' Then you're screwed." The whole notion of going somewhere and doing something simply because it was pleasurable or interesting was a concept Jay simply didn't get. "I understand how people spend money to buy things they need or they like," Jay said, summarizing his philosophy. "But spending money on an experience? That seems like an extravagance to me."

Of course, even though he always avowed that he never spent a dime of his NBC salary and lived only off the money from his stand-up dates, it didn't seem to dawn on Jay that most of the people coming to see him tell jokes were on vacation and were paying for that experience.

Critics—as well as occasionally the network and his own producers—often cited Jay's apparent lack of interest in the stories guests on the show told. Certainly most of the staff knew that Jay devoted little time preparing to speak to guests. Worse, at least for some, was a habit Jay adopted later in his *Tonight Show* run. As described by one A-level movie star guest, an appearance with Jay could be thoroughly disconcerting.

"I'm sitting there telling him a story about some damn thing that happened and I realize he's not looking at me at all," the star said. "His eyes are going straight past me. The audience can't see this because he's still looking vaguely in my direction, but his eyes are not on me at all. When he went to commercial I took a look over my shoulder. There was a guy with cue cards standing off to the side behind him. Jay was just reading the questions off the cards. Not paying attention to me at all. The whole thing was so artificial; I was totally put off by it."

Jay's day was so consumed with reading and deciding on jokes that he usually had to be clued in that it was time to stop. "By the afternoon he would have been reading jokes for about five hours," one longtime staff member said. "He would have culled them down to about a hundred fifty by that point from at least five hundred. Then about four p.m. someone would go to him and say, 'You can't read any more jokes.' He would go down to rehearsal, but while rehearsing whatever the comedy bit was in act two, Jay would still be reading more jokes right through the rehearsal." Throughout the process, Jay would rarely, if ever, laugh.

But for Jay his method worked. Forget the Emmy Awards, the critics, the comparisons to Dave or anybody else. Others might watch him and shake their heads in wonder. Some might call him a robot, with no apparent inner life at all. Jay didn't care, nor did he even seem to disagree all that much. He had boiled it all down to the most basic level, in a way that made others in the field of comedy sometimes wince and moan. No matter; Jay stuck steadfastly to his approach. After all, it was the secret to his success:

"Write joke; tell joke; get check."

CHAPTER FIVE

SEIZE THE JAY

F or six months or so Jay Leno would be fine. Throughout the fall of 2004 and early 2005 his routine would be as it always had been. Around first light he would climb into his chosen vehicle for the day (1937 Bugatti, 1955 Buick Roadmaster, 1915 Hispano-Suiza, 1987 Lamborghini Countach, 1934 Rolls, 1996 Dodge Viper, 1926 Bentley, 1932 Duesenberg, 1909 Stanley Steamer—whatever choice from his ever expanding collection he and his garagemates had most recently restored to full driving condition) and make his way over the hill to Burbank from his home in Beverly Hills. Upon arriving on the NBC lot he would park in his designated spot adjacent to the entry ramp, pull out his battered leather saddlebag of a briefcase stuffed with jokes and the research the staff had provided on news stories and guests, and roll on in to work.

Many mornings the first one in, he'd settle down at his desk and pore over the jokes he and his head writer Joe Medeiros had committed to index cards late the night before in Jay's home office. At the same time he would be culling printouts of the e-mailed jokes that had been submitted by the group still known as the faxers (a holdover from a bygone techno-logical day), the pay-by-the-joke freelance contributors who got seventy-five or a hundred dollars apiece for every gag Jay used on the air.

When Debbie Vickers arrived hours later, she would take a reading of Jay's demeanor. Most days she could discern the familiar attributes:

steady, purposeful, joke obsessed. It didn't mean Jay was no longer feeling the disappointment, resentment, and regret that NBC's long-range termination notice had planted inside him. It meant only that, for the moment anyway, he was living by what he called "the first rule of show business: Don't create anything bigger than your act." Jay interpreted the rule to mean that, if you found yourself consumed by something bigger than what you are known for, your downfall was assured. If something distracting or dispiriting was going on in his life, his duty was to shrug it off, get back in the game of telling jokes, and be funny, day in, day out.

But after those initial six months passed, Vickers knew that every day would no longer be conventional. There came a morning, and then several mornings, when Jay's demeanor was clearly different: sullen, chagrined, joke obsessed. On those days Leno would unburden himself to Vickers, spilling out his undissipated confusion over NBC's decision. His unhappiness was only exacerbated if he played a gig somewhere and faced bewildered fans asking, "Why are you retiring, Jay?" He would try to laugh it off, tell them of course he wasn't really retiring, he would still tour and be around plenty. But the exercise was excruciating. So was having to deal with the guests who brought up the subject on the air, with cracks about being put out to pasture or some other dopey expression.

"I'm just sick of lying," Leno told Vickers.

On the bad days he would openly kick around his options. At worst, he would announce, he would end up a really rich person. Or he just might decide to defect; maybe he would go down the road to ABC. They might be interested in him over there.

That was the scenario that eventually filtered back to Rick Ludwin from his contacts on the show. In his capacity as supervisor of late night for NBC, Ludwin always spent a great deal of time around the *Tonight* studio, but Jay wasn't sending a message to NBC about his litany of unhappiness through Rick—maybe because Jay had begun to suspect that Ludwin had been one of the architects of the Conan elevation.

Inside the confines of the *Tonight Show* world, Ludwin heard Jay had been telling staff members things like: "Instead of getting off the freeway off-ramp for Bob Hope Drive and turning left, we'll just turn right and go up to the Disney lot on Buena Vista. We'll take the whole staff and just move on up to Disney and ABC."

Ludwin would dutifully report back to his management about Jay's prospective driving directions. The news didn't really surprise anyone; Ludwin and the others at NBC hardly expected Jay was going to pack it in and take up gardening.

Jay's message could also come through at times in his monologue. More jokes began to appear about NBC's expertise in coming in fourth in the network rankings. A failure by a politician or sports team in the news somehow led to comparisons to NBC. When he returned from a dark week and NBC had done some redecorating on his stage, including installing a new desk, Jay feigned surprise, saying, "It's not like NBC to get rid of something that's worked perfectly well for fifteen years."

When Brett Favre of the Green Bay Packers was let go by his team after long years of exceptional play, Jay remarked, with an obvious edge, "His bosses don't want him anymore—even though he was doing a really good job." Later, during the 2008 presidential primaries, Jay went through the news of the day, which included a story about Hillary Clinton's camp making a secret offer to Barack Obama to run with her as vice presidential nominee. Jay's joke: "Obama is wondering why he's being offered the second position when he's still in first place." Pause. "I've been wondering the same thing myself."

And occasionally Conan would get a pointed reference, as in one holiday-period show when Jay turned to his bandleader, Kevin Eubanks, and asked, "Kev, you ever regift?" (Pause.) "I do. I regifted; I gave Conan something I got fifteen years ago."

At least Jay could derive a little cathartic satisfaction from nailing NBC with a good shot every once in a while. It was fun for him—in a small way. But it wasn't as though it was going to make any difference. Leno had resigned himself to the fact that nobody was going to reverse the decision. The NBC executives were hardly going to change their minds.

In meetings of his entertainment group, Jeff Zucker enjoyed putting people on the spot, usually in jest, though for the most part the executives under him never really believed he was kidding. When late night was being considered, Zucker truly was only needling his executives through 2005 and 2006, raising questions about how things were shaping up. He was feeling no regrets. Profits were still pouring in from both of his hour-long shows, profits he had protected by locking in both stars; ABC and Fox still weren't in the entertainment game in late night. All seemed right in that world.

But as the years rolled by, with all the players back on their isolated islands, the endgame, once a blip on the horizon, began to come into focus, gather shape—and the shape looked dark and smoky, like a distant storm.

Zucker, whose prime-time headaches had gone from annoying to chronic to blindingly intense, now had to endure a faint but growing buzzing in his ear: the sound of Jay Leno humming, "Na, na, na, na. Na, na, na, na. Hey, hey, hey, good-bye."

So as 2006 rolled into 2007, Zucker began calculating what losing Jay Leno might really mean—especially if he landed in the late-night arms of a competitor. Zucker, an eye on the long-range calendar, began foraging for kernels of ideas that might grow into a feasible possibility to keep Jay attached to NBC in some capacity.

So Zucker, whenever he dropped in on his entertainment staff in Burbank, running the meetings as always, had sharpened his late-night focus. He would turn to Rick Ludwin, employing his usual half-puckish, half-pointed tone.

"So, Rick, how're you sleeping at night?" Zucker would ask, and then scan the table, letting the group know how playfully pregnant the question really was. Ludwin, looking bookish as usual, was flanked almost always by his late-night deputy Nick Bernstein, so boyish next to the much taller Ludwin that they were affectionately known as Batman and Robin. Ludwin had a ready answer: "Like a baby."

The cause for Zucker's concern about the degree of Ludwin's restfulness was no mystery to anyone at the meetings. Jay was still winning handily; Conan was . . . well, doing fine. Rick—backed by Nick—never backed down, never wavered in supporting Conan's ascension to *The Tonight Show*. The two NBC late-night executives had complete faith in O'Brien and were willing to defend that faith against any doubters.

In these meetings doubters had begun to speak up with questions about Conan, and they always sprang from the same concern: Should we worry that he's a little too narrow, a little too hip, a little too New York, a little too young male college guy and not enough middle America, middle age, middle brow?

Ludwin always went to the same place to answer the doubters. The Conan you will see on *The Tonight Show* is that guy who stood up on that stage at the Emmy Awards and charmed people with broad, easily accessible humor. Conan went into the Emmys with the intention to entertain not only the audience in the Shrine Auditorium but the millions more watching at home. He killed doing bits that were all Conan, bits that pleased his hard-core fans and yet didn't require newcomers to know any of the backstory to get the comedy. He would do the same at eleven thirty, Ludwin promised.

His stout defense may not have swayed everyone at the meeting, but it certainly did persuade them all that Rick Ludwin had strength in his convictions—and he was unalterably convinced that Conan O'Brien was the right guy at the right time for NBC.

If they had had a vote, a group of television executives from the other networks would have happily stumped for Conan as well. To the hierarchy of ABC and Fox, NBC's move had the look of a free ticket on the late-night gravy train. Were they *really* going to usher the dominant late-night star out the door? And leave him open to sign elsewhere, bringing along the $50 million to $100 million in profits that had previously gone to NBC? Was there a catch?

Maybe. It would certainly take strenuous wooing to land Leno, who was famous for his reluctance to change any habit (like those denim shirts and Payless shoes), never mind one as big as whom he would work for. And there was that ungodly long wait. Who knew what NBC might pull in the end, if it really looked as though a competitor was about to grab Leno? Still, it was surely worth trying.

ABC still had its *Nightline* issue, but the network had shown its hand in 2002 when it chased Letterman. For the right talent the 11:35 hour would be offered up, no matter how loudly the news division might howl to the moon (and the press). Leno was clearly the right talent. It went beyond a no-brainer; if ABC *didn't* pursue Jay, the Disney shareholders would have a right to sue them for malfeasance. Bob Iger, who had been named chief executive of Disney in 2005, personally took charge of supervising the Leno courtship, with help from Anne Sweeney, the top ABC corporate executive, and Steve McPherson, the head of entertainment.

Over at Fox, Peter Chernin, still eager to fill the network's late-night void, might still have preferred Conan, in terms of matching the sensibility of his network. But how could any network pass on the opportunity to sign the biggest dog in the yard? How could Fox stay on the sidelines? Chernin decided again to head up the Fox effort to lure away an NBC late-night star.

Fox's hunger to grab a slice of late night had not abated since the disappointment of failing to land Conan in 2001. The network had sniffed around for other potential candidates, and in 2007 made a full-frontal assault on what it considered to be a potential game-changing name in late night when Chernin and Fox took a serious run at Billy Crystal.

The well-respected comic, whose already soaring career went stratospheric thanks to his eight-time much-celebrated hosting performances at the Academy Awards, had not previously been part of the big late-night derbies. With movies, one-man Broadway shows, and Oscar duties, Crystal hardly needed the profile boost of his own talk show. But when Fox came calling, he listened.

For one thing, Fox presented a compelling case. It had put together a PowerPoint presentation of what it called a late-night deck, which broke down what the comic could expect in terms of station clearances and advertising sales, and even a guess at what size audience might be available. (Once again, the pitch was to launch a show at eleven p.m., giving Crystal a half-hour jump on Leno and Letterman.) And then there was the $20 million–plus potential payday.

The Fox executives were convinced they had gotten close, really close, to making a deal with Billy. He asked all the right questions; the interest was there. But if he hadn't already been aware of just how much effort went into these jobs, having done the late-night rounds himself—including, famously, being the first ever guest on Leno's *Tonight Show*—it hardly took much due diligence to learn. "When Billy found out how much you have to work," said one Fox entertainment executive, "he thought, *No way.*"

Workload was never going to be an issue with Jay Leno, of course, whose reputation preceded him. The product might not always be fresh or exciting or new to the critics, but it was going to be pumped out on a regular basis and it was going to generate numbers—and dollars. NBC's competitors knew if they somehow could lure Jay away, the tectonic plates in the late-night world would slide and shift with devastating results.

But the rules had to be observed. NBC held exclusive rights to Jay Leno's television work for the full period of his contract. That meant that any flirtations that went over the line into an actual pass—as in, anything resembling a real offer of future employment for Jay elsewhere—would be grounds for a legitimate claim of tampering, or tortious interference, if it ever got to court.

Hollywood deals generally hold only loosely to such legal niceties. Agents and managers test the waters of future associations for their clients all the time, and studios and networks have their ways of letting talent know how much they love the idea of getting together someday. Everyone in the late-night game remembered how David Letterman's team had handled his contractual complications with NBC when the star looked to flee in 1993. Though bound by limitations stipulating when Letterman would be free to negotiate any kind of new deal, his agents at CAA simply told suitors to make their best pitch—and all Dave would do was listen.

Now Leno found himself in a similar position: He was all ears.

The approaches from ABC and Fox were general at first. Interest was conveyed; discreet conversations were held. Everyone understood the terms. Jay was locked in at NBC through January 1, 2010, and NBC retained exclusive negotiating rights with him until late November 2009. No outside entity could engage in any negotiation with him before that time. Jay, of course, had no formal representation, so the only way to get to him was either directly or through his lawyer, Ken Ziffren. Quiet though it was, none of this activity caught NBC by surprise in the least. "I expect Bob Iger and Peter Chernin are camped out at Leno's garage," one top NBC Entertainment executive said.

If they were not there exactly, they were certainly cruising the neighborhood. And if NBC didn't get word of Jay's courtship some other way, Leno had his own means of communication—like the night when he was doing his act two "Headlines" segment and put up a local newspaper's Sunday TV listings insert. The cover featured a picture of Jay himself, with the tagline "Starring Jay Leno of ABC."

Jay, swallowed-canary grin firmly in place, peered into the camera and said: "Like a headline from the future."

On November 5, 2007, the monologues stopped—for everybody. Looking to press the networks and studios for a bigger payday from their material being used on new media like Internet videos and webisodes, writers walked off their jobs, shutting down every scripted show on television. That included the late-night shows, all of which relied on a stable of twelve to twenty writers.

The late-night hosts felt the pressure almost immediately. They were all writers themselves, of course, and members of the Writers Guild of America. But they were also signature stars for their networks, and so usually much closer to the network management than stars of sitcoms in Hollywood were. The top network executives, sensing one way to undermine the solidarity of the union and its supporters among actors, directors, and the other Hollywood guilds, almost immediately pushed for the late-night hosts to return to work. They argued that the hosts could mount shows without the writers.

The hosts had to add that pressure to the pain the strike was inflicting on their nonwriting staff members. Segment producers, researchers, assistants, and artists would all go without pay as the result of a game in which they had no stake. NBC told the producers of its two late-night shows that it would pay the staff through November, but after that layoffs would begin.

O'Brien was the first host to pledge that he would pay the staff out of his own pocket, if it came to that. Jeff Ross made that promise public but tried to shame the network a bit by adding, "We're hoping it will not be necessary because GE's pockets are a lot deeper than Conan's."

O'Brien was not the only host taking steps to protect his staff. Jon Stewart had already given his group a similar assurance. David Letterman's Worldwide Pants was already responsible for paying his staff directly, because in his unique arrangement with CBS, Letterman owned his show. The company announced that the staff of Letterman's *Late Show* as well as that of *The Late Late Show*—which had installed Craig Ferguson as the new host less than a year earlier—would continue to be paid, but not in full. (Rob Burnett was already plotting a special course of action for Worldwide Pants.)

Quietly several of the shows in New York began back-channel talks among themselves, hoping that there might be safety in numbers if they acted in concert in returning to the air. Letterman had to be looked to as the leader—he was the longest-serving host and obviously the prime mover in New York. All the shows wanted to return to the air, but they also wanted to respect the writers and their cause, and they also didn't want to run afoul of any union strictures about what would be allowed on the air if they did return. (In essence, no written material, only ad libs, would be permitted.)

Meanwhile, out west, Jay Leno was looking to do a little back-channeling of his own. While he made some gestures of support for the writers, including turning up on the picket lines with a stash of doughnuts, being off the air always drove Jay a little buggy. If there was going to be a way to get back on TV, Jay wanted to explore it. He reached out to a guy he suspected might be a kindred spirit, at least during the strike: ABC's Jimmy Kimmel.

That Jay could even have a civil discussion of any kind with Kimmel seemed beyond imagining only a short time earlier. Late-night competitors may have a history of barbed comments about each other; Kimmel's early remarks about Jay were barbarous. A lifelong Letterman disciple, Jimmy had arrived in the late-night cauldron in 2003 spilling over with disdain for Leno and his brand of comedy.

First Kimmel gave an interview in which he said of his upcoming ABC show, "I want to do the comedy version of *The Tonight Show.*" Then, after Jay called Kimmel's publicist to complain, Kimmel said he had only been goofing around, though he couldn't help reacting publicly to the phone call by saying, "It's just amazing how insecure he is." Kimmel clearly had the prevailing view of most Letterman devotees: "Leno was so great when he was a guest on Letterman. Great, great. I just think he worked it too hard. I think he turned comedy into factory work—and it comes across."

Kimmel even rationalized about becoming a competitor to the great Dave himself by turning it against Leno. "I figure this: The people who like Leno are largely the stupid group. The people who root for Letterman are the smarter group. The people who like me? Also stupid. I figure I cut into the dummies." And he suggested that his greatest fear in starting up his own talk show was the bad example the late-night audience was already setting. "In a world where Jay Leno beats David Letterman every night, you can't be sure of anything."

Leno, who seemed to read everything written about him, was flabbergasted by the trashing Kimmel was dishing out—before he even had a show on the air. Jay was never one to flinch from picking up the phone and seeking an explanation from people who maligned him, even occasionally viewers who wrote letters of complaint. He dialed up Kimmel.

Jay didn't spew anger in these calls. He usually presented himself as mystified about the impetus for the attack and interested in knowing if he had done anything to provoke it. Put on the spot, Kimmel told Jay he had been wrong to make comments like that. He explained that he was coming into late-night with a morning-radio mentality, because that was where he had spent most of his young career. In that venue, everybody looks to gut the other guy. And then, of course, Kimmel admitted he was a huge Letterman fan and as such was angry at Jay because of what had happened with Dave at NBC, which, he said, he later came to realize he had no right to be. Kimmel acknowledged he had a chip on his shoulder with regard to Jay, and maybe that was silly.

As it turned out, they had a pleasant conversation that set up a rapprochement. Kimmel concluded that Leno, who seemed to have no real emotional investment in any of this, wanted to patch things up, just move on. That made sense. Leno was on top; it was in his interest to snuff out any conflict.

Kimmel was willing to go along with that—for now.

Maybe it had to do with growing up in Las Vegas. From a young age, Jimmy Kimmel liked to put it all out there and let it ride. He was born in Brooklyn—that may have factored into the bravado as well—moving west to Nevada at age nine. His father, also James—German-Irish side and wryly witty—worked for IBM. His mom, Joan—from the Italian side of the family and a pistol—raised a close clan of J-offspring, her sons Jimmy and Jon and their sister Jill.

In his youth Kimmel had two all-consuming fascinations: art and David Letterman. The art he pursued in school, when he wasn't indulging his wiseass nature. When he was eight, still in Brooklyn, a teacher suggested a career in comedy. In high school, then in Vegas, he cut up in class so persistently that one teacher ordered a strict limit of one joke a week. That was good for comic discipline: Kimmel knew he had to get off a memorable line with that single shot.

He generally stayed up well past midnight, mesmerized by the show on the little black-and-white set on the desk in his room. If David Letterman was on, Jimmy Kimmel was watching. For his seventeenth birthday, his mother surprised him with a cake in the shape of the *Late Night* logo, along with a "Late Night with David Letterman" jacket she had made for him. When he got his first car in high school, the license plate read, "L8 NITE."

His parents expected Kimmel to pursue his talent for drawing; he had other ideas. Because Letterman had started in radio, that was where Jimmy would try to break in. (Letterman had actually started in TV as a local weatherman in Indianapolis, and his radio career was a poor choice to emulate in any case, because Dave had bombed when he did a year's stint in talk radio.)

By then Kimmel already had unusual responsibilities: a wife and family. He had married his college sweetheart at twenty-one, and three years later they had a daughter, adding a son two years after that. Career objectives got filed deep behind bill-paying concerns. The radio jobs came—and mostly went: Seattle, Tampa, Palm Springs, Tucson. Kimmel usually blazed in and then flamed out, mainly because he got on the wrong side of somebody.

But the demands of radio helped define his work ethic. With no staff and no resources, Kimmel had to put together hours of material for the daily schedule on his own. He arrived each morning terrified because he was making $25,000 and supporting a family of four. If he got fired, he would have to move them all again, because there really was no other radio station in any of these towns that would want what he did. So he planned and wrote and somehow produced five or six hours of content a day. Every waking hour had to be devoted to gathering material for the following day. He didn't even have time to relax and watch Letterman for an hour—not when he had to be up and at the station by five a.m.

When Kimmel finally landed at K-Rock (KROQ-FM) in LA, he found a niche that stabilized his peripatetic career, becoming "Jimmy the Sports Guy" for a popular morning drive team, Kevin and the Bean. Finally somewhat secure, he sought out side gigs for extra money. Among others, he won a spot as a writer for a would-be game show that the legendary former programmer for multiple networks Fred Silverman was putting together.

"Gossip" had the rather preposterous premise of asking contestants to watch a series of bizarre events involving celebrities, only one of which was real. Kimmel thought the show had no shot at ever seeing the light of a TV screen—they were going to shoot it six months in advance and expect the real gossip items either to be still unknown or still relevant? But it was a paying job, so he didn't care.

At the time of the initial run-throughs, "Gossip" had no host, so the producer asked Kimmel to stand in for a day. Within a few minutes of taking charge of the stage, Kimmel got it into his head that he could surely lead this stupid thing—a suggestion the producer dismissed when

Kimmel offered it. But Jimmy raised his energy level and performed in the run-through as though the show belonged to him. Silverman was sitting in the empty audience seats sipping a glass of iced tea. This kid suddenly got his attention; he watched for a while and then called out:

"Cancel the host auditions! This guy's the host!"

Silverman brought the show to a series of meetings with potential buyers, with Jimmy fronting the presentations. A young executive with ABC's production studio named Michael Davies sat in on one of them. Davies, an Englishman who knew from British television that game shows were not the lowest form of TV life, as most American producers believed, didn't care at all for "Gossip." But he recognized a game-show host when he saw one.

From that moment on, Michael Davies became Jimmy Kimmel's unofficial career placement officer. Convinced of his talent, Davies laid a series of potential projects out for Kimmel, who shocked Davies by rejecting them all. Jimmy, just hitting thirty, needed money desperately, but he knew the next move was a crucial one for him. He couldn't jump into television in some throwaway slice of processed cheese. That was a ticket back to radio, maybe forever.

Then Davies showed up with an offbeat project called *Win Ben Stein's Money*. The premise was a spin on a quiz show in which every week contestants played against Stein, the dry and wry conservative commentator, writer, and actor, for (supposedly) his own money. Davies set up Kimmel to audition, and no one needed to see any other candidates. During the presentation for network buyers, Kimmel lit up the stage, providing a comic edge that made the show distinctive. Comedy Central outbid other networks. Kimmel suddenly had a television career.

He didn't exactly fit the usual physical prerequisites of a TV star. Not really overweight but always slightly puffy, Kimmel looked less like a leading man than a relaxed-fit jeans model. Medium height, often rumpled around the edges, with a thatch of black hair that always trailed off this way or that and hooded eyes that made him look perpetually sleepy (perhaps because he actually suffered from narcolepsy), Jimmy didn't figure to win a lot of face roles from casting directors—or style points from the fashion police. But he made up for those shortcomings with spirit. Outgoing, boisterous, and far, far smarter than a first impression might convey, Kimmel exuded a sense of fun that never seemed faked.

He plainly enjoyed what he was doing, which seemed to consist largely of taking any and every opportunity to spread the fun around. He also had that Vegas penchant for daring, which could lead to both breakthrough comic ideas and occasional transgressions in taste. Mainly he seemed on television to be exactly who he was in life: the wiseass kid grown up. Deeply into sports and music (he even played bass clarinet), he was a guy's guy, up for anything that had a shot to be either laugh-your-ass-off funny or just outrageous enough to disturb the universe in some way.

The Davies connection came into play again two years later when Kimmel and his pal Adam Carolla devised a show aimed to be "the anti-Oprah." Kimmel had been told by a producer that he would never appeal to women, so he and Carolla, another radio-based comic, planned a show to appeal to the most basic (and debased) instincts of guys. Davies loved *The Man Show* and pushed it to the ABC programming division. But the network was appalled. "It was the most poorly received pilot ever," Davies recalled.

Given the British executive's classy deportment and accent—not to mention suits—his advocacy for this project, as well as for an apparently rude character like Kimmel, may have seemed unexpected. But Davies, who went on to import and then produce for ABC the biggest game-show hit of all time, *Who Wants to Be a Millionaire?*, simply got Kimmel. Once *The Man Show* was on Comedy Central and a hit, he never lost contact with his discovery, and that connection would pay off again, bigger than ever, for Jimmy.

In the meantime Kimmel climbed another step up on his own. Playing off his sports-guy persona on K-Rock, Kimmel worked a deal with Fox Sports to provide a comedy sketch for the network's pregame show every Sunday. While making half-serious picks on the games, Kimmel found ways to tweak both the NFL and the roundtable of ex-jocks that populated the show. The bumptious crew, led by Terry Bradshaw, quickly came to sneer at Kimmel's weekly presence, but the quarter hour when he appeared demonstrated a clear ratings uptick.

Kimmel, whose deal with Fox was freelance, got a call out of the blue from CBS Sports, the other network with a Sunday NFL show. Surprised but intrigued, Kimmel quietly flew to New York to meet with Sean McManus, the president of the division. McManus, son of the legendary ABC sportscaster Jim McKay, pitched Jimmy hard about coming on as a regular on *The NFL Today*. When Kimmel got back to LA, still mulling the CBS offer, Leslie Moonves, the capo of capos at CBS, asked to meet with him, a gesture that signaled an overture of real substance. After explaining how ardently CBS wanted him for the football package, and all the great things Jimmy could do on the Sunday football show, Les, who had clearly done his homework, came at Kimmel in the place where his deepest dreams resided.

"I know you love Letterman," Moonves told Jimmy, surprising him with that little bit of research. "Maybe we could put something else on the table for you down the road."

Moonves told Kimmel that he didn't much like what Craig Kilborn was doing in the 12:35 show. (Moonves seemed to have a different take on late-night talent than the experts at Worldwide Pants.) He tried to tempt Kimmel by suggesting that Kilborn was not going to be around forever. And if Jimmy was in the CBS family when that 12:35 show opened up, it would certainly be something Les and the network would consider for Jimmy.

If Moonves meant to flatter Kimmel, he succeeded—maybe a little too well. Kimmel had a lifetime of reasons to want to be in the CBS lineup behind Letterman. Instead, the gauzy promise that Moonves had floated failed to send even a shiver of anticipation up his spine. To the contrary, here he was, a total stranger to CBS, and the network boss had a plan that sounded like he was taking candy away from one baby and offering it to another. Something about it put Kimmel off, and he declined.

A few other offers drifted in: the funny neighbor/boyfriend/bartender in that year's crop of pedestrian sitcoms. Jimmy talked them over with his agent—the same James Dixon who worked with Jon Stewart—and both agreed that they were not the right fit, not the direction they wanted for Jimmy's career. Then Fox came at them with an idea for what Jimmy really wanted: a late-night show. There was one catch. Because Fox had such a dismal history in late night, it couldn't just launch a new entry with a virtual unknown as the star. Fox offered to start Jimmy off at a local station the company owned in Minnesota. If he worked out there, they could expand station by station until he was ready for the network.

Kimmel and Dixon thought the Fox offer was insulting, not to mention borderline insane. How was this better than trying a sitcom?

He had no reason to mention it to Jimmy, but about the same time

Dixon found himself in the middle of a late-night chess game going on elsewhere. In the wake of the failed mission to land David Letterman, ABC had in 2003 made contact about a possible post-*Nightline* slot for Stewart. *The Daily Show* had elevated Jon's profile immensely by that point. Still, this would be a network show, which meant more cachet—and more money. Jon was at least interested enough to listen.

The man at ABC plotting the late-night moves was Lloyd Braun, the same executive who had led the charge to win Letterman. Like everyone else in television, Braun was hugely impressed with how Stewart had transformed *The Daily Show* into a nightly must-see for news (and comedy) junkies. The circumstance seemed like it might be a simple game of pitch and catch. ABC had only to toss the offer out there in a formal way, Stewart would pull it in, and they would be in business.

But Braun hesitated. As great as Jon was in this new show, it was still cable. And some might argue that it was, of all things, *too* smart. Would Jon's scintillating wit and scalpel-sharp puncturing of politics and media play at a network level? Was he too New York and LA?

And given the public strikeout with Dave, would anyone who could be identified as a "usual suspect" in late night escape a label of second choice? Would a totally new name be better? In his late forties, Braun was a onetime entertainment lawyer who had climbed up the Hollywood ladder from management company to studio head to the top of ABC's entertainment division, and he could not afford to make a choice that flopped. With ABC's prime time near moribund, he had to make this move work.

Roiled by uncertainty, Lloyd went to play golf at the Riviera Club with a friend whose views he had come to trust. Braun waited until midround to bring the issue up. As they stepped onto the ninth green, Braun laid out his late-night dilemma and hit his playing partner with the question he had been waiting with:

"Knowing it could be anyone, someone I've never heard of—someone without a name—and knowing I have the luxury of offering the midnight show, if you could pick anyone, anyone at all, who would it be?"

With no hesitation at all, Michael Davies said, "I know the guy."

By the end of the day, Davies had sent Braun a cassette with Kimmel highlights on it, including an appearance with Letterman. Braun found himself charmed. He needed to learn more about this guy quickly, but there was a troublesome problem. Braun couldn't simply ask Jimmy's agent for material, because that agent, Dixon, also represented Stewart, and Braun did not want to spook a guy who was still his first choice. It was an awkward situation, even for the frequently conflicted business of showbiz agenting.

So Braun accumulated the material he needed elsewhere. Even amid the depths of taste the comedy sometimes reached on *The Man Show*, Braun thought he detected a real intelligence at work. Kimmel seemed much cleverer than the material. He needed to talk to him.

The feint was that ABC might consider Kimmel for a show at one a.m. That was better than a show in Minneapolis, so Jimmy went to lunch with Braun. He knocked Lloyd's socks off with his "wicked smarts" and his blue-collar charm.

At home with a stack of tapes, Braun tried to weigh the options. He watched fifteen minutes of Stewart followed by fifteen minutes of Kimmel—back and forth, most of the night. He kept reaching the same conclusion: Both great; Kimmel had a more everyman appeal. Braun surprised himself with that conclusion, so much so that he asked a question out loud: "Am I really going to pass on Jon Stewart?" The answer came when he invited Kimmel to his office and broke the news: ABC wanted Jimmy Kimmel to host its midnight show.

The news stunned Kimmel—this time in a good way. The offer also put James Dixon in a potentially touchy position, because ABC had chosen one of his guys over another. When Braun called Jon to let him know, Stewart did not hold back his displeasure—he was especially consternated by how ABC had gone about the process, jerking him around. Remarkably, considering how personally hosts had taken such tugs-of-war over late-night shows in the past, Stewart blamed Kimmel not at all. He praised Kimmel's talent, saying he was happy for him to get this chance, "even though I was disappointed for myself."

Perhaps more remarkably, Stewart never wavered in his continued allegiance to James Dixon. One deal that didn't happen was hardly going to disarrange what had become the closest and most important professional partnership of Jon's life (Dixon's as well). One thing it did mean, though: James Dixon, now with two clients installed as hosts—and other assorted late-night players on his roster, including Winstead and Smithberg, the creators of *The Daily Show*, and Stephen Colbert, then emerging as the hottest comedy correspondent on that show—was positioning himself as a kingmaker for late night. Dixon, a savvy, aggressive Cornell graduate seemingly escaped from a Damon Runyon tale, spoke like a New York cabdriver from a 1940s movie—both in accent and colorfully descriptive vocabulary. A contemporary of Stewart in age and a match in physical stature, Dixon engendered an unusual degree of loyalty and actual, identifiable fondness from his otherwise cynical comic clients. He routinely called them all "Baby Doll," to a point where that became his own nickname. It occasionally turned heads when a client like Kimmel addressed the dark-haired, always moving, often smoking Dixon as "Baby Doll."

During the writers' strike the late-night hosts found themselves pushed together by a combination of forces, which included their networks, their union, and, on a different level, David Letterman.

The networks continued to try to squeeze the hosts in every way possible to come back to work, because it could only erode the union's position to get at least some original programming on the air. The union, meanwhile, did everything possible to oppose the shows' returning, because the strikers needed to hurt the employers in every way they could. So the Guild underscored its prohibition against the hosts doing any writing at all, even for themselves, and they pressured actors to refuse to appear on the shows as guests.

But the tack that the Letterman camp took to deal with the strike managed to unite the other hosts. Most of them were still wavering over whether to try to get back to work but had agreed in their back-channel conversations, that if they did return, they would try to do so en masse, as protection against union unhappiness. Letterman's top executive, Rob Burnett, had been part of the discussions with the other shows, but all that changed when Worldwide Pants decided to take advantage of Letterman's unique position with CBS.

Because Dave owned his show as well as the 12:35 *Late Late Show*, he had an opportunity to make a separate peace with the Writers Guild. In December 2007, with the strike past the one-month mark, word leaked that Letterman's company was in talks to secure an "interim agreement" with the union. That meant Letterman and Ferguson could come back on the air—with their writers.

Besides infuriating the hosts and producers of the other shows—as one producer complained, "Dave is Dave, it always has to be about Dave;

and Rob Burnett always has to be a dick"—the move created an urgency for the other networks and hosts to respond. With the Letterman and Ferguson shows poised to return on January 2, NBC announced its two competitors, Leno and O'Brien, would come back the same night—though without any writers. Jon Stewart and his late-night partner, Stephen Colbert, tried to forge their own interim agreement, with no success. They agreed to return, writerless, on January 8.

On the West Coast Jimmy Kimmel got a call of solidarity: Jay Leno checked in again to commiserate about the bind they both found themselves in. Kimmel felt more pressure perhaps than any of the other hosts. Not only was he still struggling in the ratings, and not nearly as well paid, but he had a string of relatives on his payroll who would be going without income for the duration of the strike.

Jimmy's need to get back on the air tied him closer than he had ever been to Leno, who also wanted to return to work without delay. The two hosts kicked around the news of Letterman's special deal and agreed it was "fucking ridiculous." Kimmel had also been talking almost daily with Stewart. None of the other hosts could believe their own union was giving a competitor an unfair advantage through some bullshit loophole. Leno and Kimmel also wound up speaking almost daily, with Jay providing advice. Some of his suggestions involved telling publicists the Guild had cleared the shows to book actors as guests, a recommendation that led to confusion over whether the union had said any such thing.

When they finally got back on the air, however, the two hosts took decidedly different approaches. Kimmel, hewing to the letter of the restrictions, tried to do a show along the lines of his old radio work or what Regis Philbin did on his morning show, just winging it out of pieces from the papers and other odds and ends. Jay had urged him to perform a monologue; Kimmel thought that would be crossing a line. From his first night back, Leno did a full-on twenty-five-joke monologue. No writers; twenty-five jokes. Like all the other hosts, Jay went out of his way to express support for his writing team. But the show, even with no big-name stars—during his first week back Letterman, thanks to his waiver, had plenty of those, including Tom Hanks—and guests that largely consisted of NBC News personnel, animal acts, and assorted chefs and other oddballs, had to go on.

The early highlight was a crossover Jay suggested to Kimmel: They would go on each other's shows on the same night. Leno told Kimmel on the air that there was one good thing about the strike: "At least we don't have to see a lot of stupid movies and pretend they're good." Off the air he continued to counsel the younger host: "Don't get too excited; don't worry too much." Kimmel was so tense he thought he might lose his mind. Jay told him, "Let it pass." He also urged Jimmy again to start doing monologue jokes.

Kimmel still fretted about taking a step like that. "I don't feel comfortable," he told Leno. "I'm not you. I'm not in the position you're in." Kimmel wrote nothing down, just to be safe.

With no written material and no real guests, the late-night shows were supposed to come on, flop, and embarrass the networks into forcing a settlement. But Jay wasn't about to allow *The Tonight Show* to be damaged that way. And of course, he was eager to show up the critics who predicted a train wreck if he tried to ad-lib his way through a show. Jay made up his mind: He was not doing a strike show; he was doing *The Tonight Show*, and it would not be a *Tonight Show* without an opening monologue.

How he did it quickly became a matter of both conjecture and condemnation from the union's many supporters. Jay said he was merely writing for himself, which is precisely what Johnny Carson had done when he came back on the air during a previous strike. But the Guild had expressly forbidden the hosts from writing material of any kind. They were supposed to sit there scriptless and hack their way through an hour of television.

Many of the jokes on the *Tonight* strike shows certainly *sounded* fresh, as Jay poked at figures in the news, the president, Congress, and the latest bit of outré behavior by some Hollywood starlet or reality-show contestant. At the same time, some of the gags did seem like ancient material dredged up from some joke crypt. "Doctors in China have confirmed the existence of a man born with three eyes. Three eyes! And today LensCrafters announced they can make him glasses in about an hour and a half."

Jay swore he was getting no help, not even from the faxers who could have made more than the usual hundred bucks (though at the risk of never being accepted into the Guild). One of Jay's longtime writers, out on strike but watching carefully, explained his method. "Jay takes the premise from some old joke, plugs in a current name from the news, and sells it as a new joke."

Even that process seemed to violate the spirit of the rules the Guild had set down, though Jay argued (supported by one of his writers who was present) that he had been given assurances in a private meeting with union leaders that they would not "hassle him." After the strike Leno was called to a hearing by the disciplinary committee of the Guild and was unanimously cleared.

During the strike Leno proved again how sturdy and loyal his audience really was. A couple of weeks in, he averaged 5.2 million viewers to Letterman's 4.1, despite all the advantages Dave enjoyed. In private Jay took great pride in that achievement. He was enjoying himself, feeling resourceful, and even took to comparing it to another moment when he had had to rely on his own devices when under the gun. In 1993, when NBC engaged in last-minute dithering about whether to dump Jay and install Letterman in *The Tonight Show*, Leno had initiated his own little espionage mission, listening in surreptitiously on a conference call during which NBC executives thrashed out the relative merits of the two comics. Jay reveled in that episode because he was able to tweak NBC's executives with the information gleaned from his eavesdropping, leaving them flummoxed about how he had learned what had gone on in a meeting on the other side of the country.

What became known as Jay's "closet moment" did carry a little stigma, one he largely ignored. However, a number of his friends, like Jerry Seinfeld, occasionally brought it to his attention, warning him that some of the characterizations in the press, and those of other comics, of Jay as an unprincipled schemer sprang from the closet story. Instead of making him look wily and determined, they suggested, the tale made him come across to some as sneaky and guileful. That didn't really bother Leno, any more than did questions about whether he really was putting together those long, polished monologues all by himself. During the strike he had symbolically hidden in a closet again, refusing to let events control him. People had looked forward to tuning in to see him die on the air—and he had showed them. One competing host shrugged at the issue, saying, "Jay was cheating." No one ever proved that. But the strike proved something else: Jay was still winning.

In New York, Conan O'Brien did not reconstruct old jokes, but the strike did seem to inspire him to reconstruct the old Conan a bit. Left completely to his own devices, O'Brien became more instinctive and inventive, with results that energized him. He found humor in the picayune—like spinning his wedding ring on his desk each night, timing it in the control booth as if it were an Olympic event, trying to set a new record each attempt. He led audience members out into the halls to the vending machines. He flashed a light to try to turn the studio into a German disco. One night he set up his desk in the back row of the studio, presenting the show from a reverse angle and interacting with the fans in the upper rows. (He even brought them doughnuts.)

For guests, he marched through the same assortment of animal trainers, athletes, and NBC standbys, with the *Today* show's Al Roker piling up more appearances on top of his already impressive total. One night the show booked a sex expert named Sue Johanson. She brought along a display of sex toys and talked about sex games for couples. O'Brien, even redder than usual, wove magic out of how flustered the frank sex talk was making him. "I blacked out there for a minute," he said at one point. Mostly Conan cannily took advantage of anything a guest or unscripted moment offered him.

Among those watching closely, and totally approving, was Rick Ludwin. In his capacity as the executive in charge of late night, Ludwin had the assignment of nudging Conan and his team toward expanding his act in anticipation of moving up to *The Tonight Show*. It wasn't often an easy task. While receptive to Rick, whom they all respected, the corps around Conan always believed they knew best what made their comedy work. When Ludwin offered suggestions, the Conan staff was invariably polite and professional, but little changed.

The biggest area of concern for Ludwin had always been Conan's apparent reluctance to get out from behind his desk and do something—anything. The show continued to love its set pieces—"If They Mated" (mash-ups of celebrity photos); "SAT Analogies" (Jordin Sparks is to "I grew up on *American Idol*" as Paula Abdul is to "I threw up on *American Idol*"); and "Celebrity Survey" (for the question "My Kids Won't Shut Up About," Sarah Jessica Parker wrote *G-Force*; Brad Pitt wrote *Harry Potter*; and Britney Spears wrote, "Their immediate need for food, shelter, and medical care, y'all"). But Ludwin laid out some research for Conan and his team indicating that every survey revealed that the audience loved it when a late-night host interacted with the audience. He suggested often

that the show find its version of the old Carson "Stump the Band" bit—
something they could go to periodically to get Conan off the stage and in
with the fans. Rick pointed out that Conan always scored when he riffed
with regular people. (That was as true in America as it was in Finland,
where he did a week of memorable shows built largely around his playful
communicating with Finnish folk.)

That's why the strike shows so warmed Ludwin's heart: Conan now
had no choice but to mix it up with the audience. He told Ludwin and
others that the experience was teaching him what had been missing from
his show. When the writers returned, he promised Ludwin, "We're going
to do this kind of stuff and more."

When the writers did return, however, Ludwin took immediate note.
Suddenly the show was right back to doing "New State Quarters" (mot-
toes on the back of new quarters, like "Nebraska—A great place to be butt-
ugly"). As funny and creative as such bits could be, they were all about
art cards in front of the camera and Conan reading cue cards from behind
his desk. Ludwin knew Conan thought like a writer, *was* a writer, and so
leaned toward fully scripted material. It looked as though the strike was
not going to inspire the lasting changes Ludwin was hoping for.

In the end, the strike didn't really change any of the late-night equations.
The numbers rolled out pretty much as they always had, with one exception: The networks had taken in a lot more cash. With no production costs
for three months and ratings not that much worse for the repeats they
were putting on, network balance sheets, battered for years by sinking
ratings and rising expenses, started to look suddenly favorable

"It was like this gold mine for the networks," one late-night host said.
"I went to the Guild and told them, you're not hurting them, you're help-
ing them. They're not even bothered by this. They don't care."

At NBC the strike benefits had become apparent almost immediately
even as the news from prime-time continued to be miserable. The latest
savior selected by Jeff Zucker to head the entertainment division, Ben
Silverman (replacing Kevin Reilly), saw the sizzle of his announcement
fizzle almost immediately thanks to a combination of the dead calm the
strike imposed on the creation of new programming and his own procliv-
ity for attracting unflattering PR.

With all that going on, NBC all but welcomed the infusion of extra money the strike guaranteed. "I never saw Jeff happier than during the writers' strike," said one of his entertainment executives. "The books were amazing. We were still selling DVDs and other things." At the quarterly review, the executive reported, Zucker's announcement that "these numbers are great" prompted one of the other executives in the room to pipe up, "Well, if we never produce anything, we'll be in great shape."

One week in April 2008, just over a year from the expected date when Conan O'Brien would take over *The Tonight Show*, the late-night ratings arrived as usual, and a few eyebrows popped up inside offices at two addresses on Sixth Avenue in Manhattan.

At CBS, on Fifty-second Street, they looked at the numbers and saw a headline: *Craig Ferguson Beats Conan O'Brien.* At NBC, down the block between Forty-ninth and Fiftieth streets, they looked at the same numbers and saw a need for a rapid response: *Big Deal, Conan Trounced Him Where It Counts—As Usual.*

Both versions of reality had the virtue of truth. For one week, for the first time ever, Ferguson, the third and latest CBS 12:35 a.m. host to take on Conan during his fifteen-year run, had got his Scottish nose ahead of Conan's Irish pompadour in the category of most viewers. That this meant less than it seemed was a quirk of the television business, where having the most almost always mattered less than having the most *select.* So the fact that Ferguson had more viewers than O'Brien—1.88 million to 1.77 million—was thoroughly mitigated by the fact that Conan still ruled bigtime with the under-fifty crowd.

But still . . .

NBC had already broken ground on the Universal lot in LA, commencing its capital investment of tens of millions on a grand new studio for *The Tonight Show* with Conan O'Brien. It still had no answer to the oft-repeated question "Are you really going to allow ABC to steal Jay Leno?" other than "We believe in Conan." Craig Ferguson's just happening to have more people watching him in a week than the guy NBC had that massive a bet riding on had to be worth at least a *Huh?*

The official line from NBC was: No worries. A blip.

Craig Ferguson had been called a lot of things in his turbulent life, including "Bing Hitler," but "a blip"? Not bloody likely.

The path of most late-night hosts traversed familiar terrain: watched a lot of Carson/Letterman; decided "I could do that"; found an agent/manager/producer who could open the right door; jumped on a break and made it happen.

Craig Ferguson's path touched none of those mileposts—except the last. Instead, his course followed no familiar pattern at all, having started in Scotland, of all places. The fact that his accent sounded so alien, at least to most Americans, was one more reason why Ferguson's successful entry into the world of late-night television had a hint of hallucination to it.

Ferguson had done enough alcohol and drugs in his youth to hallucinate just about anything, but not this. This was the product of accidental timing meeting unforeseen talent. That he did have abundant talent was apparent in his résumé: rock drummer, stand-up, sketch satirist, film actor, stage actor, screenwriter, director, sitcom actor, novelist. And much of that had been accomplished while he was barely able to stand on his feet.

Ferguson had a theory about why Scotland was such a drinking society, and its climate was a major factor. "Anywhere you go where it's cold, people drink like crazy," Ferguson observed. But his homeland was different, in that the drinking there was all but pathological. "It was excessive; it was ridiculous," Ferguson said. A Scottish politician Ferguson once met offered an explanation Craig came to embrace as telling. "Scotland is a country in mourning," he said, "ever since World War II. So many died. It changed the society."

The Glasgow of Ferguson's youth—he was born in 1962—was a sorry place, riven by animosity between Protestants and Catholics and prone to casual violence that seemed impossible to escape. Ferguson often cited getting beaten up as a youth, though that wasn't the worst experience of his childhood. For him, nothing could top the horror of school. Ferguson's family was blue collar and lived in a soulless Glasgow area called Cumbernauld, mostly government housing built to absorb the overflow from the city, but it was a family that respected learning and education. Not Craig, though. Every early encounter with a teacher—nasty, disinterested, burned out, cruel to the students—soured his psyche. "I couldn't take it. It was awful. Bad company and mean people doing horrible things to each other."

He escaped in his teens, but the scars lasted. Ferguson could never sit for training of any kind because of his "abhorrence of the early years of my academic life. I couldn't trust anyone who was willing to give me information." That left him to pursue interests he could teach himself, like drumming, a hobby he fell into mostly because the punk world attracted him and playing in a punk rock band had the perfect subversive appeal. As with most things he tried, Ferguson proved himself to be quickly adept and he landed in a band called Bastards from Hell (later softened to Dreamboys). He was funny, too, of course, but humor had been of so little use in his life to that point that he considered it unworthy of his time or attention, except in the pursuit of girls who dug guys who could make them laugh. The band's lead singer, Peter Capaldi (who later enjoyed a successful career as an actor), pushed Ferguson to give comedy a shot.

That meant standing up in pubs and trying to get irascible drunks to laugh—fierce but useful training. Ferguson had a Scottish comedy model in Billy Connolly, known in Scotland as the Big Yin (the Big One). He was "like Elvis" to Ferguson. "I'd never seen people from my socioeconomic group make it big, and suddenly there was *this* guy."

And soon after, Bing Hitler was born. Bing was a product of the terror Ferguson felt getting up there as himself in front of those drunks. "I had to create a voice, because then if you fail, it's not you who fail." He also wanted a name with marquee shock value. And he got it. Just twenty-four, Ferguson debuted Bing Hitler at the Edinburgh Festival Fringe in 1986 and for a time became a Scottish sensation, filling three-thousand-seat theaters in Glasgow. Wearing too tight jackets, his hair teased up into a Scottish fro, Bing bellowed at his audiences, a crude caricature of an angry, obnoxious Scottish jingoist. Bing railed furiously about everything that annoyed him in life, from people to insects. "I may have gone a little too far with that name," Ferguson conceded. "But there was no crooning or fascism."

What the character did was provide the confidence for Craig to emerge as a stand-up on his own terms. He was club toughened and ready for a big comedy career, but the combination of drink and his restless nature pushed him in different directions. The drink led all the way down to contemplation of suicide; the restlessness, out onto the stage, first as Brad Majors in *The Rocky Horror Show* and then as Oscar Madison in an all-

Scottish version of *The Odd Couple*. (With the simple substitute of soccer for baseball, it all worked.)

Tall, with piercing blue eyes and a head of dense dark hair, Ferguson morphed from slightly pudgy to moodily handsome as he hit his thirties. He had little trouble landing roles—or women. He was in and out of a string of relationships and a couple of marriages. The drink and drugs sabotaged most of his personal dealings, but he still got work. Finally, in 1992, the sheer enormity of the degradation he was visiting upon himself overwhelmed him, and he got sober, once and forever. "I proved to myself to my own satisfaction that I am madder than I think and I just can't do that. I really can't. It was a realization that there's a darkness in here that's bigger than you. I just don't go to that part of the house."

Ferguson moved to the United States two years later, a lifelong dream after having visited an uncle in Long Island as a boy. Work followed in short order: a role in a sitcom, *Maybe This Time*, with Betty White and Marie Osmond, that busted out quickly. But a year later he was back in a sitcom, and this one lasted. He put in seven seasons as the eccentric British boss Mr. Wick on *The Drew Carey Show*. "I liked the money, but, man, was it boring," Ferguson recalled. He was bored enough to write movies he could act in during his spare time, one of which, *Saving Grace*, about a proper British widow who escapes debt by growing marijuana, turned into a rosy little hit.

Craig went along chasing his muddled muse (he also took up writing a novel at around this time) when he got a call out of the blue from a producer named Peter Lassally, who worked for David Letterman's Worldwide Pants. Ferguson had no idea that this was the same man who had guided Johnny Carson's *Tonight Show* before serving as professional father to Dave himself. The offer Lassally was floating sounded utterly preposterous to Ferguson: Would he like to take part in a series of tryouts for a new host for CBS's 12:35 talk show?

Craig knew the talk-show gig solely from having been a guest on them. His best appearances had been with Conan, whose comedy Craig greatly admired. (The admiration was mutual; during at least one appearance Ferguson set O'Brien to laughing so hard he had to throw to a commercial.) But hosting? Did this guy know Ferguson was from Scotland, not Cleveland?

Lassally assured him there had been no mistake. "This is what I do," Lassally told him. "I find people like you. And if I'm right, you're it."

To Ferguson, that sounded like so much showbiz blather—nothing would come of it; but why not do it for a laugh? That was his prevailing feeling until approximately five seconds after the red camera light came on—and then it all changed for Craig Ferguson. "It was like showbusiness crack. I was hooked. I was like, *This is it. This is what I do. I'm a talk-show host.*"

His two-night stand sold Lassally cold. The producer found this lanky Scotsman completely fresh and original, just as he had hoped he would. "And he was a grown-up," Lassally concluded, something out of the ordinary for would-be late-night hosts, who mostly were arrested youths, playing to audiences of similar young men. Lassally was convinced this guy could build an audience around women, and maybe change that late-night advertiser preference.

Ferguson loved the job extravagantly from the start, even though he felt at sea for a while. The ratings were passable almost immediately, but Craig felt "weirded out" for at least six months, trying to find his own voice in late night and sensing that he needed to do something to make the show his own. A symbolic turning point came in an apparently unconnected circumstance. With the show on a break, Craig was in New York visiting a movie actress he was then dating. "She was a fucking pain in the ass," as Ferguson described her. "She wound up a great friend, but she was a rotten girlfriend. I found myself in bed about three o'clock in the morning. I sat up and I said out loud, 'I think I've got it. I'm not going to wear a tie anymore!' She looked up and said, 'OK, that's great.' And I remember thinking, *And you're fucking toast as well.*"

What the tie business was about—Ferguson skipped a tie for about a year—was "not just doing what was available," Ferguson decided. A period of time went by before he put that urge into a real innovation: He chucked the whole idea of scripted monologues. They sounded forced and pedestrian to him, and most nights he wandered away from the jokes anyway. Instead, he would put together a list of topics, gather his own thoughts on them, and then riff away on the air—comedy as improvisational jazz. Risky as hell, yes, but the move had the potential to generate rhythms no other late-night show had ever had. Some nights the notes might not fit together as a melody. But when they did, the laughs had a music of their own.

Attention and better ratings followed, and then came a deal from CBS—one no other late-night host, first at NBC and now at CBS, had ever had. Ferguson won a guarantee that he would be the successor to David Letterman, should there ever—heaven forbid—be a sudden need for a new host of *Late Show*. It wasn't anything like a five-year ticket to the big chair, but it was the CBS version of the Prince of Wales clause. Or in this case maybe, the Prince of Scots.

On another April day in that spring of 2008, Dick Ebersol invited Jeff Ross to lunch. The NBC Sports chief told O'Brien's producer that they ought to start kicking around some ideas for how Conan could be incorporated into NBC's Winter Olympics coverage from Vancouver, which would be taking place about six months into Conan's new *Tonight Show*.

The suggestion sounded reasonable to Ross, who, if he thought much about Dick Ebersol at all, regarded him as part of the long-established Bob Wright team, which meant he was likely a Conan supporter. Nothing coming from Dick had ever caused Ross to think otherwise. And a regular shot for Conan during the Olympics certainly sounded like a promising idea.

Ebersol had never hesitated to jump into situations involving NBC's late night because for long stretches of his career he had had serious skin in the game. In 1975, as the NBC executive in charge of late night, he pushed to get *Saturday Night Live* on the air and hired Lorne Michaels to run it. After that he left the network and became an independent producer, heavily involved with late-night programming. That began with a show called *The Midnight Special*, which ran on Friday nights after Carson in the late 1970s. In 1981, Dick's closest friend at NBC, Brandon Tartikoff, recruited Ebersol in desperation when *SNL*, in its first year after the departure of Michaels, was collapsing under a producer named Jean Doumanian. Ebersol stepped in and righted the *SNL* ship, running it successfully for four seasons—when the cast included Eddie Murphy, Billy Crystal, and Martin Short—until Michaels returned. After that Ebersol created another late-night series, *Friday Night Videos*, which became a hit in the Letterman time period. (Dave's show ran only four days a week on NBC.)

Early on in Conan's then tenuous tenure, Michaels, whom Ebersol loved like a professional brother, approached him and explained, "Conan is under siege. He needs friends. Will you talk to him?" Ebersol did, mostly advising Conan to listen to Lorne as much as he could and to trust himself. When Conan asked if there was anything about the show he would change, Ebersol said there was just one thing: Andy Richter. Playing around too much with Andy was preventing Conan from connecting with the audience. He should dump him. Conan had obviously not taken that advice, and Andy emerged as a fan favorite later. But Ebersol came away generally thinking Conan was a terrific kid, smart and hardworking.

At his lunch with Ross, Dick had some other advice he wanted to impart. "You've really got to be careful at eleven thirty," Ebersol told him. "You don't want to have him dancing around, flopping the hair, and touching the nipple and all that stuff." Of course, the "string dance," which Conan performed many nights, shifting side to side and then cutting an imaginary string on one hip while touching a finger to a nipple with a sizzle sound, amounted to his signature move on the *Late Night* show.

"This is the time to experiment," Ebersol said. "The twelve thirty audience is never going to desert him. They adore him. But eleven thirty is a whole other game."

To illustrate his point, Ebersol launched into a story about the starting days of *Saturday Night Live*. Because the show would be sitting in a time period owned by Carson during the week, he and Michaels were summoned to meet the King.

In Burbank, in the same cavelike office that became Leno's dungeon, Carson greeted them, not yet dressed for the night's show—he was in a sleeveless white undershirt of the kind Brando wore as Stanley Kowalski. Carson mainly wanted to feel out these two kids to make sure they weren't planning something too radical. But Johnny had words of advice that Ebersol wanted to repeat for Ross.

Johnny urged that whatever else *SNL* did, the guest host should come out early and have something funny to say. And he emphasized that playing at eleven thirty you had to always be aware that in the center of the country the show would come on at ten thirty. More viewers would be awake and available, and so "you better be able to play in Chicago and St. Louis or you won't have a chance."

What Conan should take from this story, Ebersol explained, was to emphasize the opening monologue and make sure he pitched his show to appeal to middle America.

Ross received the advice equably. He said that everyone on the show knew they had to adjust when they got to eleven thirty and predicted Conan would adapt organically, cutting back on the jumping around because he would recognize this was new territory. "Did you have a problem with how he did the Emmys?" Ross asked.

Ebersol said he hadn't, but Ross wondered if Dick had actually seen Conan that night. In the end, the men felt the lunch had gone just fine. It was completely friendly. Like everyone else, Ebersol found Ross open, smart, and generous of spirit. They both went back to work.

That spring, on one of his usual trips out to the West Coast, Jeff Zucker called Jay Leno and said, "Hey, I'm coming out and I want to come by."

By now Zucker knew two things for certain: Jay was being fervidly wooed by ABC and Fox, and time was starting to get short if he was going to dredge up that brilliant idea that might induce Jay to stay. Not that Jeff lacked confidence that he could do so; he just had to find a way to breach Jay's resistance to any kind of change in his life or routine.

What Zucker meant to propose that spring was actually a relic from his trunkful of unused notions. As early as 2002 Zucker had stood on the sidelines of Letterman's negotiations for a new contract, looking for an opportunity to spring if Dave showed the slightest sign of being willing to bolt CBS. When he did, with ABC entering the picture, Zucker leapt into back-channel action and logged in a call to Rob Burnett at Letterman's shop.

Zucker pitched an intriguing concept: a comeback for Dave to NBC— only not in late night. What Zucker proposed for Dave was an hour each night of prime time, at eight p.m. (except for Thursday, because in 2002 NBC still had the hit *Friends* there). The plan had several beautiful angles for Zucker. Besides removing Letterman as a late-night competitor, it would address what had become one of Zucker's bêtes noires since taking over the entertainment side of NBC: the network's chronic issue with finding eight p.m. shows. *Friends*, he had to admit, had little life left, and after that it was a lot of questions for NBC at eight.

Zucker believed that NBC's core audience of young professionals brought with them certain limitations—namely, they weren't really available to watch much television at eight p.m. (seven p.m. central). Instead they were just getting home from work, or having a late dinner in town, or putting kiddies to bed. What was needed, Zucker decided in one of his first potential game-changing solutions for network television, was a less expensive show that could be slotted in at eight p.m. multiple nights of the week. But it had to be a reliable show that would generate steady if not necessarily spectacular ratings at that hour. Zucker might have publicly written off Letterman as an old-hat loser in late night, but he wasn't blind to his talent, or to his smart, sophisticated following, which had always fit NBC's profile better than it had CBS's.

Had he studied Dave closely, Zucker might have also discovered that Letterman had a lifelong aversion to prime time, believing his act was strictly a late-night animal. Some forays in prime for anniversary shows at NBC had done well, but not so well that Dave was likely to risk his career on so great a gamble at age fifty-five.

Still, Burnett listened to the pitch with interest. At the time he was in business with Zucker on a side project, a prime-time hour-long comedy drama he had cocreated called *Ed*—which, ironically enough, was then parked at eight p.m. on NBC's Wednesday night schedule. Burnett knew the economics of trying to survive at eight as a costly hour-long series, so he could have been convinced that moving elsewhere was better in the long run for *Ed*, which was close to his heart. Burnett concluded that Zucker had come up with "a very smart idea" and was impressed by the NBC boss's "outside the box" thinking.

But he couldn't help tweaking Zucker with a little counterproposal: Suppose NBC moved Jay to eight; then surely Dave would come back and take over *The Tonight Show*. Zucker dismissed that idea as the joke both men knew it really was.

A short time later Burnett did run the NBC proposal by Letterman, and they discussed it briefly. Mostly, Burnett reported, "Dave had a good laugh over it."

Zucker had never completely abandoned the eight p.m. strip idea. He later even ran it by Oprah Winfrey, trying to lure her away from syndication and onto NBC. She hadn't been tempted, either, though she let Zucker down gently, telling him that if the offer had come ten years earlier in her career she might well have jumped at it.

Now it was Jay's turn.

When Zucker sat down with Leno in Burbank, he started out with an earnest expression of the network's undying commitment to keep their biggest star in the NBC family.

"Why do you want to keep me?" a skeptical Jay replied. "I already got canned."

Zucker had heard that kneejerk response before, whenever he had casually suggested to Jay that NBC still loved him and wanted him to stay in the family; he regarded it no more seriously than he did the jokes Jay was telling about NBC every night on the air. Zucker plowed on, telling Jay the network would come up with something right for him, something that would keep him happy.

"I mean, why?" Jay shrugged off the solicitous words. "You should have kept me before."

Zucker assured him that NBC still had big plans for Jay. He pitched Jay his new wrinkle on the five-night-a-week show at eight: not an hour-long show, but a half-hour one. Jay could do his monologue every night, maybe even a slightly longer one, then go to commercials, then a second comedy piece, another commercial, followed by a short piece, either an interview or, even better (since the interview portions were not Jay's strong suit), something with a corps of comedy correspondents, and then—we're out. Done. No forced chat with some starlet hawking one of those movies Jay didn't like having to see anyway; no music act that never pulled in viewers because music tastes had become so stratified.

Jay listened politely; even though still carrying a grudge for what NBC had done to him, he was unfailingly polite to management. But his instant reaction to the eight p.m. idea was that it was "way wrong." The idea of just doing the monologue and a second comedy bit may have seemed to play to Jay's predilection for those parts of the show, but Jay actually did worry about trying to make each individual show stand out. That's what the guests were really for. You brought in different people on different nights because audiences wanted to see the hot young actor, or the latest *American Idol* winner (or loser). On a guestless show there would be no chance for a Hugh Grant moment, that famous guest appearance in 1995, right after the British film star's arrest for doing business with a prostitute. Grant's willingness to show up for his long-scheduled appearance and take Jay's questions—most famously, "What the hell were you thinking?"—turned things around in one big night for Leno.

As Jay analyzed it, "I'm not vain enough to believe that people want to watch a fifty-eight-year-old guy every single night. There have to be other elements in the show."

At the end of this meeting and all his conversations where he expressed his commitment to finding a new place for Jay at NBC, Zucker would always ask if Jay had any suggestions for what might tempt him to stay with NBC; what else did he want to do? Jay always had the same reply: "I tell jokes at eleven thirty at night."

Back in New York, Jeff Ross kept in touch as usual with his friendly counterpart on *The Tonight Show*, Debbie Vickers. Debbie would never go over any of the details of Jay's meetings with Zucker, but both producers knew the NBC boss had begun his campaign to throw at Leno anything he could conjure up to see if Jay might bite. Neither of them could imagine a scenario where Jay would.

But they differed about what was likely to happen. Debbie was convinced Jay would end up at ABC; it was the only thing that made sense. Ross insisted, on more than one occasion, "I think he's gonna retire."

And Vickers always had the same answer: "You're out of your mind. I mean, you are *out* of your mind."

CHAPTER SIX

THE TEN O'CLOCK
SOLUTION

J immy Kimmel had come to expect the calls, and throughout the early months of 2008, even after the strike had ended, they came in steadily on his personal line. Never in his life would Kimmel have suspected that it would have come to this, but Jay Leno seemed to be his new BFF.

"You really need to do something about your start time," Jay would tell Kimmel in a familiar line of helpful advice. "It's killing you."

Jay had noticed that, despite its officially listed start time of 12:05 a.m., after the half-hour *Nightline*, Kimmel's ABC show rarely ever began until 12:06, and sometimes as late as 12:08. Kimmel, who taped the show around seven p.m. in LA and then virtually never saw it on the air (it made him uncomfortable to watch himself), had not noticed how much the start time was sliding.

"You need to press them on this," Jay advised Kimmel. "The start time has to be consistent." How would Jimmy's viewers know what time to change channels, or even start their DVRs, if the start time contained that much variation?

Kimmel never failed to be impressed with Leno's thorough knowledge of late-night ratings across the board, and he was not a little flattered that Jay seemed to be including him in his comprehensive evaluation of the time period. Jay had also taken to complimenting Kimmel on how much his show had progressed, and how Jimmy himself was growing as a host—and a comic. With Jay, the quality of material always ranked as the highest priority, and he told Jimmy he was more and more impressed by how funny the show was night after night.

But after the advice and the compliments, Jay had another message for Kimmel. He wanted to tell him how much better everything would be, including that start-time issue, if the two of them could get together—like back-to-back on ABC, with Jay at 11:35 and Jimmy at 12:35. It would be a late-night package, he said, just like what he and Conan had had at NBC.

The unspoken implication, of course, was that Jay was far down the road in his consideration of jumping to ABC, and he knew one bit of fallout from a decision in that direction would involve *Jimmy Kimmel Live*: Jimmy would have to slide back a half hour to make this scenario work. More accurately, Jimmy would have to not make a stink about moving back a half hour. The last thing Jay needed was another displaced host pointing fingers at him for wanting to stay on the air at 11:35.

As Jay pointed out, the 12:35 start time would be better in some ways than what Kimmel had now, both because of that variable in the start time that ABC was throwing in every night and because Jay would be providing a more compatible lead-in than *Nightline*. Having to follow some depressing or distressing news story was like sticking a knife in any comedy that was set up to open a show. This could really work, Leno insisted.

Jay didn't really know the terms of Kimmel's deal with ABC, but a different outside party did: the management of the Fox network. The truth was, Kimmel could not simply be assigned the 12:35 show after Leno if ABC did sign the NBC star, because his deal contained time-period specificity. If ABC tried to move him backward, Kimmel would automatically become a free agent.

Did it make sense, Kimmel wondered, to go backward a half hour after five years on the air? Wouldn't that play like a demotion? Alternately, there might be a plus to pushing back against the shove to a later hour. Breaking off from ABC would make Kimmel fair game for Fox and the eleven p.m. spot on that network. Jimmy's agent, James Dixon, had made sure Fox had all the information regarding that point.

Kimmel believed he fit Fox even more snugly than Conan would have. His audience was also young, and more male than any other network's late-night show. Kimmel also retained some of his connections from his days needling the Fox jocks on Sundays, including the most important one of all—David Hill, who ran Fox Sports and who had hired him for the

Sunday football gig. Hill had once headed all of Fox television and still played a powerful role behind the scenes at the company. The welcome at Fox could be sweet.

And maybe sweetly lucrative. Kimmel and Dixon had heard about the $20 million plus that Fox had offered to Conan in 2001. If the network was going to make Kimmel some crazy offer like $50 million over three years, sticking around for less than $5 million a year to play behind Jay Leno was not going to have much curb appeal. Still, none of these balls was going to be put in play unless and until Jay made his move to ABC.

The bottom line for Kimmel was: Follow a guy likely to keep winning big in late night, or move on and roll the dice at another network. Kimmel realized the smart play was to stick around as the next act after the top guy; that path promised security and a steady paycheck. If Jay took 11:35, Kimmel didn't foresee himself falling into the Conan role and asking, "When the fuck is this guy going to retire?" Sure, it might come to that someday, but there was an even bigger age gap between him and Leno: seventeen years.

In their phone conversations Kimmel would try to press Jay on whether he really had committed to make the jump to ABC. Leno would not say— and couldn't really, because no firm deal could even be discussed—but Kimmel always came away with the strong impression that Jay was either taking the ABC option seriously or at least pretending to do so.

As usual Jay mostly kept his own counsel. Aside from his real counsel, Ken Ziffren, he had no hired help to kick the options around with. He had the general sense that ABC presented the best choice for him. It had, at least, a lineup of stations that competed hard in the late local news. But Jay didn't swallow ABC's blandishments whole. While the network touted its potent lineup of prime-time hits, Jay knew that *Desperate Housewives* was on Sunday and of no help to him there, that *Grey's Anatomy* played at nine, not ten, and that *Lost* was on the air for less than twenty weeks. The truth was, ABC's ten p.m. lineup—his network lead-in—was barren. NBC, in its sorry state as the fourth-place network, had more strength at ten with the solid *Law & Order: SVU* on Tuesday and the ancient but still viable *ER* on Thursday.

Fox was still out there with an offer as well, but even some Fox executives questioned whether Jay would be interested in a show that started at eleven p.m. Not only was that alien territory for him, but it meant he would not be facing off head-to-head with Dave and Conan on *The Tonight Show*. The ratings might get parsed; the leader might not be clear cut. At ABC he could win big and make NBC face the full consequences of the decision to evict him.

As one of the top executives who was then chasing Jay put it, "I expect money will play a secondary role to revenge, and Jay will look to prove to everybody that NBC was wrong. In whatever deal Jay takes, there has to be a big, badass 'fuck you' to NBC."

Even as he leaned toward ABC and away from Fox, another possibility floated Jay's way. Sony Pictures Television was looking for a big syndicated late-night franchise to match what it had in the daytime hours with Oprah, with whom the company had a distribution deal. Sony laid a goody-laden package under Jay's nose: the biggest payday in late night, more than $40 million a year; ownership of his own show and a companion twelve thirty show (the match of Letterman's deal with CBS); and a landmark new studio on Sony's Culver City lot. "When he walks on the lot, there'll be a Yellow Brick Road to the Jay Leno Theater," said one Sony executive, adding that it would become "the centerpiece of the Sony lot."

Sony was even dangling connections to Sony's music division—if Jay broke new artists on the show he might get cut in on a percentage of their sales. The company promised to think of ways to associate Jay with its PlayStation franchise, maybe promotions in the products, something to help Jay reach the young men obsessed with video games.

Even with all the perks, Sony's executives knew their proposal was a long shot, simply because it didn't come with a network attached. To make syndication work Sony would have to canvass the country to line up stations. And while entirely confident of success in that endeavor, the Sony representatives expected that Jay would squirm at the notion that his national station lineup was not instantly certain and secure.

To make that kind of complicated sale, therefore, Sony needed an ally in Jay's camp. But Jay was agentless, and no one could easily name even an intimate friend who ranked as a professional confidant. Then some Sony executives remembered Jerry Seinfeld's long-professed friendship with Jay. Sony was in business with Jerry as distributor of the *Seinfeld* reruns and DVDs. Maybe Jerry was the influencer they needed.

They approached Jerry's longtime managers, George Shapiro and

Howard West, and struck gold. Jay had already turned to Jerry for advice and he had brought George and Howard in as (quiet) consultants. Classic comic managers from the old school, Shapiro and West, both men in their seventies who seemed like the best sort of showbiz characters from a Woody Allen movie, could be counted on to do only what was in Jay's best interests.

One thing everybody involved knew was that, when the time came, Jay would not lack for offers. Of course, not all the bidders were convinced they would even get a crack at Leno, not if NBC blinked and wound up paying off Conan, as some strongly suspected they would. With that in mind, a negotiator for one of the suitors figured it made sense to make another move, purely as a hedge. The executive contacted Ari Emanuel with a message: "Not if but when NBC fucks Conan, we want you to know we've got a pile of money to offer your client."

When Jeff Zucker met with Rick Ludwin to thrash out the status of the effort to keep Jay in house, nobody fretted about Sony or any other syndication deal. All those people had to offer was money, but with Jay, it was never really about money. He wanted to count people more than bills. He wanted to work someplace where he could win. For Zucker, that had to mean ABC. It fit Jay's needs, and ABC surely would want a shot at late-night entertainment after all these years on the sideline with *Nightline*.

As the early months of 2008 rolled by, Zucker heard from Ludwin that Jay's hints about taking that left off the freeway and heading over to the Disney lot were only growing louder. Leno gave an interview to *USA Today* about his auto collection and put an exclamation point on it, telling the reporter, "I am definitely done next year with NBC." And when asked if he would head out for another network, he offered his version of a cocky comeback. "I'm not a beach guy, and the last time I was in my pool was to fix a light. Don't worry. I'll find a job somewhere."

This amounted to Jay's waving a scimitar over Jeff Zucker's head. Jeff's calculation was simple: If—really, when—Jay refused all NBC's various offers, he would take up residence at ABC, and money would surely follow him. Zucker had already received estimates from the network's research and sales departments of what a Jay-at-ABC outcome would mean: NBC would take a monetary pasting. Despite that, Zucker clung, at least in what he was saying out loud, to the conviction that Conan could still win the young demos, figuring Leno and Letterman would then split the older crowd.

That might mitigate the financial hit a bit, but if Conan was finishing second—or, heaven forbid, *third*—among total viewers in late night, it would likely be viewed throughout most of the television world as a calamity for the institution of *The Tonight Show*. And, of course, a ratings quake like that would kick up a PR tsunami directed at NBC—and Zucker. Having to sell the notion that a *Tonight Show* attracting fewer viewers than either CBS or ABC was just fine, no problem at all, because NBC still had a .2 rating margin in men eighteen to thirty-four, while at the same time shrugging off finishing dead last in prime time again, might have required more spin than a tropical storm.

Zucker had assumed the job of chief executive of NBC Universal a year earlier, when Bob Wright retired. GE's chairman, Jeff Immelt, had said at the time that NBC's struggles had actually enhanced Zucker's reputation with the board of directors. "The board and I particularly liked the way that Jeff has handled tough times," Immelt explained. "He never got down. He always drove the company harder, inspired the team to do better."

That was all well and good in 2007, before another year with the NBC network locked in the ratings cellar and before the best-laid late-night plan of 2004 for the seamless transition from Jay to Conan—all completely the inspiration and personal handiwork of Jeffrey Zucker, CEO—took a turn downhill and, in the nightmare scenario with Jay at ABC, headed for the edge of a ravine.

It was time to run another scenario by Jay.

Every three months or so Zucker was still making his pilgrimage out to the Burbank dungeon, shining up Jay as best he could, trotting out NBC's latest version of an attractive alternative to hosting *The Tonight Show*.

He offered him the Bob Hope deal: permanent employment with the network, high-profile specials—maybe even a road named after him in Burbank. Jay didn't even think twice. A few times on TV a year, after being on every weeknight? Not happening.

Zucker came back a short time later with what seemed like a more promising solution: a big show every Sunday night, in prime time or maybe in late night, like his own version of *SNL*—but with a different *S*.

"Once a week is death," Jay said. Not only would every good topical joke have been done on the other shows all week—anathema to Leno—but the process of making that kind of show would have made him go boing like an overwound watch.

"The idea is you write jokes literally until it's pencils down," Jay said. "If you do it once a week, then you're writing jokes twenty-four hours a day and you go batty. And every time you put your pencil down you feel incredibly guilty that you're not doing a joke. It has to be every day." For one thing the forced regularity of jokes delivered daily relieved some of the pressure to perform on some extraordinary level. "It's a little like a newspaper versus a magazine," Leno explained. "Your standard doesn't have to be quite as high when you write a story every single day."

The answer really boiled down to what it had always boiled down to: "I tell jokes at eleven thirty at night—every night."

Back in his New York office, Zucker continued to play a game of Rubik's Cube with the parts of the NBC Universal empire, looking for the key that would make the colors line up for Jay. There had to be a way, without reaching all the way to the bottom for that last trick in his bag. He was holding out as long as he could, hoping he would never have to unload that one.

Zucker wasn't surprised the first time the whispers circulating around the corners of NBC's Rock Center executive suite reached him—with no names attached. Would NBC consider, for even half a second, the outrageous? Pay off Conan, wish him well, and keep Jay? That was *not* the last trick in Zucker's bag; and for many reasons—at least 45 million of them— he didn't waste any time responding to the rumors.

On his next trip west, Zucker tried to address Jay's baseline concern of telling jokes every night in late night. He offered him a real weeknight late-night show—on cable TV. Jay could have a traditional comedy talk show on the USA Network (owned by NBC Universal, of course), which had the biggest audience in all of cable television. Zucker emphasized that there was only one catch—it would have to start at eleven, not eleven thirty, because they couldn't undermine Conan by having Jay go on head-to-head with him.

The NBC boss had arguments to marshal on behalf of this concept, but again, he never really got a chance. Jay did not see himself finishing out his career on cable television, which to him sounded like "living in the basement of your own house." He was, by his own admission, an older guy who had grown up thinking network was the place to be. "Like my dad would say, 'Cadillac is the Rolls-Royce of automobiles.'" The notion of relocating to cable at that point in his life "just seemed too weird."

Jay felt old enough that he figured he shouldn't start all over in "new media." He had carefully taken note of what had become of radio's biggest comic, Howard Stern, when he "sort of went to cable," as Jay viewed it. Stern had accepted an enormous payday to abandon terrestrial radio in favor of the satellite company Sirius. To Jay, Stern had been a genuine populist—one of his highest compliments, because that was how Jay often identified his own appeal. "The truck driver, the average guy, would listen to Howard wherever, in the cafeteria, the car, the truck," Jay said. "Then when he went to Sirius, I didn't hear Howard quoted anymore. People don't ever say, 'Hey, did you hear what Howard said today?' And I'm sure he's still doing what he always did."

The difference, of course, was that in order to hear Stern now, the old truck-driving fan would have to cough up twelve dollars or whatever a month, which surely amounted to a mighty investment for the average Joes whom Jay saw as the backbone of both Stern's audience and his. If you started making it tough for the average Joes to find you, pretty soon you wouldn't be a populist anymore. "To me," Jay said, "the key to *The Tonight Show* is you're at the airport and, oh look, it's on the TV over the bar."

Not likely that a show on the USA Network was making it onto many TVs in the airport in, say, Reno. Jay told Zucker his cable idea was a nonstarter.

As the 2008 calendar rolled through spring, May becoming June, Conan O'Brien could not help but think of the date looming one year in the future. His first night on *The Tonight Show* was set for June 1, 2009.

The prospect filled him with a real thrill because O'Brien, despite his long-held Letterman worship, also had a deep personal connection to Johnny Carson's *Tonight Show*. He associated Carson directly with his dad and the fondly remembered experience of watching *The Tonight Show* as a twelve-year-old in 1975, in his den, next to his father, and recalling how his father laughed and enjoyed Carson's matchless delivery and timing.

That reverence only deepened when Conan had occasion later—just a few times—to interact with Johnny. The first came before he even went on the air with *Late Night* in 1993. As a thirty-year-old kid, just named out of nowhere to replace Letterman, Conan met Carson at a celebrity-strewn lunch that the Center for Communication in New York held in Johnny's honor—an event at which Johnny performed his final topical stand-up in public (though no one knew that at the time). Johnny's best line of the afternoon: "I'm optimistic about television. Of course, you know, in the entertainment business, an optimist is an accordion player with a beeper."

After the lunch, Carson greeted Conan amiably and offered a snippet of advice: "Just be yourself—it's the only way it can work." The comment seemed nothing but generous to O'Brien, though he later had a rueful second thought: And even *then* it might not work.

Later O'Brien contacted Carson—and all the other giants of late night, including Steve Allen, Jack Paar, and, yes, Letterman—when he was hosting an NBC special about fifty years of late night on the network. Conan asked for Johnny's input on the clips chosen for the special. He said they looked fine.

Most memorably for Conan, Carson had checked in with a call after NBC had named Conan as Leno's successor (officially, that is). That brief conversation, which took place only a few months before Carson died in 2005, mainly consisted of congratulations. Conan joked that getting the show was a great honor, "if I live to see it." Johnny agreed that "it does seem like a long engagement before the marriage."

The exchanges with Carson may have been fleeting, but they were enough to validate for Conan the emotion he felt for Johnny and the show that had made him famous. O'Brien took to calling *The Tonight Show* "sacred ground."

In many of his private moments, Conan felt the surge of adrenalin—he was getting *The Tonight Show, Johnny's* show. How exciting was this? And eager as he was to get it, he continued to have flashes of doubt: *This is about me? And I'm that kid from that elementary school whose pants don't fit? And do they know that I had acne as a teenager? Do they know that I don't always know exactly what I'm doing?*

Those moments, which had come in abundance in his early days of *Late Night*, were much more sporadic now. Still, he recognized that ever proximate condition: the imposter syndrome—the thought that, no matter how successful you became, "they're about to catch up to you." Conan encountered it with some frequency, but was comforted by knowing the syndrome affected everyone in show business, as he became aware one night when the comic Chris Rock visited *Late Night* as a guest. At the time

Rock mania had gripped the land, and Chris was being celebrated everywhere as the comic genius of a generation.

On the show Rock sat down next to Conan and within seconds had the crowd by the throat, wringing gales of laughter out of them with just the slightest effort. Conan felt blown back by the power Rock commanded over the audience, shooting out one explosive line after another. It seemed to Conan that everything around Rock had turned liquid, the air around him was so blazing hot.

Then the commercial break arrived, and Conan leaned over to tell Rock, "Man, that was fantastic!" And Rock stretched close to Conan's ear and said, "I just hope they don't catch on."

To outsiders Conan mostly kept his guard up in revealing any cracks in his confidence about the coming change in his professional life. But sometimes the lingering insecurity seeped out unexpectedly, as in a moment after he performed for advertisers at NBC's infront presentation in the spring of 2008. While chatting with a small group that included Lorne Michaels and Tina Fey, celebrating the renewal of their *30 Rock* sitcom, O'Brien got a sudden faraway look in his eye. He pulled aside one of the group, someone Conan had known since his first year at NBC.

"Can I ask you something?" Conan leaned in to whisper. "Will you root for me?"

Those shaky moments hardly dominated Conan's days and nights, though, for he had far too much to do and think about. Beyond daily preparation for the *Late Night* show, Conan and his staff, led by head writer Mike Sweeney, had begun noodling, even a year in advance, with ideas for the coming *Tonight Show*. They sorted out what bits they might retain (definitely "Conando," the wildly exaggerated takeoff on a Spanish-language *telenovela*, with Conan in pencil mustache) and what they might have to abandon ("the Masturbating Bear," "Vomiting Kermit").

Already Sweeney had beefed up the writing staff with a few additional monologue specialists. They knew *The Tonight Show* would demand a longer monologue than Conan had ever performed on *Late Night*. There he had mostly followed Letterman's precedent from his days on that show and tossed out just four or five gags before moving on to the more creative comedy.

But over the course of this last year, the monologue began to creep up to eight to ten jokes a night. That did not begin to approach Jay, who often hit the thirty-five mark, but Conan was stretching, a concession to the need for a substantial top-of-the-show joke barrage at 11:35. The additional jokes tested the limit of Conan's stand-up technique, which he had never really needed to perfect before, since it wasn't his signature thing. Now he had to work on the necessary moves—while dropping some of the unnecessary tics.

For years Conan had told his few opening jokes in the same almost throwaway manner. He would stand at center stage and read the setup off his cue cards in a kind of singsong delivery.

"Despite protests from conservatives, President Bush today appointed an openly gay man as his assistant secretary of commerce. . . ."

Stop, pause, head nod, and throw each hand out to the side, as if to signal in a kind of stand-up semaphore: *OK, folks, the punch line is on the way. . . .*

"Yeah, Bush claimed a gay man is perfect for the commerce department because 'those people love to shop.'" Outthrust hands brought together with an audible clap.

Conan executed this exercise so routinely that few on the show were even aware he told most jokes this way. With the longer monologue, however, varying the delivery became imperative, and Conan set to work on it.

Rick Ludwin still sent notes, of course, and Conan and staff dutifully read and considered them. Mostly, the suggestions—still always along the lines of more interaction with the audience—did not result in any changes. Not that Conan didn't appreciate Ludwin's efforts. He knew how important Rick had been in steering *The Tonight Show* into his hands. But comedy writers and performers are rarely disposed to believe that "civilians" know what's best in comedy.

The NBC suggestions all had a whiff of mothballs to them: Be broader, be more traditional, more eleven thirty than twelve thirty. "I think people are overthinking the twelve-thirty-to-eleven-thirty shift," O'Brien said. "Because television is so different now." The younger people who favored Conan were more and more watching the show in new ways: on DVR playback, where they sped through to the favored moments, or catching up to it online rather than watching every night. As Conan analyzed it, he needed to kick-start *The Tonight Show* into a new century with new media and new audiences. He had to put his own stamp on the show, no matter how much tradition was draped all over it.

He didn't accept that the show had to be stodgy or hidebound. In several published accounts he compared the show to a classic but sleek, fast, and sexy sports car. "They're handing me the keys to this beautiful Ferrari of *The Tonight Show*," Conan told the Cleveland *Plain Dealer*. "I've been driving around in a Jeep Wrangler called the *Late Night* show. A fine Jeep Wrangler with a busted radio, but now they're handing me the keys to a Ferrari called *The Tonight Show*. And I don't want to just gently put it into gear and drive it at fifty-five miles an hour down the highway so I don't burn out the clutch."

No, he had other plans. "I want to see what this baby can do. I want to get this thing up over a hundred miles an hour. I want to clip some fire hydrants. I want to get it up on two wheels, on its side, like James Bond in that alley."

As the days of 2008 dwindled down, the ever nearing prospect of losing Jay Leno cast a threatening shadow over every other decision on Jeff Zucker's plate. After all his masterful maneuvering—the coup of keeping Jay and Conan together for five more years as the network's late-night profit juggernaut—Zucker and NBC were back where they had started. They still found themselves on the verge of playing the sad-sack victims in an old familiar horror movie, menaced by the same intractable bogeyman, apparently every bit as unkillable as Michael Myers in a *Halloween* movie: the chair that two men wanted, but only one could sit in.

Where the hell did Zucker go from here? That last option, the one he'd kept in reserve, had not quite burned a hole through Zucker's pocket, but it had been in there smoldering for a long time. Before he gave in, pulled it out, and threw it on the table, he needed backup, and so he commissioned some special studies from NBC's research department.

Out in Burbank, Jay was still telling his pointed jokes. He did a bit about car navigation systems and the programmed voices they used. The conceit was that the voice, rather than some disembodied robot character, was someone you know, in this case a nagging mother: "When are you going to get a new job?" (Pause.) "ABC would be nice!"

Meanwhile, Rick Ludwin was still doing his job. Whenever he chatted with Jay, as he routinely did, he had a message: The cash might be greener elsewhere, but that didn't mean the grass was. Just look at the other examples of stars jumping from their home networks, Ludwin urged him, citing the one Jay would be most viscerally familiar with: Dave. Look what happened when Letterman went to CBS, Ludwin pointed out. Sure, he beat Jay's brains out for a couple of years, but once NBC retook the late-night title, Dave was a loser for the next fifteen years. And the examples extended beyond late night. How about news stars, like Katie Couric? She was America's sweetheart in the mornings on the *Today* show. Now look at her—last place on the *CBS Evening News*.

How much impact these arguments had on Jay, Ludwin could not be sure, but he felt he had at least planted some seeds of doubt about a happy switch to ABC.

Those seeds might have fallen on stony ground, but others had already dug some deep roots in Jay's consciousness. More than anything else, what gnawed at Leno about his contract situation was NBC's ability—and now intention—to beach him for at least six months. Conan would start June 1; Jay couldn't get back on the air until after January 1.

When NBC agreed to Jay's five-year extension back in 2004, it had carefully included, along with the obligation to pay him in full for the life of the deal, the right to shelve the comic at any time the network desired. In other words, NBC had Jay Leno for five years, and if at any point during that time it decided to replace him, it was completely within its rights to put him on a (symbolic) beach for as long as it wanted for the duration of that five-year period. Jay could work Vegas, Reno, and every Native American casino from Temecula, California, to Ledyard, Connecticut—but nowhere else on television until after January 1, 2010. Now, it was true that NBC had basically agreed up front that it would not exercise the right to shelve Jay until June 2009, when Conan was slated to start. But that was more handshake than handwritten.

Nobody was more aware of this situation—and obsessed by it—than Jay Leno. As he looked forward and considered his options, he could not help but look backward and chafe under his limitations. ABC's desirability as a destination was undercut by a sobering realization: Before he could reach it, he would have to endure the test—torture test, really—of an enforced absence of six months or more from television.

One top Hollywood agent, a strong Jay supporter, found himself befogged when Jay told him of this dilemma. With the clear leverage Jay had had back when NBC came to him with this cockamamie five-year plan, the agent knew Jay could have protected himself against getting boxed in like this. "The guy always went in by himself to make his deals," the agent said. "He was the big dog. Somebody representing him would have said, 'OK, five-year deal, you're making Jay leave. But the *minute* you take him off the air, he's free to go anywhere he likes.' "

Jay usually couched his concern about being off the air for so long in terms of what it would mean for his staff. If NBC really did send him into enforced exile starting in June, that meant months of no pay for his writers and other staff members. He conjured a worst-case scenario in which he got stuck in neutral all the way until April. That would be the case, he estimated, if he couldn't hook up with anyone at ABC or Fox until January and couldn't even talk to anyone before that. He couldn't be expected to launch a new show overnight.

But the circumstances were actually quite different. From his conversations with Kimmel, it was clear Jay had a reasonably good idea that ABC had an 11:35 spot laid out for his arrival. As for the staff worries, could he not push his suitors for some assurance that nobody would lose income for that interregnum? A raise or advance in salary for key staff could have covered that issue.

And it wasn't as if Jay was going to reinvent his show. Take away the *Tonight* title, adjust the network designation, and what else would change? Not the performance. One executive who had worked with Jay in the past laughed off the notion that a network transfer would set him back months, saying, "Jay would probably be ready to go after a weekend."

His close associates knew the truth: Jay would do almost anything to avoid the prolonged nightmare of going without nightly monologues to prepare and deliver to millions on TV. Boiled down, Jay's philosophy was: "Anytime you're on the air, you're winning." Even a short absence increased the chances that people might forget about you and drift away. In Jay's view, attention spans were simply too short to gamble with.

Debbie Vickers knew Jay best of all, and she had her own back-channel connection to Zucker. Her quiet message: Jay is a creature of habit. If anything tempts him at all, he will stay where he is most comfortable.

Jeff Zucker was known within NBC to be research friendly. He didn't make calls strictly based on what the research department predicted the outcome would be, but he certainly wanted all the data he could get his hands on before he made those calls.

In support of his original idea of moving Jay to eight p.m. Zucker had commissioned research head Alan Wurtzel to answer one big question: Was the idea of Jay Leno in prime time something the audience would dismiss out of hand? Questions like that defied simple analysis. All Wurtzel could reasonably determine was if the notion would raise any flaming red flags, such as viewers indicating that they would simply have no interest at all in such a proposition.

What he found, in fact, was the opposite: An alternative to the traditional prime-time fare, like a new comedy show with Jay Leno, came across as intriguing and appealing when suggested to focus groups.

In March of 2008 Zucker had dispatched Wurtzel to try to sell Jay on the idea of the prime-time half hour at eight. Jay had been polite as always but direct. "Alan, I go into late night and I'm number one. That's what I do. I don't know how to do prime time."

Wurtzel worked him as best he could. "Look, one of the reasons this makes sense to us is you really are iconic. And when people are in a surfing environment and go by and see Jay Leno, they know exactly who he is. They stop; they know where he comes from. If anybody could do this in prime time it would be you."

Jay appreciated the flattery. But prime time didn't look like it was going to be the temptation Debbie Vickers had prescribed.

When Wurtzel got back from Burbank, Zucker had some other questions for him to work on. A big one: What will happen if Jay is at ABC?

That was a concrete concept that Wurtzel's department could quantify. The number they came up with looked very good for Jay. If he landed at ABC, he was still going to win. But more than anything, the research suggested, a three-way network pileup in late night would likely produce mutually assured destruction: diluted numbers, diluted profits. NBC might be left with the show with the youngest appeal—but perhaps also the least overall appeal.

When one of his top lieutenants kicked the situation around with Zucker, he came away convinced that Jeff's goal now was two-pronged: find a way to retain Leno, yes, but also find a way to protect Conan. Of course, the executive concluded, Zucker's protecting Conan translated to Zucker's protecting himself. He was the father of the five-year plan, after all. If it all went wrong it would set up one easy—and unpleasant—paternity test.

So there was that daunting possibility to confront. There was also a raft of other information from Alan Wurtzel for Zucker to digest—information that could make the prospect of having to drag that last option out of his pocket a little more tolerable.

If Zucker solicited private advice, he usually went to Dick Ebersol, the man he had looked to for career counseling since his earliest days at NBC. They had a regular routine, if Dick happened to be in New York. Very early, seven thirty or so, Ebersol would turn up at Zucker's sprawling, always overheated office (they could never take the Miami totally out of Jeff Zucker) on the fifty-second floor. There they would discuss anything having to do with NBC. Not just NBC Sports, Ebersol's main purview, but everything. On a morning in mid-2008, when Dick sat down on Jeff's big pillow-packed couch to hash things out as usual, the NBC boss gave him the word: It looked like he had to go for broke with Leno.

"The only thing left in my drawer is ten o'clock," Zucker told him.

Zucker saw the situation as a confluence of events, all coming together to compel him to move in a direction he had strenuously resisted. He needed something to offer Jay Leno that would keep him at NBC, while at the same time he had in front of him a ratings track for prime-time shows at ten p.m. dating back to the 2003–2004 television season. Its message seemed clear: Ten p.m. had become a graveyard for network series. Few or none qualified as real hits anymore. Where onetime giant hits like *Law & Order* and *ER* averaged audiences at ten that surpassed 25 million viewers, now few ten p.m. shows were topping 10 million. And the news was worse in that advertiser-preferred eighteen-to-forty-nine-year-old age group.

In 2004–2005, CBS's ten p.m. shows had averaged a network-best 4.17 rating in the age group eighteen to forty-nine. The same year NBC's ten p.m. shows had averaged a 3.9 rating and ABC's a 2.82. Every year since, the numbers had dropped precipitously, to the point where Wurtzel's department was projecting the ten p.m. shows in 2008–2009 to fall below a 2.0 rating for both NBC and ABC, with CBS at just 2.43. Those were massive falloffs of approaching 50 percent for each network. And this shrinkage was affecting shows generally among the most expensive in television, cop and medical dramas, with high-cost actors and writers and demanding production values.

It only figured to get worse. The widespread and increasing use of

DVRs was wreaking havoc on network schedules, and nowhere more so than at ten p.m. Viewers had clearly developed the habit of playing back favored shows from earlier in the evening, or earlier in the week, at that hour instead of watching the offerings on the three networks (Fox being an eight-to-ten network only). The last real hit show airing at ten p.m. was CBS's *CSI: Miami,* and that had been introduced in 2002. NBC had ridden those warhorses *ER* and *Law & Order* almost into the ground. It still had *Law & Order: SVU,* but beyond that it looked bleak for the new entries that first Kevin Reilly and then Ben Silverman had selected for ten p.m.

What the data suggested to Zucker was that he might be on the cusp of another paradigm shift. Maybe he could perceive the groundbreaking changes that would have to be made earlier than other network executives precisely because of NBC's long travails in prime time. As he had often said before, "It's sometimes easier to see the world when you're flat on your back."

The other flow feeding into the confluence came from Conan's direction. Zucker had an unsettling nervous twitch regarding Conan. Nothing seemed drastically wrong and yet something felt unmistakably off. Conan had yet to show real signs of transforming his act into something more mainstream. And there were those more competitive numbers that continued to be put up by CBS's Craig Ferguson, who was never far from Conan now in viewers. Conan always won easily in the contest for the young demos, but taking all these factors into account, it seemed to Zucker that signs were growing that the heat under Conan, so intense in 2004, had been turned down to a simmer.

Zucker certainly didn't like continually getting reports from Ludwin that Conan and his team were resisting the notes he was giving them about breaking away from behind the desk, getting out into the audience. Was it arrogance, Zucker wondered, that fed the urge to reject the network's suggestions? Or maybe just an inability to make the changes because Conan couldn't perform any other way but the way he already knew?

Meanwhile, though the internal anxiety about the impending shift to Conan was only increasing, Rick Ludwin and Nick Bernstein, the two executives closest to NBC's late-night lineup, never lost faith. Bernstein, in his early thirties, had watched Conan with a fan's fervor beginning in high school. He supported *The Tonight Show* shift in a circle-of-life kind of way, though he deeply respected and admired Leno. For his part, Ludwin found the second-guessing of the move to Conan all too familiar, reminiscent of the last-minute hedging that went on in the nineties when NBC almost threw over Leno for Letterman. If the network had listened to some strident voices back then, Ludwin concluded, Jay would never have survived to be the dominant force he became. So Ludwin argued forcefully for sticking by the decision that had been so thoughtfully worked out.

Besides, Ludwin didn't have any overall reservations about the content of Conan's 12:35 show. To Ludwin, Conan had long since proved how inventive and creative he could be—and of course how damn smart he was. He knew that Conan considered everything carefully. The last thing that made sense to Ludwin was to try to force something on a host that he believed he wouldn't execute well, which could easily lead to a performance without conviction.

Ludwin patiently countered the Conan doubters whenever the discussion drifted toward a suggestion that NBC not go through with the shift, though he knew he didn't convince all of them. As one top NBC executive described the sentiment being expressed privately inside some offices in New York and Burbank, "I don't know how with anyone still successful you can be creating a situation where there would be a finite end to that success. I mean, Barbara Walters stays on the air until she's eighty. You gotta pay Conan off. But Jeff had that relationship with Conan and Jeff Ross."

Zucker shrugged off all the under-the-breath questions about whether Conan should be paid off. His stance was simple: He'd made a commitment to O'Brien and he was going to stand by it. With any ousting-Conan option off the table, Zucker was left standing in the middle of his confluence. He decided to go with the flow; he pulled out the ten o'clock solution, ready at last to lay it at Jay's feet.

Despite all the on-air jokes about running off to ABC and his serious private comments about how wounded he felt by NBC's decision to point him toward the door, Jay Leno recoiled from what he saw as the potential consequences of a change of professional address.

As usual, he had a ready line for it: "The czar you have is always better than the czar you're going to get." A new place meant new camera operators, new pages, new everything. Worse, he foresaw an ugly scenario taking shape, with his long relationships at NBC turning hostile the moment he announced he was moving on. "Then the mysterious sandbag falls on your head," he said. "I'm Italian. I know how this works."

Jay elaborated: "Suddenly little stories appear in the papers: 'The arrogant Mr. Leno refused to . . .' Or 'Jay took a private jet to go to . . .' And you're like, where did this come from?" Staff members who might have felt slighted by some little incident that had taken place fifteen years earlier would suddenly be out there peddling nasty stories. "You get fragged. Your own troops are shooting at you—that's the worst thing."

While he remained unhappy with what NBC had done, Jay never directed that unhappiness toward Conan. Conan might well become his competitor if he was forced to join ABC, but Jay had long argued that the late-night comics should all get along in spite of their competitiveness. It was all just show business. He wasn't about to nullify that position now by making it openly personal with Conan, which was a primary reason why he turned down one extremely provocative offer.

Word got to him from the Letterman camp that a true television event could be set up after he ended his *Tonight Show* run: They invited Jay to come on the show as Dave's guest. A chance to relive old times and to begin a rapprochement with Dave—that had great appeal for Jay. But then the Letterman people clarified the invitation: They wanted Jay to sit down with Dave on the very night that Conan premiered. They didn't consider it a personal attack on Conan, whom all the Letterman people liked. It was simply business, a way to block a competitor right out of the starting gate. Conan would surely be swamped, his debut reduced to rubble by the monster late-night event over on CBS.

"I couldn't insult Conan that way," Jay said, in explaining how he had declined the Letterman bookers. But he made certain they knew he would love to do it any another time, when the damage to Conan—and the chances of igniting a PR backlash against himself—would be dissipated. After all, it looked as though he would be off television for months.

On October 18, 2008, NBC seized the attention of the nation with the biggest edition of *Saturday Night Live* in fourteen years: a guest appearance by vice presidential candidate Sarah Palin, with Tina Fey on hand to perform her devastating impression of Palin. The show would attract 17 million viewers, a stunning number, far more than all but a few of the prime-time shows on all of television that week—or any week.

For an event of that magnitude, Jeff Zucker had to be a presence. He would often turn up backstage during the live broadcasts on Saturday night because of his close friendship with Lorne Michaels. For Zucker it was a fun diversion just to sit in on the production of a live show. But this was more like a command appearance. The event had national significance.

Many of NBC's top executives, some in from the West Coast, circulated in the long hallway that led back from Studio 8H. With security forces, Palin handlers, and VIP guests everywhere, the atmosphere crackled with tension and excitement. Zucker, however, floated through the scene with aplomb, greeting people, talking about the expectations for Palin's appearance, acting the part of host. Shortly before the countdown to the live show, when Zucker intended to repair to his natural habitat, the control room, he gathered a few select executives for a private, hushed conversation.

"Don't tell anyone this," Zucker told the little group. "But Jay's interested in ten o'clock—and we think we're going to be able to make a deal."

His listeners had to restrain their surprise. To one it seemed near incredible, virtually a 180 from what they had been hearing to that point: that Jay wouldn't do prime time; that he wouldn't know how to take on the cops or Dr. McDreamy or whoever else the other networks would throw at him.

Zucker seemed more than positive; he almost oozed self-satisfaction. But he repeated his warning. "We have to stay quiet about this until it's done."

Staying quiet clearly meant keeping this news to the tight circle Zucker had just informed—and not, say, leaking word to anyone connected to Conan O'Brien. No one was surprised by that stricture. They all knew there was reason to have concern about how Conan would react. But the deal had not been completed. Everyone in television knew of endless numbers of occasions when agreements hatched behind closed doors never came to fruition.

For Zucker, holding off on informing Conan of his intentions only made sense. This was his final play with Jay. Why disrupt Conan if, in the end, nothing would come of it?

Zucker had made his pilgrimage to Burbank several more times, armed with new research from Alan Wurtzel. Jay did not embrace even this idea without initial resistance. "I don't need phony research," Jay first told Zucker. "I have research that shows I was number one since 1994. My research shows over a billion dollars in sales."

But over the course of several meetings, Zucker had been able to make an impression. The ten p.m. hour had become the place where dramas went to die, he argued. ABC kept shoveling show after show into ten p.m. holes—*October Road, Cashmere Mafia, Big Shots, Eli Stone, Life on Mars,* and on and on—succeeding only in digging the holes deeper and wasting tens of millions of dollars in the process.

Jay, of course, kept his own eye on the numbers, especially for the shows at ten, because they provided his network lead-in (and Dave's). He could see what was happening at his own network. Its big new highly promoted entry, *My Own Worst Enemy,* starring Christian Slater, had been given the plum ten p.m. slot after NBC's one newish (though fading) hit, *Heroes;* but it had already caved in, with barely a 1.7 rating in the young-adult demo. Jay was averaging about a 1.4 running well past midnight, for a fraction of the cost.

Maybe, he finally concluded, he really could do some business at ten p.m.

By the late fall of 2008, down to his last three months as host of *Late Night,* Conan O'Brien felt the pull of history. Not so much from his own show, though the process of going back through highlights of more than twenty-five hundred programs certainly struck an emotional chord. No, what was hitting O'Brien hardest was his imminent change of venue. It had been the same for David Letterman when his days in 30 Rock were melting away. Saying good-bye to the most famous building in the history of broadcasting was more than sweet sorrow, it was gut-wrenching.

Conan responded by trying to absorb every moment he had left. For him that meant changing a routine he had followed from his first days at NBC, when he would grab a cab from the apartment he rented off the park near Tavern on the Green and jump out on Forty-ninth and Sixth.

Close by the entrance was an auxiliary elevator bank that took him up to his office on the seventh floor.

Now eager to drink in all of 30 Rock that he could, he decided to start his days by wandering in slowly through the ornate entrance on the plaza side of the building. In December that meant weaving through the streams of tourists lined up to take pictures of the giant evergreen, just lit in all its glory in the annual celebration that NBC had turned into a holiday special.

Even in baseball cap and sunglasses, and with his head down, Conan was always recognized. That profile, the red hair, the storklike gait—who could miss him? "Hey, Conan!" The shouts were predictable: "Conan! What's going on?" or "Conan! Love the show!"

O'Brien always shouted back, "Thanks, great to see you." He didn't mind the notice; he still remembered when there hadn't been any.

Conan walked into that grand art deco lobby because he wanted to see the murals every day he had remaining, the massive wraparound painting *American Progress* by Jose Maria Sert, depicting straining men and women building a nation. As he walked by, Conan looked up at the murals and found himself lost in scenes from the movies *Quiz Show* and *My Favorite Year.*

O'Brien, who probably knew more television history than anyone else who'd made a piece of it, could recite details about the 30 Rock–based inspirations for those films, the scandal of the rigged answers on the quiz show *Twenty-One* and the raucous nights of ninety minutes' worth of live weekly comedy from Sid Caesar and Carl Reiner on *Your Show of Shows* that were the model for *My Favorite Year.*

He thought about watching Rob Petrie in *The Dick Van Dyke Show,* a writer for an ersatz Caesar (played by Reiner) whose fictive workplace would have been 30 Rock (though it was never expressly mentioned). And the birth of *Saturday Night Live,* so essential to his own career. It was from this location that breaking historic news had been broadcast to the nation since the 1930s. Of course, Steve Allen had begun *The Tonight Show* here, with Paar and Carson following, all commanding America's attention every night. And this was where Letterman lit the fuse that turned Conan into a late-night host.

To O'Brien the place was ground zero—the place where television was invented. Walking in through that imposing lobby and looking all around, he could feel it. He was there.

Having worked sixteen years in the building, Conan felt that so much of his life had been gifted to him through his television show. He had, after all, met his wife because of the show, and now they had two children. In 2000 Elizabeth Ann (Liza) Powel had been working in advertising at the Foote, Cone & Belding agency in New York, at a time when Conan's show had taken to mocking some truly preposterous local commercials. When they saw one in Houston featuring a store owner who brandished a whirring chain saw while promising to "slash prices," they knew they had an ideal foil.

Their idea was to bring this guy to New York to a legitimate ad agency for a commercial makeover. On the segment, Conan walked into the agency with his Houston friend and started riffing with several of the ad execs about what they might be able do for him. Very quickly he noticed the stunning blonde behind one desk. She wound up featured in the bit and soon in his life. (Conan boasted that he was one father who truly could show his kids footage some day of "How I Met Your Mother.")

Conan knew NBC was already deep into the construction of his new space in LA on the Universal lot, an investment of $50 million, which certainly spoke to their confidence in him. Given all that was happening to television, O'Brien found himself wondering how long a building like 30 Rock would still be in use for television, whether within only a few years everyone would be doing television shows out of their own living rooms.

Even in the hallway outside his studio on the sixth floor, the resonance was unmistakable for Conan. He had only to look at the studio across the hall, 6B, where for years NBC's local station, Channel 4 in New York, had produced its newscasts. (They had been relocated to NBC News's state-of-the-art studios on the eleventh floor.) Now 6B was being remade back into a late-night studio, as it had once been for the young Johnny Carson, with new seats and a proscenium-style arch, all for the next tenant.

It was always going to be up to Lorne Michaels to pick Conan's successor. Though his day-to-day connection with it had long since ended, he still had production rights to the 12:35 show (and still carried an executive producer credit on Conan's show).

When NBC signed Jimmy Fallon to a holding deal in early 2007, speculation spread that Michaels, still close to Jimmy from his days as one of the
most popular players on *SNL*, had made his choice. The sniping quickly
followed. Fallon had gotten on the wrong side of some Internet snark-
meisters on sites like Gawker and Defamer, mainly for his penchant for
breaking up during sketches and for his short-lived movie career.

But Michaels had supreme confidence in Fallon, mainly because he
had a quality that could not be either manufactured or faked. "People
really like him," as Lorne put it. "When he was on *Saturday Night Live*, he
had enormous appeal to young girls. That means young men are going to
be a bit ambivalent. But they'll come around."

James Thomas Fallon Jr. was born in Brooklyn in 1974, a year before *Saturday Night Live* went on the air. Recognizing they had a funny kid on
their hands (actually two, counting Jimmy's sister Gloria), his accommodating parents, who enjoyed *SNL* themselves, taped segments of the
show (the safer ones) in the mid-1980s to replay for their kids, who would
try to re-create some of the sketches. The family, just as Irish Catholic as
Conan's (if more black Irish than red), had moved to the upstate New York
town of Saugerties, just up the Hudson from Kingston, where Jimmy's
dad, James Sr., worked at the IBM plant. Fallon attended Catholic school
(St. Mary of the Snow—not a joke) and was popular and clearly talented.
He learned guitar quickly and demonstrated an early facility for voices
and impressions.

His mother had heard Jimmy do killer knockoffs of enough celebrities to know that when the Bananas Comedy Club down the river in
Poughkeepsie announced it was holding an impressions contest she had
a potential winner in the family. Fallon got inspiration from a high school
graduation gift of a troll doll. He put together a routine based on celebrity
endorsers of troll dolls—and he killed. He won the contest, of course,
and jumped right into a stand-up career, often accompanying himself on
guitar, even as he was starting college.

Fallon started out majoring in computer science at the College of Saint
Rose, a onetime girls' school in Albany, and barely stayed above water in
his grades, eventually abandoning the computer stuff for communications. That he could fake his way through while pursuing his comedy.
Mostly Fallon was known in college for his obsessive viewing of *SNL*. No

one who knew him doubted he would chase the dream of making the cast of the show that had all but defined his life.

Fallon was good enough in his stand-up by twenty-one that he secured an agent, got bookings, and eventually dropped out of college. He made his way to LA and, in the Conan pattern, took improv classes with the Groundlings. Only a year later he won an audition at one of the showcases that Lorne Michaels held for potential new talent for *SNL*. Fallon did some of his impressions, including a dynamite Jerry Seinfeld, but he didn't make the cut. Grievously disappointed, he at least heard later that Lorne had kind of liked him and might take a second look when Jimmy got some of the green off him.

He worked his way back into an invitation to another showcase the following year. Now only twenty-three, not quite as tall as he seemed because of his gawky posture, but puckishly handsome, with the look of a choirboy who'd been sneaking sips of the altar wine, Fallon was convinced he was ready. Before the audition, one of the advance men, talking to all those trying out, offered some advice: Don't look for Lorne in the audience. If you see him he won't be laughing, and you may get thrown. It won't mean he doesn't like you; it's just that he *never* laughs.

Fallon had no more than ten minutes to change his life. He came prepared; he even had some of his old troll material. But he couldn't help checking out the audience, looking for Lorne. Fallon spotted him easily, sitting quietly in the dark a few rows back. Then Jimmy hit him with his Adam Sandler impression. It was undeniable: Lorne Michaels was laughing.

On the show Fallon scored early with his versatility and his infectious likeability. In Fallon's first season, 1998–1999, *SNL* was entering one of its periodic upswings. Will Ferrell was emerging as a star; the cast also included Darrell Hammond, Tracy Morgan, Molly Shannon, Maya Rudolph, and Colin Quinn. Fallon broke out almost immediately, moving from feature player to regular cast member in one season, with characters like Jarret, the stoner with his own Internet show; Sully, the wiseass Boston high schooler who constantly makes out with Denise (Rachel Dratch) but mostly is in love with "No-mah" on the "Sawks"; and perhaps most memorably, a perpetually pissed-off, dead-on Barry Gibb, who hosted his own irrationally enraged talk show with his brother Robin (played with equally devastating accuracy by Justin Timberlake).

By his second year Fallon was among the busiest members of the cast, and was getting noticed—and not only by Lorne. One on of their trips to the show, Rick Ludwin and Nick Bernstein, always on the lookout for potential future late-night hosts, began to see real possibilities in Fallon. He was clearly a big young talent, immensely prepossessing. When Ludwin got into a conversation with Lorne about potential hosts for the "Weekend Update" segment to replace the departing Quinn, Ludwin recommended Fallon. Michaels, who was going to be in sole charge of this choice no matter what any late-night executive suggested, had been kicking around a notion of inserting the show's head writer, Tina Fey, in that role. Now he saw intriguing potential in a male-female coanchor team, something the show had not had (under Lorne) since Jane Curtin matched up first with Dan Aykroyd, then with Bill Murray, in the late 1970s.

The following season, the team of Fey and Fallon became the hottest act on television. Writers reached for comparisons: Hepburn and Tracy, because she was so smart and he so everyman likeable; Nichols and May, because they were both so spontaneously funny; Astaire and Rogers, because "she gave him sex and he gave her class." Michaels himself suggested the last one, though only the sex part seemed apt. Fallon provided more sass than class; he came across as kind of the cute-and-I-know-it bad boy of the act. What mostly worked was that the jokes—one part smart satire, one part ribaldry—had real bite. "After experiencing chest pains Monday, Vice President Dick Cheney was rushed to George Washington Medical Center," Tina intoned one week in her mock-serious newsbabe voice. "When asked how Cheney's angina would affect the administration, President Bush confidently told reporters, 'Boys don't have anginas!' "

Jimmy could occasionally push the limits: "Sesame Street Workshop announced this week they are laying off sixty workers. News of the firings was brought to employees by the letters F and U."

The team hit all the magazine covers; they pushed SNL back into the national conversation. Jimmy hosted the MTV awards; he was named one of People magazine's fifty most beautiful people; he started getting movie offers. Many other SNL grads had followed the latter path, of course—everyone from Chevy Chase to Adam Sandler (and eventually Tina, as well). But Fallon's decision to try films played, for some reason, as presumptuous arrogance to many of the growing legion of his detractors. It was too soon for Fallon to run off to Hollywood, the argument went. What made him think he was a movie star?

None of that quibbling would have mattered if the movies were hits. Instead Fallon picked losers like *Taxi*, a misbegotten comedy with Queen Latifah. *Fever Pitch*, about an obsessive Boston fan, was a reasonable success—it might have helped that he had established credibility as a Red Sox fan thanks to Sully—but overall, Fallon's film career was going nowhere.

That did nothing to dissuade Lorne Michaels, who, in pondering possible replacements for Conan, never had another thought after Jimmy, whom he saw as having "a natural appeal for the audience." That and his real comedy chops would see him through. Lorne backed Fallon with the best producer at his disposal. Mike Shoemaker was one of Lorne's top lieutenants at *SNL*, who had run the "Weekend Update" segment when Fallon was there.

Lorne's idea was to go back to *Late Night*'s roots—an experimental comedy show for a different generation. The target would be the college crowd that had anointed first Letterman and then Conan. Now, of course, because that group had infinitely more diversions for its time, most of them tech based, a new young host would have to be adaptable to the tech world. Even with his truncated computer science background, Fallon filled that bill as well as anybody in comedy at the moment.

Michaels still believed that what worked on late-night talk shows was a host people could identify with and like. "The more time you fill on television, the more and more of you comes out," Michaels said. "These jobs define overexposure." He had total confidence that he had a new team that would step in smoothly to *Late Night*—far more so than had been the case with the installation of Conan sixteen years earlier.

"That," Lorne recalled, "was a difficult birth."

In early December, Jeff Zucker gathered his West Coast entertainment chiefs, Ben Silverman and Marc Graboff, to announce some important news: Jay Leno had agreed, in principle, to stay with NBC and move to a new show, airing five nights a week at ten p.m.

Both men were flabbergasted; neither had played a direct role in NBC's effort to retain Leno because Zucker had taken full hands-on responsibility. Silverman, who had been heavily preoccupied with fending off attacks from other quarters of Hollywood and the press for NBC's latest roster of prime-time misses, had tried to build a relationship with Jay, but he had never really penetrated Jay's self-protective shell. Graboff was widely liked but mainly restricted himself to the business side, which kept him from confronting many personnel and talent issues.

Zucker took obvious pleasure in the announcement, and Graboff could see why. A move like this would accomplish several goals at once. It would take Jay off the market, while at the same time protecting Conan and *The Tonight Show*. It also had the potential to solve a few problems for Silverman and his development team. A weeknight strip of five editions of Jay at ten would effectively refashion NBC in the Fox model, needing only to fill the eight-to-ten p.m. hours with other entertainment programming. With five fewer hours a week for NBC Entertainment to supply, the cost savings would surely be significant. It sounded to Graboff like a very interesting play.

Both Silverman and Graboff immediately wanted to know, however, what this would mean for Conan. As the three men discussed it, they agreed that he surely would not be thrilled with this development. Graboff asked Zucker who was going to break the news to Conan, and Zucker immediately acknowledged it was his responsibility and promised to do it—but first they needed to get Jay signed.

With Zucker having already secured Jay's verbal agreement to a new deal for ten p.m., Graboff approached Ken Ziffren with a simple enough proposal—an extension for Jay, with more money because he would now be in prime time.

Ziffren responded with a request like none other Graboff had ever heard in more than twenty years in the business. He asked for a four-year pay-*and*-play contract. Everybody in Hollywood knew what a pay-*or*-play deal meant: The performer was paid in full for his two-year or four-year or whatever commitment, even if he was removed from the job at an earlier date. When shows got canceled, stars and writers with pay-or-play deals got their checks for the amounts negotiated at the start, and they couldn't sue for damages, claiming their career had been ruined; if a network chose to, it could also bench the performer for the life of the deal. If they decreed the star would sit at home for eighteen months, he would sit at home for eighteen months.

What Ziffren wanted for Leno was substantially different. Pay *and* play meant that for the agreed-upon time the network guaranteed both to pay the negotiated salary *and* to keep the star's show on the air. And if the contract were to be breached in that time, the performer had the right to sue, claiming damage to his career. In addition, a breach would mean instantaneous freedom for the star: no being sent to the beach.

Clearly the last element had been on Jay's mind. He wanted no possibility that NBC could keep him off television again.

Graboff blanched at both the pay-and-play notion and, especially, its four-year duration. That provision, fortunately, he was able to negotiate down to only the first two years of the four-year deal; after that, specific ratings considerations were put in place that would determine whether NBC could cancel the show. The message Graboff took away with him, which he assumed came indirectly from Jay, was that this new show might take time to build and that NBC needed to agree to leave it alone, without getting worked up about things like "making the quarter."

But after accepting the cut-down to two years, there would be no further concessions coming from Jay's side. NBC had to accede to his terms or watch Jay Leno disappear. Graboff, faced with a new, unrecognizable animal, wanted all the official clearance he could get. He requested that he be given assurance, in writing, from NBC's general counsel—as well as from Jeff Zucker himself—that the pay-and-play arrangement with Jay Leno, while unprecedented, had been vetted and approved. Graboff printed out the e-mail acknowledgements from the general counsel and Zucker—who in his message signed off on how unusual the deal truly was, but described the decision to do it as "the price of admission"—and stuck them in the files with the contracts.

On December 8, 2008, Conan O'Brien took his little journey past the holiday tableaux outside in Rockefeller Plaza and made his way to the elevator bank up to his offices. It was a Monday, which meant the writers would have some fresh ideas from the weekend. Conan was especially looking forward to an unbilled walk-on: Stephen Colbert had agreed to drop in and do a "Year 2000" bit with him at the desk. Otherwise it looked like another day to work on stretching the monologue out a bit, maybe kick around some other ideas for *The Tonight Show* with Jeff Ross, head writer Mike Sweeney, and the rest of the writing staff.

Conan and Ross had heard that Rick Ludwin was coming to town, maybe something related to *Saturday Night Live*, which Ludwin always attended when he was in New York.

In fact, Ludwin was scheduled to arrive later in the day to meet with Zucker, but the issue had nothing to do with the *SNL* of two nights previous. The two of them were going down to visit with Conan and break the news: Jay had accepted NBC's offer of a five-night-a-week show at ten p.m.

The two executives knew the conversation had the potential to be long, or tense, or maybe contentious. In essence space had been cleared for Jay to move ahead of Conan again. NBC was building Jay a beachfront house right between Conan's and the shoreline. Certainly they expected Conan to be more than a little surprised—he had not heard anything about this proposal. For all those reasons, and just good business judgment in how to break possibly bad news to a performer, Zucker had resolved to wait until the taping of that day's show had been completed and Conan had made it back from the stage to his office.

Out on the West Coast, meanwhile, Jay Leno had some business of his own to conduct. His deal now set, Jay felt an obligation of professional correctness. At around midday in LA, during a break from the usual joke rundown, Jay first called Peter Chernin at Fox, thanking him for his generous interest but letting him know he was staying at NBC, because the network was handing him the ten p.m. weeknight slot. Chernin, generally taciturn about all business matters, simply thanked Jay for the call.

Then Jay called Bob Iger at Disney. Clearly the matter had gone farther with Disney and ABC, and Jay had spent a lot of time laying the groundwork with Jimmy Kimmel for a possible tag-team effort. So with Iger he was more expansive, describing how deeply he had appreciated the interest, how impressed he was with ABC's proposal, and how close he came to accepting. But in the end, NBC had come up with something that he felt he could not turn down: ten p.m. each weeknight.

Iger took the news equably; in truth, he wasn't all that disappointed. Switching networks was always a crapshoot. Maybe Jay wouldn't have provided a surefire windfall, and at least he didn't have to face an immediate confrontation with the ABC news division over *Nightline*.

By now it was getting on toward evening in the east, and Conan was backstage ready to go on. He had no clue about Jay's calls, or the ones that followed. Iger was making a few, to notify some of the people who had been with him in the Leno hunt that it was over. These calls, naturally, set in motion talk around the ABC headquarters, and the news of NBC's bold move quickly seemed too delicious to withhold.

Around six p.m., Cory Shields, the top corporate communications executive for NBC executive, got a call from *The New York Times*: They had the information about Jay Leno and ten o'clock.

When Zucker heard the news had leaked, he realized he had to act fast. If Conan happened to read about Jay's getting ten p.m. on the *Times's* Web site before Zucker had a chance to break the news to him, it could become a dreaded "This is how I find out?" moment. Zucker and Ludwin made their way down to Conan's offices to meet him directly after the show.

In California Rick Rosen, Conan's principal agent, sat behind the wheel of his car, cruising south on 101 back from Santa Barbara to LA. He had spent the morning checking out a possible new home. No business matters pressed; the drive was lovely. When his cell phone rang he picked up the call, which was from Kevin Reilly, now ensconced as the entertainment chief at Fox. Reilly, of course, had heard the news from Chernin.

"Is this true about Jay and Conan?" Reilly asked.

"Is what true?" Rick said, feeling a little tremble at the question.

"I hear they're gonna move Jay to ten o'clock."

In New York, as soon as he left the stage, Conan heard Zucker and Ludwin were coming down to Jeff Ross's office and wanted him to stop by for a chat. No real worries there; could be about anything. Conan arrived and splayed himself out on Ross's couch, as he normally did. The two NBC executives were soon escorted in. Zucker greeted both men cheerfully and got right to the point.

"I've figured out a way to keep Jay," he said, with just a little note of triumph in his voice. "At ten o'clock."

Conan and Ross glanced at each other, a bit unsure what this meant. Finally Ross spoke.

"So . . . ten o'clock? You don't mean, like, every night?"

Zucker assured them that was the plan. Ross could not restrain his surprise. "He's going to be on five nights a week at ten?"

"Look," Zucker said. "This is good for you guys, because he was going to go someplace else."

Conan, as he often did at big moments, contained himself, letting Ross speak for both of them. When they had discussed it between themselves previously, he and Ross had never conceded the point that Jay was certain to land somewhere else. It always seemed to them that Jay's hints of leaving were merely leverage to force NBC to come across with something that might finally make him happy. Ross had still leaned toward Jay's stepping away from television altogether, because if he did defect and then fail at ABC, it would be a notably bad end to his career. Conan likewise couldn't imagine Jay's making that ultimate call to leave NBC, given his borderline obsessive-compulsive attachment to the routines of his work schedule. When they had batted it around previously, Conan had always told Ross that, if Jay really wanted to go to ABC, let him. If Jay wanted to end his legacy by jumping to another network and taking on *The Tonight Show*, he should go right ahead. Game on.

The two men pressed Zucker for details on how long this arrangement would be in place. Zucker glossed over the question without offering specifics, but he did allude to its not necessarily being long term—two years, maybe.

In full spin cycle Zucker stressed, emphasized, underscored that Conan was still getting *The Tonight Show*, at 11:35 each weeknight; nothing in the least would change for him.

Although Zucker didn't say it, he believed that just about everyone, including Conan's agents at Endeavor, preferred this outcome to that three-headed competitive monster, with Letterman factored in. It made no real sense to him to go into that now, though. He had always steered clear of any Dave vs. Jay comparisons in front of Conan and his team, having long since picked up from Conan and his staff what Jeff perceived as a visceral dislike of Leno. They all more or less dismissed him as a hack. It bothered and disappointed Zucker that at the same time they openly celebrated and embraced David Letterman, they denigrated NBC's guy. Zucker put it down to their artistic, higher-brow, New York–centric point of view; but to him it merely meant that they never understood or appreciated Jay Leno's broad appeal. Still, he expected Conan and his people to be better team players than that. You're on the team, you shouldn't be revering the other guy and disrespecting your own guy.

The meeting broke up quickly, with Conan saying little and revealing even less.

After Zucker and Ludwin left, the somewhat dazed Ross and Conan took stock. Ross couldn't help but think back to a phone conversation he had had with Fox's Gail Berman years earlier when Conan had turned down their offer, preferring the long-range chase of *The Tonight Show.*

"Remember I said this to you," Gail had told Ross. "You're never gonna get *The Tonight Show.*" At the time Ross had been convinced he was dealing with honorable people and promises would be kept. Who could have foreseen this? Jay at ten? What did it mean, really?

As for Conan, he instantly had a bad feeling. After sixteen years of following Jay Leno, after finally being released into the free air of 11:35, Conan had been hit with the news that NBC was reviving the old lineup order. This was more like a time shift than a programming change; certainly it wasn't a commitment to a new star over the old. It amounted to going from daylight savings time back to eastern standard time—move the clocks back an hour. For Conan, the decision reeked of NBC's apparent ongoing strategy, which was like a car with headlights that shone only three inches in front of it, leaving the driver always reacting only to anything appearing a few feet ahead—look out, jerk the wheel this way or that. Never would they try a brighter light, shine it farther down the road, scan the horizon for what's really ahead.

For almost two hours Conan, Ross, Mike Sweeney, and some of the other writers sat around Ross's office parsing the decision out, trying to discern what it really meant for them, until Conan's assistant buzzed with some news: Jay Leno was on the line.

Jay did everything he could to be gracious, saying all the right things. "Are you all right with this, Conan?" he asked. "Is this good for you?"

Conan returned the graciousness; he knew it was the right thing to do. Jay ended the call by saying he was sure they'd be seeing each other down the road.

Even after he put down the phone, Conan could not get past the uneasiness he was feeling. But what were his options? Quit and go to ABC himself? Or Fox? On what basis? He had a contract, and NBC had not taken *The Tonight Show* away from him.

That realization calmed him a bit, and he told himself that something had changed for NBC, but nothing had substantially changed for him. Finally he asked Jeff Ross, "In this scenario, am I still hosting that show that Johnny Carson had that I watched with my father in my living room in Brookline, Massachusetts?"

"Yes, you are," Ross said, looking for the right message.

"Then, I'm good," Conan replied.

In the remaining weeks before he closed shop on his *Late Night* show, O'Brien offered several explanations of his feelings about how it all went down with Jay and the whole ten o'clock plan. Mostly, he was at pains to say how much he preferred this outcome, with Jay not driven from the home he loved.

"I had always hoped that something could be worked out where Jay could stay, because it's just a better scenario for all of us—just on a human level. On a human level I'm not comfortable with people being unhappy. It's not in my makeup." Conan never wanted to "walk into some restaurant and have to avoid anybody."

He said that he liked Jay and that Jay was doing "a great job." It was important, he said, that no matter what happened, he could always "feel like I didn't say anything or do anything to get *The Tonight Show* that I couldn't happily tell anybody about. And Jay knows that; I've always had great rapport with Jay."

If the ten o'clock solution still left him with an uneasy feeling, he wasn't expressing it publicly. "Of all the alternatives in the universe, this one does honestly work the best for me," Conan said. "I've known Jay for a long time, and we've been friends. I was not going to be comfortable in some Hatfields-McCoys situation. I don't think Jay would be comfortable in that situation. So life is short and I'm getting to host *The Tonight Show,* and the fact that Jay Leno and I can still be friends is the best resolution for me."

O'Brien acknowledged the competitive environment would be different, but that was OK too. "I think a lot of it is up to me. If I do a good, funny, and fresh *Tonight Show* every night at 11:35, I think that's going to be successful, and I think it's going to be irrelevant what everybody else is doing."

That was not a prediction, however. "Anyone who sits back and tells you exactly how this is going to play out is crazy."

On February 20, Conan O'Brien said farewell to *Late Night* after sixteen years and 2,725 shows.

The emotion was all-consuming. Andy Richter returned to a warm embrace from the fans—and the host. Will Ferrell, who had been probably the signature guest on the show, the ideal match of emerging talent with growing audience, did one final turn by stripping down to outrageous leprechaun undies.

Conan played the last of several weeks of highlight clips, including probably the archetypal taped remote of the Conan era, when the host covered—and then played in—a game of old-time baseball, circa 1864. He called it his favorite piece of all time.

In the best anarchic spirit of the show, Conan had a work crew come in and rip a section of the set's backdrop apart, to hand out tiny pieces to members of the final studio audience. Later his brother Neal walked off with the Conan half-moon logo from the set. His dad was there, as was his mom, hobbling with a cane. Liza waited in the hall outside with Missy, Jeff Ross's wife, and several of the other staff's family members. Tears flowed.

On the air Conan fought them. In the closing moments, he summoned up thanks for everyone from Bob Wright to Lorne Michaels, whom Conan credited with rolling the dice on one of "the most ridiculous chances in the history of the medium."

Conan said, "Lorne Michaels single-handedly made my career in television. I don't know what I did. I must have saved his life at some point. He certainly saved mine."

Then it was time for Jay:

"Jay Leno from day one has called me constantly and offered his support. Every night at the end of *The Tonight Show*, Jay Leno says, 'Stay tuned for Conan O'Brien,' and he has done that since 1993. *The Tonight Show* under Jay Leno has been a powerhouse. His success turned into success for us. I owe that man a great deal. I'm thrilled that we get to be friends for all of our time in television and that he will continue to be my lead-in, and I'm thrilled that we are on the same network."

But O'Brien brought out the unreserved encomiums for a different late-night host:

"David Letterman invented this *Late Night* show, and he is one of the most brilliant broadcasters of the last century—and certainly this century and for all time. I have a terrific amount of respect for him and what he did. He set the bar absurdly high for everyone in my generation who does this. Living in his shadow has been a burden and an inspiration for me for years, and I think we need to acknowledge that it all started with David Letterman."

Conan saved the last heartfelt thanks for his forever producer and friend Jeff Ross, "the man who gets the show on every night."

Struggling with his emotion to the end, Conan closed with a message, to his fans and anyone else who wanted to know what to expect from a Conan O'Brien *Tonight* show:

"There are people that have hosted these kinds of shows who are better than I am. Nobody has enjoyed it more than I do. It's an incredible, amazing honor to do this show for you people. We're going on to this next gig, and sometimes I read that it's time for Conan to grow up because he's going to eleven thirty." And here he paused for maximum effect.

"I assure you, that's just *not* going to happen. It can't. This is who I am—for better or for worse."

CHAPTER SEVEN

CONAN ROCKS

W hen he finally got to work inside the vast, sparkling new studio created for NBC's *Tonight Show,* just inside the Universal gate off Lankershim Boulevard, where the studio had resided for the eighty-five years since Carl Laemmle settled his fledgling film company there, Conan O'Brien could feel his psyche shift down into a familiar gear.

After weeks of pushing, straining, and grinding his way through meet-and-greet sessions with affiliates from Cleveland to Oklahoma City, through rounds of interviews with the supportive but sometimes skeptical press, through the slog of buying a home, moving the staff, relocating his family, nesting in a new office, Conan was finally back to what he called "the organizing principle" of his and his staff's lives, "the magnet that organizes all the particles": making a funny show.

The weeks between the end of February and mid-May of 2009 had represented the longest period he had been off TV in the last third of his life. And yet he had never worked harder. People would see him and say, "Hey, so you've had a nice break." And he would respond, "You have no idea." Despite all the logistical heavy lifting, Conan had not slackened his creative efforts in the intervening weeks, throwing himself into preparing comedy pieces for the first weeks of the new show. Again taking inspiration from David Letterman, who charged out of the gate in his remade 11:35 CBS show with a series of tightly edited taped segments that had electrified late night and compelled the nation to tune in, Conan was banking a similar store of taped bits. He was extravagantly proud of them and confident they would help create the opening buzz the new show needed.

But best of all, in mid-May Conan, Jeff Ross, Mike Sweeney, and all the guys got down to doing what they loved best: late-night shows in front of regular people. To break in the studio—the sound, the lighting, the camera angles—Ross wanted to produce a series of test shows. The first couple had a few ragged moments, but that was to be expected. It didn't matter to Conan, who was invigorated by them. It felt so good to be back. The new space, open, ornately decorated—even including a little art deco mural rimming the top of the stage design, harkening back to 30 Rock's lobby—was much more expansive than good old 6A in 30 Rock. "Elegant" was how Conan summed it up, though he added that he was sure he would have no trouble being "a jackass in an elegant space." When he stepped out onto the new stage for the first test show, it came on him like a rush: *Oh yeah, this is what we really do.*

More than anything else, Conan expected the lavish new lighting to shock people. He'd been told often enough by fans how much better he looked in person and had concluded that that was because they had only seen him performing in a shoe box with a light on him from about two feet away.

The experience of coast-to-coast relocation did have one big advantage, Conan decided. Almost nothing really captured people's imagination anymore, but somehow this pasty Irishman pulling up stakes in New York and having a go in sunny LA struck a nerve. Everywhere that Conan had been, the talk was all about his moving to California—what would that be like? Conan pictured Osama bin Laden in a cave somewhere saying, "I wonder how it will be for Conan in LA. It'll be different. We'll have to see."

On the other hand, the massive buildup did have its downside. Conan had the impression that some people expected to see him "jump the Snake River Canyon" on his first night, instead of what they would actually get: "a guy making a few adjustments in a better-lit space."

The move of Jay Leno to ten had certainly altered some of the equations and expectations. What had begun as Conan vs. Dave was now Jay-into-Conan vs. Dave. "There's a period of realignment now," Conan explained. "These things aren't decided in a night or a week. It's a marathon. We're going to bring some people with us and we're going to have to find some new people, and it's not going to happen right away. But I'm interested in getting to that part. Let's get to that part."

Not that the present didn't offer some stop-the-heart moments, like seeing crates rolling by to be installed in the new studio or office building, all reading on the side: "The Tonight Show with Conan O'Brien."

Conan pulled back to remind himself, "It's unbelievable that I got here. It's a Catholic word, but sometimes it's a sin not to acknowledge, sometimes, for just a minute: *Hey, you got this far.*"

But of course, the dark nights could provide their own distractions. Conan also acknowledged spending his share of time wide awake at three in the morning, picturing Martin Sheen in the movie *Apocalypse Now*. In those moments, Conan said, he stared up at the ceiling fan in his bedroom, "thinking about my trip upriver—and we all know how that worked out!"

Team Conan had its own share of concerns, not about how Conan would perform on *Tonight*—they all believed in him without reservation—but about how committed NBC really was to him. The move of Jay Leno to ten p.m. had stunned Rick Rosen and the rest of the Conan support group, and set them to thinking through all the implications of that decision.

Rosen had quickly called Ari Emanuel and Gavin Polone to discuss the issue. Ari told Rick he thought NBC was fucking Conan over, pure and simple. Gavin believed it was partly the result of Conan's always agreeing, "OK, I'll play ball"—a pattern he had long established with his employer: *OK, I won't take the Fox offer because I want to chase* The Tonight Show. *OK, I'll hang around for five more years and take way less money even when they do give me* The Tonight Show. Now, Polone concluded, Conan was swallowing the network's latest bow to Leno because it was all still worth it to host *The Tonight Show*.

NBC continued to insist that the show Jay would be doing had no chance to affect Conan's show, because it would be so different. Polone and the others didn't buy this disingenuous portrait of Leno, how he would steer clear of conflict with Conan over guests or content.

Conan did worry about it anyway despite the network's assurances. Conan told Polone he suspected NBC might still try to pay him off the $45 million and give the show back to Jay. Polone was accustomed to glimpses of Conan's darker side, when he would get down and start worrying about things that weren't really about to happen. Polone simply dismissed the payoff idea as absurd. How could anybody think of doing that? Only a complete idiot would think of doing that.

Rosen, for one, didn't write off NBC's potential for possessing an idiot factor. When he pressed Zucker on the payoff issue, Zucker flicked away the notion. "It's never going to happen," he told Rosen. The people talking about it were just "those Hollywood people." Zucker repeated, "It's never going to happen to you guys. There's nothing to worry about."

Conan did his best to embrace the idea that ultimately this Jay stuff didn't matter. What mattered was hosting *The Tonight Show*. His representatives would assure him: of course, that was true. But among themselves, with Conan out of earshot, they all agreed: Jay at ten was bad, and it was going to stay bad. Not one of them could offer a single positive note about NBC's plan—other than that Jay wouldn't be at ABC at 11:35, of course. Sure, it might be better to be in the same boat with Jay, rather than on opposing warships; but it would be better still if Jay sailed away entirely.

For Jeff Ross, the situation was much more complicated. He had to get a show—and his guy—ready to knock America dead, so it did no good to waste time stewing over getting leap-frogged by Leno.

He had made his own discomfort plain to his pal Zucker and then moved on. For the sake of the show, and Conan, Ross allowed himself a few sips of the Kool-Aid.

Maybe it would *mean a broader audience for Conan,* Ross told himself. *Who the fuck knows?*

On May 12, less than a month before Conan's premiere, and only a week before Conan's trip to New York for the comedy showcase for the advertisers, Dick Ebersol, in LA for some other business, dropped by the new *Tonight* studio. The ostensible reason for the meeting was to nail down ideas for Conan's participation in NBC's coverage of the Winter Olympics from Vancouver, set for February 2010. Ebersol was more than just the executive in charge of the Olympic telecasts—he would personally produce every hour of prime time for the games. Both Conan and Jeff Ross were enthusiastic about the additional exposure Conan was sure to get during those hugely watched events.

But Ebersol had another message he wanted to convey, one he had told Jeff Zucker he was determined to get across to Conan. Since his lunch with Jeff Ross in April 2008, Ebersol had only grown more worried about whether Conan & Co. grasped the nuances of difference between shows at 11:35 and 12:35. Ebersol became especially worried after he watched Conan's farewell show on *Late Night* in February and heard him promise, straight out, in his closing address to his fans—one that, to Ebersol, seemed to ring of defiance—that he didn't care what people suggested, he wasn't about to change.

A conversation about Olympics exposure would serve as a convenient pretext for Ebersol to offer his theories of what made for late-night success or failure directly to Conan.

Ebersol had fond feelings toward Conan—almost everyone at NBC did, of course. But Dick's affection touched another level. When Ebersol and his wife, the actress Susan Saint James, had suffered the shattering tragedy of losing their young son Teddy in a private plane crash—one that had almost killed Dick as well—Conan had handwritten a note to the couple that they remembered as extraordinarily moving. So Ebersol put Conan, as a person, at the highest level.

But this was business, and from a television executive's perspective he saw Conan as possibly naive, or maybe just too insulated on one of those little islands that seemed to spring up and form spontaneously around every late-night star. Whatever it was, Ebersol meant to break through with some down-to-earth business-reality talk.

After touring the *Tonight* set, Ebersol, favorably impressed, repaired to Jeff Ross's still unfinished new quarters upstairs in the adjacent office building, where he sat down with Ross and Conan. Ebersol first laid out some suggestions for how they could team up in Vancouver. The first week of the games Conan would not be preempted by a late-night Olympics show, so he would get a week of regular shows with skaters and skiers providing likely the biggest lead-ins of his life. Ebersol promised to deliver some Olympics guests for the shows—and with those tie-ins NBC would be able to charge a premium to advertisers for Olympics-themed programming.

For the second week, with a late-night Olympics program taking over for *The Tonight Show*, Ebersol had been mulling a plan for a two- or three-minute Conan feature each night, something that would capture Conan's take on the big news from the games the day before. They would find a special sponsor and sell it separately. Ebersol would insert the bit somewhere within the first ninety minutes of each night's coverage.

The proposal sounded great to O'Brien and Ross, and Conan had every confidence he could pull something like that off.

The preliminaries out of the way, Ebersol moved on to the central purpose of his visit. "I want you guys to know, I'm really here to say, one more time, how important it is to broaden out the comedy and think of those Midwest markets."

Then Ebersol launched again into the story of his 1975 visit with Lorne Michaels to the undershirted Johnny Carson in his Burbank lair, and Johnny's advice about slotting the best comedy at the top of the show—and playing well in Topeka and Des Moines.

Ebersol believed he detected that both men were well aware of the Carson anecdote, so he presumed Ross had filled Conan in on it.

The conversation remained entirely collegial, but Conan made much the same point he had made on the air on his farewell *Late Night* show. He had made up his mind to do the things he had always done, to be himself.

"I'm not telling you not to be Conan O'Brien," Ebersol said. "I'm suggesting things to change at the top of the show."

None of this advice struck either O'Brien or Ross as either unusual or new. Broaden your appeal? Conan's internal reaction was the same as it had always been: *OK, good; thanks for that.* It didn't seem that Ebersol was delivering anything like actionable notes. It reminded Conan of typical network chitchat. The meeting didn't last more than fifteen minutes. As it broke up they all promised to talk more about the Olympics idea when Dick's plans were further down the road.

After he left, Conan and Ross thought little of the meeting in terms of what it meant for *Tonight*, other than that Ebersol, whom they both basically liked, came across as someone else professing to know more about their show than they did—and that he was awfully full of himself.

Ebersol, for his part, got into his car and drove off the lot, a riffle of foreboding running through his stomach.

At ABC, Jimmy Kimmel had more than a little natural curiosity about how Conan O'Brien would fare—and some reason to regret what might have been.

If there really had been a might have been, that is.

What Kimmel and a number of executives both inside and outside ABC knew was that back in January, a short time after the announcement that Leno was moving to ten, there had been a frisson of activity surrounding ABC's late night—activity that surely would have involved Jimmy. Maybe it was just the network's entertainment division spinning out potential alternatives, having missed out on Leno, as ABC executives later claimed. But executives conversant with ABC's late-night plans concluded that the network was working on a plan to go after Conan on NBC by moving Jimmy to 11:35. Of course, none of that had been run by ABC's news division, which would have risen up in righteous anger at another assault on *Nightline*.

The executives aware of ABC's planning said that Kimmel and his agent, James Dixon, had had quiet discussions and meetings with ABC executives, and several network insiders presumed that an offer to move Kimmel up to 11:35 was imminent. By that point ABC had some results from the extensive late-night research it had commissioned. One finding was that a Conan O'Brien *Tonight Show* would likely be vulnerable to a show on a competing network with another young host. At that point ABC was considering which of three potential moves to take advantage of this situation made most sense: to have Kimmel go for broke and jump ahead of Conan in the 11:35 slot by months, probably starting as early as March; to sneak ahead of him just by a week or so in May, in order to steal some of his thunder; or, alternately, to hold off until October, when, if the research estimates proved out, Conan would be struggling.

"ABC can deny whatever they want," said a longtime network executive connected to the discussions about Kimmel, "but they met with Kimmel and he really thought he was going to 11:35."

When word of the possible move for Kimmel leaked, ABC did deny it. Anne Sweeney, the network's chief executive, wrote the notion off as too unlikely to qualify even as far-fetched—words that comforted the news division.

The maneuvering was complicated by the dysfunctional chain of command at the network. Most staff members (and indeed much of the rest of Hollywood) knew that the entertainment division boss, Steve McPherson, technically reported to Sweeney, but in practice the two didn't get along at all and barely spoke to one another. "At ABC, there's Bob Iger, Anne Sweeney, and Steve McPherson," said one long-serving ABC employee, explaining the network hierarchy. "Anne and Steve hate each other. Bob gets along with both of them."

One hint of ABC's possible late-night intentions was revealed when Iger, the Disney chairman, led a little hunting foray into the territory of the E! cable channel in pursuit of that network's late-night host and signature star, Chelsea Handler. That approach may have been totally serious, or merely a little fun for Iger. The fun theory held that Iger might simply have been messing with—or perhaps doing a favor for—one of his oldest Hollywood cronies, Ted Harbert, a former ABC and NBC Entertainment executive, now the head of the E! channel (and, not coincidentally, the man in Chelsea Handler's life at that point). What was indisputable was that ABC executives did meet, rather publicly, with Handler at the Beverly Hills Polo Lounge.

Handler, blond, toned, and thirty-five, from Livingston, New Jersey, had made a splash—and a name—with a series of best-selling books about her outrageous (in a funny way) drinking and sex habits. She became immensely important to E! (and Harbert) because her show, *Chelsea Lately*, was scoring with an audience of women between the ages of eighteen and thirty-four, a demographic that was not being reached in as big numbers by any of the guys in late night.

After the meeting between ABC and Handler and her agents, she was able to land a new, more lucrative contract at E!. Handler later alluded to her dealings with ABC when she acknowledged in a Web interview with CBS's Katie Couric that she had, in fact, been approached for a network job, but admitted she didn't think she was "ready to graduate to that particular point." For one thing, Handler said she didn't think she would be able to say the things on network television that she routinely got away with on cable. (Her show chewed up low-rung celebrities.) For another, she wanted to be able to express views that were "more pointed" than "somebody like Jay Leno, who has to be nice to everybody."

The job Handler's backers reported ABC had pitched to her was as follow-up act to an upgraded Kimmel, in an 11:35 to 12:35 pairing. But there may, in fact, have been no real spot for her at ABC. One proposal for Kimmel that ABC executives had discussed internally would have re-created the original format of *The Tonight Show* at ninety minutes. In the shrinking economy of late night, a ninety-minute show could have real appeal. The costs would be negligibly higher than an hour show, but the extra half hour would easily cover that and more with the additional commercial time it could sell. Jettisoning *Nightline* would also have wiped out the high cost of that show.

But at the same time these machinations were roiling behind the scenes at ABC Entertainment, *Nightline* was quietly restoring itself to competitive health at 11:35. With a new format that worked more as a newsmagazine than as an interview show, *Nightline* had grabbed a core audience that, while not overpowering, was sizable enough to defy expectations that the show was sliding toward cancelation.

ABC often hawked ratings numbers that showed *Nightline* approaching or even beating the late-night entertainment shows on NBC and CBS. But the network always compared its half-hour score for *Nightline* to the hour score for Leno and Letterman. Of course, both those shows lost viewers every minute they were on the air because they were running late into the night. In a fairer comparison of the viewership for the first half hour of each show, *Nightline* almost always came in third. Still, because the entertainment shows were clearly fading in ratings, *Nightline* became more viable.

Kimmel, meanwhile, remained a personal favorite of ABC executives, who were more and more convinced of his growing talent. He made a tradition of appearing at every ABC upfront in May, where he would invariably deliver an outstanding (and scathing) monologue. In 2009, on May 18, the same day Jay Leno crashed and burned onstage downtown, Kimmel, up at Lincoln Center, told advertisers, "Everything you hear this week is bullshit. Let's get real here. Let's get Dr. Phil here. These new fall shows? We're going to cancel about 90 percent of them, maybe more. Every year we lie to you, and every year you come back for more. You don't need an upfront; you need therapy." He also took a little shot at the age of the likely fans for NBC's upcoming ten p.m. star, saying that NBC was giving "Jay's viewers exactly what they want: an early-bird special."

In reality ABC could not have been more excited about the upcoming changes at NBC both in late night and at ten p.m. Its research had come back with a strong answer to the question of whether ABC should feel compelled to follow NBC's lead: Don't even think about it. An ABC executive made a prediction: "We know it's going to be bad. It's going to be a disaster. They can say whatever they want about saving money, but they are going to kill their local news and this is not going to last."

As smoothly as all the deal points had gone with Conan's shift to *The Tonight Show*, one thread of his old deal had been left dangling—and on the end of that line was an awfully big fish.

Lorne Michaels had more than discovered Conan O'Brien; he had basically sprinkled magic dust on him and created a star. Part of his reward for that was an ongoing financial stake in *Late Night*. Michaels retained an executive producer credit on *Late Night* that provided him with a weekly fee of about $25,000.

From the start no one disputed there was real value in this arrangement, even though Lorne did not sustain any direct day-to-day role on the show after its initial years. Lorne had put Conan on the air, fought for the show, and protected it as best he could in its rocky early days, influencing its style from its conception. But as he saw it, *Late Night* then became Conan's show, in the same way that the sitcom Lorne had helped create, *30 Rock*, became Tina Fey's show.

Still, as the start of *The Tonight Show* loomed, the question of whether Lorne's financial association would continue lingered for some time unresolved. NBC's position was that some members of the Conan side had sent a message indicating that they were cool to the idea of keeping Lorne on. For their part, Conan's reps swore that they steered clear of any and all financial arrangements between NBC and Michaels, because the network paid the fee; they didn't.

However the process unfolded, the result was that Lorne Michaels received no EP credit on *The Tonight Show* and no weekly fee.

Michaels raised no protest. *The Tonight Show* was going to be in LA, three thousand miles away from New York, where he was already deeply involved with *SNL* and Jimmy Fallon's new 12:35 show. Michaels himself interpreted the decision as Conan simply deciding to leave the nest. Conan had tossed that bouquet of gratitude Lorne's way on the last *Late Night* show, and Michaels had been moved by it.

Lorne never said a word to Conan or Jeff Ross about the change in the arrangement. But Zucker, for one, concluded Michaels was hurt more than he ever would say to have that association with Conan and his show cut off.

He was right: Michaels would never say. Lorne concluded that, even without any contractual arrangement, Conan and Jeff Ross would always know he was on their side—because he was.

When Johnny Carson was counting down the days to his final edition of *The Tonight Show*, a cavalcade of favorite guests dropped by for one last visit with the King. David Letterman had been on the list; Jay Leno had not.

Jay had been determined never to repeat the rancor that accompanied that changeover, when neither Carson in his final show, nor Leno in his first, saw fit to mention the other. As always seemed to happen with Jay, he took all the heat for that snub—and even he later came to agree with that judgment. It had been an unconscionable faux pas, one that took years for him to live down. He had apologized for it, laying the misbegotten decision at the feet of his tyrannical manager, Helen Kushnick, who had all but gotten him fired from the show with that and other scorched-earth personal dealings. (And that, in turn, had always played to some as an especially egregious example of the ritual of blaming the manager or agent. As one of Jay's late-night competitors put it, "If my manager told me to jump off a bridge, I wouldn't jump off a bridge.")

The bitter aftermath of that transition influenced many of Jay's decisions about how to end his own *Tonight* run. The parade of familiar guests in the final weeks was inevitable; but Jay insisted that the finale needed to go down exactly opposite of how it had transpired with Carson. Not only would Jay acknowledge Conan on the last show, he would have him as his final guest.

So on Friday, May 29, 2009, Conan and Jeff Ross left their new studio and the preparations for Conan's premiere the following Monday to make the short drive east on the 134 to Burbank.

Conan had done numerous appearances on *Tonight*, always with strong results. Whenever he was booked, his West Coast fans seemed to make a point to get there. Some of Conan's support group took note of the raucous reaction he would attract sitting up there with Jay and concluded that it made Jay uncomfortable for Conan to bring all that passionate popularity into his house.

On the finale, his 3,775th *Tonight Show* as host, Jay got a huge ovation, which he had to tamp down to leave enough time for the usual joke-intensive monologue. Jay dug from some best hits: Bill Clinton, George

Bush, Michael Jackson, even O.J. Of course, NBC's travails were not ignored. "I'm going off to a safe, secluded spot where no one can find me. Prime time on NBC!"

After a collage of the best of "Jaywalking" segments drew some big laughs, Jay brought out Conan, to another thunderous ovation. Conan looked cool and professional in his dark suit and royal blue shirt—a stark contrast to the gawky kid in blazer over jeans who first visited Leno in 1993. (Jay showed a clip of that visit.)

Conan teased his incipient *Tonight Show* run with a snippet from an upcoming remote segment: Conan in disguise leading a focus group analyzing the prospects of . . . Conan O'Brien.

As he handed off the symbolic baton, Jay declared, "I couldn't be happier" with the selection of his successor. "You were the only choice; you were the perfect choice. You are an absolute gentleman . . ."

Someone in the audience shouted out, "Conan rocks!"

"I agree: Conan rocks," Jay said. "Good luck, my friend."

Conan shook his hand, saying, "Jay, thank you for everything."

At his close Jay offered thank-yous to Debbie Vickers, of course, whom he identified as his executive producer "from day one." (Actually Helen Kushnick had been the original top executive producer for Jay.) He singled out Warren Littlefield, the former NBC Entertainment chief who fought to keep Jay in the chair. He thanked his longtime head writer Joe Medeiros and NBC's top late-night executive, Rick Ludwin, for being steadfast "when we were getting our ass kicked." Jeff Zucker got a mention, too, with thanks for "giving us another opportunity." And then, of course, an affectionate shout-out to Mavis. "I'm leaving this dance with the same girl I came in with," Jay said.

A cold open had worked well in 1993; why not try it again in 2009?

In what dedicated fans surely recognized as a thematic reference to his introduction to American television, Conan O'Brien burst onto the screen in his first moments as *Tonight Show* host on another symbolic journey, this time not through Manhattan, but all the way across the country.

Fast, arresting, funny, and oddly patriotic at the same time, the run from New York to LA included shots of Conan going full tilt everywhere from the Amish country to across the Wrigley Field outfield in mid-inning—all real, no green screen—backed by the pounding and utterly unconnected theme music, "Surrender," by Cheap Trick. The opening carried an electrical charge unlike anything seen on the Jay Leno version of *Tonight*. This show was going to be 100 percent Conan, right off the bat.

The voice of Andy Richter, back as sidekick/announcer—and sounding a little less than fully committed—rose up behind the wailing theme song: "Here's your host, Conan O'Briiii-en!" The first audience, the early LA adapters, already whipped into a frenzy, erupted as Conan strode out, looking leaner, certainly more mature, hewing to the lesson he'd learned from Jack Paar: classic dark suit, light blue shirt, striped tie. As the squeals went on and on, the more mature Conan almost had to give them a little taste, even if he hadn't planned to, even if it wasn't really broad-based and middle American—just a few moves from the string dance.

Tall as he was, Conan looked somewhat dwarfed by the capacious new set. When the camera pulled back to show a glimpse of the adoring fans, the space looked deep and cavernous. The next day Tom Shales in *The Washington Post* would call it a "Circus Maximus," and indeed this frenzied crowd might well have fit in there, rooting on the chariots. After letting them go on a bit too long, Conan finally started the monologue, the first joke about his great timing, coming to California just as it was going bankrupt and being sponsored by the equally bankrupt General Motors. He tossed out a few others, but this was not a night to try a string of hot topical jokes. That wasn't what he and his guys had worked on all these months; that wasn't going to be the signature of the Conan *Tonight Show*. The opening—that had the Conan touch, and he had more.

He introduced another taped segment, clearly one he and the staff saw as a high card they wanted to play right at the start. It would also stamp the new location in which they had landed: Conan took over a tourist tram shuttling around the Universal lot.

Later, most critics would be rapturous, but a few first-night viewers with vested interests would express some reservations about this choice: a taped piece that early? And one that long? And one that didn't quite work for some (such as a contingent of associates from 30 Rock)? And one that was so clearly—maybe too clearly—Lettermanesque: the host exploring the new neighborhood, riffing with regular folks, relying on spontaneous wit and quick tape cuts?

But OK, it was the first night, and not everything had been locked in yet. If Conan's nerve ends seemed a bit jangly to some of his old colleagues in New York, it was understandable.

After the first commercial, when he took his seat behind his new elegantly S-shaped cherry-toned desk, Conan had the obligatory exchange with Andy, now revealed in an unexpected location: standing behind a wooden podium that made him look like an exiled candidate from a presidential debate. But after a comfortable bit of business with the always reliable Andy, Conan would go no further without checking off the next critical item on his to-do list.

"I want to take a second," he said. "I want to acknowledge somebody, a very good friend of mine, a true gentleman, a very gracious man, a man who hosted this show for seventeen years, took good care of the franchise. Ladies and gentlemen, let's all give it up for Mr. Jay Leno!" As the obligatory applause rained down, Conan added, "He's going to come back on the air—in two days, three days maybe, tops!" Then he slipped into the high-pitched Jay voice: "You know, got to get back in there!"

After the laugh, Conan added one more thought: "He's been a very good friend to me. And so I'm looking forward to him being our lead-in once again."

A few moments later Conan brought on his sole guest for the night— Will Ferrell again—and got a huge kick out of Ferrell's apparent disbelief that someone actually went through with it and gave Conan the job.

"Don't get me wrong—I'm pulling for you," Ferrell said. "But this whole thing is a crapshoot at best."

The overnight, unofficial Nielsen numbers attested to just how big a deal *Tonight* remained in the United States. Conan's premiere pulled over 9 million viewers, more than triple David Letterman's audience for the night, and more than anything on television that evening in prime time—on a night in June, no less. He utterly dominated among the younger audience segments, which was exactly what his network wanted him to do. Conan's 3.8 rating among the eighteen to forty-nine audience would have been a hit number for any show in prime time at any time of year. In late night it looked like something from a time machine—a throwback to the 1980s.

But over the course of the premiere week a pattern seemed to emerge. Viewers over the age of fifty, many of them presumably Jay Leno fans, started to check out—steadily, night by night. It wasn't as though Conan hadn't anticipated a reaction like that. The focus group bit he had teased on Jay's last show (and would run on his own during the second week) had been conceived specifically to address the lingering questions about whether older viewers would ever embrace Conan. In concealing makeup that made him look a little like the Popeye character Wimpy, O'Brien, posing as a researcher named Stuart Wexler, led a group of senior citizens ("crusty, crotchety old people," as Conan put it) in discussions about a series of clips involving this comic named Conan O'Brien. The most outstanding of the many pretaped pieces the show had banked, the hilarious focus-group bit showed Conan at his smartest and best: interacting with people and getting laughs without making fun of them, and landing a point at the same time. One woman suggested this guy didn't belong on TV, he belonged in a mental institution. Another said simply, "I can see why some younger men who watch a lot of pornography might like this."

Later, some at NBC would suggest the piece carried particular irony. The night it aired, Tuesday, June 9, was Conan's seventh edition of *The Tonight Show*, and it wound up being the first night David Letterman attracted more viewers. The difference was tiny, and Conan still commanded all the younger demographic groups by huge margins. But he had dropped in terms of the overall number of viewers watching on each night since his huge premiere. A few NBC executives, even while they shrugged off the competitive results—with predictable comments like "Let Letterman take all the old people; the young demos, that's where the money is"—did mention they hoped to see the total viewer number level off soon. (*The Tonight Show* was not accustomed to losing in any area, *ever*.)

Naturally, with the unrelenting scrutiny being applied to all things late night, Conan's first night trailing Dave was going to receive wide coverage. NBC moved quickly to the defensive: Marc Graboff gave interviews emphasizing that late night was always about the long term, "a marathon, not a sprint."

Jeff Zucker checked in with Conan by phone, offering congratulations based on how spectacularly he had dropped the show's median age—a full decade in just a week. Zucker had been stressing to other NBC executives, as Conan's first numbers came in, that this was the goal of the five-year plan—generational change. He told Conan much the same, assuring him that this was what NBC cared about and urging him not to worry about that mass number.

That was comforting news and especially appreciated, because a few details around the edges were already nagging at Conan. It seemed to him that the promo spigot had been turned off. Right up until he went on the air, notices of the new *Tonight Show* appeared to be everywhere: billboards, sides of buses and trucks, all over NBC's shows. (A banner six stories high had floated outside NBC's main office building in Burbank, consisting of a shot of Conan, only from the hairline up.) Now, suddenly, the promotions seemed to have ended—all at once. Jeff Ross, meanwhile, had been watching some prime-time show on NBC and noticed that the promotions for what was coming up on *The Tonight Show* had suddenly become double promotions, including what was going to be on that night on Jimmy Fallon. Promos were a disquieting issue to all Conan people because they had chafed for years under NBC's long-term promo policy, which devoted all the airtime to clips from what Leno had on that night, followed by a rushed announcer voice-over at the end: "And Conan's got Al Roker!" But Ross, too, received assurances from his good friend in New York that the demo numbers were exciting—and all that really mattered.

In reality, not every NBC executive was so sanguine, even at that early date. In New York Dick Ebersol watched the first few Conan *Tonight* shows and felt his queasy feelings were being validated: This was not going over well. When the early spectacular ratings came in, Ebersol felt compelled to warn Zucker and others at NBC, "Don't celebrate this."

That advice also died aborning. Two days after *Tonight* first slipped behind Letterman, the weekly late-night numbers arrived. (Nielsen, still a monopoly and thus under no real burden to be timely, delivered a week's official national late-night ratings on the Thursday after a previous week had been completed.) Even though he had shown some declines each night, Conan's first week remained truly spectacular.

Conan averaged over 6 million viewers for the premiere week, about 900,000 less than Jay had scored in his final week at *Tonight*. But those young demos! Conan posted eye-popping numbers for the crowd eighteen to forty-nine, averaging a 2.3 rating, about a full rating point above Jay's average for the previous year. And he crushed Letterman across the board, by more than 2.5 million viewers and 1.4 rating points in those demos.

The weekly numbers gave NBC all the ammunition it needed to shoot back at those in the press eager to start questioning the wisdom of the big late-night shift, given Conan's slide in the mass viewer totals. And Jeff Zucker intended to fire that ammo at will. When the NBC press department put together its release celebrating Conan's mighty inaugural week, Zucker, who from his earliest *Today* show days knew how to ride a good PR story, decided to stick a big headline on the release: "Conan Is the New King of Late Night."

In Burbank, the NBC press department shuddered. Did NBC really want to go out with that message? One week on the air, and Conan had already earned a crown? Phone calls flew back and forth between the network press people and other executives.

In the offices of their late-night department, Rick Ludwin and Nick Bernstein were deeply worried about the release. It was unfair and unwise to stick a label like that on Conan this early. They urged that it be changed, as did many of the PR executives, concerned about the inevitable instant backlash in the press. Even Jay Leno, after all his years of winning, never really claimed that royal title; it belonged to Johnny Carson, once and always. Jay was too smart to ever allow NBC to stick it on him. It would only serve as an invitation to mockery.

Ludwin understood the motivation behind Zucker's aggressive promotional effort. But to Ludwin it recalled how the Fed chairman Alan Greenspan had described what had motivated overenthusiastic investors during the stock market boom: "irrational exuberance." This amounted to the Conan boom. One week in, and Conan had lost one night to Letterman—in the ultimately meaningless category of total viewers. That only meant Dave was adding the old people who simply didn't get Conan. One night, and already the press was jumping on Conan for not being broad-based enough. Ludwin saw it as nothing more than a self-fulfilling prophecy, the narrative the press had been gunning to write even before Conan uttered one word on *The Tonight Show*. That didn't make him any less certain that Zucker had made a mistake.

Other NBC executives reached the same conclusion; but they quickly got the message: Jeff wanted that headline. For one executive, the move captured a salient Zucker trait: "He's the kind of guy who is so smart and so capable that he thinks he can do everyone else's job better than they can, from the entertainment boss to bookers to the PR department. That's why he insisted on 'King of Late Night' when the PR executives argued against it."

Later Zucker himself, with the benefit of hindsight, would agree with Ludwin's assessment. The press release was mistake. That Thursday, though, it went out.

When Jeff Ross received an e-mail with the release, he strenuously disapproved. In truth, he went insane, and immediately called Rebecca Marks, who ran the LA press department.

"Please tell me this is a draft," he said to her.

"No," she replied, not fully concealing her own reservations. "It went out."

"It went out!" Ross shouted. "We're going to get fucking *killed!*" He spent the rest of the morning calling NBC executives, unloading an earful to each of them about how absolutely stupid this move was.

A short while later Conan strolled in, ready to start his day, and Ross showed him the release. All the new king could do was roll his eyes and shake his head.

Conan was proud of the *Tonight* shows they were putting on night after night, and he was happy and fulfilled to be living his dream. He didn't sweat the early ratings much—not the irrational exuberance of the first week, nor the turbulence in the total-viewer numbers—calculating that fluctuation was normal: You settle in, find a groove, grow from there. That it might take some time to find that groove didn't throw him in the least. He recognized that, unlike anybody else in the history of this iconic show, he was taking it over while squaring off against an established late-night star, one who had been on television twenty-seven years and who was, by most estimates (including his own), one of the greatest comic talents in the history of the medium. David Letterman was also a star of the baby-boom generation, the audience least likely to be spending a lot of time on computers and other gadgets. They watched their entertainment the old-fashioned way, on a television set.

So Conan figured that with his younger-skewing style it was always going to be hard to recruit the Dave fans and the Jay fans—especially the latter. They had enjoyed years of a different sort of *Tonight Show* than the one Conan was going to offer, and besides, now they could wait the summer out and get back to their chosen comic in September.

As satisfied as Conan was with so much of the *Tonight Show* experience, something about the decision to keep Jay continued to distress him. Jay didn't really feel gone, thanks to NBC's decision to give him ten p.m., and his presence lingered—like the long-graduated college alum who still wanted to hang around the dorm and party.

Conan knew his late-night history. Every other *Tonight* host had enjoyed the unconditional support of the brass in New York and LA: The network lined their big clanking machine behind their choice and went full bore on his behalf. In his case it felt as if they were somehow hedging their bet. But Conan believed that tentativeness had to change; they couldn't half give anybody *The Tonight Show*. Nobody half married somebody. You're in or you're not, right? All he could do for now was accept NBC's protestations of good faith and hope Jay and ten would work out. He had to root for Jay.

Meanwhile, stick to the knitting. For Conan, that meant hitting the notes he knew best how to sing. Yes, he wanted to build a mass audience following, but at what risk? He found himself confronting a fundamental question: Did they really expect him to grab a broad-based viewership immediately without alienating his core fans? To him it made no sense to send a signal to all those college kids and seventeen-year-olds secretly staying up late to watch him in their bedrooms, or following his bits online, that he wasn't their guy anymore.

The problem was this: By the time Conan loped out onstage every night at 11:35 p.m., another late-night host, with increasingly potent appeal to those same college kids and teens in front of their video and computer screens, was already five minutes into his act, one that was being widely admired for both its comedy and its "truthiness."

Stephen Colbert had so quickly thrust his comic character and his blowhard vocabulary into the national consciousness that the Merriam-Webster dictionary editors had selected "truthiness"—according to Colbert, "what you want the facts to be, as opposed to what the facts are"—as its Word of the Year in 2006. A year earlier, after Colbert had been on the air only a few months, another group, the American Dialect Society, had awarded it the same honor, while clarifying truthiness as a "stunt word."

In a way, the whole *Colbert Report* on the Comedy Central cable channel was a stunt, the first late-night entry to flout the premise that nightly talk-show exposure inevitably reveals the real personality of the host. Stephen Colbert wasn't doing faux news like his pal Jon Stewart; he was doing faux personality. His on-air character started out as a full-blown satirical take on Fox News's Bill O'Reilly, only bigger and more bloviating. The show's conceit had distinct advantages. Colbert could mock the excesses and bizarre stances taken by right-wing talk-show hosts by celebrating them instead of denigrating them. (And indeed some conservatives—like the former House majority leader Tom DeLay—didn't quite get the joke for a time, thinking maybe they finally had a really funny guy on their side.)

It was a filament-fine line, but Colbert danced agilely on it most nights thanks to laser-sharp writing and his own consummate improv skills. That was never more apparent than during his transformative perfor-mance at the 2006 White House Correspondents Dinner. Booked, as com-ics had always been, to provide a little humor—and *maybe* a dig or two at the current chief executive—Colbert brought out the biggest sword he could find and laid waste. Capturing much of the prevailing national take on the Bush administration, Colbert took his pretend admiration to the heights of absurdity that national opinion demanded.

In one of his most quoted lines, Colbert, citing Bush's then-32 percent approval rating, said, "We know that polls are just a collection of statistics that reflect what people are thinking in 'reality.' And reality has a well-known liberal bias."

The bit accomplished something rare in the clubby atmosphere of Washington politics and press: It disturbed people. Colbert was only vaguely aware that night of the stir he was causing, by his audience's avoiding making eye contact with him. But over the next few days he got the message. He had dared disturb the universe, and the level of oppro-brium he attracted stunned him. "I didn't want to be subversive," he said. "I just wanted to be funny." Still, for every accusation hurled at him of having violated the dinner's unspoken code of gentlemanliness, there were an equal number of plaudits from fans who realized that they now had their own champion of truthiness.

In many ways, Colbert was closer to O'Brien in background and training than anyone else in late night: never a stand-up, intellectually gifted, and balls-out fearless in pursuit of a laugh. Born in Washington, D.C., almost exactly a year after Conan, and raised on James Island near Charleston, South Carolina, Stephen Tyrone Colbert was also Irish Catholic, from a huge family, and the son of a doctor. Conan tried tap; Stephen tried ballet.

What separated them—really what separated Colbert from almost everyone else in his youth—was a tragedy. When he was ten, his father and the two brothers closest to him in age (he had eleven siblings in all) were killed in a plane crash on their way to enroll the boys in a boarding school. Colbert could never fully calculate the devastation that the loss wrought, on his family or his own young psyche.

Stephen all but shut down academically, turning instead to fantasy books, which he escaped into by devouring them at breakneck pace. "Nothing seemed important after that," Colbert said of the tragedy, a feeling that sparked a lifelong resistance to "blind acceptance of authority." He felt detached from the standard interests and behavior of children. Nothing a teacher could say could inspire any discipline, because after what had happened to his family "nothing seemed threatening to me." He did try to make his mother laugh, as humor was respected, even valued in the family. But the young Colbert wanted to be less ham than Hamlet, "so I could share my misery with the world."

He started at Hampden-Sydney College in Virginia, where he finally got a little serious about using his intellect—when he wasn't consumed by playing Dungeons and Dragons, which he later credited with fueling his character-creation skills. After two years he transferred to Northwestern to chase his serious acting muse.

On his flight to Chicago to enroll, he fell into conversation with a fellow passenger—an unnamed astronaut, in Colbert's telling—and described how his dad at one time considered shifting the second syllable of their name to the French pronunciation, but didn't out of deference to his own father, "who lacked the pretentious gene I have." Advised by his seatmate to go for it if he really wanted to change his life, COLE-burt landed in Chicago as Cole-BEAR.

Acting at Northwestern, he discovered that he appreciated comic roles—and being around the funnier people—more than that grim, tragic stuff. After trying other groups in Chicago, Colbert eventually signed on to the famous Second City improv troupe and truly found his form. He met some significant future contacts there, including Steve Carell (Colbert became his understudy) and Amy Sedaris. With Amy and Paul Dinello,

Colbert went on to create a sketch comedy show for Comedy Central in 1995, *Exit 57*. (Later the threesome would also launch the surreal series *Strangers with Candy* for the channel, which gained a cult following, mainly for Sedaris.)

Though Colbert had not quite broken through, he was finding a consistent theme for his characters: totally sure of themselves and completely ignorant, or as he put it, "poorly informed, high-status idiots." Something about that combination sounded like a perfect profile for television news correspondent, or at least ABC's *Good Morning America* thought so. In one of network news's periodic attempts to try something different—or funny—*GMA* hired Colbert as a comedy correspondent to play off the serious anchorman Charlie Gibson.

Colbert certainly looked the part. He had a bookish demeanor behind his spectacles, wore a suit well, like a professional *something*, and kept his dark hair shortish and precisely in place. Of average height, weight, and appearance, Stephen could have found a niche in the fifties playing Jim Anderson's best friend from the insurance office on *Father Knows Best*. Except he was really funny—and, yes, kind of subversive. (That didn't describe his personal life, which really did seem right out of *Father Knows Best*. Colbert, happily married to Evelyn McGee, also a South Carolinian, was the father of three and lived in suburban conventionality in Montclair, New Jersey, where he also taught Sunday school in his local Catholic parish.)

Ultimately Colbert was apparently too funny—or subversive—for *Good Morning America*, which didn't dare try many of his ideas on their show. (Two of about twenty he proposed were filmed; only one aired.) But the experience did leave him with a real press credential, which helped land him a tryout on the just emerging *Daily Show* in 1997, when Craig Kilborn was still the host. The faux, full-of-it correspondent turned out to be the ideal expression of the Colbert character, but he hit his full stride only when Jon Stewart took over the show in 1999 and raised the show's comedy threat level from broad to biting. Colbert's smug, know-nothing know-it-all began to take shape, and after the show's first star correspondent, Colbert's former Second City mate Steve Carell, left for movie fame, Stephen became the breakout feature player for the show's growing legion of fans.

Colbert's pompous conservative egotist eventually took over for the merely moronic correspondent. Comedy Central had been looking for a companion series to run at eleven thirty following *The Daily Show*. Stewart had by this time become more or less Colbert's professional brother (among other things, they also shared an agent, the ultra-ubiquitous James Dixon), and Jon's Busboy Productions became the producing entity for the new show. Success came instantly; Comedy Central commissioned a study in 2008 showing that the degree of passion and loyalty expressed toward Stewart and Colbert dwarfed anything else in late-night television. For a time Colbert faced some questions about whether he could possibly sustain a talk show essentially acting every night instead of presenting himself and his own views. Five years in, he answered those questions nightly, modifying his character slowly and subtly over time to add dimension to the show—and to the host's future possibilities.

Some of those close to Stewart and Colbert suggested that Jon was now well settled and needed nothing more from his career than continuing what had become, professionally and culturally, the job of a lifetime. But Stephen Colbert? He might be up for much bigger ambitions, colleagues said—like reinventing what it was the networks were doing with their late-night shows. If they ever decided to break the form—the couch, the desk, the band, the jokey monologue—Colbert had by 2009 earned a spot high on the candidate list; he had certainly proved he had the creative nerviness to do it.

A few weeks into Conan's run, a single dark-shaded cloud began to drift across the Manhattan sky, sinking just low enough to pose a threat of interfering, ever so slightly, with the spectacular views outside the CEO's office on the fifty-second floor of 30 Rock. Jeff Zucker was starting to feel less than thrilled with the way *The Tonight Show* was going, an opinion he had already expressed to NBC's late-night executives on the West Coast, Rick Ludwin and Nick Bernstein.

There were two issues, as Zucker saw it. One was Conan's performance. By his reckoning, Conan looked tentative, not relaxed enough. That could be expected and tolerated, to a point. People get a case of nerves starting a huge career move like this.

But as far as Zucker was concerned, there was less excuse for the second issue: missteps in guest bookings. Zucker, of course, had a great deal of accrued experience from running *Today*, where bookings were the lifeblood of the program (and the ratings). While each show had its own booking staff that made most of the calls, landing the biggest names often required the intervention of a star like a Katie Couric (or a star producer, like Jeff Zucker). Even close to ten years past his *Today* tenure, if there was one thing Zucker knew as well as or better than anybody else in the business, it was how to book for numbers. And he thought Conan and his team weren't doing it.

To what extent that was purely Zucker's view as opposed to how much he was being influenced by what was being murmured in his ear wasn't totally clear to those on whom Jeff unloaded this opinion. Others at NBC were already aware that Dick Ebersol, the man whose judgment Zucker was most apt to rely on and trust, had tipped over entirely to the negative side about Conan. Ebersol's reservations—and unhappiness at how Conan had reacted to his voluntary consultant role—had hardened, within days of the premiere.

As the shows piled up, Ebersol's critique grew only more pointed. The focus group tape late in the first week was funny, but it almost seemed designed to offend older viewers—however many were left by that point. The music performances in the last act of the show seemed calculated to encourage the nonhip to hit the road. Even Pearl Jam, which seemed like a booking coup on Conan's first night, had irritated Ebersol. He knew the group had many great songs, but what they played ("Get Some") seemed to Dick—admittedly, at sixty-two, not the precise target audience for that brand of rock—to push past entertainment and toward a test of how much hearing loss a human could comfortably suffer. Alienating music acts were not going to help drive *Tonight* audiences into Jimmy Fallon either, Ebersol, who was already most impressed with Fallon's early efforts, concluded.

Dick's concerns actually started at the very top of the show—with Andy. Conan had managed just fine, it seemed to Dick, after Richter left the *Late Night* show in 2000. That Conan had decided to bring him back when he was starting up *Tonight* boggled Ebersol's mind. He could not conceive of a thing Andy brought to the show, other than serving as a baby blanket for Conan. The interaction between Conan and Andy made Ebersol wince. During the monologue Conan would hit a joke, and Andy—off camera, to Conan's right, audibly mic'd—would occasionally respond with a comeback, almost every one of which cracked Conan up. (Indeed, one star of another late-night show was in awe of Richter because "he scored every time he opened his mouth.")

Andy didn't crack up Ebersol. Worse, Dick thought the nightly remarks from Andy, which Conan would then respond to, had the effect of a bouncer shooing would-be attendees away. Their exchanges played to Dick like two guys having a conversation the audience wasn't a part of, with Conan glancing off camera for a significant portion of his mono-logue, checking Andy's reaction. Every second he was doing that, he wasn't talking directly to the people lying in their beds with the TV on.

But more than anything else, what had raised Ebersol's finely attuned late-night hackles was precisely what had alarmed Zucker: the booking issue. Here was Conan, assuming control of the biggest platform in show business, and in his second week—on only his ninth *Tonight Show*—his lead guest was, incredibly, Norm MacDonald. The onetime *SNL* player had not, as far as Ebersol knew, had a prominent show-business job in years. Ebersol thought the show might as well have booked Norm Crosby.

Of course, for Conan's true fans, the MacDonald booking was cause for real excitement. He had always been one of O'Brien's signature guests, and he always seemed to delight Conan. (And that night, he killed Conan again, at one point driving the host to stand up and flee the desk after some banter with Andy.) To not appreciate Norm, and what he brought every time he visited, was to not be a Conan fan at all.

Again, to Ebersol, that attitude seemed a signal that Conan had circled the wagons and was including within the circle only those who shared the faith and had signed a religious pact to travel west with him. That did not include Jay's fans, of course, who were effectively being disin-vited. When Kevin Nealon, another long-absent *SNL* vet, turned up on the couch the next night, Ebersol was simply dumbfounded.

In general, Ludwin did not disagree with these concerns. But he always approached his role in trying to manage Conan and his team from a point of unfettered admiration for the comic's talent. He believed Conan was brilliant, pure and simple; he saw Conan as the future. Still, even in the *Late Night* days, Ludwin himself had felt the need to prod the staff in terms of bookings. It seemed to Rick that Conan's booking depart-ment still had a 12:35 mentality, that they sought out what he saw as the more quirky, less mainstream kind of showbiz guest. He wasn't sure they understood, or simply didn't embrace, the arm-twisting clout that *The Tonight Show* could wield over top guests.

In theory Ludwin had no issue with someone like Norm MacDonald as a lead guest. He knew how funny Norm had been with Conan on many occasions, and every host had those guests who simply played so well with them that they made for attractive and frequent bookings. For years Letterman had booked Charles Grodin because of the killer shtick the two of them had developed, not because Grodin was a big star. Rick's own reservation was about the approach Norm sometimes took to his visitations with Conan, when he would come on and simply tell old jokes, rather than extending himself a bit and being more topical, which might lure in a larger audience.

The disconnect over booking policy did not spring from arrogance, Ludwin was sure. Conan and his staff wanted the show to be organic, he believed, always consistent within Conan's sensibility. Nothing should look as though he was merely taking network notes, because then the fans really might believe he was selling out. And Ludwin never underestimated the effects of the heat from the cauldron Conan had stepped into. *The Tonight Show* remained the pinnacle of show business for the NBC late-night executive. As he saw it, only five men could ever really know what it was like to assume the mantle of hosting that institution—and how much pressure that inflicted. So he continued to nudge Conan and Jeff Ross gently toward broader, more 11:35-style guests, toward finding ways to "make the show bigger."

Lorne Michaels, meanwhile, was watching the show and having a different reaction: In some ways it looked *too* big. The move to a soundstage had undoubtedly opened up the show, but maybe not all to the good. In New York, with its tight quarters, set builders and directors did everything they could to make studios look larger, the same way New Yorkers try to use space wisely to make their apartments look more spacious. In LA, the soundstage space was so wide open, the show did not look intimate anyway. Michaels knew the center of the show was always going to be Conan O'Brien, not some sprawling set that some viewers might suspect came from a page in *Architectural Digest*.

Once, when filming a scene from a movie in an Indian casino in the Southwest, Michaels and his cast and crew had been struck by how grim and tawdry the setting seemed, with old women betting quarters and six-hundred-pound people playing slots. But in that room at night, on every TV monitor, Lorne noticed that Leno was playing—and that seemed right. "Oh, this is America," Michaels concluded. Picturing Conan on those monitors threw the imagery off somehow, for Michaels. Something about it sent a message that this old familiar show had gone upmarket.

Knowing and recognizing television was like knowing and recognizing candy bars, Michaels reasoned. You anticipated what you would get for your dime or quarter or dollar (depending on how old you were). Snickers? That was the one with nuts. If somehow that relationship changed, because the wrapper made it odder or more expensive looking, you might get confused and think maybe that wasn't the candy bar you wanted after all. It might still be a good one, of course, but it wasn't the one you knew. If it had the look of having gone upmarket, maybe you'd look around for a different candy bar.

The accumulated wisdom of all this analysis reached the Conan team in drips and splashes. Jeff Ross was having lunch a lot at the Grill on the Universal lot with Marc Graboff and listening to what Marc was hearing from New York—nothing really different from what was in the notes Ludwin and Bernstein were delivering in LA. Graboff didn't think Jeff had slipped on a pair of rose-colored glasses; he always seemed to appreciate the inside intelligence.

But the heavy-rotation concentration on the bookings drove Ross a little mad. Of course they were trying to book the best names they could; they weren't idiots. They always sought the A-list. But it was early summer, and how many A-list stars were making the rounds unless they were in summer popcorn movies, which were usually about robots anyway?

The music complaints seemed even sillier to Ross. The notes said, put on more music with wide appeal. Like who? Ross asked. There were only so many *American Idol* losers available. He checked his list: The music acts seemed to have a high quotient of crossover artists, with many singers Leno had previously booked.

One note from the network did get addressed quickly. As early as the first night no one had liked the way Andy did the voice-over opening. To many inside NBC it sounded like Richter was putting a little ironic topspin in his inflection of "Conan O'Briii-en," with the last syllable trailing off like the fade-out at the end of a song—as though Andy was partly spoofing the role of the announcer. That element got fixed

One other element—and a significant one, as far as Jeff Zucker was concerned—did not.

Jeff Zucker had never completely hung up his *Today* show cleats—the ones he had used, with recurring glee, to stomp on competitors when he produced the show in the nineties. Even as CEO of the far-flung NBC Universal entertainment empire (cable channels, broadcast network, movie studio, theme parks), he was still known to check in on occasion with the *Today* producer Jim Bell to suggest a segment—or, more frequently, a booking. Zucker prided himself on knowing a great story when he saw one, and the best way for a television show to take advantage of that story.

So as June rolled by with the press taking note of Conan's shrinking margins over Letterman—and by week three Dave had edged past Conan in viewers for a full week (though Conan continued to crush Dave in the young demos)—Zucker saw the kind of wide-open opportunity that used to ring his wake-up alarm in the mornings:

Sarah Palin.

Always a magnet for press attention, Palin had jumped on an insult to her young daughter to launch a summer publicity offensive. And the target of her righteous parental wrath was none other than David Letterman, who had stumbled into Palin's PR gunsights by cracking a joke that would have wandered dangerously close to offensive even if it had been accurate. The fact that it wasn't only set Letterman up as easy prey for the former governor of Alaska.

On June 9, with Conan just starting his second week on his show, Dave told a joke about Palin's visiting Yankee Stadium with her daughter. "One awkward moment for Sarah Palin," Letterman said. "During the seventh-inning stretch her daughter was knocked up by Alex Rodriguez."

Everyone knew Palin's unmarried eighteen-year-old daughter, Bristol, had gotten pregnant by her boyfriend and now had a child. Bristol wasn't the daughter who accompanied Palin to the stadium, however. It was Palin's fourteen-year-old, Willow.

Palin seized the moment. While she and her husband, Todd, took turns volleying fire at Letterman, accusing him of being "sexually perverted" for telling a joke "about raping" their young daughter, the backlash against Letterman, especially in the conservative media world of Fox News and talk radio, threatened to blow up into a wildfire. Two days later Letterman spent more than seven minutes during his at-the-desk segment in act two defending himself and explaining the mistake that had made the Rodriguez joke go wrong. In a tone of self-mockery that the audience took for humor—because they laughed all through it—Letterman acknowledged that the jokes were ugly.

"These are actually ugly. These are borderline," he acknowledged, laying the reason down to "an act of desperation to get cheap laughs, which is what I've been doing for the last thirty years." He also apologized—after a fashion—for the mix-up about the two daughters. But he adamantly defended himself against the charge that he had suggested that Willow might have sex with a grown baseball player.

"These are not jokes made about her fourteen-year-old daughter. I would never, never make jokes about raping or having sex of any description with a fourteen-year-old girl."

Letterman summed up: "Am I guilty of poor taste? Yes. Did I suggest that it was OK for her fourteen-year-old daughter to be having promiscuous sex? No."

And then, signaling he was not going to prostrate himself before a woman he seemed to believe was a grandstanding politician, Letterman also mentioned a line—one Palin had labeled in an interview as "pretty pathetic"—that he had used the same night as the Rodriguez joke in a top ten "Highlights of Sarah Palin's Visit to New York": "Bought makeup at Bloomingdale's to update her slutty flight attendant look."

No apology for that one. "I kind of like that joke," Letterman said.

Palin supporters bombarded CBS and Letterman's office with calls of complaint and demands that he be fired. FireDavidLetterman.com, a Web site launched by Palin supporters, tried to gin up a rally to take place the following week outside the Letterman theater on Broadway.

The concern was real inside the Letterman camp. They took the protest seriously enough for Dave to take the unusual step of offering a second apology on the air the next Monday, made directly to Palin, admitting that his own intent was meaningless compared to how the joke had been perceived. That was good enough for Palin, who, having gotten as much as she could have possibly hoped to squeeze out of this episode, accepted the apology. The planned protest fizzled; only about fifteen people showed up carrying signs. They were vastly outnumbered by the media assembled to cover the event.

But if that protest was flaming out, another was still in full blaze.

As soon as the first news of the Palin-Letterman contretemps began breaking, Jeff Zucker sent a message to his Conan team: The perfect move in this circumstance was to book Sarah Palin as quickly as possible.

There was only one problem with this plan: O'Brien didn't want to do it.

Conan explained it as best he could to some of his West Coast colleagues: He didn't want to appear to be taking advantage of a situation Dave had gotten himself into; he didn't want to come across as a pawn in some machination of Palin's. If the show booked her at that moment, Conan told one associate, it would be obvious she was on only because of the news in the David Letterman world, and Conan would be vulnerable to the perception that he had been suckered into doing it. Not only would the press accuse him of pandering for ratings, but his fans would likely judge the move unseemly.

As both a producer and a boss, this reaction drove Zucker nuts. As a producer, he knew how to manipulate audiences—that was simply what you did as part of the job. He looked at Palin as the first of-the-moment guest who could change the game for Conan. As a boss, he couldn't believe Conan would stand in the way of what was obviously the smart business move—for him and his network.

Zucker pressed the issue with Jeff Ross: Letterman wants to kill you. He wants to bash your brains in. And you're bringing a knife to a gunfight. This guy wants to kill you, and you guys aren't doing all that well.

The *Today* show, still under Zucker's direct aegis, did book Palin in the middle of the Letterman fracas. In her interview, Palin told Matt Lauer, the show's biggest star, that he would have to be "extremely naive" to believe Letterman's "convenient excuse" that he was not referring to Willow but Bristol Palin in the joke. She also backed a statement by her spokesperson that it would be wise to keep Willow away from David Letterman. And when pressed by Lauer about what that statement was meant to imply about Letterman, she added, "You can interpret that however you want to interpret it."

At NBC it was taken for granted that Jay would have booked Palin without a moment's hesitation. That was certainly what Ebersol thought O'Brien should do. His argument: "This is your fucking competition. This is a business. You're making eight figures."

The Palin issue came up in meetings between the Conan staff, Ludwin and Bernstein, and other NBC executives. As Jeff Ross heard it later, there was not one person in these discussions who did not comprehend why Conan balked at booking Palin at that moment. The move had the potential to blow up in his face. No one questioned how seriously Conan took this situation—he had clearly thought it through, as he did everything involving his career. He was making a judgment based on what he believed was best for his show.

When Conan laid out his reasoning, Rick Ludwin, for one, could not find a reason to challenge it. In general, Ludwin believed it was wrong to try to force hosts to do something they were clearly opposed to doing. That could lead only to bad moments on the air. The network's job was to make the host look good.

One Conan supporter did acknowledge that the show was forsaking the "ratings pop" that would have come with a Palin appearance. "Conan didn't want to dictate what his *Tonight Show* would be based on someone else's late-night show. The challenge for late-night shows, forever and always, is: At what price is the pop?"

For Jeff Zucker there was a much simpler—and less justifiable— explanation for Conan's decision to bypass a Palin guest shot: He didn't want to piss off David Letterman.

CHAPTER EIGHT

STILL DAVE, AFTER ALL THESE YEARS

O n the morning of December 9, 2008—six months earlier to the day of its host's controversial Palin joke—excitement coursed through the usually sedate offices of *Late Show with David Letterman*, and it had nothing to do with Christmas season in New York.

Among the staff who actually interacted with the star on a daily basis—and that was a limited number, it was true—Dave's arrival that day was much more than usually anticipated. The burning question passed around over coffee: What is Dave going to say about *this*?

"This" was NBC's announcement that it had reached its agreement with Jay Leno to keep him on, transferring him to prime time, of all places, ten p.m. each weeknight. That move seemed to resolve, once and for all, the head-to-head rivalry between Jay and Dave, which reached back sixteen years to the decision over the Carson succession—and even further than that, to nights as stand-ups on stages like the Comedy Store on Sunset Boulevard in LA in the seventies.

Letterman had said little on the subject since NBC had installed its five-year layaway plan for *The Tonight Show*, with Conan O'Brien the designated heir to Jay. But then, he said little on how he felt about most topics, especially in public. On this matter, he had deigned to speak for the record only once, in a *Rolling Stone* interview the previous September.

At that time he had made the remarkable statement—remarkable at least to those still guessing how Dave might feel about Jay—that he no

longer harbored any hope of ever topping Leno in the ratings. His acceptance of that fact was remarkable mainly for the reason Letterman cited,
an explanation for his ratings shortcomings that defied all previous efforts
by his own entourage to blame uncontrollable factors like CBS's lead-in
shows and NBC's stronger local stations (as well as the well-known limited artistic tastes of the American public).

"The answer is me," Dave said. "I just think that Jay has wider appeal
than I do."

His admission likely stunned those at NBC who had been hammering
away at that same argument for years in the face of the litany of excuses
being thrown up by Letterman's defenders. With Dave himself conceding, "I think more people are responding to Jay than will ever respond to
me," the excuse well had officially run dry.

Given Jay's now acknowledged victory in what, by that point, seemed
like the Hundred Years War of Late Night, NBC's decision to relieve Leno
of his *Tonight* chair in favor of Conan left Letterman nonplussed. While
he recognized that the network may have been attempting to find a "less
messy way to handle what happened to me at NBC," he still seemed
thrown by the whole concept. Maybe because he knew his counterpart
so well—perhaps as well as anyone who had interacted with the near
impenetrable Leno in his long career—Letterman suspected (correctly, of
course) that Jay would have preferred to stay exactly where he was.

So even then, ten months before the switchover was due to take place,
Letterman found himself wondering whether it was really going to happen. The few times he would talk about it around the office with his producers and writers, Dave tended to agree with those who speculated that
NBC would find some way not to go through with the handover to Conan.
The pattern seemed far too similar to how the network had tried to handle
Dave's departure for CBS. NBC had offered him *The Tonight Show* at the
last minute, but only if he waited eighteen months to get it. All his advisers at the time had warned him that NBC would have stiffed him in the
end if Jay's numbers looked good.

Here they were, fifteen years later, and with the numbers still looking
good for Jay, a stiffing seemed in the offing—this time for Conan. Either
that or NBC would be inviting Jay to pull a Dave and launch another
separate franchise, probably at ABC this time.

In either case, Dave knew for certain that the balance in late night might shift for the first time since the early nineties. For his staff, it felt like a potential reversal in the earth's rotation—back toward Dave.

When Dave arrived that December day, summoning a few of his key people together in his office for a regular morning meeting, anticipation hung in the air like swirling smoke from a lit fuse. Then Dave walked in, sat down, and said not a word about any of it. His number one nemesis was not only leaving the field but was going to prime time, and Dave was shrugging it off, as if . . . whatever. All he said to the group was "So what are we doing on the show today?"

Conan's now certain arrival in six months was not quite so easy to ignore. The departure of Jay might mean opportunity for Letterman, it was true, but it also carried risk—huge, momentous risk. Losing to Jay, conceding Jay's ultimate ratings superiority, had been tough enough to swallow. No one at *Late Show* wanted to ponder what it would mean if Dave now lost again—to Conan.

Rob Burnett, still an executive producer on the show and the executive in charge of Worldwide Pants, whose tenure extended all the way back to Letterman's days at NBC, never stopped being a true believer. For him NBC's selection of Leno over Letterman could be linked to the concept of original sin: NBC picked Jay over Dave and had never really overcome plucking the apple from the wrong tree.

Had NBC seized the moment back then and elevated Dave, as this virtually religious tenet posited it, the premier late-night network would likely have preserved the utter dominance of *The Tonight Show* that Johnny Carson and all his predecessors had enjoyed. How? By ensuring that another network did not secure the one star capable of a successful late-night schism: Dave. Surely, this dogma went, Jay Leno, without the built-in loyalty of the *Tonight Show* viewership, could not have set up his tent at CBS and pulled in the same kind of crowds that he did at NBC. And if CBS had tried Jay and he had misfired, then NBC with Letterman would have owned the eleven thirty time period exclusively for who knows how long.

Of course, this doctrinal wisdom did not take into account the part where Dave would have refused to work the affiliates, court the advertisers, massage the press, and give succor to his network whenever it was in need. Letterman would likely have shut all that out at NBC, just as he did at CBS—one big reason why he didn't win the *Tonight* job in the first place.

Many in the Letterman camp never fully accepted that particular downside of Dave's persnickety personality. For them, it was all black and white: Dave, a comedy genius; Jay, a machine politician. Dave playing Mozart; Jay playing Salieri.

Or in Rob Burnett's favored metaphor: Jay equals Coke; Dave equals Pepsi. Burnett's answer to NBC's attempted dismissals of Dave's heroic efforts at CBS was to cite Pepsi's entering the soft-drink market as rival to Coke. Maybe Coke still outsold Pepsi overall, but there was now a Pepsi where there was none before—which enabled people to let their tastes decide between two more or less equal choices. (It would not be the last time Coca-Cola raised its metaphoric head in the late-night saga.)

But with Jay now bowing out of late night, Letterman's people were concerned that Conan might well represent an all-new brand of soft drink. Dr. Pepper? Maybe even Mountain Dew? People had grown accustomed to Coke and Pepsi. If Mountain Dew was now going to try to grab some slice of their market, Letterman's team couldn't just sit around and let it happen.

The question for the *Late Show* brain trust was this: How could they best prepare to prevent Conan from doing the unthinkable—beating them?

Initially there was some general discomfort with that entire idea. Dave had always been personally fond of Conan and admired his fresh, impressive comedy work. He had more or less blessed Conan as his successor by appearing as a guest on *Late Night* in February 1994, when Conan was barely surviving NBC's attempts to smother him in his crib. Later, when Conan was finally starting to break through, Dave turned up again as an unbilled walk-on during Conan's third-anniversary show with some advice for Conan and Andy: "In nine years you guys can switch networks and start making some real money."

Even though they shared New York and thus had likely booking conflicts, there had never been friction between the two shows. Quietly Dave had even called Conan personally when he was leaving the *Late Night* show to wish him well, which had meant a lot to Conan. And of course everyone knew the level of Conan's idolatry regarding Dave.

But leaving aside the issue of not really wanting to go after Conan, the staff had to confront another question: the limitations on exactly what steps Dave might take to elevate his game. He certainly wasn't going to go back to monkeycams (handheld cameras on the back of chimps), or create some new adventures for "The Strong Guy, The Fat Guy, The Genius," or take a camera back into the souvenir shop up the street to banter with Sirajul and Mujibur. (For one thing, their Rock America store had long since closed.)

Through the choices he had made in recent years about what he would and would not do on the show, Dave had been sending a clear message: He was no longer the guy breaking new ground in late night. As Burnett put it, "You can't be on the cutting edge forever or you start to look ridiculous."

That didn't mean Dave was any less Dave; it only meant he relied more on the pure essence of wit extracted nightly from his brain. He had taken to building act two largely around a conversation he had with the audience every night from behind his desk. Some nights, when he had a prepared piece of comedy laid out in front of him, he would choose instead to discuss what had happened over the weekend at the house or out on the ranch in Montana. (Most famously, a grizzly bear once made his way into the kitchen for some snacking.) These impromptu asides were often far more hilarious than whatever the writers had come up with.

The most ambitious reinvention Dave and his team did adopt in the months before Conan's hour-long time shift was much more throwback than leap forward. He started telling more—lots more—monologue jokes.

For most of his run at CBS Dave had averaged about eight jokes a night—more than he had during his *Late Night* days at NBC (three or four, tops), but still nothing like the fusillade (thirtyish) Jay was firing off every night. In trying to keep the show as much Dave as possible, while also not requiring him to run around town on his time off as he used to do during the nineties, the staff looked to the opening monologue as a target of opportunity.

In their no-concessions way, Letterman's team had for years resisted any notion that Jay was the master monologist and hence the natural heir to Carson in that regard. Dave had just as much talent for standing on that mark and delivering a finely crafted one-liner, they argued. Of course, Jay pounded his point home every night in a gag barrage, and Letterman himself had never hesitated to grant Jay his props as a stand-up; Dave would routinely say Jay had been the best he'd seen at the joke-telling craft. In the meantime, Dave limited his nightly joke total, believing it was better to tell a few polished jokes than spray the room with a joke hose.

In the early days, however, Dave did fill the show with those ambitious cutting-edge comedy concepts. Not only was he disinclined to do them anymore, but it now seemed those innovations that he had introduced had all become staples of everyone else's late-night shows. Conan went everywhere, from bartending school to Finland. Jimmy Kimmel had a recurring piece at a black barber shop that scored for him every time. Jay sent his "Ross the Intern" character to the same places—award shows, big sporting events—where Dave had sent his stage manager, Biff Henderson, for years. If those ideas were now to be relegated to the scrapbooks, then Letterman needed something else to freshen the show. So the monologue made a comeback.

"It was so hot in New York that when I was driving home last night, the navigation lady says to me, 'So you want to stop for a beer?' "

"It was an especially fine day today, a day like a New York cabdriver: only a slight chance of a shower."

"Jenna Bush is getting married over the weekend. I thought this was nice. For their wedding night, President Bush is loaning the groom his 'Mission Accomplished' banner."

Only privately did some Letterman acolytes mention one ulterior motive for the new direction: It might be another way to distinguish Dave from Conan, who had never done all that nightclub slogging—basic training in the art of monologue.

In mid-2008 another factor was compelling Dave to add jokes at the top of the show. It was a presidential election year, populated with a host of characters inviting comment every night, from John McCain and Hillary Clinton to side players like John Edwards, Fred Thompson, and, once the summer hit, Sarah Palin—all of them offering rich material for monologues.

"At last night's debate John McCain brought up Barack Obama's relationship with sixties radical William Ayers. Then Barack Obama brought up McCain's relationship with John Brown at Harper's Ferry."

Letterman found himself at the center of the news on September 24, during the height of the presidential race, when McCain, who was scheduled to make his thirteenth appearance as a guest, abruptly canceled because he said he was being forced to suspend his campaign to rush to Washington to deal with the collapsing economy.

Dave first made some generous remarks about McCain, citing his war heroism and noting that the senator had called him personally to apologize for this last-minute emergency that was forcing him to cancel. McCain had actually announced his plan to run for president on Letterman's show in 2007; the two men had a comfortable relationship.

But then Dave learned that McCain, instead of rushing to the airport, had turned up at CBS News headquarters for a quick sit-down with Katie Couric. The interview was taking place at the precise time Dave had begun his taping, and because it was on CBS, he could pick it up on the internal network feed. The audience, brought in on this breaking event, pushed Letterman on with their laughter.

"Hey, John," Letterman yelled into the monitor, only starting to get revved up. "I've got a question! You need a ride to the airport?" Egged on by his fill-in guest, the pro-Democratic MSNBC host Keith Olbermann, Letterman questioned McCain's motivation for what seemed to Dave like a PR stunt. "You don't suspend your campaign," Dave said, mixing comic delivery with righteous anger. "No, because that makes me think, well, you know, maybe there will be other things down the road. If he's in the White House, he might just suspend being president. I mean, we've got a guy like that now!"

The event became part of the news cycle in the race. McCain had stiffed Letterman, and Dave made him pay. He got more licks in on McCain for several nights after, and McCain ultimately had to make a date in his otherwise packed calendar to return to New York (a state he was hardly going to win) on October 16 to formally seek Dave's pardon.

For the Lettermanites, the McCain episode underscored what they saw as the gravitas Dave now brought to the role of late-night host, another quality they believed set him apart. No one could picture Jay, for example, rising up and chastising a presidential candidate for reneging on a booking.

"He's bigger now than almost anyone who sits across from him," Rob Burnett said. "On his home turf, sitting behind that desk, where he's sat for so many years, you get the feeling that with whoever it is there, sitting across from him, Dave has the upper hand."

That kind of framing was no accident. What Burnett and other staff members of the show and Worldwide Pants sought to convey was that Letterman had assumed, formally, the mantle held for so long by Carson. Not the "King" thing, but rather the cultural relevance thing. The monologues Dave began performing—Johnny-style ones—played right along with that. Dave not only did more jokes, but more pointed jokes, sharper, tougher material.

The lengthening of the monologue brought with it a reshaping of the first act of the show. For years, the format had been: Dave's opening routine, followed by a brief piece of music from Paul Shaffer and the band while Dave did his walkover to his desk. From there he would jump into whatever had been planned for the next piece of comedy. The act had gotten so long that the first commercial break came much deeper into the show, a fact that actually hurt Letterman's ratings, because shows had started to be measured by how many people were watching the commercials, not the programs themselves. On *Tonight*, Jay had always ended his monologue and thrown right to a commercial—so that first ad was invariably on earlier than Dave's. That had become another ratings advantage Jay's show enjoyed. With the longer monologue, *Late Show* could switch to a similar commercial rotation, with the first ad following the monologue. It might even help in the ratings.

To feed the new structure, *Late Show* began hiring more writers specifically to work on the monologue. Dave started stretching out the joke quotient, eventually pushing it up to sixteen, then eighteen, then twenty a night. When some in the press noticed, they leapt to the immediate conclusion that Dave was intent on stealing away Jay viewers, who liked to hear a lot of topical material.

The reason for the monologue expansion had more to do with Dave looking for a way to reinvent his television act—again. He had done that with resounding success in 1993 when he jumped to CBS, but more significantly, invaded the eleven thirty time period.

The prevailing challenge for Dave in 1993 was supposed to be—as Conan's was—broadening out the show, though even then the concept was difficult to define. Should Dave be less edgy, more conventional, less innovative? At the time, one of Letterman's top producers, Robert Morton, had tried to simplify what the move up an hour was really all about. "The new show has to be about success. It can't be about failure," Morton had said. The old show had celebrated failure: If something about the show went wrong, the camera went right for it, zoomed in on it. As in a memorable night when a trick by Kamar the Discount Magician had failed spectacularly (because he forgot to plug in his levitation table).

If the same act was being done on a show playing at 11:35, Morton argued to Letterman, "You want to see the trick work; you want to see the best trick ever."

Dave had levitated the expectations of the show in just that way when he moved up an hour and over to CBS. But this latest reinvention was not going to be a question of success or failure so much as it would be a question of age. Dave needed to find an age-appropriate way for a sixty-one-year-old guy to keep being funny in late night.

That didn't mean the staff dismissed what Conan was up to. The booking department kept one eye on the guest list Conan's staff had lined up for week one. As expected, it contained big names every night. With the odds pointing to a blowout for Conan (especially now that Jay wasn't going to be available as a guest for Dave on the first night of Conan's *Tonight Show*), the Letterman squad decided to borrow a little strategy from Muhammad Ali for their own guests that week. They would go for the rope-a-dope.

That was Ali's scheme in the famous "Rumble in the Jungle" against George Foreman in Zaire in 1974. Ali essentially laid back against the ropes in the early rounds, allowing Foreman to whale away with his heaviest blows. Then, with Foreman's best shots exhausted, Ali came back with a vengeance—and knocked big George out.

Citing that precedent, the *Late Show* strategists decided to stay away from Conan during his premiere week. They had the show's booking staff, in effect, lay back on the ropes while Conan went for the big swings early. It almost might make it worse for Conan, they guessed, to have a monster first week and then have to start listening to everyone talk about how the numbers were dropping.

"Let's go after the second week," Rob Burnett told the show's bookers. The show—and Dave—would be loaded for bear.

In his early days at CBS, David Letterman was doing so well, surpassing *The Tonight Show* in the ratings and winning nonstop accolades, that Dick Ebersol, one of the NBC executives who had supported the last-minute effort to dump Jay Leno and keep Dave, decided to call a friend who worked on the show and ask if everyone there was over the moon about their success.

"Not everyone," the friend reported. "The first week and a half Dave was happy. Now he's gone right back to being the most miserable person in the world."

The classic adage applied as much or more to the compelling, complicated, challenging David Letterman as it did to anyone else on the planet: You don't get older, you just get more so.

By the end of 2008 Letterman's fifteen-year run at CBS had encompassed a dizzying collection of highs and lows. He had won six Emmy Awards for outstanding comedy or variety series; he had led a driving team that won his dream race, the Indy 500, in 2004; he had experienced the unexpected joy of having a son born into his life at age fifty-six; he had won the admiration of his city and the nation for his sensitive leadership in bringing true comic relief after the horror of the terrorist attacks of 9/11; and he had shepherded countless memorable moments—foulmouthed Madonna, topless Drew Barrymore, post-slammer Paris Hilton—onto television. Oh, and CBS had paid him several hundred million dollars for his labors.

But the toll of lows was also long. Letterman had taken a battering over his one venture outside the cocoon of his show, when he hosted the Academy Awards in 1995; he had been forced to deal with a kidnap threat against his son; he had lost his idol Johnny Carson to death in 2005; whatever hope he had to prove NBC wrong for choosing Jay Leno over him had disappeared under the pile of weekly wins Jay continued to post; and a severely constricted artery had almost cost him his life in 2000, when emergency quintuple heart bypass surgery forced him off the show for seven weeks.

By 2008 Dave had been at it in late night for twenty-six years, closing in on Carson's record three-decade run. Nothing suggested Dave was about to stop, maybe because he realized, having observed Johnny, that shutting down a late-night show would pretty much entail shutting down life as he'd come to know it.

"Once you give up that chair, it's over," said one longtime Letterman associate. "It's hard to imagine him without a show and it's hard for him to imagine himself without a show."

Had Dave mellowed at all? Maybe in some ways, his colleagues suggested; not so much in others. After the heart scare, he modified some behaviors (no more cigars), but if not quite the "maniacal asshole" about the show that he once called himself, he still often made it tough on people to work for him. People got cut off; Dave stopped speaking to them for months on end. That could include anybody, from the top down. One executive producer, Maria Pope, lost favor and contact with Dave (but not her job) for a long stretch of time. Even Rob Burnett found himself ostracized on occasion. The list of advisers Dave would actually listen to grew short, almost to the nub.

Letterman still pushed himself—and others—with an irascible style that took getting used to, especially up close. "This is a guy whose anger feeds everything," said a veteran Letterman intimate. "Just in everything he did there was an underlying level of anger. He's the kind of guy who's having a cup of coffee and instead of just putting it down on the table, he'll go, *slam!* He'd open a package and go '*Raarrr!*,' tearing it apart instead of just opening it."

As he had from early in his career, Letterman directed most of his anger and disgust at himself. In the old days the staff would often hear him in his office battering his stereo equipment with a baseball bat, all of them wondering, *Is he mad at me? Did he not like my joke, or my segment?* But when one of the producers would work up the nerve to walk in and ask him if everything was all right, Dave would say, "I hate myself. I'm the biggest asshole in the world. Look how I messed this up."

For many of the staff, who stood in awe of him, these moments were almost heartbreaking. They would rather have had Dave turn to one of them and say, "You fucked up tonight, and I'm really pissed off."

The top staff tried to shield the angry Dave from the rest of the employees, but they usually got the message. "It's like always walking on eggshells," one writer recalled.

One time Dave came into the office, stepped into the elevator, and saw one of the show's interns. "Oh, hello," Dave said perfunctorily.

The intern froze and stared at the floor. She had been told by one superior never to address Dave—never to *look* at Dave. Letterman went to his producers and instructed them to tell the interns to at least speak to him. They had to assure the terrified young woman that she would be doing them all a favor if she would just say hello to the guy.

Most days, Dave remained intently focused on that one hour a day when his nerve endings would tingle with the anticipation of being fully realized. In the early days he would juice himself up just before going on the air with a ritual of high-test metabolic enhancement. After drinking enough cups of strong coffee to stimulate the economy and before going downstairs to perform, Letterman would sit at his desk surrounded by a pile of Hershey bars. Carefully unwrapping each one, Dave would break four or five of them into their separate little squares and then pile them on top of one another into a little chocolate tower. He would proceed to eat all the squares as he went over the upcoming show with the producers. By the time the sugar rush kicked into his system, he would be backstage and ready to go on the air.

Every night the show, for good or for bad, defined who he was. The act of stepping out nearly daily onto a stage and standing in front of people, millions of people, and soliciting laughs almost defined the term narcissism. Every performer would have needed an outsize ego to get through that crucible every night. Clearly the two giants of this late-night era had that in common, but they reacted to it in totally opposite ways. Jay Leno told friends and colleagues he had the easiest job in the world. One friend remembered hearing Jay say that and replying, "Jay, I know you're at ease with what you do. But you really think you have the easiest job in the world? Every night getting a report card? Nobody else's job gives them a grade every time they finish up their work. No, Jay, really this is the opposite of the easiest job."

The same friend also knew Dave well. The significant difference between them, the friend said, was that "with Jay nothing is ever wrong and with Dave nothing is ever right."

Jay's narcissism took the form of an overarching single-mindedness about his career and the material that fed it. To some close observers of Jay over the years, the *Tonight Show* star didn't seem to be living life so much as he seemed to be living comedy material.

Dave's narcissism, however, seemed more officially diagnosable. Some of Dave's associates who had interacted with him over long periods of time began to look for ways to try to help him cope better with his demons, and dug through psychological tracts looking to match the symptoms of Dave's apparent neurosis. They settled on a variant of narcissism, because the straight clinical condition—the one defined by grandiosity and egotism—didn't seem a match. Dave seemed at times the direct opposite of that. His condition was more defined by a swing between huge confidence and feelings of worthlessness.

No one who spent a lot of time with Letterman ever doubted that he had true demons. The guesses about the reasons for that were varied, although, as might be expected, some pointed to his relationship with his mother. His mom's public persona, from her numerous appearances on the show, was that of a lovely older woman from Indianapolis who baked pies every Thanksgiving. But in countless interviews Dave described her in variations of the same theme: "The least demonstrative woman God ever breathed life into." It was another thing Dave had in common with his old rival: Jay's mother seemed to have issues with showing emotion, as well.

Many of those closest to Dave urged him to seek some help, get counseling of some kind, maybe visit a psychiatrist. But that idea always unsettled him. One member of his inner circle said, "Every time I brought up over the years that he ought to see a shrink he always had the same reaction: 'I wouldn't be as funny.' There was probably no question that he was right." For the same reason Dave resisted recommendations that some kind of medication might help.

As committed as he was to staying funny, Letterman didn't completely disregard his psychological state. Many of his colleagues believed he had occasionally sought some kind of psychological assistance—either formal or through his own research—because he dropped observations like his conclusion that he suffered from anhedonia, the inability to experience pleasurable emotions. And on the air he would tell guests that he couldn't come to their play, or party, or dinner because he suffered from a social-anxiety disorder. Invariably the audience would laugh. The Letterman they knew was supremely self-confident, the master of his domain, in charge of every interaction with his guests. This guy was socially awkward?

Dave did turn up at a private party NBC held for Tom Brokaw at the Museum of Modern Art in 2004, when Tom was leaving the anchor position. Though it was well known that Letterman and Brokaw had developed a solid personal relationship, heads turned all around the room when Dave walked in, accompanied by Regina Lasko, for fifteen years the woman in his life. Regina had an even lower profile in New York social circles, but at the Brokaw event she appeared smiling at Dave's side, happily accepting congratulations on the birth of their son, Harry, less than a year before. Dave stood back stiffly from the center of the party. When someone who knew Dave well noted to Regina that a lot of people in the room were surprised to see them there, Regina replied, "So am I. It's the first social occasion we've attended in five years."

It was another case of Dave only getting more so. Years earlier, when Dave was better about talking to people, he still avoided dinners with large groups from the show. And if he was out and ran into someone he knew—a frequent guest from his show, say—he would often be thrown and not know what to do, how to go over to the other table and say a simple hello.

Even with his idol, Johnny, the awkwardness could sometimes seep out. Soon after Carson bought his estate in Malibu, which was not far from where Dave had purchased a much more modest home, Dave appeared on *The Tonight Show*. After the taping, Johnny pointed out that they were neighbors now. "Maybe we should get together," Johnny said.

"And do what?" Dave asked.

Dave was never less than eloquent when speaking *about* Johnny Carson, if not to him. He openly admitted to being "in awe" of Carson and how he felt that he literally owed his career to Johnny.

Carson's had been the vote that sent Dave off to CBS when NBC was still dangling the fever dream of *The Tonight Show* in front of him in 1993. It was Johnny who had told him that the eighteen-month hold in the deal made it sound bogus, and that he certainly would not have accepted it for himself. That was enough for Dave.

Nobody, not even Jay, really doubted who Carson believed deserved to succeed him, but Johnny himself didn't have a vote in that. He kept his opinion on the matter private, at least until it was revealed after his death that Carson had regularly submitted monologue jokes to Dave.

That was the handiwork of Peter Lassally, the longtime executive producer for Carson, who took on the same role for Letterman after Johnny retired—first while Dave was still at NBC, and then for a time at CBS. Lassally, whose expertise in broadcasting stretched back to Arthur Godfrey's days in radio, became Letterman's chief counselor, advocate, and father figure during the turbulent days after NBC threw Dave over in favor of Jay. Throughout the late nineties and into the next decade, their relationship, like most others involving Dave, cooled and warmed, warmed and cooled. At the same time Lassally, to his delight, was growing much closer to the retired, and now more relaxed, Johnny.

The separation from the show that had been his life and utter preoccupation for thirty years had proved jarring for Carson. Friends reported that it had taken at least six months after he stepped down before Johnny could have a normal day—one in which he didn't feel the withdrawal pangs. Even after he settled in to his postshow life, however, Carson could not turn off the trenchant comic instincts honed over a lifetime. He would read the paper in the morning, watch the news, hear about some zany event taking place somewhere, and the joke would simply come to him, like music. And what good is a perfectly crafted joke if you can't tell it to someone?

Johnny took to calling Peter Lassally, sometimes once a week, occasionally several times, when he had one of the monologues down. Over the phone Johnny would read his collection of carefully composed, Carsonesque jokes—*perform* them, really, just as he would have if he had driven to Burbank, put on his suit, and walked out onstage to read them off cue cards. The performance was just as amusing and appealing as it had always been, the only difference being that now Johnny was not entertaining the multitudes but performing for an audience of one.

Lassally would compliment Johnny of course. As the jokes rolled on, Peter developed another idea. "These jokes are wonderful, Johnny," Peter would tell him. "You really should start sending these in to Dave."

Carson dismissed the idea. "No, I can't do that," he would say. "I don't want to force Dave to do it. Dave would feel obligated."

Lassally could hardly dispute that, knowing how Dave idolized Johnny. Still, he urged Carson again and again. The jokes were too good to be wasting on one person. Let's send them in to Dave, he repeated.

Johnny, finally convinced, didn't flood Dave with jokes, sending in only a few here and there whenever he felt they were worthy. Letterman could not help but be moved, but promised he would judge the material as he would that from any other writer. Later he would mention that Johnny had sent some jokes to him as early as the NBC days, when they were both on the network. But this was different. This was Johnny Carson, silenced by retirement, still using his comic voice, with Dave as the mouthpiece. Dave didn't want to reveal the secret, and Johnny certainly didn't want to offend NBC by having it publicly known that he was writing for the guy competing with *The Tonight Show*. So only a few insiders knew the source of the jokes, and which ones were Johnny's when they got on the air.

Johnny himself took to watching the show each night wondering if Dave would use one of his submissions. (And if he did, yes, Johnny would be paid his seventy-five dollars.) Whenever Dave did, Johnny's joy was infectious, and he would call Lassally and excitedly tell him, "Oh my gosh. I got a joke on the air last night. Dave told one of my jokes."

Lassally could hear the pride in Carson's voice. "He was like a kid in a candy store," Lassally recalled.

After Carson died, on January 23, 2005, Dave put together a special show with Lassally and Doc Severinsen, Carson's old orchestra leader, as guests. He ended the opening monologue that night with an explanation: Every joke he had just told had been submitted by Johnny Carson. They all got laughs—and if you listened closely, you could almost hear the Carson rhythms.

"Bad day in New York, today. The cab fare in New York has gone up from two dollars to two fifty. And as any New York City cabbie can tell you, that's a twenty-two-rupee increase."

"John Kerry, you know, was criticized for throwing away his military service medals back in the seventies. So, not to be outdone, today, President Bush threw away his National Guard Spotty-Attendance Ribbon."

In 2007 David Letterman turned sixty, a fact he casually mentioned on the air, as he would when he turned sixty-one, sixty-two, and sixty-three. It was what it was. Dave was never going to change the way he looked or dressed or acted to try to counter the reality that he was now heading toward senior citizen status. The first and greatest sin for him remained phoniness. Dave would stand up and be who he was, no matter the consequences.

If anything, Letterman seemed to embrace growing older; his jokes and remarks at the desk often made reference to his age, as when he would ruefully comment that people sometimes took him for Harry's grandfather when they went out and about. Harry did bring out the youthful Dave, who seemed to delight in all the mysteries of childhood that were being played out in front of him.

But on the show the cranky old guy that Dave had frequently assumed as a role throughout his career had now become a genuine cranky old guy—a development that, as usual, he often turned on himself. "I know a lot of people regard me as a snarky putz," he said one night at the desk, joking about how he was thinking of replacing Oprah when she left her show.

Many nights he threw out lines that were some variation on the theme of his barely putting in an effort anymore and largely just mailing it in. "I quit trying ten years ago," he said during one show. "We just do the same old crap night after night."

His staff, however, saw that Dave was still tinkering, testing new ideas: obnoxious guests just showing up and sitting down next to him; bizarre phone calls from some angry guy to the phone on his desk; interactions with oddball characters like an actor playing Mike Singletary, the coach of the San Francisco 49ers. For fans who remembered the wildly inventive stuff of his early days (elevator races, show-us-your-pictures at the Fotomat, guests sitting in barber chairs), what Dave was presenting now might have seemed like thin gruel. But within the limits of the energy he was now willing to expend, he was still trying.

"If the shows were bad, we would feel differently," said one veteran writer-producer. "But Dave's still very, very good at this. He has to pick and choose now the things that he's going to work hard on." And as always, the comparison came out: "Johnny did the same thing."

That adjusted energy level was something the longtime staff members noticed early in the aught decade. It was part of Dave's genius, they told themselves, that he was always so smart about his own evolution. He knew when to stop wearing a Velcro suit and jumping into a wall, and when to shut down the remotes that were such a distinctive feature of the show and often inspired him to heights of brilliance. The truth was, Dave always hated doing those remotes—he didn't like all that attention focused on him. When they simply got too hard on him, he eliminated them. So the remotes disappeared, as he did the cold opens with some shtick involving a guest in his dressing room. Even the regular bits of business with Rupert Jee at the Hello Deli were mostly dropped.

Always averse to doing five shows a week, Dave had early on tried to build a three-day weekend into his life by eliminating Friday as a workday. He took to taping a second show later on Thursday evening, a move that got him out, free to fly Friday morning to Montana or St. Barts or wherever he desired, for some R & R.

In 2007 he decided that the two shows on Thursday were too taxing. The double assignment made it harder to enjoy fully the next three days off. So he shook up the schedule again, rejiggering the machinery of the show to make it possible to tape the Friday show on *Monday*. His energy would clearly be higher on Mondays after the three days off, and this way, he could get ready for his getaways after the single show on Thursday, which would be wrapped up by seven or so.

Another network with a different relationship with a star might have raised an objection to this schedule. It meant, after all, that the Friday show would be canned like tuna; so the jokes for Friday would have to be written very carefully. If a joke was made on the air about a certain celebrity on Monday, for example, and by Friday that celebrity had been married, fired, jailed, or was—most horribly—dead, the show would have to be clumsily edited. The comedy, as a result, had to be stepped as far back as possible from topical. And of course, this freezer-burned item would be airing in competition against a show minted fresh that day on NBC with Jay Leno joking away on whatever events were in *that* day's news.

Although the advantage being conceded to Jay seemed enormous, CBS went along with the plan. They didn't have much choice. Not only was Letterman likely to give them explicit anatomical directions for where they could stick their objections, but the network's hands were effectively tied by its deal with Dave. Because he owned the show—and Craig Ferguson's behind it—it was up to Worldwide Pants to make most decisions about it, including the production schedule. CBS executives could forward requests, of course, but they could not tell Letterman how to do his show—nor would they dare.

Over time, the impact of the stale-bread Friday episodes became noticeable. CBS, from just about that point on, saw the numbers begin to drop slightly for the Friday editions of *Late Show*. A few years later, the falloff became precipitous. Jay would bury Dave every Friday, often pulling away in the ratings even during weeks when the other nights had been close.

When CBS's researchers asked viewers if they reacted differently to the Friday Letterman shows, they answered no, but the ratings slide made it seem obvious that the perception had somehow gotten through that Dave's Friday show was, literally, old news. Late-night viewers had likely grown accustomed to checking out the top of each of the programs to see if the opening joke was of the moment—and if it wasn't, that usually signaled to them that it was a repeat. In time CBS would decide to tinker with the idea of simply offering a repeat on Fridays—at least in summer. The ratings seemed to come in at about the same level.

Around the same time that he was turning Monday into Friday, Dave also stopped showing up for rehearsal. The established pattern for late-night shows was to work on material through the morning and early afternoon, take it to the stage around two in the afternoon, and do a run-through. Dave had followed that routine for years—until he stopped. In lieu of a formal rehearsal, he simply familiarized himself with the material, never going to the stage to work through it.

One of his producers defended the practice, saying it was another way Dave pared down the demands of the job so he could keep doing it past sixty. In his own explanation, Dave referred to an interview with the former Dallas Cowboys running back Emmitt Smith, who had discussed, as he considered retirement, what it was about the job that he really couldn't do anymore—the practices. Dave still liked the time on the field; what he didn't like was the practices.

In September 2008, Letterman told *Rolling Stone*, in describing how the show was different and much more "host-friendly" than it used to be, "I'm not working as hard as I used to. All I have to do, really, is pick out a tie and sit down."

The rope-a-dope strategy paid off almost immediately for *Late Show*. Viewers (the older ones) apparently started drifting away from Conan in his second week to catch some of Dave's guest-loaded lineup: Howard Stern on Monday, Julia Roberts on Tuesday, Stupid Human Tricks on Wednesday.

Julia provided the first breakthrough, the first night when Dave pulled in more viewers than Conan. She teased Dave about his marriage to Regina the previous March, asking him, "Did she take your name?"

Dave said she did.

"So she's Mrs. Letterman?" Julia wanted to know.

"No," Letterman answered "She's Dave."

The shows that week were all crisp, with Letterman firing off the monologue jokes with high confidence and sparring with his guests with energy and wit.

Over at NBC, they were watching closely. One 30 Rock executive took note right away: "Dave is on his game."

Peter Lassally thought so, too. He checked out Dave's performance each night that week with increasing pleasure. No one had more experience evaluating what it took to make a late-night show work than Lassally, and he always put Letterman at the very top in terms of pure talent. But Dave so often tossed off shows with less than full effort, or got disgusted with himself for long periods of time and displayed that disgust—or, worse, pure anger—that the show inevitably suffered.

But when he committed, when Dave applied that potent mix of searing intelligence and scintillating wit, he could still take Peter Lassally's breath away.

"Brett Favre announced he was retiring again—but he vowed to keep fighting for the people of Alaska."

That week Lassally saw Letterman marching out each night and belting out a bravura monologue just as he had when he first came to CBS. "He's got the fever!" Lassally said by midweek. The material also sounded more biting, punchier. It was all wildly above Peter's expectations. Could it really be true? Could the old Dave be back?

Lassally couldn't resist calling Dave—and, of course, got the old Dave on the phone. When Peter told Dave how great the monologue had been every night that week, Letterman immediately deflected the compliment.

"How's Alice?" Dave asked, shifting the topic to Peter's much-loved wife.

No matter how hard Lassally tried, Dave continued to shrink away from his praise, finally saying, "I don't want to talk about that." He simply would not let Lassally express enthusiasm about his performance.

The competition for the hearts and eyeballs of viewers under fifty, meanwhile, continued to be a mismatch. In week three, when Dave finally slipped ahead in the viewer totals by 143,000, Conan buried Letterman by half a rating point (almost 700,000 people) among the younger segment of the audience. If that pattern remained consistent, no one at NBC would complain, because Conan would clean up in terms of cash—and accumulating cash, not eyeballs, was the name of the game.

What the Letterman people liked, though, was the trend. As the weeks of summer wore on, Dave's margin in viewers grew larger; he began winning weeks by totals of more than 700,000, then 800,000—one week in August Dave won by close to a million viewers.

The margin for those eighteen-to-forty-nine viewers was dropping, too—though the fact that Conan always won, even with those massive deficiencies among the overall viewing totals, spoke to the fact that some kind of sweeping generational migration was taking place.

Neither host had any real structural advantage in the summer. In general, CBS's ten p.m. repeats of cop shows provided decent lead-in audiences, but NBC had by far the biggest show of the summer months in the reality competition show *America's Got Talent*, which several nights extended all the way to eleven p.m., giving Conan a presumed boost.

One thing that was not happening was any sniping between the two shows. Conan had long since established his membership in the Letterman fan club, so his team wasn't about to start throwing stones; Letterman had clearly laid his imprimatur on Conan with his visits to his show. Whenever the subject of Conan came up, Dave went right to the heart of the matter: "He's a very funny guy."

Not that he thought Conan always appreciated the full weight of the late-night cross. He noted that when Conan came on as a guest on Dave's CBS show, about two years into his run on *Late Night*, and Dave asked him how it was going, Conan replied that things were great and he had done about eighteen tremendous shows in a row. Dave recalled thinking, *Holy Christ, he's either lying or insane.* The obvious reason: Dave couldn't think of eighteen tremendous shows he had done during his entire late-night career.

A staff member who had been with Dave through most of his career broke down the comedy of the three big network talents. He said, "Conan's comedy is whimsical, which was like Dave's, but he's moved away from that as he's gotten older. I don't know if Conan has evolved a ton since he was in his thirties. Jay doesn't really have a point of view, other than 'I'm a joke-telling machine and I'm a blue-collar guy.' Conan is very smart. He has thoughts in his head. He's got a point of view, but not like a broadcaster like Dave who just comes out and says stuff. I think Conan chooses not to have a point of view, unlike Jay, who doesn't really have the mentality to have one."

One veteran member of Letterman's writing staff had a question about whether Conan might be saddled with an inherent handicap: "Is there something about the look, the presence, the sound of his voice? The oldest credo in television is you need to have a big head to star on TV. As much as we want to get away from that stuff, we are humans and there's something that goes on there. Conan is kind of gangly, pasty looking. He's got a high voice."

Really none of that had anything to do with Conan's talent, which was all that really should have mattered, as the Letterman staff members conceded. But as the summer weeks passed and the ratings came in, and Dave looked more and more competitive with Conan, confidence suffused the *Late Show* staff. By their reckoning the timing of the move to *The Tonight Show*—that five-year wait on the sidelines—had ultimately hurt O'Brien.

"He cooled off," one Letterman staff member said. "He languished there. Five, six years ago he became the *thing*. Then he had those five years of lame-duckness."

But there was much more than that behind their growing sense of confidence. As one Letterman staff member put it, "Conan is in a very perilous position. He goes on in summer, tries to get himself established, and then—here comes Jay."

The impending arrival of Leno in the fall as the lead-in every night at ten aroused more than curiosity among Letterman's backers. They were all but counting the days. "Here's what I think is going to happen," said the writing staff veteran. "Dave's numbers will not move. But when Jay comes on, Conan is going to stay below Dave. I feel sorry for Conan. I think he's getting sandbagged."

CHAPTER NINE

THE POWER OF TEN

In the outrageously overacted scene, a cold open to a new TV show, a fake college professor, looking more like a used-car salesman in a local TV commercial, was giving a class full of girls with big hair and guys in mullets some rigorous instruction in the intricacies of network television.

One student stood up to offer his intentionally pretentious analysis of an article on how "the temporality of physical sexual attraction necessarily undermines one's prime-time viability—and the descent into cable is inevitable."

Though fraught with potential meaning for the program's host, who was seated in the back row of the class during the first moments of *The Jay Leno Show*, that supposedly funny line was not precisely predictive of the course of his career.

The entertainment that followed turned out to be a strange mix of taped segments, awkward interviews with the audience, a truncated monologue, "angry-Jay" rants, guest appearances from a lineup that included Vanna White and Doug Llewelyn, and a brief cameo from a guy in high-waisted jeans and golf shirt, ostensibly coming on to this trying-much-too-hard romp to make his "dramatic debut" in a scene from *The Glass Menagerie*.

That would be David Letterman. But he wasn't around for long. Dave walked out onstage, he greeted Jay, the lights went black, a shot rang out, and when the dust cleared, there was Letterman, stretched out onstage, allegedly shot dead. The faux-irritated but too-busy-to-care Jay made light of the moment, declaring they needed to "get this stiff out of here."

Between ultrastrained moments like Llewelyn—the onetime "court reporter" for *The People's Court*—covering a "real trial" between a creationist and an evolutionist (something having to do with a pet monkey) and Jay unaccountably (and unfunnily) breaking a parked car's window with a sledgehammer because it had a "Baby on Board" sign and he didn't see any baby inside, Leno went around finding "clues" about the Letterman "murder" in the audience. These consisted of random letters of the alphabet, which he handed to Vanna to post on a board in some kind of *Wheel of Fortune* code meant to spell out the name of the Letterman killer.

Actually, though, right after the shooting moment, Jay had told viewers—those "at home with VCRs"—to tape the show and play back the blackout scene "really slow" to see who the real killer was. If they did, they would have seen that it was in fact Jay himself who knocked Dave off—and, yes, that was the predictive highlight of *The Jay Leno Show*.

But it was not the Jay Leno show that premiered on NBC at ten p.m. in September 2009. This was a much earlier *Jay Leno Show*, also on NBC, but one that aired in 1986. At that time NBC had already cast its eye on Jay as a potential late-night talent, mainly thanks to his many killer (in a different sense of that word) appearances with Letterman on *Late Night*. The network agreed to set Jay up in a pilot, his second for NBC. (The first, also an embarrassing miss, had been intended specifically to be considered for prime time.) This one was designed to showcase Jay's varied comedy talents for possible use as part of what NBC viewed as its "late-night wheel" on Saturday nights—*Saturday Night Live* and shows they could use on the weeks when *SNL* was dark.

That was the plan until they got a look at *The Jay Leno Show*. Shot, for obscure reasons, on a pier under the Ben Franklin Bridge in Philadelphia, the concept and the material impressed no one. Jay did do a monologue, but it was the furthest thing imaginable from the topical Leno joke fests he would come to be famous for. Wearing what was then his signature hip-guy gear—black pants, reddish blazer, sleeves rolled a quarter up—Jay told jokes about bad air travel and railed about corporations. But the laughs he got from an audience spread out around tables to create an ersatz nightclub effect were perfunctory. Rick Ludwin, even then NBC's designated executive in the world of late night, watched the proceedings from backstage. He had a simple verdict: It didn't work.

Other assessments were harsher. One of Jay's bigger supporters of that era among NBC's late-night participants, based on Leno's many jousts with Letterman, was astonished by the overwhelming lameness of the production, which the supporter knew had been shepherded by Jay's then manager Helen Kushnick. (Helen and her husband, Jerry, both received executive producer credits on the special.) "Helen got him the special," the late-night player said. "This was Jay left to his own devices. That was Jay's sensibility, everything. It was a horrible show."

Somebody else had been watching the Leno special with intense interest. Sitting around with some of his "comedy nerd" friends from the *Lampoon*, Conan O'Brien had made it a point to catch *The Jay Leno Show*. Like all hard-core Letterman devotees of that era, Conan looked forward with excitement to Leno's bookings on *Late Night*, because his spots with Dave were so consistently electric. But this? For Conan and his *Lampoon* coterie, the Leno special was a total disconnect between the hip, hilarious comic who appeared with Dave and this clearly uncomfortable, imaginatively flailing guy. He was out of his milieu.

If anyone at NBC in 2009 had dug out the old *Jay Leno Show* from some dusty network remainder bin marked "Misbegotten and Forgotten," would it have raised any questions about Jay's trying something so clearly out of his comfort zone, something so different from his *Tonight Show*? Almost surely not—because, in 2009, NBC's top executives were convinced that Jay ranked as one of the most beloved entertainers in America. That wasn't just their own opinion; the research had told them so.

As for Jay, he never had reason to worry that his upcoming ten o'clock show was going to be some stab in the dark like that ghastly 1986 effort. For one thing, the terrible ideas conjured for that show were banished from his memory. For another, he had long since learned: *Dance with the one who brung you.*

"Even though it's ten o'clock," Jay said in outlining his plans for *The Jay Leno Show* of 2009, "we're going to pretend it's eleven thirty."

As the weeks slipped away between his final *Tonight Show* in May and his big-splash premiere set for September, Jay—along with the steadfast Debbie Vickers—had to find a way to satisfy an ever expanding roster of constituencies. Left to his own, he likely would have kept most of the elements of his *Tonight Show* intact—all the way down to sticking around in the ancient studio he (and Carson) had occupied for years. But he pulled up stakes and moved a few hundred yards across the Burbank lot, from Studio 3 to Studio 11, a vast, barnlike room. NBC had sold the entire Burbank complex, moving most of its production operations over to the Universal lot, where Conan now worked. But everyone could see the potential conflict if the two shows occupied the same gated community. So NBC rented back the big Studio 11 in Burbank just for Leno. Jay, who didn't "want to go to some amusement park" (and preferred not to change his drive-in routine anyway), stuck around his old digs, kicking around the potential changes for ten p.m.

Some seemed utterly cosmetic. He would enter from what looked like the glass doors of an insurance agency, flanked by huge, square wooden columns—which made it look like an insurance agency in the Roman forum. And of course, there would be no desk. That was the major concession to Conan and *The Tonight Show*, the program that had invented the host behind the desk. That move, like several others, was made, Vickers explained, entirely out of respect for Conan. She had great personal affection for Jeff Ross, her counterpart on Conan's show, and believed the two shows could coexist without any issues. If Conan succeeded, it would be best for Jay, the network, and everybody, Vickers was convinced.

Without his desk, though, Jay would be compelled to talk to guests sitting in a couple of low-set blue felt chairs—the kind you might find in a hotel lobby—in a little conversation nook, stage right. The most significant cosmetic change for him here involved wardrobe. He had to wear midcalf socks (which he hated), because with no desk to hide behind, his legs, and some potential skin peeking out from under his cuffs, could be visible during these interviews.

But Jay would still step out onto his little monologue platform to greet the audience and deliver the nightly volley of jokes; he would still look to his left to get reaction or support from his reliable bandleader, Kevin Eubanks. And in a pinch, they would even roll out a minidesk for him to work behind for such critical elements as the "Headlines" segment, which was still set for Monday nights—just like always.

What would not be like always was that "Headlines" was going to disappear from its traditional spot in act two, right after the show's first commercial pod. Instead it would be relegated to the final segment of the show, some comedy candy to keep the fans hanging in until the end. The decision to move that segment came directly as the result of a request by Jay's most important partners in the ten p.m. enterprise: the managers of NBC's lineup of affiliated stations. Before NBC could attempt this monumental redefinition of prime time, it had to get assurances that its stations would be on board. And they were (with that single exception of the Boston affiliate that wanted to preempt Jay but was soon browbeaten into line). The local stations had conducted their own round of research into the ten p.m. change and found the results most promising. Not only did their viewers indicate that they liked Jay and would love to see him earlier, but their answers to the research questions seemed to prove that Jay's viewers had special interest in the news, which was why they enjoyed his topical monologues so much. The stations had only one request: They wanted input into the format of the show.

In LA, Debbie Vickers read a piece in the paper about NBC's plans for the show and saw a quote from Jeff Zucker saying, "We're going to let the affiliate board have input." No one had mentioned this plan to Debbie. Her reaction: We're in trouble.

Debbie Vickers had no intention of sitting down with TV station managers—hilarious guys though they might be—to hear their ideas about how to create a comedy show. She told Rick Ludwin, "You've got to go to these meetings. I'm not meeting with affiliates." Vickers had never considered herself and her team to be production geniuses, but they certainly knew more about what Jay was comfortable doing than guys selling commercial time to supermarkets in Omaha and Orlando.

Ludwin held the meetings. Word came back: The stations wanted the strongest possible comedy material at the end of the show, to lead in to their local newscasts. That meant not just "Headlines" but also "Jaywalking" and the items from the 99-cent store—all the act two bits Jay had painstakingly assembled over time as recurring elements. Slotting them at the program's close instead of right after the monologue would necessarily change Jay's rhythm. Vickers thought it was a bad idea, but the network had agreed to it, so they went along. The plan then became to fill the now empty act two with a host of new "comedy correspondents" who would tape some energetic (and, they hoped, amusing) reports to keep the laughs rolling each night.

Another move made to enforce the distinction from *The Tonight Show* was limiting the guest interviews to one each night—on the set, in any case. The staff then came up with another idea, "10 at 10," in which Jay would interview some celebrity by satellite from a remote location with ten questions intended to evoke humorous replies and sparkling repartee. And then there was "The Green Car Challenge," designed to play off Jay's automotive avocation. Guests would be invited to take a spin in an electric-powered Ford Focus around a racetrack laid out in the area behind the studio, each recording a time. The idea was to create some competitive fun among the celebrities—while simultaneously killing some minutes on the show.

From the start Vickers fretted about how to fill this newly constructed hour five nights a week. It could not be like late night, which formatted itself easily: monologue; second comedy bit; lead guest for two segments; secondary guest; music act; "Stay tuned for Conan—good night, everybody!"

For one thing, NBC did not want much music in prime time, if any at all. The reason musical acts were always exiled to the closing minutes of late-night shows was that they rarely pulled in viewers and more often drove away those who preferred a different style. And with just one guest onstage for a single segment, the other chunks of time seemed to Vickers like massive hungry mouths waiting to be fed.

In interviews Jay adamantly described the ten p.m. entry as a "comedy show" and not—horror of horrors—a "variety show." The "variety" designation, Jay explained, "just has a bad connotation." But he acknowledged that sticking to comedy meant he would likely have to commit to producing something like three times as much comedy as he had on *The Tonight Show*—most of it generated by the host himself.

In selling the creative breakthrough of the ten p.m. idea, NBC touted the originality of offering viewers an hour of comedy rather than the standard murder investigations and doctors having sex at ten p.m. In fact, television had had plenty of history with hour-long comedy shows, many of which ranked among the all-time classics: Jackie Gleason, Red Skelton, Carol Burnett, *Your Show of Shows* (that one somehow filled ninety minutes). Of course, all those shows were on once a week, and none had been seen since the late seventies. The challenge for Jay was to produce prime-time-worthy comedy on five consecutive nights, week in, week out.

The key to success, both NBC and Jay's staff agreed, was to get the show up and running and strong enough to weather the early storm of new episodes of *CSI: Miami* on CBS and *Private Practice* on ABC; to reach December, when the dramas would go into repeats for about a month; to show what Jay could do as an alternative to repeats; and then to hang on until summer, when he would likely start to crush the all-rerun lineups he would face.

Jay promoted the logic behind NBC's strategy almost as vigorously as the network executives did. More people were going to bed these days before late night started; fans were telling him they looked forward to a chance to see him earlier; surely there was a market at ten for something lighter than tales of lurid murders and rapes. He did have reluctance about the title, though, preferring "Weeknight with Jay Leno," which NBC thought sounded like a news hour. Jay, again citing his mom's discomfort with ostentation, shrank from sticking his name out there too prominently with "The Jay Leno Show." Or maybe he remembered the one from 1986 with the same name.

But in the summer of 2009, as he made his preparations for his new show-business life, Jay Leno declared himself a realist. "It's going to be different," he said. "The key will be holding the audience through the second half of the show. That's going to be tricky."

Jeff Zucker also retained a realistic assessment of his late-night handiwork. Though he proclaimed the evident economic rationale for his move of Jay to ten o'clock, citing the desperate need for broadcast networks to reduce costs, increase revenues, or face the evolutionary grim reaper, that amounted to a bit of after-the-fact rationalizing. The plan made sense; it played perfectly to the doomed-networks scenario that prevailed in cable television circles and many places on the Internet. It even induced one remaining standard-bearer of "old media," *Time* magazine, to produce a cover story featuring a mischievous-looking Jay leaning into the frame under a headline: "Jay Leno Is the Future of Television. Seriously!"

But none of that was the dominant reason why Jeff Zucker had installed Jay Leno at ten. Privately he conceded, "I didn't make this move for economic reasons; I made this move to keep Jay from going to ABC."

The risk involved, had that happened, would not have merely made a serious dent in NBC's late-night dominance—and profits. A defection by

Jay would link back directly to Zucker's 2004 move to ask the top dog in late night to step aside so NBC could guarantee Conan *The Tonight Show*. Jeff was still on the hook for however that call was going to turn out. But besides that, by almost every external evaluation in 2008, a Jay Leno at ABC figured to more than dent NBC; it looked like he would T-bone them like one of his Duesenbergs ramming a Mini Cooper.

NBC's own research department had come up with much the same results. At ABC, Jay would do very well, and probably win.

That summer Zucker presented a different argument. With Jay at ABC, Conan still would have won, he said, or at least he would have beaten Jay where it most counted for NBC, in the young demo. Rick Ludwin had assertively made that point to Zucker: Conan was going to take away the younger viewers, while Jay and Dave would be left to divvy up an audience that was largely above fifty years old.

But the idea of slicing the late-night pizza again, with Jay eating up a sizable portion of the advertising dough—which was already being doled out among Letterman, Conan, Kimmel, Stewart, Colbert, Ferguson, etc.—gave Zucker long pause. By NBC's calculations, a number of the late-night players already faced diminishing financial futures. The network didn't think Jimmy Kimmel's show made money at all, and Craig Ferguson's, maybe a pittance—a couple of million a year, they guessed. (CBS begged to differ, without offering specifics.) NBC figured that even Jimmy Fallon, who had started up amid diminished expectations, would do no better than OK.

Of course, some measure of Fallon's fate would depend on how Conan did in the hour preceding. The 11:35 shows were still where the big advertising money gravitated, but they were no longer a source of big earnings. *The Tonight Show*, a $150 million profit machine less than a decade earlier, had begun to fall below a third of that annual total. NBC believed Conan could keep that level up if he cornered the younger adult viewers. As one senior network executive observed, "We don't believe Letterman is strong enough to take any advertising money away."

The real financial opportunity still rested with Jay. NBC concocted all kinds of story angles to put the move in the best possible light—and many did sound valid. For the cost of only one hour-long ten p.m. drama—$3 million an episode—NBC could pay for an entire week of *The Jay Leno Show*. That didn't even take account of all the money the network would save by not having to develop new shows for the ten o'clock slot, most of which would fail miserably anyway at a cost of tens of millions. It did mean, however, that NBC would have far fewer at-bats with which to attempt to hit one out of the park, as CBS had done with shows like *CSI* and *NCIS*, both of which generated hundreds of millions in syndication sales. There would be no syndication aftermarket for Jay. Still, NBC hadn't hit one of those grand slam shows in what seemed like eons—and with GE contracting the costs down to the barest of bones, nobody foresaw a slugger-savior popping up any time soon.

Zucker started to like his chances a bit—and his strategic plan even more. In one respect, the play could be seen as something of a coup. The goal all along had been to retain both Conan and Jay, to avoid any replays of the Letterman-Leno fiasco. Here it was, five years after the big dive into the future, and NBC still had both stars. And in a curious twist, both had signed on at significant risk, which could impact their future plans to flee for other pastures. If the ten p.m. plan worked, NBC would get credit for transforming the fundamental economics of the industry; if it didn't, the network had at least prevented Jay Leno from going up against them— and now he might never be able to.

As one of Zucker's close associates put it privately, "I do think Jeff made a master stroke here. He's positioned it so that if Leno goes down, no one will want him anymore. ABC will have moved on. Conan, meanwhile has a chance to take root."

Even if that didn't happen, if Conan flopped, then it would be Conan trying to reenter the late-night market as a diminished thing. And if Jay actually did succeed at ten? "Jeff solves the ten p.m. problem," the Zucker associate said, "and all his costs go down."

One of television programming's legendary names, Fred Silverman, who led first CBS, then ABC, then NBC, provided serious cover for Zucker's plan. "If the Leno show works," Silverman remarked, "it will be the most significant thing to happen in broadcast television in the last decade."

Lorne Michaels used the "master stroke" analogy as well, on what he called "the chess-move level." The ABC threat is over; cost savings could be massive. Lorne's reservations had to do with the idea behind the show: Late-night guy moves to prime time. He was old enough to remember Jack Paar, who had been huge on *The Tonight Show*, trying to make a comeback in a prime-time hour. The show lasted only a couple of years. "I don't know why it didn't work," Michaels said. "It didn't feel right." He har-bored the same doubts about Leno, though he conceded, "Fortunes have been lost underestimating Jay Leno."

Another longtime NBC executive saw Zucker's familiar fingerprints all over the move. Recalling Zucker's trademark when he ran NBC's enter-tainment division—when, faced with a threat to the network's dominant Thursday nights, he expanded the running time of the episodes of his strongest comedies—the executive said: "Jeff is supersizing late night."

Competitors ripped the plan in public, though in private some nodded at the rationale. "If you look at it on one level, win-win," one rival enter-tainment executive said. "They were stretched thin. They were failing. Nice Band-Aid."

Out in Hollywood, where Zucker was still widely seen as an alien with hostile intent, the move incited pure rage—a lot of it highly personal. Especially among writers and producers who created ten p.m. shows, the Leno invasion was taken as a belligerent affront. At a gathering of show runners during the summer press tour in LA, NBC, Zucker, and Leno were excoriated for the damage they were inflicting on the televi-sion industry—and for betraying the legacy of NBC, established by such ten p.m. classics as *Hill Street Blues*, *Law & Order*, *L.A. Law*, and *ER*.

Shawn Ryan, who created the hit cable drama *The Shield* and worked on numerous network hours, including *The Unit* for CBS, said, "The reason you're hearing a visceral backlash is specific to NBC. You have a generation of writers that grew up on their shows. It inspired them to write. That network used to stand for something better." Kurt Sutter, a *Shield* writer who went on to create *Sons of Anarchy* for the cable channel FX, called NBC and Zucker "the bastards to hate." And Peter Tolan, who skewered late night earlier in his career on *The Larry Sanders Show* and then found success in drama with *Rescue Me*, summed up the prevailing view: "I feel like they should take down the American flag from in front of their building and put up a white flag."

One top studio executive, left to contemplate a business minus five hours of drama programming that an outside production unit could potentially fill, delivered a blunt opinion: "This has all the earmarks of a train wreck." The executive zeroed in on the affiliate question. "The big-gest issue is the affiliate lead-ins. So they're putting the better comedy bits at the end. What do you do between 10:12 and 10:50? More comedy? All that comedy is impossible to write and rehearse." Citing CBS head Leslie Moonves and Disney/ABC head Bob Iger, the executive said, "Les and Iger must figure they could finish off NBC with this."

Even within NBC the Leno move did not win anywhere near unanimous consent. Something about the way the network had positioned it—the cost savings, writing off ever being able to find hit-level success at ten p.m., writing off *winning*—offended some of the network's loyal veterans. One watched it all unfold and was consumed by unhappiness: "The news conference when the idea was announced was staggering. For the first time in network history, someone acted like we didn't want to win. Someone said, 'We have a number in mind.' That really had a big impact in-house. People noticed that. It was a poor-mouthing of the network. We're supposed to work in the magic department. We do things the public can only dream about. Yet here was a guy saying, 'No, we just have to make a number and that's all we're doing.' It was terribly depressing."

Knowing how hard Zucker had tried to keep Jay with all the other proposals he had run by the comic, another of NBC's most influential players explained, "The ten o'clock idea was the worst idea of all. We all thought it was a disaster. Conan was going to get the wrong lead-in. He'd have no chance to succeed. It was a catastrophe waiting to happen."

The doomsayers kept their concerns to themselves, of course, because what was done was done, and everyone had to pull together to try to make it work. The executive with likely the most influence on Zucker, Dick Ebersol, didn't buy the doom-and-gloom talk anyway. Late that summer he said, "No one would be more shocked than I if Jay doesn't work."

Something did shock Dick Ebersol that summer—and Jeff Zucker, too. In late August they got word from Jeff Immelt that GE was in the process of negotiating the sale of a controlling interest in NBC Universal to the country's biggest cable operator, Comcast. Serious talks had been under way since April. Immelt had deliberately kept Zucker out of the loop until late in the process.

Only two years earlier the GE CEO had made a statement to the company's shareholders to tamp down rumors that the company wanted to unload NBC, perhaps sometime before the massive outlay that would be required to cover the 2008 Olympics from Beijing. "Should we sell NBCU? The answer is no!" Immelt wrote in GE's 2007 annual report. "I just don't see it happening. Not before the Olympics, not after the Olympics. It doesn't make sense."

It did start to make sense soon after, though, when Brian Roberts, the Comcast CEO, began his pursuit. GE suddenly saw what had been bruited about forever in terms of its relationship with NBC: the limited synergies between its core industrial business and a media company—one with valuable cable assets but a limping flagship, the NBC network.

For a while Zucker believed GE was trying to arrange a sale to Comcast only of the 20 percent stake in NBC Universal still held by the French company Vivendi. When he finally got a clear message from Immelt of GE's intentions, Zucker faced the obvious question: What did it mean for him?

GE promised a contract extension, which would cover Zucker financially. But even with that concession he would still be cast as a lame-duck manager until Comcast won regulatory approval for the acquisition. Zucker accordingly set out to thwart that characterization by securing assurance from the incoming Comcast executives that he would continue as NBCU's CEO.

Comcast could not officially comment, but that didn't stop many executives claiming inside knowledge of that company from suggesting Zucker was headed for an executive trapdoor as soon as Comcast took charge. As he usually did, Zucker took to shrugging off those rumors with the same confident "We'll see" attitude that he applied to most efforts to marginalize him. The regulatory process was likely to extend through 2010, giving Zucker, in essence, a year to prove to Comcast's management that he was a leader they ought to retain.

In the shorter term, Zucker had tried to initiate yet another fix in NBC's chronically stalled-out entertainment division. In late July, conceding what others in the company—and throughout much of Hollywood—had long before identified as a mismatch made far from heaven, Zucker found a way to part from Ben Silverman, the onetime "rock star" executive he had chosen in 2007 to revivify NBC's pulseless prime-time schedule. After a couple years of announcements of new directions and much cost cutting, but no real hits, the relationship finally came to the end that outsiders had been forecasting—sometimes in extravagantly vituperative terms—from the beginning. In the end each man quietly acknowledged this particular partnership had been a mistake for both parties.

In place of Silverman's flash and sizzle, Zucker opted for competence and solidity. Rather than picking anyone new, he simply added to the duties he had already piled on to one of his longest-serving lieutenants, Jeff Gaspin. No other executive at NBC possessed a more successful portfolio than Gaspin, who was in charge of NBC's entertainment cable channels, like USA, Bravo, Syfy, and Oxygen, which generated by far the largest share of NBC's earnings.

No one at NBC would ever mistake Gaspin for Ben Silverman; he did not, for example, throw parties accompanied by models in bikinis and white tigers in cages. Even though he had once worked at MTV Networks, running programming for the VH1 channel (where he introduced signature concepts like *Behind the Music* and *Pop-Up Videos*), Gaspin personally exuded conventionality more than dynamism.

But his results were invariably impressive—so much so that Gaspin believed he had deserved the job running NBC Entertainment on both previous occasions when Zucker had hired someone else (first Kevin Reilly, then Silverman). Gaspin's low-key demeanor and somewhat awkward manner held him back at times. He did not always make a strong first impression. But his apparent diffidence masked consuming ambition and drive, a match for anyone else's at NBC, or the rest of the TV business, for that matter.

Gaspin looked far younger than forty-eight; of medium height, he was thin but fit, with boyish features and shortish, carefully composed dark hair. His face and hairline had seemed unchanged for so long that some colleagues joked that he must have a nasty self-portrait hanging somewhere.

For the most part, Gaspin got high marks from those under him for his leadership skills. It was true that some noted a shifty quality to his narrow eyes and tight smile, and even some of his body language, which they thought suggested he was always calculating his next move or next word. But in interviews he fired straight and without apparent guile or pretense.

He did seem to have a bit of a jones for the glamour side of the television business, though. One NBC colleague said, "Gaspin coveted the NBC job because it's a high-profile job and it seemed like he wanted to have the town recognize him as a *macher*. He seemed to always resent that cable was considered a nice little business but never got the same press attention or attention in Hollywood. It always made him crazy."

Gaspin arrived at NBC Entertainment on July 27, 2009. By then the fall schedule was in place, of course, and he didn't hesitate to cite the highest priority for the network: "All attention is going to be on Jay." All through the months since Zucker had set in motion his ten p.m. plan for Leno, Gaspin had been busy with his cable responsibilities and had paid little attention to the new show, other than to be impressed that Zucker had found a way to keep both his late-night stars again. Now that the Jay-at-ten issue was on his own plate, Gaspin had the general conviction that it represented a perfectly reasonable attempt to try something new.

As for what might happen if it didn't work, Gaspin simply avoided discussing the subject. In his mind he knew what moves he might make if Jay's show simply cratered, but he kept them to himself. When he analyzed the possibilities for Jay, Gaspin focused on the upside. The financial part could work with a really minimal rating; it certainly seemed like a more creative solution than trying to slam five more dramas on the air when the rest of NBC's schedule was bloodied and bowed.

At the same time, Gaspin did not spend much time worrying about the condition of Conan O'Brien's *Tonight Show*. As July came to a close, the pattern seemed to be holding, with Letterman winning almost every night in terms of total viewers and Conan prevailing in the younger demographics, though his margins had narrowed a bit. For the last three weeks in July, Conan's weekly margin in the audience between eighteen to forty-nine was .2 of a rating point (about 260,000 people), and each week he trailed Dave by around 750,000 to 800,000 total viewers.

There was certainly reason for some of the concern Gaspin was hearing from New York, but not enough to panic. Early on in his new tenure, he made a point to visit with Conan and have a couple of lunches with Jeff Ross. The conversations went well, from Gaspin's point of view. Conan seemed to have a firm grasp of the situation. He told Gaspin he knew the show needed to be somewhat broader in appeal, but he assured him he was a "good Irish Catholic boy," and when the audience came to realize that about him they would join the party.

At lunch with Ross, Gaspin was impressed, as everyone always was, with the friendly, levelheaded, and unflappable producer—and, in this case, with how in touch he was with the issues concerning the show. The numbers had come down, but they were still OK. Ross underscored his belief that what mattered most was doing good shows. Gaspin had no argument with that.

Nor did he dispute Ross's other observation, that as August headed to a close he and the Conan guys were looking forward to Jay's arriving at ten. That might actually help in the numbers.

In the weeks before his ten p.m. show premiered, Jay Leno would occasionally check in with Conan O'Brien, just a call here or there to see how he was doing. They would exchange the usual pleasantries. Jay mentioned some plans for his show; they discussed a few guests. Nice to talk to you.

Conan thought nothing much of the conversations. He wasn't wasting time worrying about Jay's show. He was supremely focused on his own windscreen, where the view ahead looked sunny and clear. Overall he was well pleased with his team's early efforts. The shows felt strong; he was proud of them. Of course, he didn't expect to ease right into the groove, but they were getting there. Conan could see where the show was going and how it was growing. He had enormous fun playing with two wax figures of Tom Cruise and Henry Winkler the staff had found, placing them around the studio in various creepy poses. On August 6, outside the studio, Conan lined up a couple of the cannons that Ringling Brothers used to shoot people across the circus ring. He loaded up Tom and Henry and fired them across the broad driveway leading in from the gate to the lot. The wax figures paid the ultimate price, but Conan scored some big laughs with their explosive demise. The next day the Web site Gawker posted about the bit, calling it "awesome" and "one of the funniest sketches you'll ever see on a television show."

All seemed good.

But Rick Ludwin was still hearing from New York.

Ludwin, so long experienced in late night, always kept close tabs on his shows. With Jay yet to go on, Conan dominated his days and nights. Every day the numbers arrived; Letterman, surprisingly, was winning the viewer battle by margins that were on par with the edge Jay used to have over Dave. And most of the press—maddeningly, as far as NBC was concerned—continued to call Dave the winner every night, ignoring the category that really counted, the one where the money was made. NBC PR executives quietly decried many TV journalists for not being sophisticated enough about the business to understand the advantage of securing the younger viewers every night, and the relative worthlessness of Dave's dominating the fifty-plus category.

Of course, at the same time New York kept asking Ludwin why Conan wasn't making the show broader to draw some of those older viewers back. While never wavering in his own faith in Conan, Ludwin did understand the frustration of Jeff Zucker and his other colleagues in New York. All Rick seemed to be doing was telling and retelling the same accounts of offering up notes to Conan's team but not seeing any results.

"And they won't say why they're not taking notes?" the New York colleagues would ask, increasingly incredulous that Ludwin's suggestions had been ignored. "What do you mean, they won't do that?"

Ludwin was reminded of how Carson would describe trying to make adjustments to *The Tonight Show*: "It's like trying to change a flat tire while the car is still in motion."

Conan's ratings performance, on every radar screen in New York, was also being closely scrutinized out in LA, in the offices where Jay Leno and his team were spending long days preparing for their prime-time debut. This was hardly a new activity; Jay and Debbie Vickers had studied the *Tonight Show* ratings over seventeen years, poring over them as if they were encrypted messages from the Enigma machine. They knew which guests spiked a number (Tim Allen, say) and which ones tanked (no names on the record). They knew which act two bits held the best percentage of the monologue audience. They knew the impact a week of repeats had on the following week's numbers.

Debbie Vickers noticed, for example, that Conan's numbers had taken a serious hit the week after his first break from the show. NBC, as the American network rights holder, had a commitment to present a late-night update show for the final full week of the Wimbledon tennis tournament, which would have delayed the start of *The Tonight Show* by fifteen minutes. Nobody wanted to skew Conan's first-month numbers unfairly down as a result of delayed shows, so, though he had been doing *Tonight* for only a month, Conan took a dark week beginning on June 29.

Vickers noticed that for the week before the break Conan had hit a 1.4 rating in the eighteen-to-forty-nine demo—a still-massive .6 margin over Letterman—and he had beaten Dave for the week by about 227,000 total viewers. When Conan returned the week of July 6, his eighteen-to-forty-nine rating dropped precipitously, to a 1.1, and in so doing he lost exactly half his margin over Letterman in that category. The same week Dave swamped him in the total-viewer category, winning by 862,000 viewers.

For the rest of the summer, as Vickers tracked it, Conan never got anything higher than a 1.2 rating among those young adults, and he hit that number only once. Every other week was either a 1.1 or a 1.0. Her conclusion: The Conan *Tonight Show* should not have taken a week off that early in its run, though she knew they were never offered that option.

She and Jay also examined in precise detail how Conan was doing minute by minute in his first half hour of the show. They knew from tracking their own show for so many years that the drop in the quarter hour between eleven forty-five and midnight—when the call of sleep grew insistent—should fall in a range of 18 percent to 23 percent. When Jay did "Headlines," on Mondays, the falloff was minimal, only about 7 percent. Other bits lost a bigger percentage, but Vickers considered 24 percent high. (If a bit lost that much, it was in danger of being dumped from the regular lineup.)

Checking Conan's numbers throughout July, Vickers detected drop-offs in the second quarter hour of the show of as high as 34 percent. His audience was still there for him at the top of each show, but they were checking out in alarmingly large numbers—at least as Vickers saw it. And she knew that, if she was seeing it, so were the number freaks in NBC's research department.

When Jay was asked by reporters gathered at the NBC portion of the press tour that summer if he was following the ratings for his old show, he went big and boisterous: "It's not my fault! I was happy where I was!" At other moments he did go out of his way to try to be reassuring, saying Conan would be fine—growing pains and all that.

Debbie still chatted frequently with Jeff Ross, as often as three times a week, and she enjoyed the exchanges. She had the impression Jeff was realistic about how the show was faring that summer—which, to her mind, thanks to those quarter-hour breakdowns, wasn't all that well. More than once during those conversations, Ross, who liked Debbie enormously as well and was by nature a generous spirit, repeated to her his hope that Jay's arrival at ten might stir up noise about NBC.

"I can't wait for you guys to come on," Ross told her.

The Jay Leno Show opened on September 14, 2009, with a flourish, proving, if nothing else, that America would still respond to a frequently repeated message: Something big is happening on television tonight.

With good pal Jerry Seinfeld as a comfortable first guest (Jerry tweaked Jay, "You know, in the nineties, when we quit a show, we actually left") and a fortuitous appearance by Kanye West, just days after the singer's rant against Taylor Swift at the MTV awards (Jay asked him—not in a funny way—what his mother would have thought of his behavior), the premiere hit an extraordinary number. Ranking as the biggest show in all of television for the night, Leno attracted 18.4 million viewers, with a huge 5.3 rating among the young demos. By contrast, Conan's spectacular debut on *The Tonight Show* in June had reached 9.2 million people and got a 3.8 rating in the all-important demo.

NBC resisted the urge to call Jay the "New King of Prime Time," and critics were largely unimpressed, dismissing the show as mostly a remake of the old *Tonight* formula, a rehash, and "a bore." But critics had never left bouquets on Jay's doorstep, so he was hardly surprised.

The show also introduced its first correspondent, Dan Finnerty and his Dan Band, singing their way through a car wash. The segment did not find many enthusiasts. But it soared compared to bits from others in the group of largely unknown comics and improv artists who began filling up act two of the show.

Debbie Vickers quickly realized that NBC, in its desire to appease the concerned stations with a strong end to the show, had effectively built in failure as a regular—and early—element. The contributors were mostly tepid young performers executing uninspired ideas. And they were on in prime time—at about 10:12 p.m. (when defectors could still pick up the thread of the cop shows on the other channels). All her instincts about how to retain viewers after the monologue went on alert: This material threatened to devalue the entire show.

But she couldn't cut the segment from the show. A "comedy hour" ate up material like a ravenous beast. It seemed that every time Vickers looked up, more material they had put on the schedule had already been used. As much as she wanted to bail on some of these weak contributor spots, dropping them would start a chain reaction—and by the next day three acts would be missing. Jay couldn't physically fill up the whole hour on his own. As it was, the demands on him had escalated. Any bit Jay did outside the studio had to be shot during the few spare minutes of his life. He had committed to performing just as many gigs around the country—160 or so—as he ever had, making no concessions to his increased workload on the prime-time show. Bits inside the studio that involved Jay also demanded rehearsal time—further diversion from his primary mission: putting together twelve to fourteen minutes of monologue daily.

The contributors had to contribute—lame performances or not. Vickers soon realized she was approving material to go in act two of the prime-time show that she would never have allowed to air in late night. How did that make sense? And all because the better act two material— "Headlines" and the rest—had to be saved for the last segment to lead into local news. The bad agreements Debbie believed the show had made to win the stations over looked worse every day. Jay, usually a rock onstage, showed signs of losing his rhythm. He knew well that the key to performing successfully on a daily show was flow—flow of jokes, flow of segments. Splitting the best comedy bits off from the monologue was diverting the flow into a sad little pond.

On the morning of October 1, 2009, David Letterman, looking less like a TV icon than a visiting rancher from Montana, stood up in front of a grand jury in Manhattan, sheepish and ashamed, and revealed the details of what the district attorney's office was branding as a case of extortion. For Letterman, haggard and deadly serious, the essence of his message to the jurors was that he had been threatened and he feared for himself, his family, and his job. He quietly admitted to things that made him sound boorish but explained that he was doing so willingly in an effort to help the DA's office, which he praised and thanked, along with the grand jury. The jurors were sworn to secrecy, of course, but Letterman knew the incident would break as soon as an indictment was handed down. As he had throughout his incident-dense career (and life), Letterman decided to take the matter straight to his audience.

One of the unique properties of the late-night television show in America is that daily events in the private lives of its hosts become an inescapable part of the presentation, because the presentation is, in almost every case, the host himself. Letterman, more than any of his peers, had raised that act of public self-examination to a level of comedic—and sometimes dramatic—soliloquy. He simply didn't talk about himself in any other context, which made his desk commentary in act two take on more and more of the aspect of a personal confessional. Most recently he had twice contorted himself, with apparent reluctance, into a regretful posture to apologize to Sarah Palin. But in his years on the show Dave had discussed everything from his encounters with his famous stalker, to the deaths of important people on the show and in his life, to 9/11, his bypass surgery, the birth of his son, and his marriage—all sitting behind his desk communicating directly into the camera.

In this case he might as well have been kneeling like a penitent.

Letterman told the audience assembled for that night's entertainment that he was glad they were there and apparently in "a pleasant mood" because he had a story he wanted to lay out for them. The story traced his grand jury appearance and the charge of blackmail it involved. Letterman filled in many details: the mysterious package left in his car at six a.m. three weeks earlier containing material that claimed proof of "terrible, terrible things" Dave had done—Dave conceded, "Sure enough, there was some stuff in the pages that proved I did those terrible things"—and the threat that this evidence would come out in the form of a screenplay if Letterman didn't pay up.

Dave related the steps he took, contacting his lawyer, the two of them meeting with the man behind the plot, the decision to go to the DA's office, the sting, which included Dave's lawyer, Jim Jackoway, wearing a wire and handing over a bogus check for $2 million, and the resulting arrest of the blackmailer, whom Letterman described as menacing.

Throughout the account Letterman maintained a mesmerizing tone that mixed seriousness with a kind of "Can you believe this?" incredulity. The studio audience, not having a clue if what they were hearing was the truth, some tall tale, or maybe the intro to some comedy bit, was obviously thoroughly entertained, releasing regular bursts of laughter, sometimes at inappropriate moments.

"I had to tell them all the creepy things I had done," Letterman said of his grand jury testimony, which ignited a huge laugh. "Now why is that funny?" Dave asked. But he continued, because it was time to discuss precisely what he had been accused of.

"I have had sex with women who work with me on this show," he said, this time to silence. He recounted how the grand jury had asked whether this was true. "Yes, I have," he said.

"Would it be embarrassing if it were made public? Perhaps it would," he said, adding his only real joke: "Especially for the women." But to go public and talk about it would be a decision for them, Letterman said.

He got to the essence of the issue: his need to protect his family, himself, and his job. When the smoke cleared, he brought out Woody Harrelson.

For those who had known and worked with Letterman throughout his career, the revelation was at once stunning and yet not unexpected. One longtime Letterman associate said, "I was surprised at how he confronted it. That was a shock to me. In my wildest dreams, I would never imagine David Letterman going on TV saying those things."

Not because his admissions seemed incredible, the associate said. Everyone who worked around Dave, starting early in his career, was aware that he certainly took a healthy interest in women. They also knew he tended to meet and converse with only women he worked with, because his awkwardness in social settings made it unlikely he would meet them anywhere else. It began with the early love of his professional life, Merrill Markoe, the extraordinarily talented writer who inspired many of his breakthrough ideas and shared his personal life (to her eventual regret) for about a decade. It continued with Regina Lasko, whom Letterman also met at 30 Rock, and who had been his life partner for more than twenty years before they married in 2009.

But as one woman who interacted with Dave in his *Late Night* days put it, "Everybody was after him; he was so cute and sexy."

The longtime associate who'd been so surprised by how Dave went so public said, "Isn't that why some people go into show business? Isn't that why half these guys become comics? So they can fuck around? Isn't that why rock stars become rock stars? Yes, Dave had his flings over the years, but never once did anyone hear him say he wanted so-and-so to get a raise. He was never like that."

What was most extraordinary about his confession that October was the fact that Letterman spoke so directly about the situation—on television. One friend from his early TV days said, "This is a guy who used to not like to say the word 'sex.' He was skittish about it. It was shocking to me to hear him talk like that. Shocking."

A big part of the reason for that shock was that Letterman had an almost physical revulsion against anything that he perceived as personally humiliating. One colleague from the show remembered Letterman's distress over things like a bad haircut. "He would come in on Monday and people would ask how his weekend was. He would say, 'I had to hide under the house the whole weekend. This fucking haircut. I couldn't let people see me with this haircut. I look like Howdy Doody."

Among Letterman's colleagues, friends, staff members, rivals, old enemies, fans, and nonfans alike, the reaction fell along similar lines: Dave took a situation suffused in negative, even career-threatening, connotations and somehow revealed it, dissected it, and neutralized it in one remarkable performance. It was like a scene out of *The Hurt Locker*: Letterman carefully, systematically defused a time bomb sitting in his own lap. "He went right into it, cut the wires, and left," said a veteran staff member.

"Not only did he defuse the bomb," said Jimmy Kimmel, "he then threw the bomb into enemy barracks and fucking blew everybody else up by making himself front and center again."

The question of course, remained: While it might result in Dave's getting a little more immediate attention, what would his confession mean for the show long term? Inside the offices at Worldwide Pants—and at CBS—nobody was really certain. What if a parade of former girlfriends marched forth to condemn Dave as a serial womanizer? Worse, what if some women came forward to say Dave either hit on them obnoxiously or took advantage of his position as the boss to get them into bed? No one really knew precisely what Dave meant when he said he had had affairs with women—plural—on the staff.

Some people knew about Stephanie, of course. For years Dave's evident infatuation with one of his assistants, Stephanie Birkitt, had been the subject of gossip around the office—and even among some viewers. Stephanie, who at thirty-four was about half Dave's age (sixty-two), had appeared on the show more than 250 times. Dave, who had pet names for her like Monty, Smitty, and Dutch, had her dress in cute costumes or dance goofily for him, or even serve as a comedy correspondent. She interviewed *Survivor* losers, always asking, "Did you see or touch any monkeys?" And she got to take trips to places like Turin, Italy, where she served as the show's feature reporter for the Winter Olympics in 2006.

When it was revealed that the man accused of blackmailing Letterman, Robert (Joe) Halderman—a CBS News producer—had shared a house in Connecticut with Birkitt, the connection to Stephanie as one of the in-house paramours was easy to make. Much of Halderman's information on Dave had come from Birkitt's diary, which he later admitted to reading.

Letterman, stated in his chat on that night of Thursday, October 1, that he would have nothing more to say on the subject. But between the boss-employee relationship and the age difference, the scandal sent out some potent tentacles. So he had to return to it on his next taping, the following Monday. (Friday's show had been in the can for a week, as usual.)

Letterman didn't flinch in the monologue, putting the incident stage center.

Referring to the sex scandal involving Mark Sanford, the governor of South Carolina, Letterman said, "Right now I would give anything to be hiking on the Appalachian Trail."

And: "It's fall in New York. I spent the weekend raking my hate mail."

Then he took his place at the desk and again announced that he had some serious business to attend to. His almost offhand reference to multiple affairs with staff members, he explained, had caused many of the women he employed to be chased by the press, looking for confessions of office passion.

"I'm terribly sorry that I put the staff in that position," Letterman said. "The staff here has been wonderfully supportive to me, not just through this furor, but through all the years that we've been on television and especially all the years here at CBS, so, again, my thanks to the staff for, once again, putting up with something stupid I've gotten myself involved in."

And then there was Regina. As his monologue implied, the revelation of the affair with Birkitt had put his recent marriage at serious risk. Letterman, who still felt overwhelming guilt about the breakup of his first marriage, twenty-five years earlier, to his college sweetheart, Michelle Cook, had obviously wrestled for years with his reluctance to marry again. The decision to go through with his marriage to Regina related directly to his commitment to Harry, now five, and the prospect of this family breaking up—and his losing daily contact with Harry—over "something stupid" he'd gotten himself into was clearly wrenching for him.

So, again, in front of a national television audience, Dave apologized, abjectly. Of Regina, he said, "She has been horribly hurt by my behavior, and when something happens like that, if you hurt a person and it's your responsibility, you try to fix it. At that point, there's only two things that can happen. Either you're going to make some progress and get it fixed, or you're going to fall short and perhaps not get it fixed. So let me tell you, folks, I got my work cut out for me."

As the days went by, no other women came forward (with the exception of one who admitted to a brief fling with Letterman more than a decade earlier, one she had only fond memories of). One associate who had observed Dave up close for years said, "This is where Dave is brilliant; he knows the kind of girl who isn't going to betray him." Still, no one at the show minimized the implications of the revelations. Some were thankful Dave had steered clear of product endorsements, so they were spared the litany of high-minded companies saying Dave could no longer speak for their razor/car/beer/tires.

But overall, according to one of the show's producers, "It was tense. It was scary." The biggest break was having a villain to point to so Dave didn't catch all the heat. Dave was a victim, after all, as well as a perpetrator of "terrible things." And to his credit, he didn't pay, but willingly exposed himself to public flogging rather than give in to blackmail.

As the producer put it, "Dave didn't buckle. This guy had no idea who he was dealing with. You can't exert power over Dave that way. He is not the right guy for that."

The timing was hardly ideal. While Dave did become the talk of the country again, the show didn't really need the attention at that particular moment—and certainly not this kind of attention. The day before the scandal broke, the ratings for the week prior had arrived. That week, President Obama had been a guest, marking only the second appearance ever by a sitting president on a late-night show. (Obama had visited Leno earlier.) Letterman had scored the biggest weekly win for his show in fifteen years, topping *Tonight* by a gargantuan 2.6 million viewers, winning the eighteen to forty-nine category by .3 and taking every night of the week over Conan.

In retrospect, when Jay Leno assessed how long it had taken him to realize his ten o'clock show was in a little trouble, he concluded: maybe twenty minutes in.

That represented only slight hyperbole. Within about a month a sense of uneasiness had begun to drift low and slow along the corridors of NBC's executive offices. Objectively, not much looked shockingly different from what the network had been expecting. Jay finished third at ten most nights, but wasn't he supposed to have done so for a while, until some repeats came on the other networks? In fact, Jay was managing to beat ABC on several nights, mainly because that network had again handed NBC the gift of some dreadful ten p.m. entries like *Eastwick* and *The Forgotten*. On Tuesdays, when NBC was able to deliver a healthy lead-in number to Jay from the nine p.m. hour, thanks to its reality weight-loss hit, *The Biggest Loser*, Leno was regularly grabbing second place, and often with a demo number that started with a two.

Jay was on the whole keeping his famous chin above the water line. Admittedly, NBC had set that line as low as credibility would allow. Before the show launched, Jeff Gaspin had publicly established the viability number for Jay at a 1.5 for the eighteen-to-forty-nine audience. By averaging that number, Jay could have made money, but it was still a minuscule performance for a prime-time show, far below what would be grounds for cancelation anywhere else. NBC would have had to import a barrelful of snake oil to convince anyone Jay was a success at that level, no matter what the financial breakdown said.

Privately, NBC executives conceded they were playing the lower-the-expectations game. In truth, they had been hoping for an ultimate average that started with a two, and they believed they could get there over the course of a year because the indefatigable Jay would produce so many more weeks of original shows than the dramas he was competing against—maybe even twice as many. For that fall, the realistic demo number the network wanted to see Jay average was a 1.8. That looked respectable, especially with ABC's expensive new dramas already free-falling below that level; it was also a number Gaspin believed the NBC affiliates could live with.

The stations had already become pestiferous bystanders, reading every number over the network's shoulder, offering an occasional nudge and a question: "Is that really *all* he's going to do?" Clearly the stations had not believed Gaspin's 1.5 target. By mid-October, in the big markets that received ratings figures daily, high anxiety was setting in. Some stations were already seeing their eleven p.m. newscast numbers slide. Gaspin and Zucker both started to hear from Michael Fiorile, the head of the affiliate board, which represented the entire body of NBC stations.

Fiorile, who ran Dispatch Broadcasting, based in Columbus, had backed Jay Leno with the enthusiasm of a true fan leading up to his ten p.m. debut and did not want to send out a message of panic. But Fiorile had no choice but to clue his NBC partners in to the increasing rumbling among the stations.

Gaspin examined the numbers carefully and concluded NBC had made a wrong assumption going in. The network had expected Jay to be a second choice at ten p.m. If your favored show at that hour, on either network or cable, wasn't offering a new episode, Leno would provide a pleasant alternative. But the DVR, which was wreaking so much havoc across the medium, seemed to be devastating the ten p.m. hour. Jay didn't rank as second choice. He was at best third, after the primary drama that a viewer liked at ten and whatever had been recorded on the DVR. Instead of benefiting from the fact that he was DVR-proof (because nobody really recorded the nightly comedy talk shows), Jay was getting hammered by the damn machines. And, ominously, the DVR choice did not figure to vanish when repeats started among the ten p.m. dramas, so it seemed unlikely that Jay would be making any hay against the reruns after all. He would still be second choice.

Gaspin told Fiorile that he understood the stations' concerns, but it was still relatively early. What he didn't tell him was that the network had some incipient jitters as well.

Conan O'Brien saw no reason to be nervous yet for himself, but he and his staff certainly had noticed what was happening in the ten p.m. hour and the concomitant fallout during the local newscasts—in other words, his lead-in.

Before Jay joined the fray at ten, Conan's *Tonight Show* had never failed to beat David Letterman by at least two-tenths of a point in that eighteen-to-forty-nine-year-old group NBC so favored. But since Jay had pitched camp at ten (not counting his curiosity-fed first week), Conan had never even once beaten Dave by more than .1 among those younger adults. Dave had won outright three times (including his big Obama week), and the two shows were tying many other weeks. By now Dave was also routinely running away with the mass audience, winning every week by well over a million viewers.

As Conan's team saw it, no explanation could account for this scenario other than that the weak performance at ten was infecting everything that followed. Conan also noticed he was no longer getting any calls from Jay.

Over in Burbank, Debbie Vickers was getting some calls, and they were informing her the affiliates were starting to quaver. She made up her mind not to say anything to Jay—because you don't burden the talent with extra worries.

One important NBC observer, however, who had no dog in the fight but an intense interest in seeing the network survive, had, even in early October, already rendered a definitive judgment on Jay's relocation to ten. "The show is awful," the influential network player said. "It's not a case of 'This needs to change, or that part's not working.' This is a situation where a nine-year-old at the back of the room stands up and says, 'It's awful.' It's not ten p.m. or anything else. It's just not a good show. It's not going to work. By March, it's over."

Another significant player, Dick Ebersol, equally appalled, did not pin the blame on Jay. After containing himself for a month, he finally let loose during a video conference call with West Coast executives, asking, "Has anybody really looked at the minute-by-minute of what's going on with Jay's show?"

Someone in research said they had determined what was working, and that included the monologue and the late bits, like "Jaywalking."

"That's my point," Ebersol replied. "You've got to move those segments up. The show is losing people because they never get to those segments."

It couldn't be done, he was told; the affiliates were already grumbling. You couldn't pull a strong segment away from the start of their newscasts.

Ebersol continued to complain about that and another point: the way the show was using its primary guests. He pointed out that in the *Tonight* days, when Jay had a guest he clicked with, like Terry Bradshaw, he could keep him around and bounce things off him through the other segments. Here—thanks to some overly polite decision to ensure the interview segments looked different from those on *The Tonight Show*—he was on for just six minutes and gone. "That's just fucking crazy," Ebersol said.

But nothing got changed. Outside NBC the situation took on the look of one of those slow-motion implosions of a crumbling old building. A new term got passed around the TV industry: the Leno effect. Beyond its impact on the local news, and Conan, and Jimmy Fallon after that, the decision to replace the full ten p.m. slate with all Jay, all the time, had damaged existing NBC shows, and the hopes the network had for finding new hits.

Without any ten p.m. slots available NBC had abruptly decided to cancel its best-reviewed new drama in years, a cop show called *Southland*—even though the series had already finished filming six episodes of a second season and was ready to air in late October. Gaspin, who had not participated in developing or ordering the show, had a sound rationale: The drama was expensive and slated for Friday at nine, where it would almost surely die. (Nothing on Friday attracted much of an audience anymore.)

Had NBC needed ten p.m. shows, *Southland* would clearly have received a second shot to try to grow, as earlier high-quality NBC dramas, from *St. Elsewhere* to *Hill Street Blues*, had. The decision meant NBC was also turning its back on John Wells, one of the creative forces behind *Southland* and the man who provided the biggest hit NBC had seen in a generation, *ER*. A disheartened Wells remarked, "I'm disappointed that NBC no longer has time periods available to support that kind of critically acclaimed series that was for so many years a hallmark of their success."

In clearing out Wednesdays at ten for Jay, the network had also transformed a time-period-winning drama into a show finishing dead last in its new time period. That series was *Law & Order: SVU*, a potent ratings draw for NBC for most of a decade. Sliding the show up to nine had apparently dispersed its loyal viewers, who knew a ten o'clock show when they saw one.

No one was more dismayed than the show's loud and proud creator, Dick Wolf, though his comprehensive deal with NBC Universal prevented him from responding publicly to the move. Friends and colleagues who spoke with Wolf knew he was quietly seething, flabbergasted by a network that could undermine one of its dwindling store of hits, leaving him to calculate the damage this ham-handed move would do to his show's future profits.

Beyond Wells and Wolf, other producers and studio heads railed in private about how NBC was treating their precious content. The group had a prevailing opinion: In looking to contain costs, NBC was throwing its few remaining floating toys out with the bath water. One longtime producer of several shows for NBC and other networks called the Leno-at-ten decision "one of the biggest con jobs in the history of American business. Their revenues are down 30 percent, and they have destroyed the local news in fifty stations and Conan O'Brien in just a few weeks. They used to be the place you wanted to be. What's truly horrifying now is their highest-rated show is two hours of disgusting fat people."

Taking fire from Hollywood, the press, and even some inside his own network, Jay Leno decided to try to clear the air a bit by granting an interview to the television trade publication *Broadcasting & Cable*. Sitting down in his greenroom at about ten a.m. on October 29 with the affable but aggressive *B&C* editor Ben Grossman, Jay offered up a defense of his show to that point.

Mostly Jay accepted whatever shots the show was taking because his name was on it, though he agreed that some of the anger it had attracted could be tied simply to NBC's decision to block out five nights at ten o'clock. Jay promised the show had bottomed out, and "we're not going below that."

He declined to take satisfaction in Conan's falloff from the numbers Jay had previously posted on *Tonight*, saying, "There's nothing that kills creativity more than bitterness." But he did acknowledge again that he would have preferred to stay at 11:35. "I think it's too soon to say whether I regret anything or not," Jay added. He also said he was a mainstream guy, not a niche one, that he wasn't going to whine, and that he liked "being on TV and writing jokes."

It was pretty much the standard Jay take, except for his answer to one deliberately provocative question: "Do you want to go back to 11:35?"

On the page, Jay's answer read simple and direct: "If it were offered to me, would I take it? If that's what they wanted to do, sure. That would be fine if they wanted to."

He went on to endorse Conan for still beating Dave in the demo. "Personally, I think Conan is doing fine," Jay said.

When the piece ran, no one really paid attention to anything but Leno's assurance that, yes, he would take 11:35 back if offered. Jay and NBC's PR department both later complained about the interview, insisting that Grossman had hounded Jay with the question over and over until he reluctantly answered it. While Grossman did acknowledge having asked it three or four times in different ways, he explained that Jay was always matter-of-fact in the interview, never pissed off by any of the questions, certainly in no way contentious. And, Grossman pointed out, no one at NBC disputed that Jay had said precisely those words.

Jay swore he meant to send no signal with the comment. But a signal was received all the same.

Conan O'Brien read the interview—and the widespread coverage it received—and could only shake his head. The line didn't worry or intimidate him but made him reflect on how different he was from Jay. In the same situation, Conan was convinced he would never have said anything like that. He didn't hear from Leno about it and simply decided to go about his business.

A short while later, though, Jay's remark came up again during an interview Andy Richter gave to the online magazine TV Squad. Andy generally had pleasant things to say about Jay in the interview until that business about taking 11:35 back came up. "That was a weird answer," Richter said. "Because nobody actually asked him if it was offered, the question was just sort of like, 'Would you like to be back on?' And he was the one who went on to say, 'If they asked me, would I take it?' That's certainly not the classy answer to that question. The classy answer is, 'Oh, well, that's a silly question to ask, because somebody already has that job.' That's what you say if you're classy."

Richter's comment attracted none of the attention that Jay's had—except from Jay himself. Displeased at being called "unclassy," he called Rick Ludwin to complain. Ludwin took the issue up with Jeff Ross, to see if Andy would call Jay to work it out. Richter hardly relished a chat with Jay on this particular subject, but Jeff Ross asked so he complied. Richter called Jay, who, as always, made an effort to be lighthearted and pleasant. Andy explained that he had said what he did because the job was important to him, and that Jay's remarks about going back to 11:35 made it seem his job was being threatened. Jay took it equably and told Andy it had been a good idea to call and work things like this out.

Andy agreed and then, turning Jay's observation around, asked him if he had called Conan to clear up his intentions in the B&C interview. Jay indicated he had spoken to Conan to smooth things over.

Richter, of course, checked in with Conan almost the moment he got off the phone. Conan had still received not a single call from Jay since the start of the ten p.m. show. Jay's attempt at deflection didn't really surprise Conan; people on the spot often said things like that. But not to realize Andy would immediately run the conversation by him? How does that happen, Conan wondered.

When Debbie Vickers heard later that the Conan side had taken offense at Jay's "I'd take it" comment, she had her first small moment of disappointment with the *Tonight Show* team. To blow that comment up into some kind of sign indicating that Jay was trying to push Conan out seemed to her to be the showbiz equivalent of rabbit ears in baseball: paranoid ears. She believed she knew Jay as thoroughly as any other human being could, and she did not detect a manipulative motive in what he he had said in the interview. If she had perceived he was engaging in any kind of Machiavellian maneuver, she would not have backed it for a second.

In the wake of the interview a cold front began to descend midway on the 134 freeway between Burbank and Universal City.

On Jeff Gaspin's plate, 11:35 remained an untouched side dish. The ten p.m. problem was already so pressing that Gaspin simply couldn't have cared less about 11:35. His message to the anxious affiliates was: We're going to give Jay November and then see where we are. That was a risky position to take, because November was a sweep month, one of four annual ratings periods when all the television markets in the country, down to the very smallest, get measured by the Nielsen company. Even with vastly improved techniques for achieving reach, some national advertisers still paid special attention to sweep-month numbers and bought the local markets based on those results. The local station owners considered them vital to their economic survival.

NBC didn't really get the breathing space through early November that it had wanted, in any case. The stations that were receiving daily numbers were still there, questioning the network—having noticed, for example, that Leno had played against some repeats during the last week in October, but the ratings hadn't budged. By now the affiliate noise level was growing loud enough that Zucker started hearing it in New York.

As Gaspin's anxiety level began to tick up, he checked his development slate. What did he have? One drama, *Parenthood*, was ready and looked kind of promising. It could fill one night at ten. But what else? He began to contemplate alternatives. Could Jay go down to four days a week? Three? Would the affiliates accept that?

Inside *The Jay Leno Show* the messages were coming fast and confusing. NBC had guaranteed them two years at the start, but Jay and his staff realized that really meant just one for sure. So the show's strategy, based on advice from the network, had been geared toward getting through the expected rough early patch and into summer, when they could flex some muscle competing against repeats. Then, after the faltering start, the advice had shifted: Focus all your big guns on December. You can score then because the ten p.m. shows would go to several straight weeks of reruns during the holidays.

Debbie Vickers pressed her booking department: Chase after every big name you can dredge up and confirm them for December. *The Jay Leno Show* would stand and fight in December.

On November 4 Rick Ludwin came to see her. The rules had changed again. "You have until the end of November," he told her.

Vickers felt poleaxed. She had just moved every big name on their booking board to the following month, because she had been told it was going to be life or death for the show in December. Now they had concluded: Forget it—it's all or nothing in November. This was bullshit, Vickers decided.

But it wasn't as if she had any choice. Well, she did have one. She didn't tell Jay that their show, less than two months in, had just had its yearlong guarantee reduced to four weeks.

On November 6, with some research analysis on the ten p.m. situation just starting to come in, Jeff Gaspin opened up an e-mail from the sales division and read a suggestion: What about cutting Jay back to a half hour, moving him to 11:35 again, and pushing Conan back?

At first blush this idea sounded far short of viable to Gaspin, not with all the complications it would entail. Would Jay even consider a half hour? Would that necessarily mean Conan also shrank to a half hour? And then what—an hour of Jimmy Fallon? That made no sense. What about forty-five minutes of Jay, forty-five minutes of Conan, and then a half hour of Fallon? Absurd. Gaspin quickly dismissed this wispy notion that somebody had floated out there with little thought.

In New York, meanwhile, Jeff Zucker was meeting for some private dinners with someone whose judgment he had long trusted: Lorne Michaels. The main topic of discussion: the ten p.m. problem. Zucker described the mounting pressure from affiliates to do something—as well as his ongoing concerns about Conan's numbers and the show's apparent unwillingness to listen to suggestions for changes.

Michaels knew Zucker came from a place of affection for Conan and Jeff Ross. The whole ten p.m. plan for Jay, gone so precipitately wrong, could be traced back to what Michaels saw as Zucker's real motive: to protect Conan. Now, with the options to fix this overheating lemon narrowing to exclusively unpleasant ones, Lorne tried to shore up support for his guy. He made the case that if you were betting on intelligence and talent, you simply had to leave Conan alone. He would figure it out.

On the basis of these dinners, Michaels had no doubt that Zucker still stood with Conan.

One factor the internal analysts at NBC couldn't quite get their heads around was where their future proprietors stood. Comcast, still awaiting regulatory approval, could provide no insight on their plans for NBC. Lorne Michaels, for one, expected a renewed commitment to the broadcast side, after the endless GE-influenced protestations that NBC was now a "cable company." Comcast—itself a cable megacorp—had to be aware that every NBC affiliate had the ear of its Congress member; assurances that the local stations would remain vital to the enterprise were an essential part of Comcast's pitch to Washington. Suddenly what the affiliates said or did about ten o'clock had real resonance. The impression Michaels took away from his conversations with Zucker was that Comcast had a simple goal: Get this ten p.m. business behind you before the official change of management.

By mid-November, the calls from affiliate executives were coming at Gaspin at an accelerating pace. Several station managers had set up their own information network and were exchanging panicky reactions based on what they were seeing happen day by day to the eleven p.m. newscasts at the big stations—during a sweep month. Some stations were down as much as 30 percent; others had seen their first-place newscast quickly fall into third place. In their calls to Gaspin, the station representatives had a consistent plea: "You have to do something!"

With no real answer to give them, Gaspin strung them along as best he could. "Let's just get through the month," he told them. "Let's get to December. Let's get to some repeats. Let's see how it does during repeats." But ensconced with his team he began to press for potential solutions. Could there be another play here? What about that old eight o'clock idea that Jay had rejected? Would he reconsider? Was there something else

NBC could do to make ten p.m. palatable to the affiliates for the rest of the year? Was there some way to get Jay his fifty-two weeks?

Of course, any change for Jay would involve some alteration of his contract. Gaspin decided it was time to delve into that nettlesome issue. When he did, he was caught short by the deal's salient, italicized, capitalized feature: NBC had committed to a pay-*and*-play arrangement with Jay.

Jeff Gaspin had never in his life heard of granting someone a pay-and-play promise in a contract. He tried to work out what it would mean in practice to have guaranteed not only to pay a performer but also to play him—for two years. This demanded serious legal interpretation, and the one Gaspin got from NBC's legal team left him with little doubt: NBC faced risk—*big* risk. A strict reading of the contract presented the possibility that the network could be liable for damages in a suit brought by Jay's very capable attorney. As crazy as it sounded, he could even seek an injunction that would force NBC to keep Jay on the air.

Neither outcome came close to being likely, but neither could they be automatically dismissed. From what Gaspin was hearing from the lawyers, it wasn't going to be a pretty picture if they simply tried to yank Jay off the air. Gaspin grasped that before he took any action he needed to do one essential thing: get Jay on board with whatever NBC did.

Suddenly the choices narrowed. For the first time another option moved into focus: Cancel Conan, and put Jay back into *The Tonight Show*. The prime-time issue had spilled over into late night, despite Gaspin's intentions not to mix the two. Conan's performance, his numbers—all those things Gaspin had filed under "later"—became urgently relevant.

At the meeting he called to discuss the situation, Gaspin got some clarification on Conan's ratings, but he wanted more information. His late-night executives were there, Rick Ludwin and Nick Bernstein, along with NBC's chief deal man, Marc Graboff. Of course, the impact of the sharply diminished lead-ins—from Jay to the local news, the local news to Conan—was discussed. Ludwin, as always, praised Conan's effort and long-term promise. But when asked how well Conan was adapting to the earlier hour, Ludwin was just as frank with Gaspin as he had been with Zucker: "They're fighting us on some of the things we want to see happen."

This sounded to Gaspin like a significant, but not critical, concern.

He did not get the sense that Conan and his team were simply refusing to listen, only that some of Rick's and Nick's suggested changes had met with real resistance.

But the research department had some intriguing data for him, too. When they broke down Conan's results in the key category of viewers between the ages of eighteen and forty-nine, they discovered an eye-catching statistic. Conan's strength in that group was highly concentrated in the eighteen-to-thirty-four portion. (That was often broken out as a separate segment for advertising sales, especially for youth-oriented channels like MTV and Comedy Central.) Fully half of Conan's audience in the large eighteen-to-forty-nine group fell within the eighteen-to-thirty-four segment.

Having the breakdown tip that way was highly unusual—50 percent was about twice the norm for a television show. Certainly this helped explain how Conan had so drastically reduced the median age for *The Tonight Show*, from fifty-six to forty-six. In big swaths of television that would have been considered a sensational development. NBC's research department didn't think so. For them it only seemed to confirm the growing suspicion that Conan might be that dreaded item: a "niche" talent. At 12:35, that sort of hyperyoung profile was ideal. But coming in the earlier hour, it signaled to the researchers a weakness in the show's breadth of appeal: People over thirty-five had significantly less interest in it.

One NBC executive floated a notion that some others had only whispered about to that point: Was a show-business version of the Peter Principle at work here? Had Conan been perfect at the 12:35 level and mistakenly pushed himself to a level where he couldn't quite succeed?

Jeff Gaspin wasn't buying that. He resisted any scenario that posited that Conan couldn't be a winner on *The Tonight Show* and so they needed to go crawling back to Jay. NBC had designated Conan O'Brien the future of late night five years earlier, and Gaspin had no intention of reversing that decision now. There had to be a better way.

Robert Morton, long gone from the employ of David Letterman, retained many friends in the late-night world, but none closer than Jeff Ross. The two producers shared the short-hand of warriors who had been in the trenches and seen and heard things no one outside their tiny band of brothers would ever know. Morton had experienced the tumultuous ride from 12:35 to 11:35 when he was Letterman's executive producer and close adviser in the 1990s. Now his good buddy Jeff was in the middle of the same bumpy transition with Conan; naturally, they had much to talk about.

Morton had moved to LA after his ouster from Worldwide Pants, which made it convenient when Conan's show moved west. As the waters deep beneath NBC's entertainment division were just beginning to bubble and stir that holiday season, Morty and Jeff set a date to meet for dinner. Jeff said he would bring along Rick Rosen, who by that point had become much more Jeff's intimate friend than merely Conan's principal agent.

Much of the talk at that meal, as might be expected, centered on *The Tonight Show*. Ross expressed just a little sense of uneasiness about relations with the network. NBC's notes didn't seem onerous; he couldn't quite put a finger on it, but something about the situation felt a bit weird to him.

That tripped a wire for Morty. Back in the days when the Letterman team had been haggling with NBC over their exit, much turned on whether NBC, which had retained the right to match any financial offer Dave had received, could really equal CBS's terms if NBC didn't guarantee Dave the 11:35 time period—which it couldn't do, of course, as it had already filled that slot with Jay Leno. CBS and Dave's representatives had hammered out a contract that stated in explicit detail that Dave would be programmed each night directly following the late local news on CBS's stations. The time-period stipulation remained a standard part of Dave's deals, and Morty knew Jay had the same guarantee.

"You guys got that for Conan, too, I'm sure," Morton said.

He waited, while watching Rosen and Ross exchange a little look.

"You didn't?" Morty asked, holding back his next thought, which was, *You've got to be kidding me.* He was stupefied by this revelation. Why on earth take a chance like that? No fully stipulated time-period protection?

Both Rosen and Ross indicated that they knew it could be a risky situation, but they didn't dwell on it. Neither did Morton. But as he left the dinner that night he made a point to remember the conversation. There might be consequences down the road.

The end of the November sweep brought no relief for Jeff Gaspin—on the contrary, the gang with the torches and pitchforks gathering outside Jay Leno's ten p.m. castle had grown larger and louder.

As the November sweep ratings books began arriving, the spate of affiliate calls became a slew. Now the messages began to carry a note of hysteria: "Oh my god, we were *killed!*"

Gaspin, still promising something would be done, had to make his own plea to the station managers: Please do not go public. Several of the stations were threatening to open up to their local press about what a disaster Jay Leno had turned out to be at ten o'clock and how they would take action if NBC did not. The affiliate board urgently requested a conference call, which Gaspin joined in, accompanied by Rick Ludwin. The appeal from the board members was completely professional, but their stance was unequivocal: NBC needed to act on ten p.m., and whatever the new plan was going to be, it could not wait. The affiliates were demanding the action take place in January. They would not even wait for the natural break in the prime-time schedule that NBC had coming in February with the Winter Olympics from Vancouver. If something wasn't done in January, the stations themselves would seek their own remedies. They would begin preempting Jay—either by moving their newscasts up to ten and pushing Jay back into late night or by acquiring some syndicated hour to stick in at ten—and they would go public with their plans.

Gaspin realized that it was one thing to fight the preemptions with threats to place NBC programming elsewhere, but once the complaints started getting aired in public, the situation would surely descend into nastiness. If the affiliates started bad-mouthing Jay and the decision to put him at ten, Leno would surely be damaged, perhaps irrevocably. Even if the protest started with only a few stations, as few as five or ten, the blood would be in the water. And battling your own partners? What kind of place was that to be in?

Gaspin appealed to Michael Fiorile, the board chairman, to keep the complaints inside the circle for just a little while longer while NBC pursued the alternatives. Fiorile promised to try to control the station bosses as best he could. He and the other board members were pleased that NBC had taken their concerns seriously enough to acknowledge that there was a crisis. But the answer had to come soon, he stressed: "From what I'm hearing, you could start losing stations any day." What Fiorile had been hearing specifically was that stations might not dump Jay every night of the week, but they would certainly look at a few nights where they could find something higher rated.

Conan was hardly mentioned, but when the station leaders broached the idea of sliding Jay back to late night (some wanted to start him at eleven, after an hour of local news), they argued that one side benefit was that "Jay provided a better lead-out for our local news—more people stayed around after the news to hear his monologue."

"What if we cut Jay back to three days?" Gaspin proposed.

"No," Fiorile said. "Maybe two days."

"I can't convince Jay to do just two days," Gaspin replied, repeating his plea for a little more patience.

Several nights after the call with the station managers, Ludwin dropped by Leno's stage and ran into Jay. "What are you hearing about our show?" Jay asked.

"Well, since you asked me a direct question," Ludwin said, "I'm hearing that the affiliates are not happy. They are making noises about their poor lead-ins."

Jay took it in, looked resolved, and said he would call a few of the affiliates himself to try to win them over.

Meanwhile, still looking for any kind of answer, Gaspin had a wild thought about offering Jay four days a week, but making Saturday and Sunday two of them. He had no idea how the network would sell a package like that. It felt like a mess. Besides, all this desperate scrambling didn't constitute a creative solution. Instead, it had come to seem to Gaspin like nothing so much as maneuvering to satisfy Jay's contract, rather than actually solving NBC's problems.

Consulting on phone calls with Zucker about the imminent affiliate revolt they had on their hands, Gaspin ran down what he now saw as the range of options he had left: Jay cuts down to a couple of nights a week; he gets canceled and leaves altogether; or they somehow find a way to move him back into late night.

"We haven't given them enough time," Zucker protested.

"I know," Gaspin replied. But it looked as if time had run out anyway.

The alternative Gaspin did not present was canceling Conan and simply returning Jay to *The Tonight Show*. He did contemplate the possibility of the two hosts somehow sharing the time period. Alternating nights? Alternating weeks? The notions started getting crazy.

When Zucker, eager for another opinion, called Ludwin, Ludwin went right to the recommendation of pulling back Jay to just one night a week—maybe two, at most. Slot the night on Tuesday, when Jay benefited from that *Biggest Loser* lead-in, and if necessary, maybe add Friday at ten, where he could follow a stable show, the newsmagazine *Dateline NBC*.

Again the obvious question arose: Would Jay be likely to accept so dramatic a reduction in the routine he loved so much—shows five days a week, year round? Ludwin had his doubts, but, then, he had never believed Jay would accept the ten p.m. idea. He didn't think they should just rule the possibility out.

Two prominent network employees were not consulted for input or ideas on NBC's problem: Jay Leno and Conan O'Brien. No one at NBC thought it wise to tip either host that a high-speed train might be hurtling toward him. What sense did it make to spook them with these still-unsettled proposals?

So both shows continued to churn out their comedy bits and interview segments every weeknight. Debbie Vickers, now convinced more than ever that NBC should never have let the affiliate managers in the door, decided to flout the stations' wishes and go with what she believed was best for the show. She moved Jay's stronger comedy departments up into act two, where they belonged. Most of the correspondents bit the dust; the stronger ones got slots deeper into the show. She moved the "10 at 10" segment back to the caboose, leading into the local news—at least the stations would have some name celebrity on the air just before they reported the traffic accidents on the local interstate.

At *The Tonight Show*, meanwhile, Sarah Palin finally made her appearance, on December 11—five months after her feud with Letterman, but she was on. The show had found a way to include her that was consistent with Conan's style—not at the desk for an interview, but instead as a participant (and a rather good one) in a comedy bit. And her guest spot was a walk-on—there had been no advance publicity.

William Shatner, a Conan regular, came out for act two, to do a dramatic, poetry-style reading of Palin's words, as he had several times before. Accompanied by a beatnik combo featuring bass and bongos, the actor read a selection from her recent autobiography, *Going Rogue*—including the line "I looked down to see the moose's eyeballs lying in his palm, still warm from the critter's head."

Then Palin strode out to wild applause and countered with an excerpt from Shatner's memoir, *Up Till Now*, a rich trove of funny lines: "As I finished 'Mr. Tambourine Man,' I glanced over at Johnny Carson, who had a look of astonishment on his face, vaguely similar to the look on Spock's face when his brain was missing."

The ratings needle barely twitched.

Rick Rosen had a more than cordial relationship with Jeff Zucker. He liked the guy, even given Jeff's hostility to Hollywood, where Rick happily lived and worked. Zucker was bright and winning and could parry and thrust in conversation in ways that Rosen—who engaged in plenty of that as a high-end agent—could not help but enjoy. The two men bumped heads on occasion, but not often. That was more Ari Emanuel's job (though he liked Zucker, too).

A few days after the Comcast deal closed, Zucker signed a three-year contract extension with GE—with the promise of its being carried over to Comcast—and Rosen called to congratulate him. He hadn't spoken to Zucker in several weeks. When he picked up the phone, Zucker said, a little tweak in his voice, "Oh, now you're calling. I don't hear from you for weeks. I consider you my friend. I don't hear from you."

"Well, I know what it's like to go through a merger," Rick said. "I didn't want to look like a gossip. So, congratulations."

"Oh, sure," Zucker said. "You're calling because Conan's ratings aren't good. That's why you didn't want to call."

Rosen didn't take the bait. "Conan's ratings are actually good, in the eighteen to thirty-four and eighteen to forty-nine," he said. When Zucker did not respond, he continued. "Seriously, I was calling because I know what it's like when people are gossiping about a merger."

"Look, we should get together," Jeff said. "When will you be in town?" Rick said he would be in the next week.

When Rosen dropped by 30 Rock a week later, he sat down with Zucker in his saunalike office, schmoozing for a while about the business until Zucker spontaneously brought up the subject both men knew would be the main topic of discussion. "Ten o'clock's a problem," Jeff said. "I have an affiliate problem."

This came as no surprise to Rosen, who had seen what Jay's lead-in numbers were doing to his client on *The Tonight Show.*

"Listen," Zucker continued. "I'm going to be out in LA the second week of January to show the Comcast guys around. I'd like to get together with you and Conan and Jeff and just talk about the show. Because I want the show to be broader. I just want to talk about it."

"Fine," Rosen said, but his antennae were up. "Is there a message here? Is there something I need to be concerned about?"

"No," Zucker replied, dismissing the worried look on Rick's face. "I just want the show to be broader."

Later, as he stepped outside into the refreshingly brisk Manhattan air, Rosen took stock of what he'd heard. Zucker had acknowledged his ten p.m. issue and revealed that the affiliates were up in arms. Rosen tried to guess what NBC might be up to: cutting Jay back to maybe two nights a week? That sounded just fine to Rick Rosen. Anything to get Conan some better lead-in numbers.

NBC had already postponed a long-scheduled semiannual affiliate meeting that had been set for December 10 in New York. Realizing it would be faced with nonstop questions about ten o'clock, and that it still had no answers to offer, the network opted to move the session to the second week of January. Jeff Gaspin took for granted that he would find the solution before that date—he had to. The affiliates would surely be canceling Jay with preemptions by then if NBC continued to dither.

All the conversations about the coming shake-up continued to be tightly held; Gaspin trembled at the thought of NBC's intentions leaking before anything was settled definitively—and before he had stepped up to inform the two big stars who would be affected. So far the secret was holding. Nobody in the press was even speculating that NBC had to make a change soon, which astonished Gaspin.

He remained open to suggestions and was getting a steady stream of them, most not remotely feasible. Then a New York sales executive contributed an idea—a question, really—and it rang a bell: Could you ever get Jay to do a half hour? Back at 11:35?

The notion that Gaspin had dismissed a month earlier—also from sales—suddenly seemed more worthy of consideration. In a half-hour show Jay could still deliver a monologue, which was what he most wanted to do, wasn't it? How many times had he said it himself—"All I want to do is tell jokes at eleven thirty at night"? As for Conan, his mantra over the long months and years when he was the gentleman-in-waiting had been how hosting *The Tonight Show* was his ultimate dream. Maybe these two defining life choices could actually be put together. Gaspin started to work the idea out in his head: Jay back at 11:35, but only for a half hour, leading into Conan, still the star of *The Tonight Show*, now a half hour later. Jay would sacrifice a half hour but retain the essential daily ingredient of his life—telling jokes on national television every night. Conan would sacrifice his start time, but he would still have an hour-long show, still called *The Tonight Show*. Wouldn't that be the fairest outcome for all concerned?

The biggest sacrifice that Gaspin could see in this arrangement would actually have to be made by Jimmy Fallon, who would get relegated to a start time after one a.m. All Gaspin had heard around the office was how fresh and funny Fallon was. How much risk could this entail, for a guy just starting to stir up buzz, to make him start so late? But if it had to be, it had to be.

Gaspin needed ratings estimates and sales projections—fast. When he got them, the results only raised more questions. Two hosts for an hour each graded out better than three squeezed into two and a half hours, but the numbers changed when you factored in the possibility of one of them jumping ship, going somewhere else, and eating into the overall late-night ad revenue. The sales recommendation was to keep all three, take a short-term financial hit, and adjust down the line.

Gaspin kept coming back to the fairness issue. While this proposal would displace Conan by thirty minutes, he would still be on NBC in late night. He had had only seven months in which to adjust to the big show, as Gaspin analyzed it. How fair would it be to cancel his show, send him packing, and just put Jay back there? Not fair at all. And did Jay get a fair shake with only four months on at ten, even though he'd been promised— *guaranteed*—two years?

Gaspin began to lay out the scenario in more detail. Initially NBC would have to shell out more money—Jay's salary and program budget, taken together with Conan's and Fallon's, would drive late night into the red. But they could expect significant upside in the ten o'clock hour. Even the patchwork lineup Gaspin planned to scratch together figured to top Leno's numbers just about every night.

The whole reconfiguration could be in place to kick off by March, immediately after the two weeks of wall-to-wall Olympics coverage on NBC—a conveniently timed restart. And surely the revamped lineup would hold firm for the rest of the season, at which point they could figure out something else. Of course, the unspoken but compelling grace note at the center of this improvisation was that it accomplished NBC's consummate and fixed goal: holding on to both its late-night stars. This solution would again manage to avoid a repeat of the calamity of 1993.

Gaspin examined it carefully, top to bottom, side to side. He liked it. He had two loyal, hardworking stars in Jay Leno and Conan O'Brien, backed by two classy, dedicated executive producers in Debbie Vickers and Jeff Ross. Not to mention big staffs on both shows. Under this configuration, the staffs stayed in place, retained their jobs, paid their mortgages, kept their kids in the same schools.

The week before Christmas Gaspin called Zucker and laid out his plan in detail. He needed approval, but Gaspin had no qualms about claiming paternity. He had clicked the pieces into place like an elaborately designed Lego construction; he intended to see the plan through by personally informing all the players.

"We can do it now or we can wait and let everybody think about it over the holidays," Gaspin said to Zucker, who gave his nod of approval to the overall restructuring. The advantage of going out with it immediately was that all the parties involved could mull it over during the extended two-week shutdown Hollywood enjoyed every December. Zucker, happy to have his new entertainment boss take the lead, said he would also leave the decision of pre- or post-holidays in Gaspin's hands.

Gaspin examined the calendar. Christmas was closing in; people were already looking forward to their breaks. There was that to consider. Gaspin had second thoughts; maybe it was better if they dealt with it all in the new year.

Let's not ruin anybody's holiday season.

CHAPTER TEN

THE LATE
UNPLEASANTNESS

For the first weekend of 2010, the weather at the classic Riviera Country Club in Pacific Palisades, California, was beyond glorious—mid-seventies, sunny, ideal for an unhurried round of golf just before the Hollywood grind, on hold for two holiday weeks, resumed again on Monday morning.

Jeff Ross had taken up the game pretty late in life, in his forties, using the down time from his duties running *Late Night* to throw himself headlong into lessons, including weeks at intensive golf camps in Florida. By now he had become accomplished enough to score in the mid-eighties on Riviera's tough layout. He had also formed a number of strong golf friendships: in his New York days with Jeff Zucker, among others, and, once he moved to LA and was admitted as a member at Riviera, with Rick Rosen and Lloyd Braun.

That Sunday morning Ross teed it up with Braun, one of the more active television executives of the previous decade. Braun, trained as an entertainment lawyer, had worked as a talent manager for the big Brillstein-Grey firm, later joining Disney as head of its television production studio Buena Vista, and then as president of entertainment for Disney's network, ABC. After a wild ride there, Braun had moved on to work a brief stint at Yahoo! before finally starting up his own production company in partnership with Gail Berman, the well-regarded onetime president of entertainment for Fox. Now Berman-Braun had what was known as a first-look deal with NBC.

Braun, lean and athletic, played golf often and well. He had a knack for turning up in the middle of late-night action, having pursued David Letterman for ABC in 2002 and then creating the new ABC entry for Jimmy Kimmel. Naturally enough, as he walked the Riviera course that January morning with Jeff Ross, Lloyd had NBC's late-night situation on his mind. When they reached the seventeenth green, Braun finally asked Ross about the latest concerning Conan and the Jay Leno experiment at ten.

Ross told him it was becoming overwhelmingly obvious that Leno was in big trouble.

"I know," Braun said. "They've got to do something about it."

Ross nodded in agreement, but his generally dour demeanor looked even gloomier than usual. "I sure hope it doesn't affect us," he said.

Lloyd put up a hand to stop that line of thinking. "You guys have nothing to worry about," Braun pronounced. "That would be the dumbest thing ever. It would be the worst PR move ever. It's not planning for the future."

"I know," Ross said, not very convincingly. "They made a commitment to us."

"If they do something, they've got to get rid of Leno," Braun insisted, trying to reassure his friend.

"Yeah, but it would be a fortune to pay him off," Ross continued, not at all reassured.

Braun, as was his wont, worked himself up to a level of passionate indignation. "To do something with you guys would be the most ridiculous move they could make!" Lloyd declared. "They can't do it. Listen to me. Don't even think about it. It is never . . . gonna . . . happen!"

By the time he arrived at his office at Universal early the next morning, Monday, January 4, Jeff Gaspin had already made up his mind about what was going to happen. Quietly, over the holidays, Gaspin had on his own sketched out his new ten p.m. schedule and was satisfied that the results would represent an immediate and significant improvement over Jay Leno's faltering performance. Gaspin knew that Jeff Zucker had a plan to fly in to LA later that week with the two top dogs from Comcast, Brian Roberts and Steve Burke, intending to show them around the West Coast entertainment operation. The time to act was now. Gaspin put in a call to Zucker first thing that morning. "I don't want to wait until the end of the week," Gaspin told him. "I want to start the ball rolling. I want to go talk to Jay. Give Jay a week. Then I'll go talk to Conan."

In thinking through how he would present the change to the two stars, Gaspin had factored in his expectation of how each side would handle the news. It made sense for all sorts of reasons to tell Jay Leno and Debbie Vickers first, but especially because Gaspin believed he could trust them—they would not leak the plan. It would not be in their interest anyway, given that Jay's ten p.m. show was being canceled. They also seemed to have levelheaded representation who would not want to squeal to the press the first chance they got about NBC's unfairness or lack of commitment. That would not be the case with Conan's team, Gaspin feared. He took for granted that any indication he gave them of his intentions would be planted somewhere online the same day. Beyond that, Gaspin presumed that had he made the seemingly sensible move to start up a back-channel connection with Ari Emanuel or Rick Rosen (whom Gaspin liked) or Gavin Polone (whom he didn't know at all), they would have lost no time in shopping Conan to a competitor, looking to spring him from NBC.

Besides all that, Gaspin had to have evidence that Jay would go for this fallback position—a return to 11:35 in a half-hour format—before rocking Conan's world with the news that he was being herded off to 12:05. If Jay said no way, the whole plan would implode. So Gaspin's first thought was: *Get Jay squared away early in the week; go talk to Conan on Friday; let him have the weekend to process it.*

Then he had a second thought: The press tour sessions with NBC were set for Sunday. This would be Gaspin's first time sitting in front of a room of journalists answering questions as the leader of NBC Entertainment. He wanted to make the best possible impression. If Conan learned his fate on Friday, somebody on his team—probably Polone—would spin it out in the press to try to gain leverage. Then the entire Sunday news conference would be about the ten p.m. and late-night plan instead of the wider NBC story.

Gaspin made up his mind to hold off on telling Conan until the following Monday. If all went well, everything with Jay would be settled by then, and Conan's options would be clear—and stark.

Though on a much smaller scale than in royal France, Jeff Zucker had his own Cardinal Richelieu, a behind-the-scenes éminence grise, a confidant he trusted completely, even with a closely held secret like the news of the coming changes at ten and in late night. Those closest to Zucker knew well that Dick Ebersol had filled the role of minister without formal portfolio throughout Jeff's career, but it was surprising that some inside NBC, including members of Conan O'Brien's camp, were not fully aware of the significance of Ebersol's unofficial but powerful position as the most influential adviser to the throne.

As 2010 rolled in that January, Dick Ebersol was deep into his preparations for the Vancouver Olympics, but he always had time to kick around other issues pressing NBC's tottering empire. Jeff Zucker opened up to him after he had signed off on Gaspin's plan of action—and Ebersol immediately tried to talk him out of it.

"It's not fair to Jay," Dick argued, citing specifically the shift to a half hour, a format Leno had never worked in before in his life. "What's the show going to be?"

Zucker outlined the plan—a monologue, a second comedy piece, and the occasional guest. It didn't sound promising at all to Ebersol. He made an alternate suggestion: Go all the way back in the time machine. Put Jay back at 11:35 for an hour and Conan at 12:35. It would screw Jimmy Fallon in the short run, which was a shame, because Ebersol was already highly impressed with him. They would have to figure out something else good for Fallon while keeping him in line for a future in late night. Ebersol justified the move by pointing to the numbers Conan had put up in his seven months—a performance, Dick stressed, that merited demotion if any performance ever had. "Half of the audience was gone in nine weeks," Ebersol said. "That's a joke. That isn't going to change."

Zucker defended the plan, arguing that Gaspin deserved a chance to make it work. Ebersol kept to himself the decision he would have made had he been in charge: cut Conan out of the package altogether and line up Leno and Fallon. But Dick recognized how nuclear a move like that would be. Conan didn't seem to have a clue his show was in trouble, as Ebersol read the situation. Even Gaspin's measured play was going to hit him like a sledgehammer to the temple and enrage him. To lose the whole show, to be canceled outright after seven months, would be like a public execution, Ebersol thought.

Still, he disliked the half-hour move for Jay, which smacked to him of punishment. Ebersol believed that Leno should be cut a break for having taken on the doomed ten p.m. assignment. Jay at least could see the bullet coming. Ebersol found himself astonished that Conan, at forty-six, could be, as Dick judged it, so naive about the business.

One more issue needed clarification before Gaspin pushed the button on the combustible mix he had ready for the NBC blender. Gaspin had to be certain there was no contractual prohibition that might prevent him from executing his vision for a revamped ten p.m. hour and the overcrowded elevator that he was making of the network's late-night lineup.

The implications of the apparently unprecedented pay-and-play arrangement with Jay had been explained to Gaspin; he concluded he could circumvent that issue, but only by getting Jay's commitment to play along. Still, he needed unequivocal assurance from NBC's legal department that the other part of his scenario would fly. He had to have the right to move Conan and *The Tonight Show* back a half hour. That right would be available only under one condition: Conan could not have an ironclad time-period guarantee in his contact.

Gaspin pressed the NBC lawyers in Los Angeles and New York: Do I have flexibility here? After some contractual analysis, the answer came back: Absolutely yes. In the deal Conan had signed to host *Tonight*, the duration (three years) and the salary (about $12 million) were specified. All kinds of other details—producers' salaries, head writer's salary, band size, other departments—were specified. Time-period protection was *not* specified—not remotely specified, the NBC lawyers told Gaspin. As they broke it down for him, the only thing the operative contract contained was boilerplate language about the show's "being scheduled at the network's discretion."

The lawyers also emphasized to Gaspin that they were confident they stood on unassailable ground, because whenever time-period protection *was* granted in television contracts—and that was infrequently—the issue was clearly spelled out. That had been exactly the case with the previous occupant of *The Tonight Show*—Jay and Ken Ziffren had negotiated specific, unambiguous time-period protection. That kind of language had become common in contracts with late-night stars, at least ones with a shred of leverage. Letterman had the clause written in from his first day at CBS; Jon Stewart had specified the time period in his deal with Comedy Central; Jimmy Kimmel had it in his deal with ABC.

Conan doesn't have it, the lawyers assured Gaspin. He was guaranteed *The Tonight Show*. He was not guaranteed that it would start at 11:35 p.m.

The legal interpretation cemented Gaspin's resolve to go forward. Had Conan's contract had the same specific time-period protection that all those other late-night stars had, Gaspin knew his course would have been radically altered. He would not have gone through these machinations. Had Conan's *Tonight Show* been locked in at 11:35, the options would have narrowed to the elemental choice: Fire Jay or fire Conan.

Gaspin had his assistant set up the appointment for sixish, shortly after Jay finished taping his show on Tuesday, January 5. That evening, with darkness descending, Jeff got in a car with Rebecca Marks, the head of corporate communications on the West Coast (also a close friend of Debbie Vickers), and they made their way east on the freeway, over to Burbank.

The bare bones of the mission could have been delivered as a bad-news/good-news joke: You're canceled; but hey, you get to go back into late night.

Gaspin had no intention of taking it lightly. The stakes were too high for Jay—and NBC. Besides, it wasn't his style.

Jay, already in his denims, greeted them in his more spacious, less dungeony private digs in the new studio. Debbie drifted in at about the same time, saying hello a bit tensely to Gaspin and Marks. Gaspin suspected Vickers might know what was coming, thanks to a tip from her producer soul mate, Zucker.

Gaspin initiated a bit of small talk about that night's show; it was forced, and it was pretty obvious that it was forced. Finally Rebecca Marks bit the bullet, saying simply, "We have an issue."

"We have a problem," Gaspin seconded, stepping up to the task. "Our affiliates are incredibly unhappy with ten o'clock. They want us to make a change. If we don't, they're threatening to preempt. They're threatening to talk publicly, negatively, about the performance of the show. We've got a real problem here." Gaspin spoke directly to Leno, and he could read the impact of his words in Jay's face.

"What do you want to do?" Jay asked.

Gaspin, though feeling terrible, didn't hold back. "We're going to pull the show," he said.

Very quietly Leno said, "OK."

Debbie Vickers grasped the bottom line: *We've just been fired.*

The room fell silent. Finally Jay spoke up again. "What do you want to do?" he said. "How do you want to handle it?"

"I want you to go back to eleven thirty," Gaspin said.

Jay's relief, Gaspin noticed, was instantaneous. His face lifted and brightened. "Yeah, let's do it!" he said, the pitch of his voice almost as high as performance level.

Debbie Vickers, in her quiet but forceful way, got herself in between Gaspin and Jay's enthusiasm. She suggested that they hear more.

"It's not that simple," Gaspin told them. "I only want you to do a half hour."

Now Vickers jumped all the way in, clearly thrown by the proposal. What did he mean, a half hour? What kind of show is it? Just comedy material? No guests?

"Look," Gaspin said. "Some days you have guests; some days you don't." He described it as monologue, then comedy material, then maybe a guest, maybe some music. "You know that in every hour show there's a good half hour. You get to do that show every night."

Gaspin emphasized that Jay would get to do his long monologue every night—just as always. That was the prime selling point, as Gaspin saw it. Like many others, Gaspin had heard Jay's story about being dumped by an agent who told him he was a good comic but he would never get into the press. Now Jay always had jokes quoted in the press—and he kept track. In the Sunday Week in Review section of *The New York Times* Jay always counted how many of his jokes made the weekly list. It was another form of competition for him. He almost always beat Dave and he was proud of that.

Starting to put it together, Jay turned to the other obvious lingering issue. "What happens with Conan?" he asked.

"He goes at twelve," Gaspin said. "Everything just moves back."

"So I wouldn't get *The Tonight Show*?" Jay asked.

"No, Conan would keep *Tonight*," Gaspin said. Jay stared at him during another extended silence. "Look, we have a tough situation here," Gaspin finally said. "NBC is in trouble. If you leave or Conan leaves, it gets worse. We really want both of you. We think both of you are big talents. We're trying to figure out a way to keep both of you." He tried to appeal to their long loyalty to a network, now facing a real crisis. The company could fold, Gaspin told them. "We can't afford for this to fall apart."

Jay paused again, considering it all. "You think Conan will go for this?"

Gaspin indicated they were confident they could make him come around, though nothing with Conan was settled yet.

Leno told Gaspin that he didn't want Conan to be hurt, but he was still trying to get his head around what this half-hour-at-11:35-not-*The-Tonight-Show* really meant. "I've done an hour for eighteen years," he reminded Gaspin.

Vickers's head was also spinning. She pressed again: How would they do a half hour?

Gaspin said that would be an issue for another day if they could all agree on the overall plan. "I don't need an answer tonight," he said. "Think about it, and let's talk more tomorrow."

Vickers had one final question, something she had to know before she committed even to thinking about switching to a half-hour format: What would happen if they said no? "Would you release us from our contracts?" she asked. Jay wanted to know the same thing.

"No," Gaspin said. "We're not going to release you."

After his discussion with Jay, Jeff Gaspin felt sufficiently confident to bring Marc Graboff into the tight circle aware of the new late-night strategy. He needed Graboff because as NBC's chief deal man with talent, Graboff would be the one in direct talks with Ken Ziffren about any redrafting of Jay's contract.

Graboff, like most of the other top NBC executives, had spent the holidays wondering which of the several suggested scenarios to resolve the ten p.m. dilemma would be put into effect. He was mildly surprised that they had decided to take this option, but the train was leaving the station and he knew what his next stop would be: a call to Ziffren.

As Graboff set off to contact Ziffren, the small retinue of NBC executives on both coasts who were now briefed on the plan mulled over the increasingly interesting sidebar to this big news: that it was Jeff Gaspin and not Jeff Zucker driving the action.

It seemed to this group that, besides the obvious inference that Zucker probably wanted to maintain some distance from this decision, Gaspin's willingness to ride this plan to completion had much to do with his wanting to establish himself as "the guy"—the executive truly in charge of resolving this crisis.

The corporate dynamics at work fascinated some of the close NBC observers. Just as new owners were appearing on the scene, Jeff Zucker had appointed Jeff Gaspin to a job that had previously defenestrated two other promising executives, Kevin Reilly and Ben Silverman, in quick succession. Gaspin, a shrewd insider, had clearly observed this development and decided he couldn't allow himself to be seen as another puppet of Jeff Zucker in the job. In almost every move Gaspin had made since taking over the entertainment division, he had seemed to be sending a message: *I'm running programming; I'm running scheduling.* For the first time since he had moved back east, Zucker was not attending—or running—every NBC prime-time scheduling meeting. Gaspin had agreed to bring Zucker into a monthly overview of scheduling, but he had emphasized that Zucker was not leading NBC Entertainment day to day anymore.

That had struck a sizable portion of the staff as both a good and a necessary development. Somebody had to build a firewall against what the staffers saw as incessant intrusion by New York. Now, with the Comcast takeover imminent, the dynamic grew even more intriguing for the Gaspin-Zucker analysts. Gaspin had even more incentive to separate as much as possible from Zucker, because he needed to prove to the Comcast duumvirate of Brian Roberts and Steve Burke that he was not another Jeff Zucker captive. Thanks to his years managing NBC's cable networks, Gaspin even enjoyed a potential advantage: The Comcast guys knew him; they had worked with him. Who could predict what Comcast's real intentions were? It could only be to Jeff Gaspin's benefit to step away from Jeff Zucker's penumbra as much as was reasonably possible.

Marc Graboff was one of the few NBC executives with enough experience and status not to have to be preoccupied with such palace intrigues. He had shared the title of chairman of the entertainment division with

Ben Silverman and he remained a trusted lieutenant to Zucker. Now he had to face off against Ken Ziffren, knowing that he held nothing in the way of cards, while Ziffren, armed with the pay-and-play deal he had negotiated for Jay, held a fistful.

Graboff could not guess what to expect when he called Ziffren to follow up on Gaspin's meeting with Jay. NBC's legal department had advised Graboff not to blanch if Ziffren threatened to seek an injunction. Thanks to Leno's unusual contract, Ziffren might actually have some grounds to try, they told him, though no court was going to give him that. Graboff himself, having observed Leno up close for as long as he had, guessed Jay would have no stomach for a move like that anyway.

But even as Graboff was explaining to Ziffren that they couldn't be sure yet whether Jay was going to have to switch to a half-hour format, the lawyer expressed an eagerness to make a deal—right there on the phone. For Graboff it was a sign of just how badly Jay wanted the ten p.m. show in his rearview mirror. And that he wanted a new agreement secured quickly.

Graboff made a provisional deal with Ziffren, dependent on whether Jay shifted to a half hour or wound up back in an hour-long show. Ziffren told Graboff to let him know what NBC ultimately decided, and they would go from there.

What Marc Graboff didn't know was that at least one NBC executive, privy to some of the internal concerns of the Leno camp, had no doubt that Jay would have welcomed any move that might save him from disappearing from television altogether. Dick Ebersol, working the corridors of NBC in his usual fingerprintless way, had a long-established back-channel connection to Jay through Debbie Vickers. They spoke often—easily often enough for Dick to have known, since shortly after Thanksgiving, that Jay expected the worst. From Debbie, Ebersol learned that Jay knew full well the ten p.m. show was not working, and given the unhappiness of the affiliates, he didn't see how he could survive. The message Ebersol heard from Leno's camp: Jay expected to be cut off, handed a check, and sent on his way. There was no mention of lawsuits or injunctions.

Ebersol didn't know when Gaspin was actually going to lower the boom on Leno, but as soon as he did, Dick got word of it. Not more than fifteen minutes after Gaspin left Jay's dressing area that Tuesday night in Burbank, Debbie Vickers dialed him up. Dick was in Dallas, preparing for NBC's coverage of that Saturday's NFL play-off game. Debbie told him that she had been surprised—not by the news itself, which Dick, too, suspected she had been tipped about by Zucker—but by Jay's instant embrace of the network's proposal. Jay had shown a little too much leg, Debbie concluded, wishing he had resisted NBC's pretty ill-formed ploy of cutting him back to half an hour. "How will I get an audience?" she asked him. "We're not going to have time for a guest of consequence and we can't have a music act, because that will destroy Conan when he follows straight up at twelve. What's our show going to be?"

Wednesday morning, Jeff Gaspin arrived in his office to a message that Jay Leno was on the phone. As soon as the conversation started, Gaspin realized that the tone was different. Jay was waffling. Thinking about it in the hours after their meeting the day before, Jay told him, he had started to question if he could really work in a half-hour format. To Gaspin, this sounded like Debbie Vickers talking. He told Jay he understood his concerns and asked if he could drop by to discuss it with him and Debbie after that night's show.

Back in Jay's postshow enclave, Gaspin presented his rationale again, talking it through, this time adding a little high emotion. Speaking of how difficult it had been to find a solution that would not leave either Jay or Conan behind, Gaspin said, "I'm not trying to make Sophie's choice. I'm really trying to be fair to both of you."

Jay and Debbie pressed him on the Conan issue: Did Gaspin really think Conan was going to take this?

Gaspin said NBC was about 75 percent sure he would.

"What happens to the staff?" Jay asked. "Do I stay on this lot?"

"Nothing has to change," Gaspin said.

But Vickers, thinking about the limitations of a half-hour show, said she probably wouldn't need a music department anymore.

"No," Gaspin said. "That is not going to be part of the conversation. As far as I'm concerned we are doing this to you. You shouldn't have to suffer. You don't have to make a change."

Gaspin had already made all the financial calculations. All three late-night shows had budgets in place—for a year, anyway. Getting Jay out of ten and inserting a roster of dramas would surely generate a ratings lift and more revenue, which could offset the extra costs in late night. That would not be the case in future budgets, but Gaspin figured he would deal with that the following year. For now, Jay could do whatever show he wanted in the half-hour format, with everything the staff expected of the show.

"Nobody loses a paycheck?" Jay asked. Gaspin guaranteed that would not happen.

"OK," Jay said. "I'm in."

Debbie pressed the Conan issue again: Was he really going to say yes? Gaspin expressed confidence that NBC could get him to agree.

Both Leno and Vickers saw logic in that conclusion. Numbers addicts as they were, they could not imagine that Conan and his team could be unaware of the ratings he was scoring. He had to know, they believed, that he wasn't doing well—and not just because of their own woeful performance in the ten o'clock hour. After all, Conan had started to lose chunks of viewers back in the summer before Jay even came on. Vickers figured neither show was a winner. Why not try to reformulate something while both shows were still on the air? Regroup and come back in some new incarnation; that made sense to Debbie.

Jay translated it in his typical "regular-guy" fashion. He envisioned how things like this went down in the real world:

The boss gives you a job to do and it doesn't go well. So they send you to the regional office in Des Moines to get your sales up. The half hour at 11:30 for him, and the move to midnight for Conan, those amounted to the Des Moines office. You go, you get your sales up, and when your numbers look good again, you come back to the national office. As Jay saw it, that was how real life tended to work. You're a salesman. You did gangbusters in one market, so they move you to a new market and it doesn't work out. Now your old market is filled so you have to prove yourself in a different market.

Vickers did realize that they might be naive, they might be chumps. David Letterman, with his perpetual adversarial relationship with his own network, would never roll over this way. But they really did feel a debt of gratitude to NBC, as pathetic as that made them sound in this day and age.

"If Conan's in, we're in," Vickers said.

They stood up and shook hands on it.

Gaspin wasted no time. Feeling a surge of confidence, he called Jeff Zucker, who had just arrived in LA to help the Comcast team get acquainted with Hollywood. Gaspin told him he thought this was really going to work.

Jeff Zucker was thrilled.

Jeff Gaspin had another constituency he needed to reach. The affiliate meeting he had postponed in December was now imminent, set for the following Tuesday, the twelfth. But with the crucial Conan discussion planned for Monday, it seemed impossible to fly out to meet with the affiliates in New York on Tuesday morning. Besides, it only made sense to get all the ducks lined up before facing the stations. They would have their own barrage of questions. If Gaspin could get a deal with all parties buttoned up in the next week or so, all that could be avoided. He needed another postponement.

That Wednesday evening, Gaspin quickly organized a conference call with some members of the affiliate board. He asked for a delay in the New York meeting—just a short one, until the twenty-first. "Look," Gaspin told the board members. "Call your station guys and tell them we will have an answer for them if they will give us another couple of weeks. And it will likely be something they're happy with."

Conan O'Brien wrapped up what he considered another strong show on the evening of Wednesday, January 6. The interview with that night's lead guest, Matthew Broderick, had gone especially well. The overall trend felt right; the shows were getting positive press. This was nothing like those early days on the *Late Night* show when survival seemed to hinge on every guest booking, every joke. All the negative attention in the press was centering on Jay and how his ten p.m. show was wrecking the network. The new *Tonight Show*, hosted by Conan O'Brien, seemed to be a given going forward.

And yet, as he gathered his writing and production group for the postmortem, Conan felt out of sorts. He realized he was coming across as edgy and short-tempered, which was not his intention. So he dismissed the group early. Gavin Polone stayed around. The manager had dropped by the show that night as he occasionally did now that Conan was in LA.

Nothing seemed in the least wrong about the show to Polone, but he knew Conan well enough to recognize the clouds circling above his star's head.

"What's wrong?" Polone asked. "That was a really funny show. Things are going great. The show is growing; you're doing good work every night. The numbers aren't there yet, but that's because of Jay. If they move him out, they'll put some other programming in there and, you know, that can only help."

Conan's glum expression was unchanged. "I just have a bad feeling," he said. "I just think he's going to hurt me in some way."

"You're crazy!" Polone said. What could NBC do? Move Jay back? That was clearly Conan's fear.

"Why would they do that?" Polone asked. "Jay's failing. They're going to move the guy who's failing back to where he was? It makes no sense! You can't think about these jobs based on what's happening this second. You have to think about where you're going to be in five years. Jay will be nearly seventy. You're going to have a seventy-year-old man hosting *The Tonight Show*? I just don't see any of that happening. It would just be the dumbest move ever. I'm not saying these guys are my friends or that they would keep their word. I'm just saying it doesn't make any sense."

Now, if NBC somehow had a line on somebody like Jon Stewart, Polone said, there might be some cause for alarm. But they didn't, and Stewart would never listen now anyway. He was far too successful doing what he was doing to jump into this swirling uncertainty.

Conan nodded unconvincingly. His mood did not lift. The premonition was still there.

When he got home, he had a raging headache. He dropped his things and walked into the spacious country kitchen, where he collapsed onto a couch. Liza found him stretched out there.

"What's wrong?" she asked.

"I think maybe they're going to cancel Jay," Conan said. "I just think that guy is going to hurt me."

Now Liza stepped up to be reassuring. "I don't really see how that's possible," she said.

Conan got up and gobbled some Tylenol. His head was pounding—it didn't relent.

Later he went to bed, the headache lingering. Finally, still unsettled and still not sure why, he fell asleep.

At six a.m. Pacific time Thursday, Jeff Zucker was up already in his room at the Four Seasons in Beverly Hills, getting ready for his day leading his prospective new bosses on a grand tour of the Universal lot, when he got a call from the room down the hall. His top corporate communications executive and close friend Allison Gollust had received an e-mail that morning from one of Jeff's own media properties. CNBC wanted a reaction to a story someone there had just seen on an obscure Web site called FTV Live. Had *The Jay Leno Show* been canceled? Gollust reported that she had told CNBC she was looking into it. She and Zucker agreed that was all they planned to say for the moment.

It was about seven fifteen when Zucker walked outside into the crisp California morning and climbed into his limo with Roberts, Burke, and Gollust. As they settled into their seats, Zucker spoke up immediately. "There's something you might want to know that's just about to hit the papers," he said. Recognizing that the two Comcast executives could have no input into NBC's operations at that point but guessing that the news would interest them anyway, Zucker filled them in on what was happening with Jay and Conan. He also briefed them on NBC's thinking and the network's provisional plan going forward.

Roberts and Burke took the information in as though listening to a ten-day weather forecast. Gollust had the impression that they concluded NBC might be overreacting a bit in anticipation of what was going to transpire.

The car wound its way through the congested morning-rush traffic toward Universal City.

In another part of town, at just about the same hour, Jeff Gaspin was driving himself toward the same destination. Waiting at a stoplight, he heard his BlackBerry ping and quickly checked the message. It was Rebecca Marks, letting him know that the news about Jay had leaked. But she noted that it had been posted on a site that did not attract much traffic. It seemed to be from a blogger who had posted other pieces about local TV stations. Gaspin guessed that one of the affiliates, exuberant over the news that NBC had finally found a favorable solution to the ten p.m. issue, had contacted this guy with a scoop. But the site had the news a bit wrong. The leak suggested that Jay had simply been canceled and was leaving the network. The inaccuracy encouraged Gaspin—maybe nobody else was going to follow this up.

A short time later, Conan O'Brien slid behind the wheel of his own car in his driveway in Brentwood. By that point the news had made it to the radio. The first newscast Conan heard cited reports on the Internet that NBC had canceled Jay Leno's show. Conan listened intently—not a word about *The Tonight Show*.

That same morning on the Universal lot, NBC's corps of executives was arriving early, eager to get to the meet and greet with the new Comcast overseers. A group of about thirty filed into the conference room in the Lew Wasserman Building. At about eight, Zucker strode in, accompanied by Gaspin. Zucker introduced Roberts and Burke. The NBC executives quickly introduced themselves one by one and briefly described their duties. Neither Rick Ludwin nor Nick Bernstein said a word about the morning's developments, because they were completely unaware of them.

The upbeat meeting broke up a little after nine and everyone dispersed—Zucker and his companions to some waiting golf carts for a spin around the lot. The NBC contingent took off to start their workdays. As soon as many of the network executives arrived at their offices, they perceived a heightened sense of tension. The news began to come at them all at once; reports were breaking everywhere that Jay had been canceled. The executives sped to their computers and phones, seeking to make sense of what was really happening. But they resisted the urge to check with one another, because it seemed no one had any clue what had been confirmed and what was just rampant rumor. It struck one executive as "utter chaos."

Rick Ludwin had a message waiting when he arrived back at his desk: See Gaspin immediately.

Jeff got right to the point as soon as Ludwin walked in. The plan to make the change with Jay was in progress: no more ten p.m. show; Jay back to 11:35; Conan pushed to 12:05. Gaspin asked Ludwin what he thought of the idea.

Ludwin responded that the other proposal that had been discussed— cutting Jay back to one or two nights—still seemed much better to him, because it would have been far less disruptive. Ludwin stressed that his strong preference was to avoid this kind of shakeup. But Gaspin made it clear he was going ahead with his plan.

At just about that time, Jeff Ross was arriving at the *Tonight* offices inside the auxiliary gate down at the front of the lot. As usual he was at his post before Conan turned up. The show's staff was buzzing. The rumors were by now aflame all over the Internet, though NBC had not confirmed anything: Jay was supposedly getting canceled.

"Hopefully that's true," Ross said, figuring almost anything NBC came up with would improve the ten p.m. hour and help Conan. But he wasn't really sure what to think. The uncertainty was only compounded a few minutes later when he got a message from his assistant. Jeff Gaspin wanted to see Jeff—and Conan—in his office as soon as Conan arrived. This immediately struck Ross as a curious and worrisome request. To him it should have been right out of Show Business 101: The network boss can order the producer to his office, but he never demands an appearance by the star. That just isn't done.

A few minutes later Marc Graboff walked into Jeff Gaspin's office in response to a similar request for an immediate meeting. Gaspin explained that the Jay story had broken because of an apparent leak by an affiliate. It was now imperative that they break the news to Conan immediately. He told Graboff he had already summoned Conan and Jeff Ross. Graboff recognized the good intentions behind everything Gaspin had done, but he wished there had been an opportunity for the same kind of back-channel work he had put in five years earlier when he was able to bring Conan and Ross in on NBC's plan to transfer control of *The Tonight Show*. It was too late for that now.

Graboff had a more urgent concern. If Conan and Ross got this news before NBC broke it to Conan's representatives, the plan would never have a prayer of coming to fruition. On the other hand, he agreed that if Gaspin called the agents first, it would almost surely get leaked before they had a chance to break the news to Conan—and that could be an unforgivable move as well.

"So what do we do?" Gaspin asked.

Graboff had an idea. "Have Conan and Jeff let you know when they are coming over. And then, when they are on the way, we call Ari and Rick and fill them in." That was the plan they decided to put in motion.

Back in Beverly Hills, Rick Rosen was just hanging up his jacket in his office at William Morris Endeavor at about nine fifteen when he got word from his assistant that a call had come in from NBC. "You must make yourself available for Jeff Gaspin at nine forty-five." Rosen had already spoken with Jeff Ross earlier from his car, and Jeff had relayed the rumor about Jay's getting canceled. Now, Rosen concluded, something was certainly afoot. He called Ross back and said a call was coming in from Gaspin.

"Something's up," Ross said. "Gaspin wants to see Conan and me, too." Conan was just then arriving at the *Tonight* headquarters.

In Gaspin's office, the NBC Entertainment chief put in another call, this one to New York. It was time to let Lorne Michaels and the staff of *Late Night* know that their show was headed for very late night—a 1:05 a.m. start time. The feedback from Lorne, Jimmy Fallon, and Jimmy's producer, Mike Shoemaker, was all positive. Shoemaker told him, "We love what we're doing. Don't worry about us."

"I appreciate that, guys," Gaspin said. "I'm really in a shitstorm out here."

A few minutes later Rick Rosen's assistant reported that Gaspin's office had checked in again, saying the call from Gaspin had been moved up to nine thirty. When Rosen phoned Jeff Ross back quickly with that news, the *Tonight* producer noted that they were supposed to be on their way to Gaspin's office at precisely that time. Of course, Conan and Ross had no intention of leaving for Gaspin's office until they knew what Gaspin had just told Rosen over the phone.

The call to Rosen came at exactly nine thirty. Gaspin was on the line, accompanied by Marc Graboff. "This is not a good call," Gaspin said, leading off. Rosen, taking notes, wrote down a single word: "bad."

Gaspin explained how important both Conan and Jay were to NBC, and how he wanted everyone to stay.

"What's your plan?" Rosen asked.

Gaspin played his hand: Jay to 11:35; Conan to 12:05. "We really want to make this work."

"And how long are we doing this for?" Rosen asked.

"Well, we don't know. We need to discuss that," Gaspin said, adding that this was not intended to be a long-term solution. He said he was about to have a conversation with Conan and Jeff.

"I know you are," Rosen said. "We'll get back to you."

Rosen had a client waiting, one he knew was not going to enjoy this news flash. Rosen called Ross and O'Brien to clue them in on what they were about to hear when they got to Jeff Gaspin's office.

Rosen could hear the dismay in Conan's simple response: "Oh, boy."

When Conan O'Brien walked into Jeff Gaspin's office at a little after ten a.m. on Thursday, January 7, his face said everything. Marc Graboff saw it and realized at once: *Conan knows.*

Gaspin was not quite as certain, but anyone could read Conan's expression and realize something was tearing him up, either direct knowledge or anticipation of knowledge. All at once, as he prepared to deliver this blow, Gaspin sensed he might have played it all wrong. Maybe he should have brought Rosen in early, begged him to keep the information quiet, solicited his help in getting Conan on board. Now it was too late. He had a devastated star in his office about to get hit with the official haymaker.

The NBC executives greeted O'Brien and Ross formally and stiffly— there was no call for a bogus show of warmth. Conan sat across from them, but he looked off vaguely toward the window. He did not meet Gaspin's eyes. Sitting next to him, Jeff Ross could not bring himself to look Graboff in the eye. He had too much history with Graboff, a guy he had always liked.

Gaspin got right to the point. They faced a crisis with the affiliates. The press tour was around the corner. Something had to be done. So he had come up with this plan: half-hour Jay into a later *Tonight Show.* "I don't want to choose between you," Gaspin said. Once again he referred to his refusal to make a Sophie's choice out of the situation.

Conan remained calm, totally professional, which impressed both Gaspin and Graboff. Inside he was churning, of course, but part of him was struck by how surreal—farcical almost—the moment felt. *Sophie's choice?*

Still keeping his eyes averted, Conan responded, "I completely understand the difficult position you're in," but he began to lay out his case. If someone had told you six years ago what he was going to do, and you based all your actions on that promise, and then he turned around and reneged on that promise. . . .

He went through the litany of events that flowed from that initial guarantee of *The Tonight Show.* He had sacrificed a lot of money. He hadn't wanted to go to the competition; he'd wanted to be loyal to NBC.

Gaspin offered no challenge; he saw no reason to. He agreed with Conan's points.

"I get it," Gaspin said. "It's not perfect. I'm offering you both half of what you want. You get to come to work every day, same as always.

Not Jay, because he's got a half-hour show now. He's the one who's got to change his habit, a habit he's had for eighteen years. You make the same money you always made. You work with the same people."

Gaspin never mentioned the word "ratings," nor did he bring up a point he himself regarded as an advantage for Conan: At 12:05 he wouldn't have to face the pressure to broaden out. He wouldn't have to listen to NBC's endless notes on bookings and all the rest. And Jay would act as a good buffer between the news viewers and Conan. He hoped to have a chance to have that kind of fuller discussion down the road.

Now Gaspin came back to the need to make this change and his desire to do it the right way. "I want to be fair to both of you," Gaspin said. "This has been an unfair situation for both of you."

But Conan was seeing no equivalency on the fairness meter. He could not quite see how the situation could be construed as unfair to Jay. Leno had hosted *The Tonight Show* for seventeen years. He had handed it over and immediately shifted to ten o'clock, voluntarily. How, Conan asked himself, could any of this be construed as unfair to Jay?

"I know how hard I worked for this," Conan told the NBC executives. "It was promised to me. I had a shitty lead-in." His tone was soft, but the words were clipped. Graboff knew this was Conan in the raw, speaking from the heart.

Conan asked if Lorne knew; how about Jimmy Fallon? Gaspin said he had spoken to both of them already.

Graboff tried to shift the conversation, move it away from all the emotion. He said to Jeff Ross, "Come on, Jeff. Just do this show for a couple of years and then move back."

It was the only time in his experience with Ross that he had ever heard the producer really raise his voice. "That's bullshit, and you know it!" Ross said, directly to Graboff. "The only way Jay leaves now is being carried out feet first!"

Gaspin countered by continuing his soft approach, urging Conan to give the idea some time, take it in, think about it.

Listening to Gaspin, still with a faraway look in his eye, Conan began to perceive an executive who had been in the world of cable, made a lot of money for the company by being in the right place at the right time, and was now under the impression that he was smarter than he actually was—like a guy who happened to live in Texas oil country around the time the internal combustion engine was invented. To the money counters, an executive like this came across as a genius. But unlike the best entertainment impresarios, like NBC's own Brandon Tartikoff, Gaspin wasn't somebody who lived and breathed network television. And so, Conan intuited, Gaspin had little chance to understand how late night worked, the emotions of its performers, the loyalty of its audiences.

As Conan saw it, Gaspin was in over his head. He simply didn't get what he was doing here: He acted as though late-night shows were just a few board pieces to be moved around. Conan pictured Gaspin as a guy who walked into an atomic bomb factory, had never been in one before, and just started swinging a wrench around.

The one thought Conan had on the spot about the half hour at 11:35 was that it likely would exacerbate the problem he already had with Leno. "So at least now, Jay does his show, but there's the break of the news, and that's kind of a reset button," Conan said to Gaspin and Graboff. "At 11:35 Jay's going to come out and do twenty jokes. And then what's he going to do?"

When they replied that it seemed likely he would have only one guest, Conan said, "OK. And then I come out and do what?"

The NBC guys didn't really have any answer to that other than what Conan had already been doing: his own monologue. That this now seemed like a late-night pileup—three shows with monologues lined up end to end—was the implication no one had really addressed.

Finally Conan did have something he really wanted to say, something that had been almost burning a hole in his chest. "What does Jay have on you?" Conan asked, his voice still low, his tone still even. "What does this guy have on you people? What the hell is it about Jay?"

Neither of the NBC executives had an answer. They cast their heads down. Conan thought they were working at looking sympathetic, following some lesson that had been taught at corporate school.

After a pause, Gaspin suggested again that they take some time to figure out what they wanted to do. NBC would be patient. He repeated the network's desire to keep Conan in the family.

Conan listened for a bit, then stood up. Jeff Ross followed suit. They walked out. The meeting was over; it had lasted fifteen minutes.

The walk back to the *Tonight* offices required less than two minutes. In that expanse of time both Conan O'Brien and Jeff Ross realized the same thing. NBC wasn't *asking* if this move would be OK. They were simply telling them this was going to be the plan. There was no carrot being offered: no contract extension, no salary bump. And of course it had now become clear that they had been called to this hurried meeting because the news was leaking out.

"Fuck," Ross said. "Well, we know that Jay knows."

O'Brien walked into an office in an uproar. A post on the entertainment gossip site TMZ, "NBC Shakeup; Jay Leno Comes Out on Top," had basically reversed the rumor—now it was Conan who had been canceled. The first few women on the staff he encountered had tears streaming down their cheeks. O'Brien called a rushed staff meeting, gathering everyone in the studio. He grabbed a hand mic and said he just wanted to address the rumors. It was simply not true that the show had been canceled, Conan said. Yes, he explained, "there is a situation with NBC," but the show was not being threatened. "We're all going to be OK." Relief flooded the room, but did not wash away the uncertainty much of the staff was feeling.

Even more than the meeting with Gaspin and Graboff, the TMZ story upset Conan. The day had begun with sharks circling Jay's rejected show; now they had suddenly turned in Conan's direction? How had that happened? Who could have fed the Web site this bogus story? Conan didn't have to guess much to come up with a suspect. He thought about the 1993 episode when Jay hid in a closet to listen in on his fate, a move that Jay had been conspicuously proud of, seeing himself as simply resourceful, but a move that played to some as evidence of the unholy lengths he would go to in order to protect his position. To O'Brien, the timing of the leak to TMZ—coming so soon after a story that Jay had been canceled—screamed of an attempt at diversionary action.

Soon after Conan got back to his office, Ross walked in with more news. He had e-mailed a contact in New York with a simple question: "Is it true Lorne knows?" The answer had come back: Yes.

"We were the last ones to find out about this," Ross said. "This is not good."

"Nope," said O'Brien. "This is not good."

Ross was just finished comparing how not good this was with "sticking a big stick up your ass" when his assistant told him he had a call waiting from Allison Gollust.

Out on the studio tour with the Comcast team, Zucker had already checked in with Rick Rosen. "Well, what do you think?" Zucker had questioned him.

"It doesn't sound very good," Rick replied.

"How did they take it?" Zucker asked.

"Not well."

"Well, can I go over and speak to them?"

"Hey, Jeff—you run the place," Rosen replied. "You don't have to ask me."

A short time later Gollust put in the call to Ross. She had been dispatched to reach out to assure him that Zucker was indeed in town and ready to come by and talk this through with Ross and Conan. She explained to Ross that they were driving around the lot on golf carts, still stuck with the Comcast guys, and then they had a lunch scheduled with them, but they could stop by as soon as that was over.

After checking with Conan, Jeff said it would be better if Zucker came by after the show. Zucker agreed this made sense. Zucker was mainly concerned with assuring Conan and Ross that he would make every effort to get to them as soon as he could, fully aware that they would have an issue with NBC's having talked to Jay first.

That Thursday night, Conan didn't perform a show so much as simply get through one. He made no mention of the events of that day. He knew he was only half there, the other half still distracted by the anvil hanging over his head.

Jeff Ross left Conan to wind down after he left the stage and headed up to his office, anticipating Zucker's arrival. In the past, given their closeness, a visit from Zucker would have been an occasion for lightheartedness. This evening Ross found himself more than troubled—he was pissed. The news they had heard that day was bad enough, but that it had been delivered by Jeff Gaspin, a guy they barely knew, instead of Zucker himself, left Ross hugely offended.

When Zucker arrived at around seven, he saw a familiar face waiting at the lobby elevators: Gavin Polone. Conan's manager had turned up to watch the show and provide support for his client. He shook hands with Zucker and said a simple hello. Zucker went directly up to Ross's office.

For Jeff Ross, it was instantly, and inevitably, the worst meeting he had ever had with his friend. Ross felt completely uncomfortable, trying to find a balance between the personal affection he felt for Zucker and the professional distance he needed, because Conan held his first and forever loyalty. And already—even with Zucker trying to express NBC's continued commitment to Conan—Ross's gut was filling with bile over how Conan had been treated. The whole affair felt like a public vote of no confidence; they had simply bailed on Conan.

Ross signaled the formality of this occasion by sitting behind his desk rather than out in one of the chairs or on the couch across the room. Zucker settled into a chair facing the desk. After about fifteen minutes Conan, now changed out of his suit into his usual uniform of T-shirt and jeans, ambled in slowly, hands folded, eyes downcast, his face so drawn, his expression so stony blank that Zucker thought he looked catatonic. Conan sat down all the way at the far end of the couch, about as far from the chair Zucker was in as he could get.

Despite their connection stretching back to their Harvard days, the two men were not especially close, though Conan had previously felt nothing but support from Zucker. Now Zucker spoke softly, his own eyes directed toward the carpet. He spoke first about why they had decided to make this move, how they had to do what they believed was in the best interest of NBC. That had to be the primary responsibility. Zucker stressed how vitally important both Conan and Jay were to the network, how this was all about NBC trying to do everything humanly possible to keep both of them.

Conan wanted to make one point first and foremost.

"Here's the thing I regret the most," he told Zucker. "I have a great staff. I have a staff that loves this show, a young staff that really believes in it. A lot of people moved out here. They believe in what we're doing. They see what's happening. And for an hour today, for no reason, they thought they were canceled. That makes me sick to my stomach."

Zucker said he regretted that, but his broad thought was that this sort of thing happened in the blogosphere world everyone lived in now.

Conan didn't say much more, allowing Zucker to lay it all out, repeating the message: NBC did not want to lose him. This wasn't about driving him away. This was about finding a way to get him to stay.

Conan let Zucker go on, thinking only of one thing. Finally, he said it again: "What does Jay Leno have on you guys? I just don't get it."

To Zucker, the question said more about Conan than it did about

NBC. He saw it springing from Conan's deep dislike of Leno that had simmered just below the surface for years. To Zucker, the answer to that question should have been: no more than what Conan O'Brien had on NBC. In an honest evaluation, as Zucker saw it, both late-night stars would have faced the same judgment: Their shows failed.

But Zucker didn't say that to Conan. Instead, he went over in greater detail the dilemma NBC faced with the affiliate revolt—and something else. He referred to Jay's unusual contract and the impact it had on NBC's position. As both Conan and Ross heard it and interpreted it, Zucker was explaining that he had signed a contract with Leno that he would take back if he could, but that was impossible now, and what was done was done.

Conan, who grew only more silent and closed up as the conversation wore on, did not challenge this notion, or express outrage, though he found himself astonished by Zucker's almost casual tone. To Conan, it sounded a bit like a passing observation that Zucker was making about the deal that had driven NBC's decision making, even though to Conan the decision was of such monumental importance that it was a little like someone saying, "I took your son to the mall today and I gave him to a homeless person. If I could I would take it back, but what's done is done."

Overall, the talk lasted about a half hour. Zucker concluded by urging Conan to take his time, think it over, go over things with his representatives. Then Conan stood up, tossed off some parting words, and left the room.

Zucker remained with Jeff Ross. Despite the tension, their closeness opened the door to a more honest conversation, at least from Zucker's perspective. He went back over his assurances that NBC really did want them to stay, to continue producing *The Tonight Show*. But he pointed to what he said were mistakes the show had been making—the bookings, the nichey comedy. He told Ross that Lorne Michaels was on board with this idea, even though it was hardly going to be advantageous to Jimmy Fallon.

As always Jeff Ross remained calm, stoic to a point that Zucker, as he had so frequently in the past, wondered if he should check for Jeff's pulse. Ross seemed a bit shell-shocked by the events of the day, but he did not overtly dispute Zucker's analysis. Instead he sat quietly behind his desk, listening, taking it all in.

Finally Zucker stood to leave. "I'm supposed to fly home tomorrow," he told Ross. "But if you need me to fly back out here to talk to Conan, to talk to you, whatever you need me to do, you just tell me and I'll be here in one minute."

Ross nodded. Zucker started for the door. Ross stopped him. "Hey . . . me and you," Ross said. "Whatever happens, we're all right."

When Marc Graboff woke around six the next morning, Friday, January 8, he immediately checked his BlackBerry, as was his custom. He found a message from Zucker, which he noticed had also been sent to Jeff Gaspin, Rebecca Marks, and Allison Gollust. The message said that Ari Emanuel had called and roused Zucker from his bed at the Four Seasons at five thirty a.m. (the same time he called Zucker on most mornings, though that usually meant eight thirty in the east). In the e-mail, Zucker summarized the conversation: Ari said he hated the decision about Conan, but he got it. He understood NBC's thinking and why NBC thought it was the right thing to do. They would all talk it over and he was sure Conan was going to do it.

Graboff was not overly surprised by Emanuel's reaction. He thought of Ari as levelheaded and businesslike, though mainly by reputation. Ari tended to deal exclusively with the top guys like Zucker, not next-level deal makers like Marc.

When Allison Gollust awoke to the same message, she was relieved, thinking this might spell a quick and reasonable end to this little drama, which would calm the roiling press waters. Rebecca Marks, her West Coast counterpart, had a similar reaction.

Jeff Gaspin appreciated this bit of promising news from Zucker even more than the other NBC executives, not only because the revamp had been his idea, but also because he had the press tour appearance facing him in two days. If Conan's assent could be secured by then, handling questions from the reporters might turn into an unexpected breeze. But he had little time to digest fully Zucker's message, because Jay checked in first thing that morning, interested in hearing about the discussion between Zucker and O'Brien the previous evening.

Jay asked Gaspin what he thought was going to happen with Conan now. Gaspin told Jay that Conan was truly upset. But he said there were some indications that an agreement might be possible.

"Should I call him?" Jay asked.

Gaspin, recalling the edge Conan had revealed when talking about

Leno in their meeting the day before, and how personal it seemed to be getting, said, "You know what—don't call him."

On Friday morning Jeff Ross arrived at his office still offended and no warmer to NBC's plan. The night before he had engaged in a long conversation with Polone that left him even more concerned about whether the network could even be serious about this proposal.

Polone had cited the current *Tonight* budget—about $80 million—and told Ross, "Wait a second. You're telling me they're going to put on Leno, three shows in what has been a two-hour block, and spend an extra $80 million?" Just from a numbers point of view it seemed to make no sense, except as some bullshit, short-term patch job to get them through this PR nightmare.

Ross's first call was from Lloyd Braun. "I can't believe it!" Braun all but shouted. "They did it to you guys! Exactly what you were afraid of out at Riviera. I was sure they could never do this!"

All Ross could say in reply was that he wished to hell he'd been wrong—but he wasn't.

Conan came in a short time later and sat with Ross. The two men didn't speak much, but after a while looked at each other and both said a version of the same thing: "Looks like we gotta get outta here. It's over." They discussed again the absence of any kind of carrot being offered to make this pill go down any easier.

Ross left a short time later for a lunch with Jeff Gaspin at the Grill, the de rigueur meeting spot for business lunches on the Universal lot, for what amounted to a horse-out-of-the-barn back-channel effort. Gaspin arrived with apologies for how rushed the meeting had been the day before. He conceded that spending fifteen minutes trying to lay out this plan had been inadequate, but explained that the best intentions to present the idea in a formal and complete way had gone awry when the story leaked. He acknowledged that he knew this was a very big deal and needed serious consideration on the Conan side.

Ross tried to convey the impact a move like this had on a talent like Conan—NBC was in effect publicly demoting him—Gaspin attempted to relate it to his own experience, describing how he had been passed over twice for the top entertainment job at NBC but had hung in there, kept doing his job, waiting for another opportunity.

"I cannot believe you would make that analogy," Ross said. "That's not a valid analogy. You didn't get demoted." He didn't add the obvious: *You aren't a television star, either.*

And when Gaspin repeated that he didn't want to make a Sophie's choice between Jay and Conan, Ross got a bit exasperated. "Stop with the Sophie's choice," he said. "You did make a choice."

But it was always in Ross's nature to remain levelheaded and reasonable, and Gaspin believed in the same approach. They talked more calmly about whether Conan might come around and accept the idea. Ross said he wasn't sure; he had never seen him so upset.

As he left, Gaspin saw no reason to panic about where Conan was in this process. He was unhappy, but that didn't mean he would not ultimately agree to the proposal. Besides, Zucker was already reporting that Conan's top agent would work to bring him around.

Conan was not surprised that he had not had any word from Leno. That Friday he said to Ross and his head writer, Mike Sweeney, "I'm not gonna hear from that guy. I'll probably never hear from him again."

Conan had, however, spoken with Jimmy Fallon. Conan called him in the midst of the madness on Thursday just to urge him, "I don't know what's going to happen, but you should be calm." Jimmy mentioned that Jay had called earlier to take his temperature, which only hardened Conan's conviction that Leno would not phone him. Jay could commiserate with Jimmy, because Jimmy was new, and it was all "Whatever, gang; peace and love toward everybody."

Friday was at least a better day in one respect. The show got a handle on how to be funny about all this. "We've got a great show for you tonight—I have no idea when it will air, but it's gonna be a great show," Conan pronounced at the top. He went on, "NBC has finally come up with an exciting idea—they want me to follow Jay Leno." And: "When I got in today there was a 1923 Duesenberg parked in my spot." Getting laughs on the subject that was obsessing him left Conan feeling he had his sea legs under him again.

While he focused on the show, his team—which, besides his agents and manager, now included his transactional lawyer, Leigh Brecheen—invaded the *Tonight* conference room to work on their options. Gavin Polone took to calling it the war room. From the first moment they all got the news, Polone took the hardest line of anyone working for Conan. He in no sense looked at Jeff Zucker as a friend, as Ross and even Rick Rosen did.

In the war room Conan's team divided up the press contacts, strategizing how best to get Conan's message out. Polone was unrelentingly aggressive in pushing to plant attack stories against NBC. He also pronounced from the first meeting that they would win a settlement with the network. "We are going to get a lot here," Polone told the others. "We are going to get everything we want."

Polone had spent his entire career haggling over contractual details. He didn't really care what impact his outspoken style might have on negotiations. It was just something he had to do. This did not come as any secret to the NBC side, which regarded Polone as a bomb thrower from the start. If Zucker's feisty but warm relationship with Ari Emanuel and the overall intelligence of a classy agent like Rick Rosen encouraged the NBC side to believe they might win Conan over, the presence of Polone struck them as the unstable explosive element in that mix.

Friday evening, after Conan wrapped his show for the night, he joined his support group in the conference room. One crucial element remained unclear to him: How much flexibility did he even have with this contract? NBC had put out the argument that nothing in Conan's deal prevented them from taking this step. On the face of it, that was true, at least to the extent that the deal he signed to host *The Tonight Show* had no specific language that included time-period protection. But the legal side was examining that issue more closely.

As he and his team discussed it that evening, Conan found himself trying to see if he could slip that 12:05 suit on. What would it feel like? He figured he had time to let the notion marinate; NBC had assured him nothing was imminent. He could ponder his options without pressure.

As the group was breaking for the night, Rick Rosen asked Jeff Ross if he wanted to grab some dinner. They took themselves to the Brentwood Restaurant and Lounge on South Barrington in Brentwood Village. Neither man was much of a drinker, but the last two days had left them both fried to cinders. So Rick ordered a vodka. Jeff began doing tequila shots. They ordered dinner, started to mellow out.

Just before nine p.m. Rosen's cell rang. He checked the readout: restricted number. Rick had a loose rule not to answer his cell when he didn't know who was on the line, but things were so fluid he decided he had better pick this one up.

"Hello, Richard," a voice said. Jeff Zucker often used the formal first name affectionately when he greeted someone. After some pleasantries Zucker asked how everyone was doing.

"Not good," Rosen said

"Well, have you seen tomorrow's *New York Times* yet?" Zucker asked. "Let me read you something." He proceeded to share an update on the Conan situation, already available online, which included a reference to overt interest in Conan from the Fox network, expressed by an unnamed executive, as well as an assertion from representatives of Conan that the star had not accepted NBC's plan and was not likely to anytime in the near future.

"Let me explain something to you," Zucker said. "I want a fucking answer from you. If you think you are going to play me in the press, you've got the wrong guy. You're a representative of Conan O'Brien, aren't you? And you're talking to the press?"

"I haven't spoken *to The Times* at all," Rosen replied, getting a bit heated himself. "I didn't make this comment."

"Well, I guess we know who did, don't we?" Zucker replied, not quite saying the name Gavin Polone. "I want an answer from Conan and I want an answer quickly. You know I have the ability to pay him or play him, and I could ice him for two years."

Rosen chose to ignore that little shot across his nose.

"Well, Jeff," Rosen said, "we're going to give you an answer when we have thought about it. If you want an emotional answer, I'll give you an answer now. If you want the answer after we've thought about it and we've analyzed it, you'll get that answer."

Zucker remained hot. "Just let me tell you something—you are not going to fucking play me."

The conversation ended there. Rosen was stunned at this sudden blast of pressure, coming only thirty-six hours after Conan was hit with the news. He could now picture the whole deal going off the rails. He left a message immediately for Jeff Gaspin. When Gaspin got back to him, Rosen told him that he had just had a nasty conversation with his boss. "If he thinks that by intimidating us he's going to get the answer he wants, *he's* got the wrong guys. You better tell him to chill out and let the process work."

Gaspin promised he would take care of the situation.

Conan didn't know about the confrontational call from Zucker when he arrived home that Friday night. He was tense, wrestling with the decision that faced him. Conan truly had not figured out what he should—or even could—do. He tried to talk it over with Liza, unspooling the day's events. "You know, it's still *The Tonight Show*," he told her, watching her reaction closely.

Liza didn't contradict him, but she did something that was familiar to him. She gave him a look that somehow combined patience with total skepticism.

At midday Saturday, after an exchange of e-mails, Rosen spoke to Zucker again. Jeff's tone from the start was much calmer, and Rosen guessed that Gaspin might have suggested a conciliatory call. While Zucker made many of the same points as the night before, he did so in a far more sensitive way. "Look, we just want to resolve this. I know you guys have to go through your process, but there's going to be a point where I just need a decision."

Rosen, appreciating the sincere effort from Zucker, said he got it. "I know you have this affiliate thing. We're not gonna drag this out. No one wants to drag this out. He's just digesting this still."

Perhaps signaling that he wanted to keep the line of communication friendly, Zucker shifted topics and told Rosen he also wanted to thank him for steering a new pilot written by the prolific David E. Kelley (*Ali McBeal*, *The Practice*) to NBC.

Rosen accepted the thanks and they closed on familiar good terms.

Later the same day, Rosen made it out to Conan's house, where the group was set to meet. Conan had fallen into an angry phase, sitting sullenly during the gathering in his book-lined study. They were all going round and round about whether he should accept 12:05, and Conan still wasn't sure whether he really had an option to reject it.

It sounded to Conan that Leigh Brecheen, his lawyer, was suggesting they stall for time while they examined all the drafts of his deals. The issue just wasn't clear, and as they debated it, Conan started to picture himself as the olive in the middle of an olive oil press—and with every second that passed by, the crank was getting turned and the squeeze was getting tighter. But he never pushed the question of why his deal didn't contain the overt time-period protection that appeared in so many other late-night contracts.

Sensing the contractual issue was going to become central, Rosen suggested they start thinking about hiring a litigator. And that meant only one name as far as he was concerned: Patty Glaser. Perhaps the best known (and most feared) litigation lawyer in Hollywood, Glaser had represented the Endeavor agency and had faced off against NBC successfully in the past. Given the go-ahead, Rosen reached her on vacation at the California ski resort Mammoth, and she agreed to come down on Sunday night to meet with Conan and his team.

That done, the message to Conan was essentially unchanged: Sit tight. He could bide his time for a while longer.

Conan didn't feel that way. "I can tell you—as a performer—no, I can't," he told them. "I can't go out there every night and do a show when it's this unclear what's happening. It's too toxic."

But without a firm interpretation of where they stood legally, there wasn't much else they could do.

As Saturday came to an end, uncertainty prevailed on the opposite coast as well. Zucker began to question his initial read that Conan's representatives would steer the star toward the sensible resolution of accepting the deal and staying. Zucker had continued to have occasional interaction with Ari Emanuel, but now he started to wonder if that was of any real value. Ari certainly didn't seem to be as involved as the rest of them in the strategizing going on at Conan's house; if it was true that he had been pushed out, Zucker suspected it would surely have been because Ari was on the side of looking to settle the dispute and keep Conan at NBC. That likely put Ari—and maybe Rick Rosen, whom Zucker still considered a steadying influence and a voice of reason—at odds with the engineer he believed was driving the runaway train: Gavin Polone. Zucker always believed it said a lot that Polone had named his production company Pariah.

On Sunday morning Jeff Gaspin walked into the ballroom of the Langham Huntington Hotel in Pasadena, where an extra-large gathering of media waited like wolves outside a chicken farm. Surely this was going to be a merry bloodbath: a new NBC executive trying to confront questions about what now looked like the unmitigated disaster of the failed Leno show at ten, an affiliate revolt, and the apparent demotion of the star NBC had touted as the future of late night.

At about ten a.m. Gaspin took the stage, accompanied by Angela Bromstad, who ran the Universal television production studio. He opened the session with straightforward confirmation of the news most of the group had already been reporting. *The Jay Leno Show* would end just before the Olympics, and he had made offers to Jay to move to a half-hour show at 11:35 and to Conan O'Brien to slide *The Tonight Show* back to 12:05. The barrage followed; Gaspin took each question calmly, responding with complete thoughts and apparent confidence.

"What is important to me," he said, "is that I gave Conan something that is very important to him, which was *The Tonight Show*. So when I asked him to move to 12:05, I made it very clear *The Tonight Show* was moving with him. What's important to Jay is telling jokes at eleven thirty. . . . I obviously couldn't satisfy either with 100 percent of what they wanted. That's why I came up with this compromise."

Gaspin claimed complete ownership of the idea—though he said Jeff Zucker "let me pull the trigger"—and he tied it to the concerns about the affiliates, which he declined to call a threat "so much as it was a dialogue."

He didn't call Jay's show a failure, suggesting only that it hadn't done as well as NBC had hoped. As for his plan, he said his goal was to keep all three late-night stars, and "much as I'd like to tell you we have a done deal, we know that's not true." He added, "The talks are still ongoing."

The comments came across as unusually candid, just as Gaspin came across as remarkably unflinching. He impressed the reporters, many of whom noted in their stories that, contrary to some recent NBC experiences with the press, this one was handled with honesty and professionalism.

Gaspin took a lot of pride but not much solace in those reviews, because nothing was settled. The intelligence he was receiving, primarily secondhand from contacts with Rosen and Emanuel, was that Conan was having good days and bad, and the agents were not sure they could control the outcome. Gaspin still interpreted that message to mean the agents wanted Conan to stay at NBC, but they certainly weren't guaranteeing it. Polone clearly had a different agenda, Gaspin heard, and the

X-factor was Liza O'Brien. She seemed to be in the camp guiding Conan away from NBC's plan. Frankly, that made sense to Gaspin, who knew his own wife's strength of character and how she would respond if he came home declaring his bosses were trying to screw him over.

That afternoon the Conan cadre met again in Conan's study, though not much could be advanced until that night, when Patty Glaser would arrive. Conan remained restless and unhappy, eager to find some way out of the olive press. As the group was breaking up for the evening, with Rosen due to meet Glaser back at his house, his cell rang. This time he recognized the number: Zucker again.

Rosen told him it wasn't the best time; Zucker asked if Rosen could call back at his first opportunity.

In his car, on the way home, again accompanied by Jeff Ross, Rosen reached Zucker, who began once more by inquiring about Conan's state of mind. Rosen reported again that it wasn't very good.

The bad report seemed to push Zucker past the limit of his patience.

"Have you explained the contract to him?" Zucker asked. "Do you guys understand what's in the fucking contract? I'm going to tell you right now that I can pay him or play him. I can ice you guys."

"Jeff, are you threatening me?" Rosen said. "Because if you're threatening me, I better hire a litigator." Of course, Rosen was already on that path with Glaser over the contract terms. But if NBC was trying to raise the ante by threatening to fire Conan and keep him off television for the next two years, the litigation route was going to become a fast lane.

The conversation veered back and forth at high volume over NBC's ability to pay Conan off and sideline his career. Rosen now had much more to discuss with Patty Glaser.

When the blowup got back to Polone, it only confirmed for him the message he had been pounding home at these meetings: Jeff Zucker had the ability to shatter someone's career like this and then get angry at the victims for reacting to it.

Inside the lower echelons of NBC that weekend, a contingent of Conan supporters found themselves appalled at what had taken place. Conan had always put himself on the line for the network, and for many of the people who worked there.

For some staff members, it was simply hard to believe that the network hierarchy really wanted Conan to stay. How could they put something like this in motion without knowing they were likely to lose this guy? How would it all play out? Once Jay was reestablished at 11:35, did NBC even have the right to take it away from him again at some unspecified future date to give Conan another crack? Wasn't Jay now raised to the status of Regis Philbin, a television perennial, seventy-seven and still on the air? Conan had taken one leap of faith that he would inherit the show eventually. Would he ever take another?

One executive who intended at least to try to get Conan on board was Nick Bernstein, the second-ranked NBC late-night executive under Rick Ludwin. Bernstein had a good relationship with both late-night hosts, and he found himself almost too stunned to work in the immediate aftermath of that week's upheaval. If Conan could ever agree to this plan, Bernstein could certainly buy into it. So he sent several e-mails out to Conan and Jeff Ross, more or less pleading with them to see the benefit of sticking around.

At the press tour on Monday, the Fox executive session was dominated by questions about that network's interest in acquiring Conan—should there be a divorce from NBC. The two top Fox entertainment executives, Peter Rice and Kevin Reilly, did little to hide their enthusiasm for that idea.

Reilly, who took some special enjoyment in NBC's latest misery, given his own untimely ouster by Zucker, said, "Conan would be a very compatible fit for our brand. He is one of the few guys on the planet that has demonstrated he can do one of these shows every night." That, he added, "is probably the hardest form in show business." Reilly also stressed that he did not believe Conan was "damaged goods in the least" and that, as far as he was concerned, "his show was working."

Reilly made it clear, however, that acquiring Conan would not be like picking up a used car. The Fox stations had just come through a brutal financial downturn and many had invested in syndicated programs for use in late night. He said he agreed with estimates by NBC executives that the start-up costs for a new late-night show could go as high as $70 million.

Still, the gleam in his eye made him look like a guy about to buy a diamond engagement ring.

If Fox executives had reason to be upbeat that Monday, the mood was even more buoyant in another corner of the television business: NBC's affiliates, with the official news Sunday that the Leno-at-ten experiment was dead, celebrated quietly all across the country.

Michael Fiorile, the affiliate board head, took some special satisfaction in achieving his goals without having to come to blows with the network. If there was still some uncertainty about what NBC would use to fill the ten p.m. hour, at least whatever NBC came up with promised to be a likely improvement over Jay's numbers. And the proposed solution of Jay back at 11:35, with Conan moved back past midnight, sounded more than satisfactory.

From his conversations with Jeff Gaspin and Jeff Zucker in December, Fiorile had taken away the impression that NBC saw no problem with keeping Conan at 12:05—or, if it came to that, losing him altogether. As Fiorile interpreted it, NBC's position was: "If he wouldn't take it, they'd program without him."

Fiorile possessed evidence that the affiliate body did not disagree. NBC had asked him what the local stations' preference would be at 11:35. Fiorile had quietly polled the affiliate board. The stations had long experience with Jay. (And the age group most of them occupied did not fall anywhere near the core audience of eighteen-to-thirty-four-year-olds that idolized Conan.) So it was little surprise whom the station owners preferred. Not one voted for Conan

As measured in other places, however, the reaction to the proposed move leaned heavily toward Conan. That was to be expected in any form of media that played to a younger audience, like Internet postings. One nerve grew more inflamed as the standoff continued. Resentment raged among the post-baby-boom generation at what they saw as another example of the baby boomers nailing their feet to the stage and not letting go. It would grow into an ongoing theme—even a movement. Readers posting in reaction to press stories took up the theme of Jay as an old hat that should have been shelved: "Geez, Leno, retire already! What a jerk!" "NOOOO! What is this obsession NBC has with Leno? The decision shows such little foresight. It's tomorrow's ratings that matter. Think of the children!"

Much of the press commentary sympathized with O'Brien as well. Jay was being portrayed as the usurper, the guy who didn't stand by his pledge to hand the late-night chair to Conan, the old act who refused to leave the arena when his time had passed. Worst of all for Leno, he was again being tagged as a Machiavelli who had possibly set up the entire episode. As in: Give up *The Tonight Show* under protest; assail NBC on the air for years for this shoddy treatment; then accept the ten p.m. move, knowing the pathetic lead-ins it would generate would inevitably undermine Conan and force NBC to dump him. That this would entail the monumental embarrassment for Jay of a public cancelation caused no apparent cognitive dissonance.

But Jay was taking it on his ample chin from all over. Editorial cartoons popped up. In the *Dayton Daily News*, Lincoln had been erased from Mount Rushmore and Teddy Roosevelt was saying to Jefferson, "He did the Leno show last night." In *The New Yorker*, two parents watching TV were chastising their son, who had gotten up in his pajamas: "Go back to bed or we'll make you watch Jay Leno." That kind of elitist commentary was easy for Jay to swat away, pointing out that the magazine had lost about $70 million in a year. "I had a better year than *The New Yorker*. I turned a profit."

But Conan's defenders also included many in the comedy world who had never embraced Jay because of his workmanlike style. Even one voice from the Carson camp weighed in. Jeff Sotzing, Johnny's nephew, who managed all the Carson business activity after Johnny's death, called Debbie Vickers and told her he agreed with Conan.

Like most others backing Jay, Vickers questioned the logic in the pro-Conan argument, and told Sotzing, "If Conan is doing well and they have to push him back, you go, 'No, I'm not doing it.' But if you're not doing well, don't you have to look in the mirror and say, 'What's my part in this?'"

Jerry Seinfeld provided the sternest defense of his old friend. Speaking at NBC's press tour about his new reality show, *The Marriage Ref*, Jerry defended Jay's ten p.m. show as a good idea, worth trying, one that was simply ahead of its time. But he also poked holes in Conan's defense of his own ratings and how they were damaged by weak lead-ins from Jay. "I don't think anyone's preventing people from watching Conan," Seinfeld said. "Once they give you the cameras, it's on you." He added, "Conan had a chance to destroy everybody. Go ahead! You're out there. You've got to hit the ball. They can't hit the ball for you. They can only give you the bat."

The commentary back and forth—mostly nasty and mostly directed at Jay—disturbed the NBC executives, who were already getting antsy over the lack of communication from the Conan side. To them, this smacked of Team Conan trying to get a message out there that was intended not to enhance their own position, or even to challenge NBC on its decision, but purely to trash Jay. Certainly that was Zucker's view. That Monday he picked up anti-Jay threads in the media that he believed could be traced right back to Gavin Polone. This would not do.

That same Monday Conan paid a visit to the writers' room, one of the places he felt most comfortable, surrounded by like minds. He talked briefly about how wretched he felt over this Hobson's choice he faced. He took his own poll of the room, adding the option that NBC hadn't given him—at least not officially: Accept the move to post-midnight, or take a hike. This vote was almost unanimous: Tell NBC to shove it.

Conan thanked them, using a line he would dredge up again later: "I think they cured me of my addiction to *The Tonight Show.*"

At that evening's taping Conan walked onstage to thunderous applause that he finally had to stop by saying, "You keep that up, and this monologue won't start until 12:05." He had a passel of jokes related to the news on everyone's mind: "This weekend a 6.5 earthquake hit California. The earthquake was so powerful it knocked Jay Leno's show from 10 to 11:35." (Over in Burbank, Jay was firing away as well: "I take pride in one thing. I leave NBC prime time the same way I found it—a complete disaster.")

After he wrapped that night, Conan dragged himself back upstairs to the conference room next to Ross's office, where his brain trust had reconvened, this time accompanied by the formidable Patty Glaser.

Conan had found himself more and more beaten down as the days passed. He had learned of Zucker's blast directed at Rosen, including the threat to keep him from working again. Sure, it was just business, but Conan still found himself shocked by what was transpiring. He had put in almost twenty years at NBC, devoting himself body and soul to the network and its needs, and now he was being told—in effect—that soon they would be posting his picture on NBC's properties with orders to give him the bum's rush if he ever showed his face. He recalled how, when *Late Night* had finally burst through and all the heat it generated was pumping cash into the basement at 30 Rock, NBC came and asked him what kind of gift they could give him—probably expecting he'd say a Porsche or a yacht. Instead, he had asked if NBC happened to have a vintage microphone hanging around somewhere; he would like to have something like that. They managed to dig one up, an old-fashioned mic with the letters "RCA" on it. He had been thrilled and treasured it. Now, suddenly, that was another memento headed for a scrap heap somewhere as this long marriage threatened to be blown to pieces.

It struck Conan that Jay had played it well, in his passive-aggressive way, and wound up winning again. And maybe, in contrast, he himself had simply played it all wrong.

In the conference room, Glaser, accompanied by an associate, sat at one end of the big table with a Bluetooth pinned to one ear. The lawyers, Rosen, Polone, and Ross were all discussing the contract dilemma—how it might all come down to what had been in earlier drafts, and whether they could find something there to at least throw out a charge that NBC was in breach, in order to gain leverage. Conan sat silently listening, slowly getting more and more worked up, until he was all but shaking with emotion.

Finally Glaser, way at the opposite end of the table, looked to where Conan was sitting and asked him, "What do *you* want to do?"

His chest muscles were so constricted, Conan wondered briefly if he was having a heart attack. "What I want to do," he said, haltingly, his voice rough and raw, "is something that all of you are going to tell me I can't do."

He had their full attention now, all eyes pinned to him. "I want to write a statement that says exactly how I feel about it. You guys are going to tell me that I'm giving up all my leverage if I'm supposed to go to another network or something; but I can't wait. I don't want to play games here, and the whole power of this thing is that I don't really know what my options are. That's what I want to do."

During the long pause that followed, Conan was aware of the eyes on him, the uneasiness around the table. He expected that the next words he would hear would be, "That's stupid." Instead, Glaser, calm, totally in control, asked, "What would you say?"

All his life, Conan O'Brien had lived through periods of debilitating self-doubt and insecurity, knowing that when the moment came to stand up for himself, when he was truly pressed against a wall, he would find a way to push all that aside, straighten his long Irish backbone, and be at his best. He started to speak and a boiling lava of emotion spilled out.

He described how much the show meant to him, the legacy of Carson, the offers he had passed up to get this chance, and how losing it would be crushing—and unfair. Because they were never really given a chance, not with complete lack of ratings support from prime time and the obvious lack of faith on the part of a network pulling the plug only seven months in.

The words came freely; he composed them on the spot. But they flowed, syntax perfect, no hesitation between each sentence. His voice grew softer, even more strained with emotion when he got to the core of his message: He could not accept a postponement in a nightly habit Americans had participated in and shared for six decades; he would not be accomplice to the destruction that this idea of NBC's might inflict on the greatest franchise in television history. Not to mention the fallout on the other great NBC late-night showcase, the show David Letterman had created and Conan himself had devoted so much of his life to sustaining. If it truly came to this, if NBC would truly force him to decide whether to give up his dream or play a role in undermining a cultural landmark, then maybe it would be better for him to try to find someplace else to work, someplace that prized the art of late-night television more than NBC now apparently did.

When Conan finished, his group sat silent. Jeff Ross, his eyes welling up, looked around and saw no dry eyes on the Conan team. Throughout Conan's speech Ross had found himself overcome with discomfort, thinking, *They're never going to let you do this—so stop. Don't finish this.* But he knew Conan, and the powerful way he could use words. So he was not surprised at the impact he had on the room.

Patty Glaser finally broke the silence. "I like it," she said. And then she added, "If you do one thing for me, Conan, don't quit. But I like this as a statement." She paused again, then said definitively, "Let's do it."

Her quick assent was the last thing Conan expected to hear, but it stunned—and disconcerted—Jeff Ross, who still quaked at the obvious implications if Conan ever went public with those sentiments.

"Whoa, whoa, whoa," he said. "Really? We're gonna do this?"

"Why not?" Glaser said. "It's from his heart. It's what he feels." She turned back to Conan. "Why don't you write it, and we'll look at it."

That was all Conan needed to hear. He stood up, ready to leave; Ross put up a hand.

"Wait, wait, wait," he said. "I love the idea, but let's all of us in this room understand that if we do this, we're taking the toothpaste out of the tube, and it ain't going back in."

Conan nodded at Ross with assurance. He said, "I get it."

In his car driving home, Conan felt the words burning straight out through his forehead. He knew what he wanted to say: nothing self-pitying, just an honest statement—because you can't argue with the truth. And it came down to one simple truth: He did not want to be the guy who, accepting a start time past midnight, brought *The Tonight Show* into tomorrow.

At home, he gushed it out almost all at once to Liza before sitting down at the computer to write. But he struggled; the formality of actually typing out the words presented unexpected mental roadblocks, and he kept getting stuck. When he told Liza, she said, "When you talk about it, it's so clear. So I'll just sit at the computer and you just walk around and say it."

Between the tension and the pressure, Conan had been close to throwing up for several days. Now the same sensation overcame him as he tried to speak the words he knew would convulse his career.

He dictated; Liza typed; he rewrote. He tossed out an opening address of "People of Earth," because he was a comedy writer, after all. He figured he would change it later, until Liza liked it so much she urged him, "Leave it in."

After midnight he called Ross, who was already in bed with his wife, Missy. Conan told him he would be e-mailing his draft of the statement. Sitting up in bed, Jeff and Missy each read it on Jeff's BlackBerry and both were impressed. Ross called Conan with a few suggestions. Conan got back to editing and rewriting. Around one a.m., he was exhausted and decided to leave it and go to bed. But sleep was impossible with his brain chugging away like an overstoked engine. At around three he got up again and went back to the screen, playing with the words, looking for perfection.

When Jeff Ross woke around five thirty he found a message on his BlackBerry: "If you're up, call me." He did. Conan said he wanted to e-mail his more or less finished version. Ross read it while he walked his black Lab though his neighborhood. He had no doubt this was a pretty great piece of work, but he also had no idea what the lawyers would think of it.

The entire Conan group, now nine strong, counting Glaser and her several associates, gathered in the *Tonight Show* conference room again early that morning, ready to consider the message Conan wanted to deliver to the people of the planet. The sleepless Conan got in early as well and settled into his chair at the end of the table. Ross had printouts of the statement in hand for Glaser and her group to read as soon as she sat down.

One of her associates started reading and immediately set to lawyering up the language, making suggestions out loud.

"Leave it alone," Glaser commanded. "It's perfect. It's him."

The meeting quickly took the form of a strategy session. Gavin Polone assumed control of coordinating the press contacts—when they would release the statement, and to whom. Leigh Brecheen, Conan's contract lawyer, would prepare an e-mail to send to Marc Graboff stating that Conan's team believed the network was in breach of his contract, based on earlier drafts of his agreement to assume the host job of *The Tonight Show*. Rick Rosen would call Jeff Zucker minutes before the statement went out to inform him of what Conan was going to say and of the e-mail at that moment arriving in Graboff's mailbox from Brecheen.

Rereading the statement numerous times with utmost precision, Glaser had, in the end, only two minor grammatical corrections she wanted to make. She continued to endorse the statement as ideal for their purposes. It laid out Conan's point of view unequivocally, but without compromising his legal options. Nothing in there overtly said he was quitting, so he could not be accused of forsaking his contractual obligations.

Polone believed that the statement could only work out in their favor, serving to fuel what was already a growing wildfire of support for Conan—and derision for Jeff Zucker. Gavin had a metaphor for Zucker and his sojourn in Hollywood. He was the Wicked Witch in the land of Oz, and Conan was Dorothy. Even those working for the witch were grateful when Dorothy tossed water on her and made her melt, Polone explained. In the meetings that weekend, Polone and others suggested that this was finally the blunder that would melt Jeff Zucker away at NBC.

Jeff Ross could not help himself; he cringed at that notion. Was this really the reason his friend of eighteen years would lose his job? Throughout the meetings Ross had mostly sat silent as others characterized Zucker in terms that ranged from nasty to ugly. A couple of times, Ross couldn't hold back. He spoke up, saying how bad he felt that his long relationship with Zucker was sure to be damaged, probably irreparably.

The others had jumped him: "Are you nuts? He's trying to fucking kill you!" They couldn't believe Ross could actually be concerned about Zucker's fate, when it certainly seemed like Zucker didn't give a damn about his (supposed) friend's fate. But Ross did not see Zucker as a cold, calculating boss—or a witch. He saw him as his friend, who happened to be the CEO.

Ross had always accepted the fact that Zucker, no matter how good a friend, might someday have to break off the personal connection, only because Ross would possibly become a casualty of some choice Zucker felt he had to make. Ross had spent years trying to counter much of Hollywood in its often over-the-top dislike of Zucker. To the others, this move against Conan was playing like some awfully ungrateful payback for Ross's good intentions. But Ross could not completely blame Zucker. As painful as this was, it was business. Still, there was no escaping the fact that Zucker had signed off on a decision that seemed to contain nothing but disregard for the creative work Ross and Conan had put into their show. For Jeff Ross that was the worst of it—and it tore him up.

The noon hour approached. Each member of the group around the conference table had an assignment. They all gave the statement one last read, checking for potential land mines. "OK," Glaser said. "Let's send it out."

Conan and Jeff Ross had similar thoughts race through their minds at that moment: Conan was about to step off the roof of a building, not at all sure where he'd find a net to land in. Fox was all noise at this point; nothing like a serious approach had come from their direction, no matter what hints that network was floating in the press. Did any other realistic options even exist? Ones that wouldn't look like Conan was going from late-night star to hired clown making balloon animals at birthday parties? They were about to stand up, tell the world their employers had their heads up their asses, threaten to sue the network that contained all their friends and associates, the place that had been their home for seventeen years . . . and then what? Hope for the career-rescue squad to show up? How many stars had disappeared without a trace after grandstanding, breast-beating moves like this?

Conan had an urge to run. "OK," he finally said. "You guys do what you need to do. I just need to go into my office." He stood up and made for the door, intending to say not one more word about it—just let it happen.

For Ross, the room all but spun. He was light-headed; he couldn't remember the last time he felt this nauseated. "OK, everybody, hang on," he said at the last minute, before a set of fingers pressed the buttons to send out the first press leak of the statement. Ross had to speak out; he wanted one last moment of consideration of just what it was they were about to do. Conan stopped at the door.

"Let's all be aware of this—we're about to blow this fucker up," Ross said, full of portent. "This is going to blow this fucking thing up."

There was only one reaction that mattered, only one pair of eyes for Ross to check out. Conan stood outlined by the doorway of the conference room, his swoop of copper hair almost touching the frame. He looked directly at Ross, unblinking.

"Blow it up," he said.

CHAPTER ELEVEN

MANIFESTO DESTINY

J ust before noon on Tuesday, January 12, Rick Ludwin and Nick Bernstein were headed over to the *Tonight* offices, hoping for a last-ditch conversation that might convince Conan O'Brien to accept the reconfigured NBC lineup. They didn't hold out much hope, but they both valued Conan so highly they felt they had to try.

Marc Graboff was in his office, waiting to hear something more from the Conan camp. The last word he'd had from Rick Rosen was that Team Conan was arming up with a litigator in the wake of Jeff Zucker's threat to remove Conan and bench him for two years. To Graboff it sounded a bit like Mafia families going to the mattresses. He hoped he would have an opportunity to head off a war that surely would not be good for business.

In his own office at 30 Rock, Jeff Zucker remained near the edge of his patience with the Conan camp, concerned about how they were using the press to assail the network and Jay Leno.

David Letterman and all the other players in late night were meeting with their writers, continuing to follow the events at NBC with the kind of glee usually reserved for political sex scandals. Dave prepared a couple of pointed jokes for that night—"I got a call just before I came out here from NBC. And they said, 'Look, look, we still don't want you back' "—and the show was also putting together an elaborate promo parody for a series called "Law & Order: Leno Victims Unit." It opened with a stentorian announcer intoning, "In the television industry there are two kinds of talk-show hosts: Jay Leno, and those who've been victimized by Jay Leno."

Having just ignited the fire that morning, Conan O'Brien walked down the hall from the *Tonight Show* conference room, stepped into his office, and shut the door behind him. In the center of the sunny office was the same old battered wooden desk he had had back in his *Late Night* days, shipped all the way out to California—the desk that seemed to Conan to have been tossed out by some crappy insurance company in the 1930s. It had been in his office in New York when he arrived in 1993.

Feeling not too different than he had at his low point during his first year on the air, when Tom Shales in *The Washington Post* had so wittily dismissed his chances for survival, Conan approached the desk. This time, however, he didn't drop to his knees and crawl beneath it; he simply lay down and stretched out on the floor next to it, staring at the ceiling in silence, waiting for the statement to go out—and his fate to be sealed.

The television world began to read it just after noon:

People of Earth:

In the last few days, I've been getting a lot of sympathy calls, and I want to start by making it clear that no one should waste a second feeling sorry for me. For 17 years, I've been getting paid to do what I love most and, in a world with real problems, I've been absurdly lucky. That said, I've been suddenly put in a very public predicament and my bosses are demanding an immediate decision.

Six years ago, I signed a contract with NBC to take over The Tonight Show in June of 2009. Like a lot of us, I grew up watching Johnny Carson every night and the chance to one day sit in that chair has meant everything to me. I worked long and hard to get that opportunity, passed up far more lucrative offers, and since 2004 I have spent literally hundreds of hours thinking of ways to extend the franchise long into the future. It was my mistaken belief that, like my predecessor, I would have the benefit of some time and, just as important, some degree of ratings support from the prime-time schedule. Building a lasting audience at 11:30 is impossible without both.

But sadly, we were never given that chance. After only seven months, with my Tonight Show in its infancy, NBC has decided to react to their terrible difficulties in prime-time by making a change in their long-established late night schedule.

Last Thursday, NBC executives told me they intended to move the Tonight Show to 12:05 to accommodate the Jay Leno Show at 11:35. For 60 years the Tonight Show has aired immediately following the late local news. I sincerely believe that delaying the Tonight Show into the next day to accommodate another comedy program will seriously damage what I consider to be the greatest franchise in the history of broadcasting. The Tonight Show at 12:05 simply isn't the Tonight Show. Also, if I accept this move I will be knocking the Late Night show, which I inherited from David Letterman and passed on to Jimmy Fallon, out of its long-held time slot. That would hurt the other NBC franchise that I love, and it would be unfair to Jimmy.

So it has come to this: I cannot express in words how much I enjoy hosting this program and what an enormous personal disappoint-ment it is for me to consider losing it. My staff and I have worked unbelievably hard and we are very proud of our contribution to the legacy of The Tonight Show. But I cannot participate in what I honestly believe is its destruction. Some people will make the argument that with DVRs and the Internet a time slot doesn't matter. But with the Tonight Show, I believe nothing could matter more.

There has been speculation about my going to another network but, to set the record straight, I currently have no other offer and hon-estly have no idea what happens next. My hope is that NBC and I can resolve this quickly so that my staff, crew, and I can do a show we can be proud of, for a company that values our work.

Have a great day and, for the record, I am truly sorry about my hair; it's always been that way.

Yours,

Conan

Rick Ludwin and Nick Bernstein saw the statement just before they arrived at the *Tonight* offices for their desperation pitch to Conan. After reading it they turned around and returned to Burbank.

Right at noon, as the statement hit the official release time, Rick Rosen called Jeff Zucker. "I just want to let you know Conan's releasing a statement now, and we believe you are in breach of your contract. We're sending an e-mail to Marc requesting a meeting and—"

Zucker interrupted. "What does he want?"

"What he wants is *The Tonight Show* at eleven thirty."

"Well, that's not fucking going to happen," Zucker said, not really fractious so much as irritated at how rushed—and public—this affair had suddenly become. "So what does he really want? Money? He wants money."

"He wants what he bargained for, which is *The Tonight Show* at eleven thirty," Rosen repeated.

"Not going to happen," Zucker said again. "This is not what he wants. This is what Patty Glaser is telling you to say."

The conversation got nowhere. Rosen said he'd wait for NBC to set up a meeting to discuss the details.

When Marc Graboff heard Zucker's version of the conversation, it still seemed to him that Zucker made Rosen sound reluctant about this news. Not that it mattered. In the light of Conan's statement, the die seemed cast.

That was certainly Jeff Gaspin's view as well. The letter read like a shot across NBC's bow and Conan was making NBC look like the bad guys and total idiots. The game had changed. Gaspin had continued to hope for another private meeting with Conan, where the star might have been able to say the things he had in the letter and let them all think about it calmly. He had been prepared to tell Conan: "Look—let's forget about what's going on in the press. Let's just keep going. Just stay the course; do your show. Nothing changes until March 1. We have between now and then to figure this out, and if you don't want to do it, we can negotiate a settlement. But find a nice way to do it, a way to leave that you are comfortable with. Let's find something together."

But the "People of Earth" letter—the manifesto, as NBC came to call it—changed the tone. This wasn't just Conan saying no; it was Conan saying no, and you're wrong, and, by the way, go fuck yourselves.

Both Graboff and Gaspin read the statement to mean that Conan was out and out quitting, especially the part about getting the situation resolved and doing a show for a company that "values our work." When

he called Rosen to set up a meeting, Graboff shared with Rick his perception that the letter indicated Conan was quitting. Rosen adamantly
denied it.

At about three p.m., with Graboff, Gaspin, and NBC's West Coast lawyer Andrea Hartman waiting, the Conan team—Rosen, Glaser, Polone,
and Brecheen—showed up at NBC. Brecheen started the meeting off by
saying, "We believe you're in material breach of the contract."

Gaspin responded with complete politeness, saying NBC did not
believe that was the case, that it was unfortunate the dispute had gone
public in this way, but that the network honestly wanted Conan to agree
to its proposal.

Polone challenged that immediately, insisting it was NBC's bullshit
way of pushing Conan out. He spoke with emotion, but without obvious
anger, about how this treatment of his client was intolerable, and how
he had known Conan for twenty years and never seen such commitment
from him.

It still seemed to Graboff that Conan's agents might not have been
totally on board with the manifesto, but he pressed one point. This letter
Conan sent out said he was quitting, and NBC needed to know if he was
going to perform, because his contract said nothing at all about a time slot.

The lawyers made it clear that Conan would do the show at 12:05; he
would come to work and perform as a professional. But, they added, we're
going to sue you. And Polone, who never minded playing the role of bad
cop, made it clear that the process would be ugly. They would drag NBC
through the mud in every way they could. And they would win.

"We will never back down," Polone said, matter-of-factly. "I will never
allow you guys to do this, because of my relationship with Conan. And,
believe me, his wife is 100 percent behind him, too. We will go all the way
and we will take you down."

Rosen added, "We all know how crazy Gavin can be about these
things, but you know me. I'm not crazy. I've got to tell you, I have known
Conan for thirteen years, and he is so resolute and will not give in."

The NBC group dismissed all of this as total bluster, having been
assured by the corporate legal team in New York of its 100 percent confidence that NBC was not in breach of Conan's contract. Andrea Hartman
asserted the network's position that it was not in breach and asked to be
shown where it could be considered to be so.

Patty Glaser said they could have that conversation outside or in a court of law, adding, "We're very confident of our position."

As for what Conan might take to resolve this matter, Polone and the others began to toss around figures like $50 million and $100 million. NBC cut the first figure more than in half as a starting point for a settlement.

During a break, Graboff told his NBC colleagues that the promise from Team Conan that he would in fact do a show at 12:05 seemed halfhearted at best. They were not giving NBC the assurances the network was entitled to have, and as such it could be interpreted that he was defaulting on his contract. The network could enforce its exclusivity, keep Conan idle, and pay him nothing.

When they tried out that scenario back in the conference room, it drew a swift response. Graboff read it as: "Fuck you. We'll see you in court."

Rick Rosen, who had already concluded that this was the most tumultuous week of his career, had the added pressure of impending duties as one of the leaders of the William Morris Endeavor corporate retreat, which started up that same Tuesday afternoon in Palm Springs.

As he left for the desert, Rick couldn't help thinking that, back on the Universal lot, with NBC pondering its next move, Conan and Jeff Ross had to go put on a show.

By the time Rosen arrived in Palm Springs, messages had all but clogged his BlackBerry, but among the rules of the retreat was that all phones be turned off. Ari Emanuel was there as well, of course, and Rosen brought him up to speed on the Conan developments—which came down to: We may be in for a long, ugly, litigious ride.

Ari hardly had to be clued in, for though he had not attended the meetings, frequent contact with Rick, Zucker, and others had kept him informed of the state of play. That night as he sorted it out, Emanuel concluded the whole thing was headed downhill toward a precipice. Zucker, whom he still talked to (and tweaked) regularly, was directly in the middle of it and had become too emotional to work through it rationally, Ari thought. He decided to solicit other help.

Ron Meyer had been the top executive at Universal Pictures since 1995, long before GE and NBC emerged on the scene. Along with the now eclipsed Michael Ovitz, Meyer had earlier founded Creative Artists

Agency. So he knew talent and he knew NBC; he had connective tissue to both sides of this dispute. Even more than that, Meyer commanded wide respect throughout Hollywood, not just for his experience and acumen, but also because of his sterling reputation as an all-around mensch.

Emanuel put in a discreet call to Meyer that Tuesday night. "Ronnie," Emanuel said, "if you don't get involved in this fucking thing, this thing is a fucking disaster."

Meyer told Emanuel that it was not really his place to do something like this. He worked for GE and NBC. If they asked him to become involved, he might be able to do it, but he couldn't just volunteer. And besides, he had nothing to do with television.

Even that degree of willingness was enough for Ari, who put in another call, this one to Zucker. "You should let Ronnie take the lead here," Ari urged him. Zucker liked the idea.

Zucker had Gaspin set up a breakfast with Meyer for the next morning. In addition to all the other advantages Meyer enjoyed as an intermediary, he had an excellent relationship with Conan, having thrown a party in his honor at his Malibu house, and an even better one with Jeff Ross, whom he had befriended when Jeff had arrived in LA, bringing him in as his houseguest.

Ross had quietly conferred with Meyer throughout the upheaval of the previous week, so it was not surprising that Meyer checked in with Ross about this invitation to intercede. Ross also was intrigued by the idea, thinking at that point that it had come from the NBC side—he was unaware of Ari's initial call—and decided it was the one smart move the network had made during the whole process. But when Meyer asked Ross for some advice before he began to try to mediate the dispute, Jeff pulled back. "I can't talk to you about it," he told Meyer. "My guys will kill me."

At breakfast with Gaspin, Meyer let him know that he had at least made contact with Ross. His main point to Gaspin was that a deal could be made, but NBC's number was not realistic, just as Team Conan's number was not realistic. Meyer believed there was always a way to negotiate without each side being stupid and trying to sue the other.

After breakfast Meyer reached out to Rosen, who was still incommunicado in Palm Springs. Rick, leading his retreat sessions, finally broke to check his BlackBerry, which had been going nuts. He had a mass of messages, but several had come from the office marked urgent. When Rosen called in, his assistant told him Ron Meyer had called repeatedly and was on the line again.

Meyer began by telling Rick that he found the treatment of Conan egregious, but added, "Having said that, one guy I don't think is a bad guy here is Gaspin. I just had breakfast with him this morning, and he asked me to reach out to you to see if you and I can be the reasonable heads and maybe find an amicable solution."

"Ronnie, I appreciate your help," Rosen said, but he pointed out he couldn't do anything without consulting with Polone or Glaser.

"I know, I know," Meyer said. "Believe me, I got a lot of people to talk to, but maybe we can find some common ground."

Meyer had his work cut out for him. In his first efforts to find that common ground, Meyer discovered two sides with heels cemented into position, each feeling entirely righteous about it. In each case their arguments sounded valid, Meyer concluded. Whether this was their own version of the Rashomon effect—named after the classic Kurosawa film in which four characters produce entirely different but plausible accounts of the same event—or whether they both actually had valid positions, Meyer couldn't really tell. And it didn't really matter—they both believed they were right, and that was the problem.

Mainly he observed that the issue had become unnecessarily rancorous, far too smothered in emotion and accusations of who was right, who was wrong, who was smart, who was dumb. He had a lot of mediating to do.

Conan called a staff meeting after his letter was posted. They gathered in the studio: writers and producers, bookers and graphic artists, the band, the interns, Jeff and Andy—everybody. Conan struggled through a full read of the manifesto, though by then most of his listeners had read it for themselves. When he finished, the whole staff stood and applauded. Conan couldn't say any more. He quietly left with Andy, one big arm of his sidekick around his shoulders.

Back in his office, Conan felt suddenly enlivened. It was done, and now he had no more fear—or doubt. The decision felt totally right to him. He could not be with these people anymore. He thought again of his addiction, the same one that had so tormented David Letterman (and apparently still did, almost twenty years later). Conan had put Liza and his two children through a lot, in the cause of NBC and his pursuit of *The Tonight Show*. Now, in just a few days, NBC had forced him to go cold turkey, and as of that moment, he felt free of it. If NBC didn't value the show, how could he? It seemed to Conan that Jay had been perfectly happy to see the show he had hosted for seventeen years relegated to second-class status. Conan was not.

Several hours later Conan walked onstage to another extended ovation. Then, in what had to be a message in reply to all those network notes, he slid right into the string dance, before he let fly:

"When I was a little boy, I remember watching *The Tonight Show with Johnny Carson* and thinking, 'Someday, I'm going to host that show—for seven months.'

"NBC says they're planning to have the late-night situation worked out before the Winter Olympics start. And trust me, when NBC says something—you can take that to the bank!"

Later Conan brought on Howie Mandel, host of NBC's game show *Deal or No Deal*, who did a little parody, with Conan picking his career options from the silver briefcases held by gorgeous models. Conan wound up with "two tickets to see Jay Leno perform at the Luxor casino in Las Vegas"—prompting a ludicrously excited reaction from Conan.

That was hardly the night's biggest shot at Jay, however. Over on ABC, Jimmy Kimmel went all in on mocking Jay. Dressed in a bouffant gray wig and a fake chin that looked more like the goatee on Colonel Sanders, he did a full-on Leno, from the high-pitched semi-lisp of Jay's delivery to the high fives with the front row of the audience to the constant running commentary from his bandleader (here Kimmel's Cleto Escobedo played the Kevin Eubanks role). The jokes were also clearly composed to be almost funny but ultimately kind of lame—which was exactly the way many unfriendly comedians tended to see Jay's humor.

"My name is Jay Leno and let it hereby be known that I am taking over all the shows in late night," Kimmel announced, punctuated with a rim shot. "It's good to be here on ABC," Kimmel as Jay said. "Hey, Cleto, you know what ABC stands for? Always Bump Conan." Late-night aficionados knew, of course, Jay's oft-repeated line about NBC standing for "Never Believe your Contract." Then Kimmel referred to the manifesto, and how Conan had said he would not participate in the destruction of *The Tonight Show*. After a little pause to let the setup sink in, Kimmel as

Leno added, "Fortunately, though, I will!" During the laugh, he added, "I'll burn it down if I have to."

Kimmel kept up the parody for the entire show and was rewarded with comment all over the press and Internet. The upheaval at NBC kicked up the level of attention being paid to all the late-night shows. Web sites began carrying every monologue joke and other comedy bit devoted to the NBC debacle. No one benefited from the heightened interest more than Conan, however. Suddenly his numbers began to shoot up, hitting levels that surely would have stopped NBC's plan in its tracks had they only arrived a few weeks earlier. Overnight ratings among the prized eighteen-to-forty-nine audience jumped 42 percent on Tuesday thanks to all the noise about his statement.

Online, as might be expected given the discrepancy in age between the fans of the two comics, the pro-Conan movement was more like a power surge; Web comments ran heavily in his favor, and Twitter comments tipped to Conan over Jay by about fifty to one. Some commentators in the press started speculating that the battle with NBC was turning into Conan's "Hugh Grant moment"—a reference to how the *Tonight* interview with the British actor after his arrest with a prostitute had fueled Leno's march past Letterman in 1995.

If NBC cared about the rising ratings and all the attention, the Conan group didn't notice it in the ongoing wrestling over how—or whether—to extricate Conan from his NBC chains. Polone thought the tone of the talks had changed after the manifesto, because it had made Zucker crazier and Conan stronger, a point he made sure to plant around the blogs. The NBC side interpreted that as evidence of Conan's attack dog getting even more unreasonable. They were utterly convinced that Team Conan could sue all it wanted and NBC would win, because the contract Conan had signed contained no time-period protection. To the argument that earlier drafts did mention *The Tonight Show* as a program that started after the late local news, NBC's legal team replied that the clause was more than two contracts back and part of boilerplate in what had amounted to Conan's Prince of Wales clause—that he would get the show if something happened to Jay.

In the deal Conan had signed in 2004 that guaranteed him the show in five years, no such language appeared, NBC argued, and even that earlier contract spelled out that Conan would sign a new contract before he ascended to the *Tonight* job. The NBC legal team considered Conan's central pledge in his manifesto to be public posturing, because even as he declared that he would not participate in the "destruction" of the show, his legal team was stressing that he would, in fact, go on at 12:05. It frustrated Graboff and Andrea Hartman that the public didn't seem to realize that Conan's lawyers were *promising* he would go on even as he was proclaiming he would not.

They pointed to Rick Ludwin's historical perspective. He had noted that *The Tonight Show* had originally aired at eleven fifteen, so there was precedent for moving its start time. The lawyers told the NBC negotiators that if they moved the show to four in the afternoon they might run into trouble with an arbitrator, but not for a shift of half an hour.

The terms of the contract specified that any dispute would be decided by arbitration, but either side could have always tried to file suit after an arbitration decision was rendered; of course, no one really had the stomach for that kind of extended ugliness, which was why they were sitting through so many unproductive sessions trying to work out a settlement.

Outside entertainment lawyers, considering the issue, saw big risks for both sides. NBC had strength in its contract position; it still seemed unaccountable that Conan's team had overlooked the necessity of demanding time-period protection when virtually every other big star in late night had it. But the Conan side might have some tenuous standing to challenge the contract, these lawyers said, thanks to that previous deal. A more effective argument, several others emphasized, would have been that Conan had the right to expect his *Tonight Show* would remain at 11:35 because of its long history there. NBC's own lawyers didn't buy that interpretation, saying the contract trumped all.

If it came to a public legal battle, however, no one had any doubt who would win the sympathy points. Conan was a popular star apparently at the mercy of the whims of corporate executives. For NBC, the fact that he also had a public forum to make his case—one they were still paying for and *broadcasting* to the nation—was another reason to seek resolution over confrontation.

In the negotiating sessions early that week, Ron Meyer gently pressed both sides to find a way to split the difference in their financial demands, with little movement so far.

NBC's executives continued to lay the intransigence at the feet of Gavin Polone, whom they privately labeled a terrorist—even though the terrorist never stopped assuring NBC that if they would only change their minds, Conan was still ready to be their signature late-night star—bygones be bygones.

Jeff Gaspin, who had so long tried to fight for his plan and find a way for Conan to stay, could hardly believe that even Polone could have that much chutzpah. After orchestrating a battering of NBC and Jeff Zucker in the press, he was expecting the network to fall back in love with his client?

Perhaps sensing the need to soften some of the outside rhetoric in order to get something accomplished, several of the participants on the Conan side urged Polone to back off on the press assault. He didn't think he should stop, he told them, but given the internal difference of opinion, early that week he lifted a few toes off the gas pedal.

Throughout the commotion Jay Leno maintained some personal distance from Conan and his travails. He made some jokes about the situation, mostly about NBC. He took note of all the incoming jokes about him, but he maintained, at least outwardly, his mantra that, in the comic world, anything was OK "as long as it's funny."

Kimmel's show-long impression got special notice, of course—Jay could hardly have missed it. He had not once called Kimmel since their little romantic dance when ABC was wooing Jay. But the morning after the parody, when Kimmel settled into his writers' meeting, the first comment was: "Hey, how long until Jay calls?"

At that precise moment, his assistant told him Jay was on the phone.

"Oh, fuck," Kimmel said.

"Oh, yeah, saw the show last night," Jay told Jimmy when he got on the line. "I thought, 'Oh, that's funny. Hey, it's in the news.'"

"I'm glad you thought it was funny," Jimmy said. "I was hoping you'd think it was funny."

They talked a bit about Conan. Jay said he didn't understand why he wouldn't go on at 12:05. He didn't express any real emotion about it—just surprise. Jay also repeated his own position that he had agreed to take the half-hour gig to protect his staff.

Kimmel didn't find that explanation especially credible. Like many others, he had concluded Jay wanted to keep working on television, no matter what, simple as that. But he did believe Jay was probably being honest about his surprise at Conan's refusal to accept the later start time.

Kimmel didn't really disagree with Jay on that point, figuring that Conan should have taken the 12:05 spot and ridden the folk-hero status for all he could.

"Yeah, he should have done it, because how much longer are you going to do it anyway, Jay?" Kimmel asked.

"I don't know," Jay said. "Maybe I'll do it another three or four years. But I don't see myself doing it after that."

Jay also suggested that Jimmy come over to NBC and appear on the show, a suggestion Kimmel did not take seriously until some time after they hung up and Jay's booking department called. They wanted him to do a "10 at 10" spot with Jay. Leno would be in his studio; Jimmy could stay in his own.

Kimmel realized at once he had to do it. He believed in television moments, and this would surely be a television moment. If nothing else, it would be fun to poke Jay a bit over this.

Jay was not doing much poking of his own—at least not directly at Conan. He did a mild joke the night after the letter, noting that Conan was, understandably, very upset. "He had a statement in the paper. Conan said NBC had only given him seven months to make his show work. When I heard that I said, 'Seven months? How'd he get that deal? We only got four!' Who's his agent? Get that guy!"

But amid all the punch lines flying across the networks in late night that week, only one joke really mattered. Wednesday night, a clearly liberated Conan bounced out and hit his monologue spot free and on fire, again inspired by a huge outpouring of support from his studio audience.

"Ladies and gentlemen, hello there. I'm Conan O'Brien and I've been practicing the phrase 'Who ordered the mochachino grande?' Look for me, and please tip, OK?"

The next joke may have contained a more serious message. "I'm trying very hard to stay positive here, and I want to tell you something. This is honest. Hosting *The Tonight Show* has been the fulfillment of a lifelong dream for me. And I just want to say to the kids out there watching: You can do anything you want in life. Yeah, yeah—unless Jay Leno wants to do it, too."

At NBC the joke represented the point of no return. All throughout the legal wrangling, even after the manifesto, Jeff Gaspin maintained a quiet wish that Conan would examine his options one more time and decide that staying at NBC still made the most sense. Maybe Conan and Jay would finally talk, work it out; somehow Jay might assure Conan this was not a long-term proposition and he should stick it out at 12:05 for a while and come back strong after Jay stepped down.

That, of course, would once again secure the Holy Grail—keeping NBC's two late-night stars at home.

After the joke, the Grail vaporized.

Gaspin got a call from Jay about the joke. This one did *not* strike Jay as funny. He asked Gaspin, "Why the fuck am I giving up a half hour for this guy?"

And Gaspin asked himself, *How could these guys work back-to-back if Conan hates him?* There was no longer any question about resolving this in a fashion that might keep Conan at NBC, as far as Gaspin was concerned. Now all it really was about was: How does this get settled; and when does Conan go on his way?

The joke landed like a mortar shell in one other important NBC constituency. Dick Ebersol had been quietly seething as the days rolled by and the onslaught against Leno and Zucker continued in the press and on various blogs—not to mention on the other late-night shows, especially David Letterman's. It looked to Ebersol like an organized campaign of character assassination by forces on Conan's side—and, he gathered from Allison Gollust and others, that meant one name in particular: Gavin Polone.

But Conan's joke about Jay was finally too much for Ebersol. (The same night Letterman hit a similar point, saying, "Our good friend Ricky Gervais will be hosting the Golden Globes—if Jay lets him.") Ebersol called Gollust and said he wanted to go public with a defense of Leno.

She ran it by Zucker, who gave his OK. That Thursday Dick had a lunch with members of the U.S. Olympic Committee. As soon as he returned to his office, he had a call from Gollust saying she had thought Dick's plan over and run it by the NBC lawyers. They were concerned it might rebound against the network position. They didn't want him to do it.

Ebersol hung up the phone and had one thought: *Fuck that.* He couldn't stand what was happening. He was going to do this for Jay, knowing that others would interpret it as being for Zucker's benefit, as well.

The interview with Ebersol appeared the following day on the Business section dress page in *The New York Times*. Ebersol unloaded on Conan without reservation, explaining that NBC had made the late-night move because Conan's ratings had plummeted. Citing the jokes made about Jay by Conan and Letterman, Ebersol said it was "chicken-hearted and gutless to blame a guy you couldn't beat in the ratings." He called it "professional jealousy."

Ebersol related his account of his meetings with Conan during which he had advised the host to broaden his act. That hadn't happened, Ebersol said, and the result was "an astounding failure by Conan."

If NBC's fear had been that Ebersol's comments might come across as spraying lighter fluid on the brushfire raging between the network and Conan's representatives, they had miscalculated. His remarks actually had the effect of tossing the Olympic torch into an oil tanker.

Gavin Polone went into hyperdrive, immediately calling a meeting with Jeff Ross and the PR advisers for Conan. "You see what happens?" he asked them, brandishing the Ebersol piece. "You gotta let me go do what I gotta do." If NBC wanted a PR war, Polone was only too happy to oblige, because as far as he was concerned, his side had the far better story. All they needed to do was continue hammering NBC with the truth.

Even if it was decades old. Team Conan even dug up the ancient story of how Zucker had had Conan arrested at Harvard (for a *Lampoon* prank that involved stealing Zucker's chair out of the *Crimson* office), an anecdote that had been reported many times before, but which played especially effectively in the context of Zucker's threatening to fire him now.

Ebersol's broadside may have galvanized Polone, but it pulverized his client. Conan felt shocked that NBC had suddenly decided that even the insult of a public demotion wasn't enough. Now it was time to kill Conan. His show an "astounding failure"? His jokes proved he was "gutless" and "jealous" of Jay?

Conan believed he had taken the high road; few of his comments had been directed at Jay. OK, he did the one joke. But he wasn't unleashing a venomous attack on him. Compared to others—Dave, Kimmel, or Howard Stern, who said on his radio show that he felt like vomiting at the name Jay Leno—Conan had been restrained. He had simply announced that he could not participate in something that offended him; now they were coming after him, savagely.

The tenor of the negotiations now shifted. NBC began looking less for a rationale to pay Conan a smaller settlement than for ways to control him while he was still on their air—and even for a bit after that. How much time did they need to keep him off the market? How much time did they need to keep him—more to the point his people—from spewing nastiness about NBC and Jay?

The level of nastiness certainly surprised Jay. He told himself not to take it personally, because, even after Conan's poisonous joke, he believed what the other hosts were attacking was less him than the symbol of *The Tonight Show*, the pinnacle every comic aspired to achieving. Nobody was going after his wife or anything like that, so he tried to ride it out with shrugs.

That got much harder thanks to his own misread of who still might be friendly to him. He expected his "10 at 10" interchange with Jimmy Kimmel, scheduled for the fourteenth, the same day Ebersol gave his interview to *The Times*, to be a way to capitalize playfully just a little on all the late-night uproar. One associate on *Tonight* was astounded that the booking had even been made, thinking it was foolish to believe Kimmel might be a friend of the show, especially under the circumstances.

Kimmel expected the interview to kick off some typical give-and-take between comics, based on the whole NBC ferment. But when the segment producer called him to try out a few questions, they couldn't have been more bland and off the topic, like "What's your favorite snack junk food?"

"I'm hoping we can talk about everything that's going on," Kimmel told the producer. "I have a huge viral thing on my hands because of the imitation." Kimmel's impression of Leno was all over the Internet.

"Well, we don't want to beat that to death," the producer replied.

"I understand that you don't want to beat it to death," Jimmy answered. "But it's the elephant in the room. It has to be addressed."

The producer said he would talk to the higher-ups about it. But when Kimmel got the proposed questions later in the day, he saw nothing about the whole Conan dustup. His conclusion: That little fucker Jay intended to neutralize him on the show, sending a message—"Oh yeah, Jimmy and I are friends. That vicious imitation of me he did? That didn't mean anything."

Kimmel felt he had been totally up front about what he wanted to discuss, so it would be fair game for him to spin the answers in that direction, even if the questions steered far away.

Knowing the premise of the bit, Kimmel figured he had some advantages. It had to be ten questions, so they couldn't really edit a few out. And if he gauged his answers correctly, they wouldn't easily be able to edit individual moments, either. Then he set up his own cameras to tape his end so he would have that to use no matter what Jay did.

Just before they started, the on-site producer tried to tease Kimmel about his friend Adam Carolla, who had become a frequent Leno guest: "I hope you're half as funny as your buddy Adam when he's on the show."

"I'm gonna be funny," Jimmy said. "Don't you worry about it, you motherfucker."

Kimmel sat at his desk for the bit, which was being satellited all the way from Hollywood to Burbank. It began innocently enough. Jay introduced Kimmel with his usual buoyancy, asking if anything was new in late night. Kimmel said he only watched Oprah in late night. (It was an inside joke, because several ABC stations, including a big one, in Chicago, carried a rerun of Oprah at midnight and delayed Kimmel's start time, which affected his national ratings.)

Nothing much happened until question four, when Jay asked who in the world Jimmy would most want to interview. This was teed up for him: "You and Conan, together," Jimmy said.

But it was at question five when Kimmel's real purpose in the visit became clear: "What's the best prank you ever pulled?"

After a real answer about the time he painted his aunt's house orange and green, Jimmy said, "I think the best prank I ever pulled was, I told a guy once, 'Five years from now I'm going to give you my show.' And then when the five years came, I gave it to him and I took it back, almost instantly."

"Wow, wow," Jay said, trying to laugh along agreeably. "A very good friend," Jimmy said under the laughs, and then added, "I think he works at Fox or something now."

Then question six: "Did you ever order anything off the TV?"

"Like NBC ordered your show off the TV?"

Question seven was about the most number of lap dances Kimmel had ever ordered in Vegas. Jimmy first said his mother was watching, then clarified, "Wait a minute. The show's canceled, right? Nobody's watching the show." Then he added, "Strippers I don't like in general because you have this phony relationship with them for money—similar to when you and Conan were on *The Tonight Show* together? Passing the torch?"

Jay was saying, "Right, right," to play along. Next question: "What do you fear most?"

Kimmel went through volcanoes and tidal waves before he added, "I fear the network will move my show to ten o'clock."

"I had that nightmare!" Jay threw in.

At this point, number nine looked like an invitation to open hunting season: "Is there anything you haven't hosted that you want to host?"

"Oh, this is a trick, right?" Kimmel asked. "Where you get me to host *The Tonight Show* and then take it back from me?"

The final question was a multiple choice on why Jimmy came on the show (with stupid choices like "You like satellite technology" except for the last, which was about keeping Jay happy in case he decided to switch to ABC). Kimmel turned it into an all-Conan fest: "Listen, Jay. Conan and I have children. All you have to take care of is cars!"

"That's right," Jay muttered, still playing along but looking to end this thing as amicably as possible.

"We have lives to lead here," Kimmel said. "You've got eight hundred million dollars! For god's sakes, leave our shows alone!"

Jay, smiling as best he could, finished it up. "A plea from Jimmy Kimmel! Jimmy, thank you, my friend."

Kimmel had been nervous beforehand, but he was now elated. It had the feel of winning a ten-round fight. Jay's producers seemed stunned. Kimmel waited until he got out of earshot of the Leno crew, then erupted with his writers. "Oh my god, that was so uncomfortable," one said. Kimmel thought Jay might drop the whole thing, because it had gone so badly for him and there was essentially no way to edit it.

Jimmy had no remorse. As he saw it, he took what they were trying to do to him—make him Jay's boy—as a hostile act that justified rough treatment. But he had not expected Jay to just stand there and take it, never deviating from his script. Surely Jay would say something back, Kimmel had thought. But he just let Kimmel pummel him without really throwing a punch in return.

Of course, that posture had defined Jay from the earliest of ages: He'd actually tried boxing once and found all he could do was let the other guy hit him. And then, of course, there had been that incident in school with the kid and the hammer.

Back at Jay headquarters, the discomfort was acute. Jay knew he'd walked into a door being pushed in his face and could blame no one but himself. He'd let it happen, so he wasn't going to cut it from the air.

Debbie Vickers was furious. Jay accepted it as comedy, so he could not allow himself to be angry. Debbie believed it was bad manners; Kimmel had stepped over some kind of line into sheer rudeness. Jay ascribed Jimmy's motivation to a small-time guy looking to get publicity from taking on a big-time guy. Not quite the fly who lives off the back of the elephant, but something like that. For Kimmel, Jay figured, this was like the best publicity he could get.

In that, Jay was certainly right. Kimmel climbed aboard a wave of reaction the likes of which he had rarely experienced before. For three days afterward he felt like Rocky on the steps in Philadelphia. For every one who accused him of being an invited guest who'd peed on his host's carpet—and there weren't that many who did—he had thousands of claps on the back. The Internet went wild with kudos for how ballsy he was to take Jay on that way face-to-face.

Kimmel couldn't believe how it had worked out. Instead of giving him a question or two to bat this around, Leno's forces had tried to avoid it, and he'd batted Jay over the head with it. That question about his greatest prank? That was so perfect, it was almost as though God had told him he had to do it.

He still could not believe that Jay had not expected it. If anyone had paid attention to Jimmy's career, they would have seen he could be vicious if he needed to be—and that he lived for this kind of setup.

The reaction Kimmel appreciated most came from the other late-night voice reveling in the Jay-Conan saga. David Letterman sent him a brief note to tell him that his Leno bit had been really funny.

Through his steadfast massaging of each side, Ron Meyer had broken through on the main financial issues, determining the most NBC was willing to pay and the least the Conan side was willing to take. The math he could handle.

On Thursday, the day of the Kimmel "10 at 10" ambush, Meyer called Rick Rosen, who was still in Palm Springs, to inform him that he believed a deal could be made on the numbers—about $32 million to pay off Conan. Severance for the staff, which Conan had stressed as a condition as well, still had to be resolved. Meyer told Rosen they needed him back in the conference room in LA to finish things off.

When Rosen spoke to the Conan negotiating group, they agreed it was time for him to return, so he chartered a plane and flew back. He met first with Conan and Ross, then joined the group in the conference room at Universal.

There the framework of a deal seemed to be in place; the contract would be settled after one more week on the air for Conan, a concession the host had pushed for in order to set up a proper farewell for his *Tonight* show. But the NBC group needed a break to run things by New York. At that point, the forward movement slowed down. The counsel for GE got involved; GE would need to figure out how to structure the payout over a number of quarters.

NBC also had a few fine points it wanted to discuss, a primary one being an assurance that Howard Stern would not appear as a guest during Conan's last week. This struck Rosen as a comical request—Conan had no interest in booking anyone as incendiary as Stern—so it was easily accepted. There were also demands that Conan not sit down for interviews with Letterman, Oprah, or Regis Philbin until months had passed. NBC also requested to see the show's scripts for the final week, but that was never going to happen.

Nothing was finalized on Thursday, and the Friday talks got bogged down as well. Nobody wanted the negotiations to carry over into the weekend, but NBC still had issues to resolve.

On Saturday the *New York Post* ran a story saying that Conan's staffers felt betrayed. They couldn't believe Conan wouldn't at least try to live with the 12:05 idea for a while to see if it worked out, so that they could keep their jobs. They had moved across the country to work with him and now, because of his ego, they would be out of work while he basked in some big $30 million settlement.

The story, which O'Brien had no doubt was a direct plant from NBC, infuriated him, because he had worked so hard to ensure some financial security for the staff, and they had seemed to respond with nothing but support—as evidenced by the near unanimous vote of the writers that he should walk. (In truth, there was a small minority of staff members who expressed some anger about Conan's giving up the show and their jobs with it.)

Again Conan found himself appalled. The NBC people had observed his work for seventeen years and yet they had no clue about his character? Did they really think he had no regard for his staff? Even after he had paid them out of his own pocket during the writers' strike? Did they really think he would use his last week on the air to go on a trash tour of NBC? Or book himself onto some other shows to assail Jeff Zucker?

When he saw Patty Glaser at one of the meetings, Conan asked her, "Why are these guys so obsessed with this meaningless stuff?"

"These are very small people," Glaser replied.

On Saturday Gaspin called Rosen and informed him there was a new problem: NBC could not sign off on certain terms in the deal.

"You can't be doing this now," Rosen complained, but Gaspin insisted that it couldn't be helped. A conference call was set for Sunday, the day of the Golden Globe Awards (to be telecast by NBC), and would begin at eleven, early enough for everyone to get into their tuxes in time for the show.

On Sunday Rosen reached out again to Ron Meyer, telling him he needed his help one more time, because things seemed to be going off the rails. Meyer told him he was being iced out a bit by the NBC team, which had come to believe he was too favorable to the Conan side.

Rosen remained in his new home in Santa Barbara, communicating with Glaser and Brecheen, who were in a conference room at Patty's firm in Century City. The eleven a.m. start time went by, then noon. Gaspin called Rosen saying the call had to be delayed even further. The afternoon dragged on.

Gavin Polone had scheduled a date for that evening. He thought about canceling; but what were the odds something was getting done with the Golden Globes going on? Besides, it was a second date, and he was interested in this new woman.

Rosen called Meyer again; from Ron he learned that GE had now become a bigger factor. Jeffrey Immelt, the GE chairman, had suddenly started to question why they were paying so much money to a guy they were going to allow to run off to another network.

The call was put off until six p.m., meaning the meeting would surely spill into the middle of the Globes show. (It would be nine p.m. in the east.) It also meant that a gaggle of the highest-priced legal talent in LA would be sitting around doing nothing but piling up billable hours.

By six, Polone had picked up his date and was headed for the movies. He wanted to see *Avatar* in 3D. By the time he got to the theater, it was sold out. The only thing they could get into was *The Young Victoria*. Twelve minutes into that movie, his BlackBerry buzzed: an e-mail from Jeff Ross. They wanted him to call in. Gavin excused himself and fled to the lobby.

The Conan group discussed the latest developments on their own conference call. Now NBC was asking for concessions they saw as totally crazy—among them, the unilateral right to pull the show on any night of the following week if they didn't like the content. The Conan forces signed off quickly on that one; they could only imagine how it would play for NBC in the press if they decided to pull Conan off the air one night because they didn't like a joke he told.

Polone remained on the phone in the theater lobby throughout the haggling. The movie ended; his date emerged. He was still on the phone. (The relationship didn't last.)

At the Globes, amid a pelting downpour in LA, NBC threw a grand party on the roof of the Beverly Hilton. Gaspin dropped in and out of the festivities. He spent much of his time in a private room trying to get the deal finished. Issues of severance and details of what Conan could and couldn't do the following week remained unresolved. It wasn't happening.

Meanwhile, on the air, Ricky Gervais was introducing the show with the line "Let's get on with it before NBC replaces me with Jay Leno." Tom Hanks, presenting an award, remarked, "NBC said it was going to rain at ten p.m., but they moved it to eleven thirty." And Tina Fey, accepting an award, said of the rainy night, "It's God crying for NBC."

For the increasingly besieged NBC, the online support for Conan had eclipsed the term "viral"; now it was more like a plague. Groups sprang up all over the Web and across the country in individual cities. The Facebook group "I'm with Coco" organized Conan rallies in New York, Chicago, and Seattle, as well as LA for that Monday, the eighteenth.

Along with Conan's suddenly sizzling ratings, which continued to grow by the night, the rise of Coco mania served as additional annoyance for the pressed executives at NBC. Jeff Gaspin had an idea about what was happening. He theorized that when Conan moved to 11:35, he had stopped being Conan. He tried to be something he really wasn't—a somewhat broader Conan without really abandoning the antic style that had branded him. The result was too soft for the hard-core Conan fans, but still not comfortable for the Leno fans.

But once he rose up to take a stand against NBC's meddling with his career, once he went on the attack, Conan raised his game to a new level. Gaspin didn't think this phase was something that could last, because it was built around a specific event, but while Conan was caught up in it, his show had clearly improved. Conan was now producing an irreverent show, a dangerous show, and the kids in the audience loved it. Gaspin could not help but ruefully admire the irony of the situation: NBC had given Conan his mojo back, just in time for him to take it somewhere else. That didn't mean Gaspin had decided he'd been wrong, however. On the contrary, it seemed to him to prove that NBC's evaluation that Conan had lost his mojo was exactly correct.

That Monday afternoon a crowd gathered outside the entrance to the *Tonight* studio, despite more rain, a deluge of the kind that usually paralyzes LA. Like something out of a sixties protest march, the fans came out carrying signs ("Conan Saved Me from Scientology") and chanting slogans ("Jay Leno Sucks"). The star himself showed up and shook a few hands outside before making an appearance on the roof to wave to the fans, his famous pompadour doused thoroughly.

Conan was touched to his soul by the rally, which had hundreds of fans soaked to the skin chanting his name. As he stood on the roof, dripping, it struck him that this might be—appropriately enough—a watershed moment, the first giant schism between the old broadcast world and the new electronic media dominated by the Internet. He believed NBC had tried in the old-fashioned way to undermine him, in the attack by Ebersol—whom Conan dismissed as one of the "silverback gorillas" still trying to rule television—and in the story about dissension on the staff.

The outpouring of support made Conan feel as if he was starring in his own version of the movie *It's a Wonderful Life*, both because he was allowed to see a *Tonight Show* where he never existed and because the support made him realize he really was "the richest man in town."

Beneath his feet, Conan sensed the ground moving, shifting finally from a baby-boom-centric culture to one controlled by Gens X and Y. Messages on sites all over the Web were rife with sheer anger at the boomers—symbolized by Leno—refusing to cede the stage and the culture.

By the end of Monday no deal had yet emerged, but widespread reports claimed that an agreement was close. Jay remained under assault everywhere, nowhere more so than over at CBS, with Letterman banging away at him relentlessly. He featured a faux ad for Leno, citing how Jay stood for middle America, for traditional American values like "killing Indians because you want their land."

By that night Jay had had enough and decided to deliver a manifesto (of sorts) of his own. After finishing his monologue he took his seat at the desk and announced that he wanted to give "my view of what has been going on here at NBC." It was, especially for Jay, an unusually long personal statement, not much of which was played for laughs. He recalled how NBC had come to him in 2004, even with his position as top dog in late night unchallenged, and told him to make way for Conan.

"Don't blame Conan O'Brien," Jay said. "Nice guy, good family guy, great guy."

But he did seem to assign blame to other parties—"managers . . . who try to get something for their clients." That said, Jay agreed that he had announced he would retire, mainly to "avoid what happened last time"— when he and Letterman had jousted for the crown.

He then recounted the history of the ten p.m. idea, which he explained he had resisted but ultimately accepted in order to keep his staff in their jobs. Meanwhile, he said, Conan's show "was not doing well." The hope that Jay at ten would help Conan didn't work out.

Then NBC told him it wanted to make a change. Jay said he asked to be let out of his contract; NBC refused. He outlined the half-hour plan, with Conan sliding back, and described how NBC had all but guaranteed him that Conan would accept the proposal. But then, he said, he saw Conan's statement declining to go along with it. NBC came back, Jay said, and asked, if Conan decided to walk, would Jay take *The Tonight Show* back? Jay agreed, he explained, again out of consideration for his staff.

"Through all of this, Conan O'Brien has been a gentleman," Jay said. "He's a good guy. I have no animosity towards him. This is all business. If you don't get the ratings, they take you off the air."

He concluded by telling the audience that the resolution might come the following day.

It didn't, of course. The haggling over financing employee severance and the details of the limitations on Conan kept the issue unsettled yet again. But Jay's statement—as so often with his efforts, viewed as forthright by friends and Machiavellian by foes—seemed to confirm he would return to his old *Tonight* spot when the Olympics came to an end on March 1.

Given the heightened attention on everything relating to the NBC late-night tumult, Jay's statement could hardly escape comment. And once again it was David Letterman doing the most commenting. The following night Dave devoted his own desk segment—the entirety of it, despite a scripted comedy piece resting on his desk throughout—to an apparently extemporaneous analysis of Jay's "state of the network speech."

Letterman began by saying he had known Jay for thirty-five years, and used to "buddy around" with him in the old days. "What we're seeing now is sort of vintage Jay," he observed, without defining what that was exactly. "It's like, there he is; there's the guy I used to know."

The part of the Leno statement that really piqued Letterman's interest was Jay's urging to the audience: "Don't blame Conan." Dave found this especially worthy of comment, "I said to myself, 'No one is blaming Conan.'" Later he begged the audience not to blame Conan. "I know a lot of you people think Conan pushed himself out of a job," Letterman said. "He's not that kind of guy. He wouldn't do that to himself."

In his fake sincere way, Dave jumped into advice mode. "You call Fox. You don't say"—slipping into the high-pitched Jay voice—"'I'll be in the lobby if you need me.' You don't hang around. You go across the street and you punish NBC. . . . It's an early Darwinian precept," Letterman concluded. "You get fired; you get another job. You don't hang around waiting for somebody to drop dead."

This particular salvo from Dave apparently got under Jay's skin enough for him to return fire the following night with as aggressive an attack on Dave as he had ever launched in public. At the top of his monologue Jay turned to his bandleader, Kevin Eubanks, to note how the show had been appearing in the press every day—and how Letterman, especially, had been hammering him every night.

"Hey, Kev, you know the best way to get Letterman to ignore you?" Jay asked.

"No, what?" Eubanks replied.

"Marry him! He will not bother you! He won't look you in the eye!"

The well-crafted joke drew an enormous laugh, though it would also generate an unusual amount of backlash against Jay among some (including, later, Oprah Winfrey) who thought the gag crossed a taste boundary, because it dragged a civilian—Dave's obviously hurt wife—into the battle.

(Jay later defended the joke as being both [a] funny and [b] the only time he really went after Dave during the entire January late-night convulsion.

The latter point was not precisely true, however; Jay had sprinkled a number of other Dave-centric jokes into his routines, such as "Remember the more innocent days of late-night TV, when the only thing people cared about was which intern the host was nailing? What happened to that? What happened to those days?" And later in the week of the "marry him" joke, Jay did a bit with guest Chelsea Handler, pretending to be putting the moves on her by taking her to a sleazy motel, where he plugged in a vibrating bed and said, "Actually, I got this idea from Letterman.")

Perhaps because of the backlash from his one pointed Jay joke, Conan did not join Letterman in any Leno bashing as he started what was now virtually certain to be his last week at NBC. He had never really engaged in personal invective—even when his anger was at a peak after what had transpired—and he wasn't about to change that now.

Instead Conan and his writers came up with one inspired idea after another to express their outrage—and to tap into the outrage of his fans. He first put *The Tonight Show* up for sale on Craigslist ("Guaranteed to last for up to seven months; designed for 11:35, but can easily be moved!") and then himself ("Tall, slender redhead available for nighttime recreation; currently homeless, must meet at your place").

Then they came up with a plan to make it look as though they were spending outrageous amounts of NBC's money during the show's last days on the air. "We're going to introduce comedy bits that are not so much funny as they are crazy expensive," Conan declared. One night they tricked up a Bugatti Veyron (supposedly the most expensive car in the world) with mouse ears while playing the Rolling Stones' "Satisfaction"—music rights being notoriously costly, especially if a clip containing the music is downloaded over and over online—a bit that Conan announced would cost NBC $1.5 million. The next night they brought on the alleged Kentucky Derby winner, Mine That Bird, decked the nag out in a mink Snuggie, and let him watch restricted Super Bowl clips. Price tag: $4.8 million. On his finale, Conan went all out with an absurdly mobile fossil of a rare ground sloth spraying Beluga caviar on an original Picasso. That one cost $65 million, Conan proclaimed.

But a minute later he felt compelled to explain that all these had been *comedy* bits. Credulous folks all over the Web (and some even in the press) had been either celebrating this act of sticking it to The Man or decrying this horrifyingly wasteful extravagance in a battered economy, not understanding it was all a gag. (The Bugatti was on loan from a museum; the horse was not actually Mine That Bird; the Snuggie wasn't mink; the Picasso and the caviar weren't real.)

Conan continued to pound NBC in his monologues, but he also made fun of his own situation:

"It's been a busy day for me today. I spent the afternoon at Universal Studios' amusement park, enjoying their brand-new ride, the 'Tunnel of Litigation.'"

"Some papers are reporting that I'm legally prohibited from saying anything bad about NBC. But nobody said anything about speaking in Spanish. NBC esta manejado por hijos de cabras imbeciles que comen dinero y evacuan problemas." (Translation: "NBC is run by brainless sons of goats who eat money and crap trouble.")

Even as he was urging everyone from writers to other staffers to fans to make the last week all about fun, Conan found himself tortured by the endless delays in getting the final settlement accomplished. The broad parameters had been in place for days. All the picayune details of what he could say on the air, which guests he could and couldn't book, on what date he could return to television, and when and to whom he could grant interviews only underscored the pettiness of it all. He wanted it over.

But Sunday's anticipation melted into Monday, then Monday's into Tuesday. His people kept telling him they were on the one-yard line, or right at the goal. At one point Conan just shouted to his group, "If one more person tells me we're two inches from the goal line, I'm gonna fucking kill them, because I can't hear it anymore."

All he wanted at that point was to be able to announce in public that Friday would be his last show. Then they could lock the bookings they wanted and ready the show they wanted to produce as a farewell.

Wednesday began like the previous seven or eight before it, with the message that this again would almost surely be the day. Then more rumors swirled about holdups; Conan learned for the first time of GE's qualms about the settlement.

Showtime came with no resolution, so Conan could not go out and tell his audience the definitive answer; he had to keep saying, "This looks like the final week."

After the show, the lawyers told him this time they were very close and urged him to stick around the office. Conan got some food and hung out with Jeff Ross and Mike Sweeney and some other writers. By midnight all the staff had left—except Ross, of course, always by Conan's side. Leigh Brecheen was holding down the legal front in the conference room along with an associate of Glaser's. At loose ends, Conan started wandering the halls alone, playing his guitar. Occasionally he would jump up and sit on cubicles, strum a few notes, jump down, lay flat on the ground, then jump back up and continue on his way.

He stepped outside onto the deserted Universal lot. There he stood, in the dark, entirely alone, waiting to hear if he had successfully given up *The Tonight Show*. He had his cell with him, and as he ambled aimlessly he took some pictures with the phone. At one thirty a.m. he held the phone out and took a picture of himself. Behind him was one of the tiny cafés on the lot. It was closed but there were some lights on inside, just enough for the picture and enough to see a poster for some long-forgotten movie, indecipherable in the photo, illuminated behind his head in the foreground.

When he looked at the photo, Conan thought, *This is just me at one thirty in the morning, on the Universal lot, waiting to hear this news, and looking like: What the fuck?*

Conan had no way of knowing it, but at just about the time he was snapping that photo, Ron Meyer was on the phone at his home, conferenced in with Jeff Zucker and Jeff Gaspin, to let them know that at long last he had everybody agreed on a final deal. But he also had a message he wanted to convey to the two Jeffs:

"You've got about ten minutes here before I call back to say we're closed—ten minutes to say, 'We're staying with Conan, we're going to get rid of Jay.'" Meyer had witnessed the national display of Conan mania during the previous ten days. "There's a big outcry out there," he told Zucker and Gaspin. "Think about it. I'm not suggesting it. That's not my job. I'm just suggesting you think about it. There's a moment here."

Both Zucker and Gaspin had such regard for Meyer's counsel that they did pause—or at least, out of deference to Meyer, made a show of pausing—and took the opportunity to consider, one last time, the implications of sending Conan O'Brien on his way.

Then they told Meyer: No. They believed they were making the right decision and they were committed to it.

Meyer made his call.

A few minutes later Conan finally got back to his office. It was a little after two a.m. The lawyers were still there. They had the papers for him.

From NBC's point of view, Conan got a great deal. His salary had been set at $12.5 million a year; the settlement paid him for about the two and a half years remaining in his contract, with the final number coming out at a little over $32 million. Then there were payments to Jeff Ross for his own guaranteed contract, and severance for the staff, which Conan's side had held out for NBC to improve beyond standard GE levels. In total, the settlement deal cost NBC about $45 million, which, in one of the seemingly endless coincidental twists in the saga, was exactly what it would have taken for NBC to pay off Conan had the network decided at the last minute to keep Jay in his top-rated late-night spot and forget all that ten o'clock nonsense.

That scenario had been brought up again and again internally in the wake of the self-inflicted drubbing the network had been through that month—if only someone had said, "Let's just keep Jay in *The Tonight Show* and write the check to Conan."

Conan himself had come to wish they had done just that.

What NBC got for its money was a period of nine months during which Conan could not mount a competing show. Their legal strategists figured that would be long enough to get Jay reestablished at 11:35, though they obviously had a few shudders about the prospect of Conan's riding back in triumph to lead his young troops in a Fox army, storming the late-night citadel. But given the limitations that loomed at Fox, NBC did not take that as a serious long-term threat to what they expected would be—sooner or later—a return to supremacy for Jay Leno.

In addition, Conan and his minions—most pointedly Gavin Polone—could not disparage Jay Leno, NBC, or its executives in any way during what amounted to a graduated series of monthly periods. By September 1, however, Conan could say with impunity that Jeff Zucker wore women's underwear, or anything else he desired to.

Those restrictions—and especially the ones NBC imposed on O'Brien's final shows—continued to amaze the group around Conan, because to them these concerns only proved again how little NBC really knew about the man who had starred for them for seventeen years. Rick Rosen could see how someone might not respond to Conan's humor, but as a person, who was classier?

Conan himself labeled his final show "a Viking funeral." He wrote the phrase many times over on the blotter on his desk, which was always filled with his cartoon doodles and little turns of phrase. He had the guest roster he wanted, a dream lineup: Tom Hanks, Steve Carell, and Neil Young, who had called Conan to volunteer to be on the last show and to sing, appropriately, "Long May You Run." And, of course, Will Ferrell, Conan's signature guest, closed the show, with Conan onstage as well with the whole band—including guests Beck, ZZ Top, and Ben Harper—playing a long version of Lynyrd Skynyrd's "Free Bird."

By then Conan had delivered his eulogy for his brief *Tonight Show* run, and, consistent with his approach throughout, he took the high—and well-written—road. He tried to clear up any misconceptions, saying that, despite rumors, he really could say anything he wanted in his closing remarks, and what he most wanted to say was that despite his recent differences with them, he needed to thank NBC for making his career possible.

"Walking away from *The Tonight Show* is the hardest thing I have ever had to do," Conan said. "Despite this sense of loss, I really feel this should be a happy moment. Every comedian dreams of hosting *The Tonight Show*, and for seven months I got to. I did it my way, with people I love, and I do not regret a second. I've had more good fortune than anyone I know, and if our next gig is doing a show in a 7-Eleven parking lot, we'll find a way to make it fun."

He thanked his staff and his fans, and he closed out his time on late night's biggest stage by saying:

"To all the people watching, I can never thank you enough for your kindness to me and I'll think about it for the rest of my life. All I ask of you is one thing: Please don't be cynical. I hate cynicism—it's my least favorite quality and it doesn't lead anywhere. Nobody in life gets exactly what they thought they were going to get. But if you work really hard, and you're kind, amazing things will happen."

CHAPTER TWELVE

MAKE LAUGHS, NOT WAR

They used the Conan O'Brien *Tonight Show* studio one last time, for a party—of sorts—to mark the leave-taking. It was hardly festive; one participant likened it to an Irish wake, but only because Conan was Irish, and his show was dead. Nobody did shots to salute the corpse.

Mainly the staff wanted one last chance to applaud a star most of them respected and were genuinely fond of. Someone had pulled up his monologue spot from the floor and had it framed; almost the entire staff signed it. They presented it to a clearly touched O'Brien.

He stayed late, posing for pictures with anyone who asked—every camera operator, every intern. His brother Neal had flown in to stand with him; he'd been there for the closeout of Conan's *Late Night* show less than a year earlier.

Finally, totally spent, Conan got in his car with Neal, allowing his big brother to drive home. Though Conan had not drunk an ounce at the party, given the state of his emotions, it seemed wiser for someone else to be behind the wheel. When he got home, he still felt slightly in shock.

That night, before he settled to a point where he could sleep, a memory flashed by. When Conan had been unemployed for a brief time in 1987, after his first writing job at *Not Necessarily the News* had ended, he found himself sitting in a Du-pars coffee shop in LA. His writing partner Greg Daniels had already found a temporary source of income coaching an SAT prep course. Conan had no immediate prospects.

So he sat at the counter, taking an inordinate amount of time to eat his pancakes, because what the heck else did he have to do that day? Just thinking about what might become of him next, what was around the next corner, he suddenly uttered out loud (though not very loud) a little expression of personal conviction—a sort of quick, nondenominational prayer:

"I don't care what happens in my career as long as it's interesting."

Back home in his elegant home in Brentwood on this night, freshly out of another job, this time accompanied by national headlines, Conan could certainly make a case that his long-ago prayer had been answered. Though, thinking it through, he realized he could tick off a long list of accomplishments that counted as just as interesting as being the guy who walked away from *The Tonight Show* after seven months. He'd made it as a performer, leading a show on a major network for sixteen years; he'd played guitar next to Bruce Springsteen; he had a picture of himself standing on his set next to his idol, David Letterman; he'd spoken to Johnny Carson; hell, he was even a national hero in Finland.

What had just happened to him in January 2010 had surely shone a revealing klieg light on who he really was and what he believed in. Conan was OK with that. He didn't think he had a damn thing to be ashamed of.

Which was nice—except he still felt shattered to his last bone.

Over in Burbank an NBC executive visiting Jay Leno's show for the evening could feel the emotional undercurrent rippling through that set as well. It was obvious that the star and his closest staff members had been badly bruised by the experience and were hurting. They all knew Jay was being cast as the bad guy, a role he found distressing and uncomfortable, but that seemed to dog him despite what he considered his own best efforts to play nice with everybody. Even though some in the press had always taken shots at him, Jay had not experienced this level of venom since the darkest hours of the Letterman face-off, when he was charged with snatching the show away from the friend who had done so much to elevate his career.

But nothing in that episode came close to the heights of malediction he was now experiencing. The Team Coco troops accused Jay of being a liar, a traitor, and worse. Jay was truly rocked to read a piece in *The Wall Street Journal* by Joe Queenan—a satire, certainly, but on a level of viciousness Jay simply could not fathom. Queenan compared Leno to Hitler, saying he had made "secret demands for territory" (that is, the 11:35 show) just as Hitler had with the Sudetenland, and that just as Adolf saw himself as the second coming of Frederick Barbarossa, Jay wanted to be seen as the heir to Johnny Carson.

Jay was astonished that this version of events—with him cast as evil genius—got any credence at all. He thought the story could just as easily have played as a feel-good movie of the week, laying out a totally different scenario: A guy in his fifties is told he's doing a good job but gets fired anyway. Then, six years later, the boss comes back and says, "We were wrong; we'd like to give you your old job back."

Despite the exaggerated cartoon being presented by Letterman, Kimmel, and others, Jay simply could not believe people actually accepted it as true that he had walked up to NBC, snapped his fingers, and said, "My show failed; I want that show back." Still, he got e-mails every day from Team Coco supporters making accusations like "It was Conan's dream and you took it. Just 'cause your show failed." He wanted to ask them, "What are you talking about? Do you have any idea how business works?"

Did it really make sense to people that he should step aside even when NBC clearly made the call asking him to return? Was it wrong that at fifty-nine he still wanted to work? How different was this, really, from a situation where two actors are up for the same role? Tom Cruise gets it instead of Brad Pitt—should Cruise say, "No, I'm not taking this job because Brad was up for it?"

Jay looked to do repair work where he could. He called Michael Fiorile at the NBC affiliate board and abjectly apologized for failing the stations with his ten o'clock show. Fiorile, who remained a steadfast Jay backer, said, "The affiliates are still supportive, and the fact that the show didn't play at ten really wasn't your fault."

The big concern for Leno—and for NBC—was that Jay would face a backlash of blame as he tried to reestablish himself at 11:35. There would be only a few weeks between the end of the misbegotten ten o'clock show and his return to *Tonight*. NBC was concerned enough to call in a crisis-management firm, Sitrick and Company, nationally known PR experts specializing in countering bad news. *Forbes* magazine called its founder, Michael Sitrick, "The Flack for When You're Under Attack."

The network was seeking to learn just how much damage had been done, and the best way to mount a response. In this case, the advice did not get too complicated: Jay needed to bring back his loyal fans and he would be fine. That meant keeping to his steady routine of outside stand-up appearances and benefit performances.

Jay himself had some concerns about those, but he had several big houses booked in January—a good way to assess if he would encounter any fallout. One of them was the Borgata Casino in Atlantic City, a 2,500-seat house. When Jay called, offering to back out if the sales were slow, he was told the show had sold out in a day. This seemed to be a good sign.

In one desperate stab at turning things around, NBC put together a promo ad to run during the Olympics that was a direct parody of the famous "It was all a dream" twist in the old CBS show *Dallas*. Several network executives were utterly appalled at this idea—it seemed unhip, old-fashioned, and horrendously insensitive. *What?* Now Conan's term on the show wasn't supposed to have even existed? Wiser heads prevailed, and the piece was shelved.

Some of those wiser heads remained equally appalled at how personal and ugly the standoff with Conan had become. It seemed cold and crass, especially to some younger NBC staff members who had always felt an affinity toward him. The decision to return to Jay—due to turn sixty in three months—struck them as a conscious choice by the network to shift its priorities in late night toward a mass-audience strategy and away from the more targeted let's-play-young focus that had prevailed when Conan was named to the job. Jay could not be expected to change his own approach, and there was no way to "young him up." NBC seemed to be conceding that the audience for late night was going to be considerably older for the foreseeable future.

The network signaled that shift in another way. In one of the first staff meetings about how NBC could relaunch Jay at 11:35, the gathered NBC employees wanted to know if a message that was going out that day was true: Was NBC really making the suggestion that any employees who had joined the "I'm with Coco" Facebook group were expected to unfriend themselves right away? The initial answer was yes. But then Jeff Gaspin, who was running the meeting, stepped in to say that if there were people who supported the page, he would not ask them to quit.

The truth was, a horde of young NBC staff members had joined the "I'm with Coco" page, especially in New York. For at least a time, NBC, if not the Borgata showroom, looked as if it would remain a house divided.

Certainly the posturing in the aftermath of the settlement did little to bring the snark between the two sides down to a murmur. Gavin Polone went out wide immediately, declaring that Conan had won "a big victory" and saying that his star "would be better off in the long run." There might be a new set of affiliate issues at Fox, Polone conceded, but, unlike NBC, Fox knew it had the juice to stand up to its stations, juice that came from having shows its affiliates were desperate to retain, like *American Idol* and *House*. Gavin couldn't resist pointing out that NBC actually owned the big-hit medical drama *House* but had allowed it to go to Fox because, he said, Jeff Zucker had lacked the savvy to see its potential.

Polone also restated his belief that Conan should have left NBC when he had had previous opportunities to go to Fox in 2001 and 2004, but he had felt the need to chase his muddled dream of *The Tonight Show*. Still, Polone argued, these things happen for a reason, and Conan would win in the end.

Jeff Gaspin put out a different message. On the one hand, he was conciliatory, saying that the agreement worked for both sides and granting at least one of Conan's arguments—that his show had needed more time to grow.

"Could it have grown? Absolutely," Gaspin said. "We just couldn't give him the time." Not, he said, with the affiliates demanding immediate change at ten p.m.

But NBC had a more stinging message to accompany the conciliation. The move made financial sense, the network said, because in Conan's first year *The Tonight Show*, probably the most profitable program in television history, was going to fall into the red.

Gaspin didn't offer a specific number to the press, saying only that it would amount to "tens of millions of dollars." Later NBC offered a peek at some figures showing a projected $3 million loss early in Conan's run that had grown to a $23 million loss by the time the decision to make a change came down. The revelation that *The Tonight Show* had in the middle of that a sort of startling financial turnaround stunned insiders across the television industry, especially those working in late night. Within the Conan camp, however, it raised the sense of outrage to paroxysmal levels.

Jeff Ross, who ran the show's budget, communicated often with the NBC sales department, and even sometimes lined up special product placement commercials within the show, had an instant and violent reaction: "That is total bullshit." He quickly speculated that NBC must have folded in the $60 million cost of constructing the new offices and studio, or else the overall start-up costs for the show. There was no other way, Ross insisted, that the figures could have come out on the minus side.

Conan himself had a similar bout of apoplexy at this accusation, to the point where he suggested he would be willing to stand up and actually fight anyone who advanced the lie that his show was a money-loser. To Ross and O'Brien—who were well aware that their show cost much less than Jay's to produce (Conan himself was making less than half Jay's salary) and that they had brought in new sponsors like Intel—this smacked of a cheap, vindictive slur on NBC's part.

But NBC executives, representing various corporate departments stuck by this assessment, insisting that Conan's numbers had fallen to a point where the ad revenues were simply not able to meet the costs—at $23 million, not even close.

Almost nobody else in the television business bought that explanation. Executives at several other late-night shows treated it with derision. Conan's budget came in at $70 million to $80 million for the year. The other shows knew what NBC was charging for its thirty-second ads, and the revenue simply had to be there to cover that nut—unless the network indeed was throwing in costs like the studio construction or the staff's relocation.

Even one NBC executive familiar with how the network sold its late-night packages said that prior to Gaspin's comment (which followed Conan's departure) there had been no mention whatsoever of NBC's heading for a loss at *The Tonight Show*. At each quarterly sales meeting, when such subjects might be raised, this one never was. But as with everything else in television, it all depended on how the books were massaged.

There was no doubt that Conan (and Jay, for that matter) had performed at levels below what NBC had guaranteed to advertisers. Shortfalls like that were made up for with what were known as make-goods—essentially, free ads. Maybe, the NBC executive speculated, the make-good breakdown was responsible for showing that loss for Conan. And who knew what make-goods were being folded into the total? Nothing could be certain, this executive knew, because the sales department never gave anyone a straight answer.

Polone knew just who to blame for this latest insult to Conan. To him, this was one more indication that Jeff Zucker played dirty—and it demanded a response. It was all of a piece, Polone believed. Because Zucker could never engage in long-term thinking, in Polone's view, all he could do was react. He had never gotten past his news training—see the news; react to it—which had left Zucker lost in a miasma of confusion as he tried to fit the eclectic events of the entertainment business into a news context. Now that Zucker also had Comcast looking over his shoulder, Polone imagined, he first had to act in the interests of self-preservation by shaking up the late-night landscape to make up for his blunder with Jay and Conan. And he also needed to justify the move by sticking a "loser" tag on Conan's forehead.

For Zucker's part, the noxious vitriol being spewed at him by some in Conan's camp (he never blamed either Conan or Ross, or Rick Rosen, for that matter), as well as on some Hollywood blogs, and even by the competition (Letterman displayed Zucker's picture several nights earlier, launching into a diatribe on NBC pinheads, knuckle-draggers, and mouth-breathers), only added to what was a dark, unhappy experience for him—not that he expected anyone to care.

Jeff Zucker had also never expected to be ranked as some kind of Bond villain of a boss. (Conan would go on to make the white-cat-petting Ernst Stavro Blofeld associations with Zucker ever more specific.) Jeff was generous to and considerate of his staff, engaging socially, and devoted to his wife, Karen, and their four children. He never missed birthday parties or his sons' Little League games, no matter what the press of business. In private, off the firing line, his likability and decency won him a corps of loyal friends, Jeff Ross being among the most conspicuous.

But the travails of NBC under his leadership had come close to turning Zucker into a caricature, and he was far too intelligent not to be aware of that. He professed to being able to shrug it all off, but Zucker didn't have the necessary automaton characteristics. He may have been making an outrageous fortune, but he felt all the slings and arrows.

When he consented to an interview with Charlie Rose on PBS at the height of the late-night blowup, Zucker made a concerted effort to present his case, conceding the late-night plan had not worked out, but arguing that it had made sense to have given it a shot. He noted that the plan—and this was his plan all the way—had managed to keep Jay Leno and Conan O'Brien together at NBC for five more years. It ended in a mistake, he acknowledged, labeling both shows failures, but Zucker defended the overall strategy, at least, as sound.

Still, he seemed to strain in presenting his case, emphasizing a number of times that this was the kind of thing a leader does. (To some of his critics, that sounded like a pitch intended for Comcast ears.) He also introduced a startling new element to the story: He had been subjected to death threats over the Conan business. Again Zucker was undoubtedly making a point—this time to illustrate just how crazy people had become over this issue—but he ended up inviting accusations that he was in some way begging for sympathy. The enmity Zucker aroused in many Hollywood circles, certainly not solely the product of Gavin Polone's ministrations, had made it almost impossible for Zucker to make a sincere argument— he was always being seen by some as either sinister or manipulative.

Still, others stepped forward to make, in effect, some of his arguments for him. Two principals from competing late-night shows—neither of whom had any reason to hold a brief for Zucker—had reached the same conclusion: Overall, Jeff Zucker might have come out ahead.

"Did Zucker make a mistake?" one competing late-night figure said. "I think he has a good argument—he got five years of revenue out of *The Tonight Show* and *Late Night*. I don't think he's an evil genius. This wasn't something he wanted to do; it was something he felt he had to do to keep Jay in the tent. Now as a result Conan is out of the picture. He's damaged. So it's a little hard from just a business standpoint to say Jeff Zucker made a mistake here."

The other high-profile competitor put it more directly. "Jeff Zucker made tens of millions on late night. Then he had to pay $40 million. He can look at it this way: 'I badly damaged someone who could have been our competitor and made a lot of money. And what did it really cost me? Bad press.'" But he'd already survived a ton of that, the competitor added.

Because NBC executives figured they would have had Jay anyway, they did a financial analysis based on what NBC would have lost had Conan bolted for Fox in 2004. The estimate: $235 million. Some of that total the network would have made up, of course, had they chosen a promising host to replace Conan. But that figure easily surpassed the $45 million it ultimately cost NBC to resolve its Conan dilemma.

Zucker didn't expect plaudits for his perspicacity—it all came down to doing everything possible to keep one or the other of his late-night hosts from bolting. What happened with Leno and Conan would never make its way into MBA textbooks as an example of how to manage talented underlings.

Besides, the way it played out had not only been professionally unhealthy for Zucker, it was also personally wrenching. Zucker felt terrible about the way it had ended with Conan. Though they were never exactly family-dinners close, their relationship went much deeper than just professional contact—at least for Zucker. Only Lorne Michaels truly knew the extent of Zucker's commitment to Conan, and how Jeff had quietly backed O'Brien when others inside NBC wanted to bail on him.

The Jeff Ross connection went to an unusually deep emotional place for Zucker. Having to make a decision that had the potential of ending a friendship that probably meant more to him than any other he had established during his days at NBC was an almost overpowering burden for Zucker. *Almost*, because Zucker knew what was expected of CEOs—especially at GE. Sentiment didn't count for anything.

Still, in every way, a terrible experience, as Zucker saw it.

Jeff Zucker had produced thousands of hours of news shows, and the key to staying fresh in news was moving, always moving. Here he knew he had to move on; everybody had been diminished a little by this episode, but they all needed to move on to the next phase in their lives.

Of course, making sure Jay could move on unscathed became an intense preoccupation, which was why Zucker called in his chief emissary.

Dick Ebersol was due to fly west in mid-January to plant himself in Vancouver to prepare for the big push of the Winter Olympics, starting in February. Zucker asked Dick if he would stop in at Burbank on his way and have a sit-down with Jay and Debbie Vickers to discuss what their return to *Tonight* could be—and should be—especially in terms of bringing back old elements and adding some new ones.

Ebersol would have taken on the assignment in any case, because of his relationships with Zucker and Vickers, and his confidence that he could add something of value to the discussion. But he understood that NBC also needed an executive presence with Jay, because Rick Ludwin was not going to be able to perform that duty.

One of the chief inside casualties of the Jay-Conan pileup had been the man serving as NBC's executive liaison to its late-night shows for more than two decades. The episode had fractured Ludwin's long relationship with Jay, simply because Jay blamed Rick for having fired the gun that started the demolition derby in the first place. Others had tried to persuade him that Rick did not rank high enough to make a decision as big as moving Jay Leno out of *The Tonight Show*—that it had to be the master plan of someone as high up as Zucker. But Jay continued to cite Ludwin as the source of this genius idea.

Ebersol knew from Debbie that Jay felt Ludwin had betrayed him: not just by pushing for Conan to get the 11:35 job, but also because he thought Ludwin had disappeared on him during the ten o'clock mess at a time when they were so vulnerable.

It made for an uncomfortable position for Ludwin. Jay had returned as the centerpiece of NBC's late night and he was no longer speaking to the network executive in charge of late night. Ludwin, brutally aware he was being iced out, decided to give Jay space and hope they would eventually get back to their old interaction.

In the meantime, Dick Ebersol had become the network's main conduit to *The Tonight Show*. The night before he was due to fly to Burbank to meet with Jay and Debbie, Dick sat down to a dinner with the managers of the NBC affiliate board, finally in town for their long-delayed semiannual conference with the network. Now that all had been resolved in late night, the mood among the affiliates was warm, especially toward Ebersol, whom the station managers credited with providing some of the biggest, most reliable numbers NBC still attracted: NFL games on Sunday night and the Olympics, now right around the corner.

But Ebersol had more on his mind than receiving congratulations. As he sat down with the board, he told them, "The one thing I want to say about all this is that this has all worked out the way you guys wanted it to. I understand all that. But you have to remember that you're complicit in why Jay's show didn't work. We are, too. We put so many restrictions on what his show could be that it had no chance in hell to be what the audience expected it to be."

He lectured them on the wrongheadedness of the demand that Jay save his second-best comedy element until the end of the show. He acknowledged that NBC had fumbled with the idea that Jay could have only one guest each night because somehow that wouldn't be fair to *The Tonight Show*. Ebersol then returned to the unreasonable insistence on burying the established comedy bits—"Headlines," "Jaywalking," etc.—at the back, because it destroyed the rhythm of the show and forced Jay to put on what he called "unknown comedy" right in the second act.

"Let's not lose sight of that," Ebersol concluded. "Because when he gets back to his old show in his old time period, Jay's gonna be successful again."

Jay took his own first step to push the rehabilitation effort. Possibly out of the tradition of host logrolling—you come on my show, I come on yours—Jay agreed to sit down for his first big post-blowup interview with Oprah Winfrey. As she often did, Oprah skillfully combined chumminess with a somewhat pressing interrogation.

Jay went through his account of the events that had led to the shake-up of that fall, including how NBC's decision to oust him "broke my heart." He admitted to telling "a white lie on the air" when he said he'd retire at the end of the five-year waiting period. And he professed no hard feelings toward Conan, whom he said he "very much" considered a friend.

But he also bluntly denied any responsibility for Conan's disappointment. "It had nothing to do with me," Jay said. He also repeated NBC's claim that Conan's show was going to lose money for the first time in *Tonight Show* history. And he fired off his most direct and pointed response when Oprah cited Conan's assertion that moving to 12:05 would be destructive to the franchise. "If you look at what the ratings were," Jay said, "it was already destructive to the franchise."

When Oprah chided Jay about the joke about Letterman and his wife, saying it was "beneath him," Jay defended it as funny and characterized the back-and-forth between the comics as "big-time wrestling."

He also speculated that almost anything NBC could have done would have been better than the eventual outcome. "If they'd come in and shot everybody—I mean, it would have been people murdered. But at least it would have been a two-day story. I mean, yes, NBC could not have handled it worse, from 2004 onward. This whole thing was a huge mess."

Seeking further advice, Jay also reached out in a much more unexpected direction: He called Lorne Michaels.

No one at NBC had a longer or deeper connection to Conan than

Michaels, but Jay had reason—possibly as a result of his and Debbie's conversations with Ebersol—to suspect Lorne had not bought a ticket on the Jay's-to-blame train. He was right about that.

Leno and Michaels had interacted little over the years; Jay's style of comedy hardly matched Michaels's sensibilities. Lorne saw him as more of a Bob Hope–like figure—a safety valve for viewers. And while Jay's brand of setup–punch line humor would never have landed him in the cast of *Saturday Night Live*, Michaels realized that people in America tended to admire and accept a "well-made one-of-those, even if it isn't a one-of-those that they liked." And Jay had obviously been making a good one-of-those for a long time.

Lorne had made no secret to Jeff Zucker what he would have done with the late-night plan had it been his decision to make. He was the one whispering in Zucker's ear to let Jay go, because the ten o'clock show was so awful. Everyone would understand the move in that context, Lorne had told Zucker, and now you put your bet on the younger guy, give him a full run, and stand behind him.

But when it didn't fall that way, Michaels understood the rationale: Jay would still make a good one-of-those. As much as he understood the facile comparisons of Conan and Jay as Harvard versus the garage, Lorne recognized that, every once in a while, Jay was not quite the garage and Conan not quite Harvard. Jay did smart jokes as well as dumb ones. He just did a lot of jokes because, well, that's what he did. Conan remained, like Letterman, more of an attitude comedian, as Lorne saw it.

Lorne also understood on a personal level Jay's mind-set about wanting to keep working until either he dropped or they changed the locks. That was Lorne's intention as well. As long as NBC continued to pay the electricity bill for 30 Rock, Lorne would produce *Saturday Night Live*.

More than anything else, Michaels dismissed as nonsense any suggestion that the actions of recent years and months had been driven by Jay's Machiavellian genius. Lorne did not believe in the puppets moving the strings.

So he gave Jay some counsel, listened patiently as Leno laid the blame for the decision at Ludwin's door, and told him that was silly because surely Jay realized a move of this magnitude could not emanate from Rick Ludwin's pay grade.

One thing he did not discuss with Jay, but which staggered him when he finally got convincing evidence that it was true, was the fact that Jay had won a pay-*and*-play commitment. Michaels continued to be baffled by the implications of that deal and what role it actually played in the way the drama eventually unfolded.

Mostly based on what he'd gleaned from his conversation with Zucker, but also from what his representatives continued to tell him, Conan believed that Jay's pay-and-play contract had been impossibly forbidding for NBC. Polone suggested that the network had looked at the cost of extricating itself from the deal and blanched: It could ultimately have cost as much as $100 million to pay Jay off. Whatever the price, it had to be a consideration in the decision to retain him and let Conan hit the street.

Without taking a public stand on the matter, NBC's executives begged to differ. They apparently decided it was necessary to clarify that their decision was based on programming and not financial considerations— especially after Conan went public in a *60 Minutes* interview seeming to endorse the suggestion that NBC was on the hook with Jay for about $150 million. (Though Conan himself did not bring up the figure, the reporter, Steve Kroft, did, citing other reports.)

NBC argued that Jay's deal for ten p.m., while admittedly unusual, did not constitute a burden so onerous that the network could not countenance trying to pay him off. NBC's legal department stressed that the entertainment side was free to make the smartest decision, with no regard to contract implications. The reason, they said, was that the pay-and-play would have become relevant only in a situation where the talent demanded the right to stay on the air or pressed to sue for liquidated damages based on the impact a cancelation might have on a career. Neither case would likely have ever applied to Jay Leno, NBC argued, because suing would mean a bitter, drawn-out fight during which he wouldn't be on television telling jokes. And would Jay really want to stay on the air in a show the affiliates were abandoning, guaranteeing failure?

The easy answer was that Jay and his lawyer didn't have to think much about either prospect, because NBC had come to them promising to slide Jay right back into late night, thus satisfying his need to keep telling jokes on television.

Had NBC decided Conan truly was the future and bid Jay a fond fare-thee-well, resolving his contract would have been a relatively standard procedure, according to the NBC legal department's analysis. Not that it would have been cheap—certainly it would have cost more than paying off Conan. But that was principally because Jay's salary was more than double Conan's, they explained.

One NBC executive did concede that NBC had signed a bad contract with Jay Leno, but insisted that the deal had not determined the network's decision. Had Conan been tearing it up at 11:35, NBC would have stepped up and done what it had to. The advice given to Zucker and the others in New York had been simple, the executive said: Jay would not be able to get an injunction, even though it was a pay-and-play deal. Ultimately it would still come down to writing Jay a check. Yes, the check would have to be slightly bigger because of the unusual promises in the contract, but, in the end, NBC was going to have to write a guy a check—one guy or the other.

Kevin Reilly had begun Fox's courtship of Conan O'Brien even before Conan was fully settled out at NBC; he used the customary back channel: Jeff Ross.

From his days at NBC Entertainment, Reilly had developed a warm relationship with Ross, concluding, as so many others did, that Jeff was a totally appealing guy with no artifice in him, no bullshit, as straight a shooter as you were likely to find in Hollywood.

Reilly was dead serious. He was hungry to break Fox into late night at last, and here was a performer who was not only an established star—and one whose name had lately dominated the news—but also a guy with a sensibility that was a perfect fit for Fox. He met Ross at Rick Rosen's house.

"Could this be any more insane?" Reilly asked, opening the conversation. He laid his cards out quickly. Fox had an intense interest. But there were likely to be complications.

"Back of the envelope, my instinct is, I don't know if we're going to be able to clear the show," Reilly said. By "clear," he meant get the full complement—or close to it—of Fox stations to commit to carry a Conan O'Brien late-night show. "I'm gonna do the math and we'll see where we end up."

Reilly's enthusiasm fell on welcoming ears. Team Conan knew that, in the current landscape, if they were going to find a new network home for their man, Fox represented the only real option. Polone had tried to argue that a new kind of deal made sense for Conan—maybe he didn't need a network play at all, given how much of his audience found their entertainment choices online now. Many of Conan's younger viewers already watched him only in highlights the following day on the Web (a factor that had hardly helped with the ratings impression he wanted to make with NBC). But others on Conan's team leaned heavily toward locking up a base that was an actual television show and building the new media possibilities from there.

Back in his own jurisdiction, Reilly began his sales job. Chase Carey, who had replaced Peter Chernin as the top executive overseeing all of Fox's entertainment operations, made it clear he simply didn't get Conan, but he accepted that his was a business perspective more than a creative one, and he remained open to the idea. Reilly had the unqualified backing of Peter Rice, the chairman of Fox Entertainment. Rice, who had previously headed Fox Searchlight films, had forged a reputation as a keen evaluator of breakthrough material (*Bend It Like Beckham, Slumdog Millionaire*). Rice became Reilly's partner in the pursuit of Conan.

Rice and Reilly had reason for their enthusiasm. A talent of Conan's stature simply did not fall into a network's lap so conveniently. On any checklist of qualities most appropriate for a late-night host on the Fox network, Conan would have filled in virtually every box: hip, creative, irreverent, youth oriented, special appeal to male viewers. It was no accident Conan had truly broken through as a writer on *The Simpsons*. He was all but the embodiment of the Fox comic sensibility.

As the Fox team saw it, Conan most definitely did *not* embody the *Tonight* sensibility. The fit was just off, in some fundamental way, beginning with that big Vegasy stage and the long, traditional monologue. He might have gotten there over time, but the whole traditional format didn't seem built for the scrappy, off-the-wall Conan, in their view. But if he came to Fox, playing the underdog again, they were sure he would get the magic back, overnight.

Rice and Reilly were well aware of who represented the main impediment to a quick annexation of Conan: Roger Ailes. An imposing figure internally at the News Corp., Fox's parent, given the spectacular financial results for his personal baby, the boisterous Fox News Channel, Ailes had added the portfolio of the stations owned by Fox Broadcasting. He could be expected to apply his customary aggressiveness to representing the interests of the stations, no matter how rapturous the network guys might be about Conan.

Reilly knew the easiest way to get Conan in the door at Fox. All it would take would be the ultimate voice at the network, News Corp. chairman Rupert Murdoch, delivering one simple message: "I don't give a shit. This is another *Wall Street Journal*. I want it." That always produced results at Fox. But Murdoch remained noncommittal on Conan. His position boiled down to: "If you can make it work."

That quickly proved a prodigious challenge.

Though Fox in earlier years had a clause in its contracts mandating that its affiliated stations take any late-night show Fox decided to program, that clause had been dropped from more recent agreements. With the network never having made a dent in late night, the stations loaded up on syndicated reruns of recent sitcom hits like *The Office* and *Family Guy*, along with perennials like *Seinfeld*, which always rated well. The shows were expensive and, making the issue even more complicated, the stations, short of money during the recession, had secured what were known as barter deals for many of them. That meant that instead of dealing in cash, the stations offered the syndicators big chunks of commercial time in each show.

In order to insert Conan at eleven p.m., after the late local news on the Fox stations, the stations would have to relocate the sitcom reruns; in doing so, however, the barter deals would become far more complex. If the sitcoms slid back past midnight on the schedule, the prices of the commercials would change. All the deals would likely have to be renegotiated.

Peter Rice was undaunted by this prospect. By his calculation, Fox would have to buy the stations out of their expensive barter deals at a cost of something approximating $100 million. That didn't include the start-up costs for a new late-night show, which could run to another $70 million. Rice and Reilly still wanted to do it. The word from the advertising executives was positive; they had already started to receive calls from big clients like Intel, Ford, and American Express. They all wanted in on a Conan late-night show on Fox, convinced it would be a demographic home run.

Even so, the stations remained cool, approaching icy, to the idea. Like NBC's station group, Fox's tended to be led by men in their fifties and sixties—a Jay crowd. If Jay had come on the market instead, Reilly and Rice knew they could have signed him and simply flipped a switch: The stations would easily have lined up. But Conan was again proving to have a narrower appeal to station owners.

Reilly and Rice knew there was another reason they faced such a high degree of difficulty in completing a Conan deal: Fox and its stations were already on the brink of a civil war of sorts. Nationally, broadcasters had finally reached a point where they were uniting in demanding compensation from cable systems for the right to retransmit their programs onto cable. Retransmission rights suddenly became a path of survival for the struggling networks, most of which were projecting losses in their network business. (According to one inside estimate, NBC was looking at about a $300 million loss.)

Subscription fees from flush cable operators could change all that. The problem was, networks themselves could not extract sub fees from cable systems. Local stations controlled the rights the cable operators would pay for. Even though the vast majority of programs viewers wanted to see were being supplied (and paid for) by the networks, the local station was in line to claim the $1.50 and up per subscriber that the cable systems might be compelled to pay.

Fox's plan was to negotiate tough deals with its affiliates, pointing out that the leverage they had over cable systems mainly came from the programming on Fox: NFL football, *American Idol*, *House*, and *Family Guy*. The Fox network shelled out the big bucks to acquire that programming; why should it not command the largest piece of the retransmission money?

So just as Rice and Reilly were contemplating pitching the stations on the merits of removing those high-priced and high-rated sitcom repeats in favor of the guy who just disappointed NBC on *The Tonight Show*, the Fox network was readying an onerous demand on retrans fees. If a station was able to get $2.00 per subscriber from a cable operator, Fox intended to skim $1.75 off the top—that was the price for obtaining all that great network product. But Fox's executives didn't kid themselves that the stations were simply going to bend over and take this spanking without a whimper.

When Reilly and Rice had a chance to sit down with Conan's group, the message back sounded beyond promising. The other options Conan's people mentioned seemed like posturing to the Fox executives. They became convinced it was their deal to lose. In direct meetings with Conan and with his representatives, the Fox team laid out the issues clearly. Initially, the signs pointed to a heavy lift. The number of stations willing to go along would be limited for maybe two years, as the syndication deals worked their way through the system. Rice and Reilly explained that they could not be sure they could get this deal through the News Corp. hierarchy: They wanted it badly, though, and they would work at it over a period of months to see how far they could get.

Conan, naturally, expressed reservations, given what he'd just been through, largely due to pressure from NBC's stations. "I'd want to be with you," Conan said. "But frankly, I don't want to be in a place that has to jam it through." If Kevin and Peter couldn't look him in the eye and assure him this was going to work, he didn't know if he wanted to pursue it.

They all agreed to keep at it.

Reilly did have a recommendation he wanted to run by Gavin Polone: Put Conan first on Fox's sister cable network, FX, an ad-supported entertainment channel on the basic cable tier. Maybe after a year or so there, they could make a shift over to Fox on broadcast. Reilly couldn't actually guarantee that would happen, but he thought FX would be a good home for the show, and having it in the Fox family would certainly make a transfer easier. For Polone that was a nonstarter; they were not going to entertain offers from basic cable channels.

The biggest player on the other side of the retransmission issue happened to be in the process of acquiring its own broadcast network. But even though Comcast's top executives were making the rounds in Washington that winter, shaking hands, giving public testimony, doing the whole regulatory dance, their opinions on the current NBC leadership remained opaque.

Media analysts on Wall Street, in the press, and online believed one coming decision was totally transparent: Jeff Zucker had to be a dead man walking. How could he hope to survive with his GE patron, Jeff Immelt, going out the door and two media professionals like Brian Roberts and Steve Burke coming in? Surely the latest NBC misfire, this late-night fizzle—purely Zucker's handiwork—could only have hardened the resolve that big changes had to be made in the new Comcast-led NBC Universal.

But if the Comcast executives had a judgment to make about Zucker's fate or the late-night train wreck they had at least partially witnessed, they did an exceptional job of keeping it to themselves.

Although no one admitted it directly, more than a few NBC executives welcomed a management change, because GE's parsimonious ways, especially as NBC was being readied for sale, had squeezed the network dry.

Gaspin believed NBC's entertainment properties simply had no future without significant new investment. He conveyed that opinion to Zucker, and the CEO approved a plan to spend much more freely, acquiring new programs from some of the top television creative talents.

That seemed consistent with Comcast's message to Washington: They wanted to be in the business of content. They signaled that they knew that took money.

What most NBC executives presumed was that Comcast had a plan; they just didn't know what it was or who would be affected. Upon examining the broad spectrum of NBCU, they would have seen cable channels running at high efficiency, a news division that remained a dominant leader, theme parks that seemed about to post big results thanks to a new Harry Potter attraction, and a broadcast network on the skids but showing a few glimmers of financial turnaround.

How any of this would affect Zucker's future, no one inside NBC ventured to guess. Jeff himself seemed serene; he spent a lot of time with Roberts and Burke, selling NBC's strengths—and by extension his own.

Two weeks before the end of *The Jay Leno Show,* Debbie Vickers returned to her office after completing a taping and found a message waiting from Rob Burnett of the Letterman show, simply stating, "It's not bad." Vickers had remained an unabashed admirer of Dave, through all her years of work with Jay—but then again, Debbie knew, as others on the show did, that deep down Jay himself remained an unabashed Dave admirer.

"Dave has an idea," Rob said when Vickers returned the call; and he presented it to her. When Debbie finished laughing, which required several minutes, she took the idea directly to Jay—in private. She was already on board with the need for total secrecy.

"Remember the Super Bowl ad that Dave did with Oprah?" she began, as she outlined Letterman's concept for Jay.

They were back on the phone with Burnett within five minutes.

On Tuesday, February 2, 2010, Jay Leno boarded NBC's jet for New York. He had run the idea past Jeff Zucker, who embraced it just as quickly and enthusiastically as Jay had. It did mean canceling that night's edition of the ten p.m. *Jay Leno Show,* which nobody gave a second thought.

Jay landed at Teterboro in New Jersey. A waiting car contained a disguise that a Letterman producer had prepared for him: fake mustache, glasses, hooded sweatshirt. They had worked it out that Jay would arrive at Letterman's theater when Dave was in midshow so no audience hopefuls would still be lingering outside. Jay was escorted in through the Broadway entrance, under the big marquee, because crowds always lined up across from the entrance on Fifty-third Street, in case the show did some bit out on the street.

Jay was reasonably sure nobody saw his arrival; if they did, all they noticed was a guy in a hoodie. The producers brought Jay upstairs immediately, stashing him on the thirteenth floor in an unused room where he relaxed and snacked for about thirty-five minutes, listening to the distant laughter down in the theater. Then the door opened and Oprah Winfrey walked in. This was less than a week after Jay had sat down with Oprah for his much-talked-about interview, and they greeted each other warmly. Now all they had to do was wait for the show to end.

When it did, and every audience member had been cleared from the theater, Rob Burnett appeared and greeted his guests. He led them out and down to a secluded area of the building where a fake living room had been created on a set that the show used to pretape segments. And here was David Letterman. It was the first time Dave and Jay had laid eyes on each other in person in eighteen years.

The greeting wasn't exaggerated or grand, but routine, like two guys who used to hang out a bit now happening to run into each other at somebody's party. Handshakes, not hugs.

The conversation didn't even touch on the issue that had dominated entertainment news for the previous month, nor the transcontinental punch lines they had exchanged. Instead it was all "Have you seen this guy and that guy from the old days at the Comedy Store?" To Jay it seemed he was picking up with Dave exactly where he had left off in 1992—and that this Dave, though a bit older and grayer, was still the exact same guy he had always known.

Right away Jay fell into the pattern he had always followed with Letterman: He tried to make him laugh. He knew Dave's formal way with language and how certain turns of phrase amused him, so he pulled up a line that had worked on Dave before, saying, "The old Manson place has really changed." The interaction felt so right to Jay that he relaxed totally—this was going to be a snap, just like the old days on Dave's show.

Dave's idea was simple: a fifteen-second segment, a promo designed to run in the second quarter of the game that Sunday night. The concept was the worst Super Bowl party ever.

They arranged themselves on the stage couch: Dave far right, Oprah in the middle, Jay far left. It would start with a one-shot of Dave complaining about the party, expand to a two-shot to show Oprah, and then the big reveal with Jay at the other end of the couch. Jay's line: "Oh, he's just saying that 'cause I'm here." And Oprah would tell them both to be nice.

Dave asked for input. Jay suggested Dave not have his arm around Oprah in the first shot, because that might make it seem that he was complaining about her being there.

They shot it, needing only a couple of takes. It seemed to play perfectly, with both Dave and Jay looking miserable on either side of Oprah.

"Jay, you happy with this?" Dave asked. "You want to do this again?"

"No, looks good to me," Jay said.

And then the two rivals stood and exchanged another handshake. Dave thanked them both for being so generous to show up and do this for him. He hoped it would have the impact they all expected.

Dave and Jay talked just a bit more, nothing of consequence, two comics shooting the breeze. Then they said their good-byes. Jay was back in Teterboro and on a plane in time to get into LA for a late dinner.

The circle who knew the secret was small and tight at both networks. Still, somehow the same Web site that had gotten wind of the change coming for Jay's ten p.m. show, FTV Live, posted news of some kind of "secret taping" that had taken place at Letterman's studio. One of the writers on Jay's staff approached him at rehearsal with the rumor about the taping. "Why don't you try to find out more?" Jay said, enjoying the tease.

The night of the game, those in on the secret were barely distracted by the action on the field. They knew the promo was set for the first commercial break in the second quarter. Even Jay, who didn't give a hoot about sports, was at home glued to the set.

As soon as the spot appeared—Dave, then Oprah, then . . . *Jay?*— phones began ringing and e-mails began flying. Jay was contacted by e-mail from the White House—David Axelrod, the senior adviser, wanted to know, was that real? He had been watching with the president, and they all had instantly asked themselves: *Could that possibly have been real?*

So amazed were viewers that hordes on Web sites and chat rooms immediately speculated that Leno had somehow been "green-screened" into the picture. Surely these two guys who had so recently ripped each other with such abandon had not sat down together for a gag promo?

They had indeed—and it delighted Jay Leno. The whole experience had been great fun, but also something else. Jay had been moved by it. For all the competition, the endless ratings measuring out their worths on a weekly basis, Jay had never really stopped holding out hope that he and Dave could one day just get together, be guys again. For Jay, the Super Bowl promo, as elaborate and secret as it had been, really came down to that: He had gotten together with Dave again. And the years, the jokes, and the animosity melted away in an instant.

Jay acknowledged that he may have been naive, but he thought maybe Dave sensed he had gone a little too far. Dave was never going to stop by, say he was sorry, and offer to shake hands; comics didn't do that. Instead they did this: They appeared together in a bit. This was how you conducted a late-night feud. Jay decided to believe it was Dave offering an olive branch. It didn't really matter to him whether that was true or not. It felt good to believe it was.

If Letterman had had his way, the bit might have been even better. Before he invited Jay, Dave had had Rob Burnett reach out to one other potential participant: But Conan didn't get the joke. More precisely, he didn't find anything funny in the situation. Jeff Ross got the call from Burnett and brought the idea to Conan, by now out of the show and already growing his scraggly red beard.

"So, Burnett called. Dave wants to know if you want to be in a Super Bowl ad with Jay and Dave." Ross had little doubt what the answer would be.

Conan fired it back instantly. "No fucking way I'm doing that," Conan said. "It's not a joke to me—it's real."

Conan was sure that NBC—which, according to the release Conan had just signed, held the lock on his TV appearances until May—would have been only too happy to grant a onetime permit for this little foray with Jay. Of course NBC would be all for it, Conan guessed. It could only help rehabilitate Jay in the nation's eyes: all the late-night warriors, cozying up. The message, Conan believed, would be: *See? It's all just smoke and mirrors, folks.* Or, as Jay himself had put it, it would be "big-time wrestling"—all fake, all a game. Ross sent back word: Conan was a no.

One other late-night host strongly disapproved of the promo. Watching the game that night at a party at his house, Jimmy Kimmel couldn't believe his eyes. Dave was throwing Jay a life preserver. He later went on Dave's show as a guest and tweaked him about it, after Dave said how much fun he'd had bashing Jay. Jimmy said Jay had been drowning; they could have finished him off. The two of them had a laugh about it all.

Kimmel had thought about it a lot and realized the ad represented Dave sending a message: *This is still about two guys at the top; I don't need these other hangers-on cluttering up the late-night stage.* When Letterman had slammed Jay with the joke comparing him to Americans stealing the Indians' land, it had thrilled Kimmel; it was television with a real edge. Jimmy had even admired Jay for coming back with nasty stuff about Dave as well, though, as might be expected, he didn't think it was as funny as Dave's hits on Jay.

For Kimmel, the late-night war had been pure joy. There was something primally funny about it, something that played to his own instincts. His haranguing of Jay on Jay's show had been, in his estimation, the best thing that had ever happened to his own show. He had broken through into a story being dominated by two other late-night network stars, with Dave guest-starring as the outside agitator. Thrusting himself into the discussion had made Jimmy a host of new fans. Previously, he knew, Conan's fans had viewed him as something of a lummox: Conan was the smart guy; Jimmy was the jack-off. Now he was being flooded with messages and e-mails from Conan's people. Writers on Conan's show, on Letterman's show, and on *The Simpsons*, congratulated him, as did big names like Will Ferrell, Martin Short, and even Paul Shaffer, Dave's bandleader.

Kimmel at first denied Jay's charge (to Oprah) that he had sucker-punched Jay with that "10 at 10" appearance. Then, to Dave, he acknowledged that, having checked the dictionary, yeah, he had sucker-punched him. But he had to quibble with Dave's ultimate assessment that it was all fun and "nobody got hurt."

"I think Conan might disagree," Jimmy said.

In the days before his return to *The Tonight Show* on March 2, Jay Leno and his staff found themselves treading lightly. They were all feeling the heat of Team Coco and the blasts still coming over the Internet. Jay and Debbie Vickers both accepted the likelihood that they would face some damaged-goods issues. And they feared that Letterman had built up a wave of momentum that might be hard to break. Maybe it would take another eighteen months before Jay returned to the top—if he ever reached there.

Rebuilding the show seemed less challenging than rebuilding Jay's image, because they all knew how to do a *Tonight Show*. Debbie had already returned the better comedy bits to act two. The guests would come back; the familiar routine would be reestablished.

During the three-week break for the Olympics, they fiddled with the set, brought in a desk and chairs for the old panel look. The studio still had the overall ambience of *The Jay Leno Show*, because there wasn't time to make it look radically different.

One big question was how to play the return—obviously it had to be for laughs. The *Dallas* promo had been ditched, but they all kicked around that idea and eventually turned it into a *Wizard of Oz* parody: Jay would have hit his head and gone to a strange land—ten p.m.—but had now come home. It might be a screamingly obvious idea, but those were usually the kind that had the broadest appeal, and reinstalling Jay was all about recapturing that broad appeal.

Another question demanded to be addressed: Would Jay say anything in the first show about Conan, salute his efforts on the show, again toast him for being a good guy? Nick Bernstein, among others, pressed the case for some kind of mention of Conan. The issue had resonance for Jay, because one of the deepest regrets of his career had been not citing Carson on the first night when he assumed *The Tonight Show* in 1992. That had been his manager Helen's demand, though of course Jay could have overruled it had he been willing to defy her. Not mentioning Johnny had invited immediate charges that Jay was an ungracious slug who didn't deserve the job.

Jay certainly didn't want to go through anything like that again, but this situation was clearly different. Conan at seven months obviously wasn't Johnny at thirty years. But more than that, Jay was now facing a torrent of acrimony from Conan's fans. To give Conan even a tiny nod of recognition would surely be seen by some as shameless pandering.

They felt damned either way, so they decided to pass.

Other than that bit of awkwardness, Jay slipped comfortably into his old seat at *Tonight*. In a real way, the show was his baby, his only baby. His family—other than Mavis—was the staff. His personal relationships outside the show remained minimal.

Just before he resumed his old position, Jay stepped back to consider the events of 2009. One rationalized way he looked at them: He had been off the air for eight months. That other show? Somehow, that didn't constitute being on the air for Jay—not when matched against being on *The Tonight Show*. From that perspective, Jay realized he was back home in less than a year.

The numbers for the first night back reflected the continuing fascination with the rumble in late night. Jay pulled in 6.6 million viewers, a massive bump over Conan's average (but nowhere near the 10.3 million who turned out to blow Conan a kiss good-bye in January). What was notable, of course, was how big Jay's margin was over Letterman, who attracted 3.8 million that night. Of course, there was curiosity value in Jay's return, but he won the week as well, with 5.58 million viewers to Dave's 3.66. Jay cleaned up among those precious viewers eighteen to forty-nine as well, landing 1.94 million to 1.3 million for Dave.

As the weeks passed, Jay's margin held. It looked a bit like a replay of two years earlier: Jay won every week and most every night. "It's as if a collective erase button was pushed," said Robert Thompson, professor of television at Syracuse University, "with the usual suspects back in their usual locations—except Conan is gone."

Week by week Jay's total audience numbers remained about 50 percent higher than what Conan had been scoring. But he was down sharply from his own previous performance on *Tonight* two years earlier, and the edge in the younger audience groups was far less impressive. The evidence was quickly overwhelming: NBC had exchanged a smaller, mostly younger audience for a larger, mostly older audience. The median age of the Jay viewer, just over fifty-six, represented growth, virtually overnight, of more than a decade over what it had been for the Conan viewer.

The results played more ominously for Letterman. In a flash, with Jay back as his chief rival, Dave lost the number one status he had enjoyed during Conan's brief run. And a sizable slice of the additional audience he'd collected during Conan's tenure seemed to drift away and not come back. The erase button had wiped out the short, happy reign of David Letterman in late night.

Conan O'Brien had once read a story about Lyndon Johnson. After he had decided not to run for reelection and was spending his days down at his ranch in Texas, the former leader shared a day with a journalist, who noticed almost immediately that Johnson had not been able to shake the mantle of the presidency. He was no longer tackling problems of poverty or ordering the carpet bombing of Cambodia; instead he was applying the same energy and authority to fixing a small water pump that filled a cattle trough.

Though he hardly qualified as an ex-president, Conan, in the first weeks after being untimely ripped from his *Tonight Show* womb, found himself similarly diminished. Accustomed to heading a staff of people all devoted to a single cause—getting a show on the air every day—he now found himself sitting outside, waiting for his daughter's school bus, thinking in some instinctive, hostlike way: *Where is that bus?! I want nine people over here right now!*

He had things do to, like taking care of remaining issues with the staff and, more than anything, planning the live tour that would get him back to doing what the fire in his blood demanded: standing in front of people and making them laugh. One small task, writing a daily Twitter feed, had come to amuse and inspire him a bit. Though initially dismissive of the trivial nature of most items on Twitter, O'Brien could not help but be impressed by the impact of its social connections, and he came to enjoy the discipline of writing something funny every day in 140 characters or less. As long as the tweets stuck to jokes, he was able to continue doing them; NBC monitored Conan's daily messages to make sure he was not sprinkling them with anti-NBC or anti-Jay material, because its deal with him included no Internet presence for several months. But they weren't going to enforce that for a stream of funny lines.

"I just celebrated the end of Lent by eating twenty-two sleeves of Peeps. My religion rocks!"

Conan needed to flex his comedy muscles because his psyche was still lacerated. It was too soon to have any perspective on what had just transpired in his life, but he had no uncertainty about the choices he had made, dating all the way back to his turning down Fox in 2001. Chasing *The Tonight Show* had been something he had to do. Giving it up had been the hardest thing he had ever done—or likely would ever do—professionally, but that sacrifice was better than holding on to a compromised version of it.

Fox remained on his mind, though, because, in terms of future moves, there was the tour and then . . . if not Fox, what? For the most part Conan left such considerations in the hands of his representatives. He had learned of a few possibilities: Did HBO have interest? That would be only once a week, though. Conan had also heard rumblings that Leslie Moonves, the head of CBS, had made a pitch for Showtime, the pay cable channel he also supervised. Rick Rosen thought it might be either Les's way of parking a potential successor to Dave or else maybe just another move by Les to give Jeff Zucker a professional noogie.

While all that sounded mildly diverting, Conan still expected a push from Fox—though it was starting to feel awfully slow in coming.

In early April Conan began rehearsals for his tour show, which got his adrenalin pumping again. Jeff Ross was around supervising it all. Like everyone else on Team Conan, Ross assumed the Fox deal would get done. The process seemed slow and painful, but his impression was that it was far enough down the road that it was going to happen—the situation just wasn't going to be great.

Unexpectedly, just after noon on one of the first rehearsal days, Ross got a call from an old friend. Richard Plepler, who had ascended to the post of copresident of HBO, went back years with Ross, who respected Plepler as a smart guy about the business, besides being a fun guy to hang with.

Plepler said he just wanted to make a little pitch on behalf of Steve Koonin. The name rang a bell with Ross, but not too loudly. "I know you guys are meeting with him today," Plepler continued. "And I just want to urge you to take him seriously. He's got good ideas. You may wind up at Fox and all that, but hear the guy out."

The appointment had totally slipped Ross's mind; they were scheduled to meet with Steve Koonin, the head of the cable channel TBS, that same afternoon. TBS shared a corporate parent, Time Warner, with HBO, which was why Plepler was touting Koonin. Ross now recalled that when the agents had initially told Conan and him about the TBS pitch, they had both kind of shrugged, lumping TBS in with the vague offers they had been getting from the syndication crowd.

When Conan got back from lunch, Ross told him they would have to break from rehearsal early that afternoon. They had to head over to Beverly Hills to Rick Rosen's office at William Morris Endeavor to listen to a pitch.

"Why? What's this for?" Conan said.

"TBS," Ross said, adding quickly before Conan could get too skeptical, "Plepler called me about this guy. I think we should hear him out."

Steve Koonin did not have a big profile in Hollywood, probably because he lived in Atlanta, where the cable channels that had been part of the Ted Turner empire—and now belonged to Time Warner—maintained their base. But Koonin had a plan for TBS, a cable network that even Koonin conceded had a long-ingrained image in the business: not hip, not cutting edge. "It's an uphill climb from *Andy of Mayberry* and the Braves," as Koonin put it.

TBS had started as a local station in Atlanta that carried Braves baseball and lots of reruns of truly old sitcoms. But because Turner got it on satellite, TBS became one of the first so-called superstations, and thus one of the nation's inaugural cable channels. As cable matured, with networks as varied as MTV, FX, and AMC acquiring distinctive brands because of signature original programming, TBS had kept its downmarket identity as that rube channel with the Southern accent.

It had plenty of cash, though, thanks to being grandfathered into every cable system in the country, and Koonin set out to sculpt a new identity for it, essentially turning TBS into Comedy Central without the attitude, a comedy channel for older and more middlebrow tastes. He began buying up every hit sitcom that came off its network run, eventually building a stable that included *Everybody Loves Raymond*, *The Office*, *Family Guy*, and, of course, *Seinfeld*. Under Koonin, TBS's ratings grew, especially when he moved to what he called a "vertical stack" of programs in prime time: running a show like *Family Guy* for three straight hours—six episodes—in a row.

The formula was unorthodox, but so was Koonin. A big guy with a slightly nasal accent, he bore a passing resemblance to the Newman character (Wayne Knight) from *Seinfeld*. He came by his Hollywood-outsider cred legitimately, having spent much of his early career in marketing for another Atlanta-based company, Coca-Cola. Koonin would have appreciated the metaphor perhaps better than anyone else, but he probably never heard the private remarks some NBC executives made about Conan, snidely labeling him "New Coke" (the ill-fated formula that had failed so miserably trying to replace "The Real Thing" in the eighties). But even if Koonin had heard that slam, it was unlikely that it would have deterred him. When Koonin looked at Conan, what he saw was the signature star his channel so far lacked. Koonin and TBS didn't jump in initially because the Conan-to-Fox scenario had been reported as an all but done deal, but they remained patiently on the sidelines while Fox seemed to dither in its wooing process. With no Fox announcement imminent, it was time to make their own interest clear.

Koonin's pitch to Conan and his team that afternoon impressed the whole room. TBS had already tried a late-night format with George Lopez; they believed they could now expand by inserting Conan at eleven and sliding Lopez back to midnight. (Koonin assured them he had already secured George's assent, so they would not have to worry about unfortunate suggestions that Conan was now doing to Lopez what Jay had done to him.)

TBS had exceptional young male demos, Koonin pointed out—perfect for Conan. It also had big-time sports: The baseball play-offs in October would draw a huge audience. They could promote a November launch of Conan to that big crowd. By the time Koonin left Rick Rosen's office, the Conan group had moved from passively curious to borderline excited. Maybe this really did represent a real possibility for them. They all had great affection for Kevin Reilly at Fox, and Peter Rice had wowed them with his intelligence and British class. But doubts had sprung up as the Fox team struggled to close the deal. Could Conan afford to get into another dicey situation with a network and its stations? Just how low a deal could they accept? Fox was talking about dropping the budget from the $70 million they'd had at NBC to about $45 million. How would that affect the show Conan could do?

At TBS the budget would be slashed as well, but there certainly would be no issue with stations. TBS was on every cable system. In terms of reach it wouldn't quite match that of *The Tonight Show*, but it looked as though it would surpass the initial hodgepodge Fox was talking about putting together.

"So what do we know about TBS?" one of the Conan guys finally asked. "What's the channel really like?"

Nobody really knew, and someone finally suggested, "Let's turn it on now and see what's on." Reaching for the remote to flick on the set in his office, Rosen stopped and asked, "Uh, what channel is TBS?"

The rest of the group looked around at one another asking, "Do you know?"

None of them did. Rosen called in his assistant and asked the same question.

The assistant had no idea either.

At almost the same time, over in the Fox offices in Century City, Kevin Reilly took stock of the Conan situation. What he and Rice faced included a huge capital expenditure, stern resistance from a host of stations, and ratings prospects that likely would not have generated profits for a year or two, maybe longer. He and Rice had heard from New York that Roger Ailes had stiffened his opposition and likely would not be moved. To force through a Conan deal now would surely create a raft of ill will inside the company—and, not incidentally, be a risky political maneuver internally. A misstep here could well lead to vulnerability against a dangerous adversary of the likes of Roger Ailes, and maybe an unexpected career change.

Reilly e-mailed Rice, who was on vacation: "Look, this thing is going nowhere. I'm starting to feel like we're in bad faith. We're wasting a lot of our time and theirs. Let's pass."

When Reilly made the call to inform the Conan forces of Fox's decision to withdraw, they told him things had gotten close with another party. It would only hurt their leverage if Fox publicly passed now. Would Kevin mind sitting on this, just for about a week? Kevin said sure.

He couldn't for the life of him guess who the other party might be.

When the news broke on April 12 that Conan had signed with TBS, it rocked the television business. It was shocking enough that such a huge, news-making deal could be consummated under complete radio silence, but the match itself—Conan and *TBS*? How would that work?

It worked for Jeff Ross and the other Conan backers because it afforded a national platform and a network that would truly commit all it had to making Conan successful—and it didn't hurt that Conan would now have complete control of the show, including ownership.

But surely some Team Coco fans, in the words of a writer on the *New York* magazine blog Vulture, let loose "a dejected sigh." Instead of creating a new paradigm for the digital age, "Conan will now be featured as a lead-in for *Lopez Tonight* (a show you don't watch) on TBS (a cable channel you don't watch, or at least never notice when you're watching it). It's not just basic cable, it's unsexy basic cable."

That was certainly not how Jeff Ross viewed it. On TBS, accessible in more than 85 million homes, enough viewers would be available to go out and beat Letterman, especially in the key demo, and maybe even—if things broke right—Leno. That would never be a stated goal, of course, and cable versus a network still constituted an unfair fight.

That didn't mean Team Coco wouldn't be thinking about it.

As Conan headed out on tour, arenas from Eugene, Oregon, to Los Angeles, from New York to Manchester, Tennessee, were packed with screaming, ecstatic fans. They waited in the rain, bought Team Coco T-shirts and posters, crawled over one another to touch Conan as he worked the aisles with his guitar. It was the full rock star treatment, one difficult to imagine any other late-night star matching.

Except maybe the pair on Comedy Central. And in a shift certain to add to the intrigue surrounding Conan's return, he would now be going head-to-head in the basic cable universe against those two now-celebrated hosts Jon Stewart and Stephen Colbert. The cross-channel adulation for all three late-night hosts was never more apparent than at Conan's June 1 stop at Radio City Music Hall—right under the shadow of NBC's 30 Rock headquarters across Fiftieth Street.

Conan, his voice strained by weeks of touring—much of the show consisted of singing, which Conan did surprisingly well—welcomed a couple of special guests that night: first Colbert, then Stewart. It was a love fest for the comics, who had also appeared together during the writers' strike. But it gave some veteran Conan watchers in the audience pause, envisioning the competition to come.

"Can Conan kill Jon Stewart?" one of Conan's old NBC associates asked. "With intent—I mean, can he stand over the body? Because, you know, that's what he has to do now. And we know Jon can definitely kill Conan."

Another longtime New York–based Conanite observed, "The young audience loves Conan—we know that. But they'll take a bullet for Stewart. It's not going to be easy for Conan."

If Conan's switch to the cable world set up new challenges for him, it had the opposite effect at NBC—at least as far as Jeff Gaspin was concerned. He stated his position point-blank: "Late night's not my problem anymore."

Jay was back; he was winning, and while he was down in the ratings, he was back ahead of Letterman, which was all Gaspin cared about. He shrugged off any suggestions that Jay's numbers were perilously close to what Conan had been scoring. "Where would Conan's numbers be now?" Gaspin asked.

Best of all from Gaspin's point of view was that Conan had signed on to move to cable. "That's over," Gaspin said of his not so excellent late-night adventure. "Conan's going to cable. I don't have to wait for the next shoe to drop."

Gaspin admitted that had Conan jumped to Fox, it would have again meant daily scrutiny of the late-night numbers. "I would have had the whole Jay versus Conan thing again," Gaspin said. "Now I don't have to worry about that. Now it's Conan versus Jon Stewart. So I'm out of that game." And he reinforced the competitive point: It was less a question of ratings than it was of who was winning, or at least who could be widely identified as winning. "Leno is beating Letterman. I don't care if his ratings are a third of what they are, as long as he's beating Letterman."

All in all, Gaspin judged the late-night cup to have come out half full; maybe, in the long run, as he explained, "It's better for Conan. It's better for all of us."

While it was surely better that Jay Leno had escaped his exile in the Siberian wastes of ten o'clock, as he resumed the routine of his life, monologues every night, was it really all back to normal for Jay? Just like that? Hadn't Jay been part of NBC's ritual of human sacrifice? How many pieces of his spirit had the experience carved away?

In his appearance on Oprah, Jay had looked almost shattered—puffy faced and profoundly sad. Was that the real Jay? Nobody masked emotion better than Jay; he was so good at it, many people accused him of having none to mask. How much of that flat, emotionless disposition was real and how much was just another part of the persona he presented to the world? Even many of those close to him had trouble sorting out that question.

One NBC executive who was truly fond of Jay called him "a strange, strange guy." Dick Ebersol called him "almost guileless," while competitors used words like "conniving" and even "diabolical." How could one guy fit two such opposite descriptions?

Jay seemed to defy Carson's central maxim about hosting a late-night show: Whoever you truly are comes out eventually. Even after thousands of hours behind the desk, Jay defied that transparency; few viewers had a clue who he really was.

What Jay had to say about the rough ride of 2009 sounded at once sincere and somehow calculated, depending on who was doing the listening. He expressed surprise that things had turned so bitter on the Conan side and said that he found it truly sad that he and Conan would likely never speak again. He really had tried, he said, to put in a call to Conan when it all started to unravel, but was dissuaded by NBC executives who told him that Conan would not take the call.

At the same time, when Jay discussed with his staff all the actions and reactions of that chaotic month, the one thing none of them really understood was that whole dream-destroying theme that Conan had expressed so eloquently. When Jay was a kid, he'd dreamed of hosting *The Tonight Show*, too. But as an adult it became his employment. Debbie Vickers questioned why Conan persisted in seeing the show as a dream when it was, in reality, a job—and one that required bringing in winning ratings. On Jay's side of the late-night divide, pretending that ratings didn't matter so much qualified as a form of arrogance, something they just could not subscribe to, because, as they saw it, they were too busy doing shows.

Jay intended to settle back in and stay busy doing shows for the foreseeable future, but he swore he was open to considering a true end date now, though one he could pick at his own discretion—not NBC's. He cited what he called the Midwestern model: put twenty or more years into a job, get to sixty-three, sixty-five, or so, and that's retirement time. Reminded that Carson went until he hit sixty-six, Jay conceded that sounded OK, too. He even volunteered to try on a plan he had always opposed: opening up some nights to allow guest hosts to replace him—a way for NBC to identify potential new host prospects. This kind of talk was totally new for Jay, who more often talked of working until the lights went out—literally. As in: "I'm Scottish; we die in the mine."

The course of events that fall and winter did throw Jay off his stride, he admitted, and not just because of all the body blows he'd suffered. There was something a bit eerie about it all, or maybe it was just déjà vu. But at times Jay felt as if he were back in 1993, trying to hold on to the show because some people at NBC wanted to give it to Dave. Jay would never have believed he would be caught up in a replay of that unhappy time again.

But here he was, again forced to defend himself against charges of being an unworthy schemer—even though he had been the top-rated comic in late night for sixteen years.

One of his NBC associates, who had a good if somewhat superficial relationship with Jay, said that in the wake of what had taken place in the previous five months, Jay spoke more openly about his feelings when he returned to *The Tonight Show*. He made it clear that he wanted to get back in the good graces of those who still held ill feelings toward him because of the Conan business. But the heart-on-sleeve moments didn't last. Jay could never be someone who waxed philosophical, the associate said. He simply didn't look back. Seeking perspective might deflect his focus, and Jay believed that to stay on top it was essential to be single-mindedly focused on the job and the job alone. "The fact that he's still number one alleviates most of the grief he takes," the associate said. "He does his gigs; people eat it up. That justifies everything for Jay."

Not that he believed anything he had done really required justification. The fact that show-business people, who really should have known better, could possibly conclude that it was somehow incumbent on him to walk away from *The Tonight Show* simply stunned Jay. His take remained: The show was taken from him, which was fair and square; somebody else got it. But the wheel had spun and, totally unexpectedly, the show came around again.

There was no deal in a back room. Circumstances played out; NBC moved him back where he had always wanted to be.

Jay slept well at night.

The tour, with all the spontaneous outpourings of love and support he encountered in every venue, surely helped Conan O'Brien get past some of his anger, but he was realistic. It would take time, longer than he probably could guess, to process completely the cosmic event that had crashed into his life.

Conan couldn't help but look back, like someone wondering just what it was that had hit him over the head while he was honestly going about his business. In the end he accepted Liza's analysis: NBC had never really given him *The Tonight Show*. It was a Potemkin version; they gave him the outline of *The Tonight Show*, but left out the guts.

He perceived the analysis emerging from certain corners of show business: Conan had played the patsy. At the very moment his career was exploding—when Fox and ABC would have torn up their floorboards to build a fire to attract him—he had allowed himself to be lured into staying where he was, because NBC had dangled *The Tonight Show* far in the distance.

But he had no second thoughts—not about any of that. The most important question for him had been and remained: Where can I do good work? Hanging on at NBC and *Late Night* all but guaranteed he would have every opportunity to do good work as he waited out the promise of *The Tonight Show* in his future.

Conan could not imagine doing anything different, either in his initial call to accept confinement in the waiting room for five years or in his final call to reject the ultimate insult of NBC's wait-and-switch maneuver—the thirty-minute delay.

O'Brien took solace in his conviction that he was the only individual in the whole fucking mess who could say with total honesty that he'd held up his end of the bargain.

Could Jay Leno really claim that?

Conan had already thought about what he might say to Jay if he ever did chance to run into him again: "I know you think you've won, but you have no idea what you've lost."

It wouldn't have the slightest impact on Jay, Conan knew, because Jay would simply shrug and say, "Hey, I'm getting my numbers."

Between the tour, keeping up with his growing legion of fans via Twitter, and prepping for the new show on TBS, Conan had plenty to occupy his mind and keep it from drifting again and again to fantasy confrontations with NBC executives, imaginary exchanges with Jay.

Conan was thankful for that, and immensely thankful for Liza and the kids, and for Jeff Ross and the others who had stood beside him in this sandstorm and never took a step sideways. They would all be back for the next ride in his career carnival, no questions asked, no regrets.

All of that helped in his sensible commitment to move on.

But still, sometimes, in the middle of the night, when the house was quiet and the bed was warm, Conan would lie awake, sleep impossible, the replay machine running in his mind, generating scenes wilder and more stunning than anything his always blazing imagination could ever have conjured.

Liza would wake and watch him for a while, just lying there, staring blankly. And then Conan O'Brien would softly say:

"What the fuck happened?"

EPILOGUE

WE'RE THE NETWORK

A few years after he stepped down from *The Tonight Show*, Johnny Carson met Jerry Seinfeld for dinner in Los Angeles. As one of the many comics who broke through into public consciousness thanks to a showcase on Johnny's show, Jerry was thrilled at the invitation.

As they talked about the comedy business they both loved, Jerry said to Johnny, "In my entire career as a stand-up, one of the things endlessly debated in every comedy club I was ever in was: Who do you think is going to take over *The Tonight Show* when Johnny leaves? For like twenty years I had that conversation. And the one thing none of us realized was that, when you left, you were taking it with you."

Johnny had broadly agreed, Jerry said later. The point, Jerry explained, was that the show—the way Johnny did it; "the institution," as people called it—effectively ended the day he walked off that stage. After that, what was left? A time slot, another guy in it, and a name that essentially meant nothing. Because, Seinfeld pointed out, nobody in the business ever said, "I'm doing *The Tonight Show*." Instead they all said, "I'm doing Jay; I'm doing Dave; I'm doing Conan."

Observing the NBC events of late 2009 and early 2010, Seinfeld found himself astonished at the psychic bloodletting that had taken place, and all of it over a chair on a studio set, a television show, and whether that show would begin at this time or another time, a half hour later.

"Nobody ever uses these show names," Jerry said, his voice hitting the high register familiar from his routines when he addressed the most mind-boggling absurdities of life. "These names are bullshit words! How do you not get that this whole thing is phony? It's all fake! There's no institution to offend! All of this 'I won't sit by and watch the institution damaged.' What institution? Ripping off the public? That's the only institution! We tell jokes and they give us millions! Who's going to take over *Late Night* or *Late Show* or whatever the hell it's called? Nobody's going to take it over! It's Dave! When Dave's done, that's the end of that! And then another guy comes along and has to do his thing. That, to me, is an obvious essential of show business that you eventually grasp. Somehow that seems to have been missed by some of the people here."

Obviously Seinfeld directed most of his amazement toward Conan O'Brien and his team for taking a position that Jerry, a contemporary comic with distinctly old-school values, simply couldn't fathom. "I don't really understand why they were so offended," Jerry said. "Jay's show isn't working; your show isn't working—how about a new idea? To me, when I see the numbers those two guys were getting, yes, it's time to sit down at the idea table." And why put a career on the line over a shift of thirty minutes, he wondered. "A half hour is a half hour no matter where it is. It goes by forty-eight times a day! Who cares where it is?" As for the passionate defense of the tradition of *The Tonight Show,* Seinfeld observed, "There is no tradition! This is what I didn't get. Conan has been on television for sixteen years. At that point you should get it: There are no shows! It's all made up! The TV show is just a card! Somebody printed the words on it!"

Jerry admired Conan's talent, wished him the best, and predicted he would do well "because he's great." But why on earth it had come to a point where he felt he had to leave NBC for TBS—that simply made no sense. "I couldn't believe he walked away," Seinfeld said. "I thought he should just say, 'Yeah, let me go at midnight. Let me work this differently. Let me hang around.' Here's big point number two in show business: Hang around! Just stay there, just be there! The old cliché: 95 percent is just showing up. OK, I'm on at twelve; I'm still showing up. You never leave!"

At least one Conan loyalist, Lorne Michaels, found that argument sound. Lorne had never stopped believing in Conan, in his talent and his wit, and never wavered in his certainty that, left alone with his imposing intelligence, Conan would have composed his show as well as he composed his matchless comedy writing.

Michaels was convinced that the Conan he knew and had worked with would have reacted differently had NBC's approach been better planned—if only it had been Jeff Zucker who turned up on Conan's doorstep, saying, "Listen, what do I do here? I did this to protect you. Whether I was right or wrong, I did it for what I believed were the right reasons. I need your help now."

The earlier Conan, Lorne believed, would have responded to that plea, because he was nothing if not pragmatic. In the panicky early days at *Late Night*, Conan had told a previous crew of bomb-throwing colleagues to stay calm, and they'd weathered that storm.

This time, it seemed to Michaels, Conan had been too beaten up to maintain perspective, and he had no one around him to provide the perspective he needed. Lorne didn't know Gavin Polone at all; his frame of reference on managers was dominated by his own, the legendary Bernie Brillstein. Bernie, as Lorne recalled, used to say there were two kinds of managers: the ones who walked through kitchens and the ones who didn't.

"The ones who walked through kitchens" referred to old-time managers who made a point to show up in every grimy club where a client performed, to the point where "they knew the guys with the hairnets working in the back."

That kind of manager, as Michaels saw it, would have been in there talking to the guys in hairnets—and everybody else—at NBC, finding out what was really going on, getting the information he needed to warn his client that he faced serious trouble. From at least October on, Michaels believed, a Bernie kind of manager would have been asking the necessary questions: Are we OK? What do we need to do?

It was of no use simply to make the argument that Conan was superior to Jay, had paid his dues, and deserved the job more. In television, Michaels knew from deep experience, in the contest of numbers versus taste, it was no contest. To allow the situation to get caught up in "They misled me" or "I was lied to" or "They did the wrong thing and I'm doing the right thing" had the effect of turning it toxic.

There was no way that Bernie Brillstein would have allowed that to happen, Michaels knew. Instead, he would have been right there agreeing with Seinfeld: Stay on the air. You're still on NBC—stay on and figure it out. Your position might not be idyllic, but complaining that "they've deceived me and they betrayed me" could result only in martyrdom. And, as Lorne pointed out, underscoring his and Brillstein's (and Seinfeld's) frame of reference, "Jews do not celebrate martyrdom."

Conan also had a raft of fervent supporters online, and many in the press, who feted his show as a gem that NBC had treated as if it were a chewed-over olive pit. In one delicious twist for him, Conan's *Tonight Show* was nominated for an Emmy (he lost again to Jon Stewart, who won for an astounding eighth straight year), while Jay was totally shut out. And of course, the stand Conan took to walk rather than be downgraded was widely celebrated as courageous and justified.

Among others in the comedy business, Conan had enormous support. His old friend and summer roommate Jeff Garlin linked the outcome to character issues—as in, Conan had character and Jay didn't: "Jay should have had the character to say, 'No, I said I was leaving and I'm going to stand by what I said.' Instead he pretended like it never happened,"Garlin said.

Like some others, though, Garlin was not convinced Conan had found his rhythm yet on *The Tonight Show*—or at least not until his last two cant-miss weeks of shows. "Conan is extraordinarily talented," Garlin observed. "He's totally different. He should play up those things." Instead, on *Tonight*, Garlin argued, Conan was trying to be both outrageous and mainstream. "You can't be both things. He didn't have enough time. He was three-quarters of the way there."

Even Garlin conceded that NBC was probably right in believing that Jay would have beaten Conan in the ratings if he had left to go to ABC rather than move to ten p.m. But Garlin insisted that that proved nothing: Jay already beat Letterman with regularity, "and you can't tell me that *The Tonight Show* with Leno is funnier than *Late Show* with Letterman." Jay's dominance, Garlin said, went back to the taste vs. numbers debate. "The people that Jay appeals to are not comedy *fans*," Garlin argued. "It's just the general public. Letterman and Conan appeal to people who are comedy *fans*. It's like comparing John Coltrane to Kenny G. One of Kenny G's albums probably sold more than all of John Coltrane's library. But you can't tell me for a second that Kenny G is better than John Coltrane."

NBC didn't care if Conan O'Brien was funnier, just as in 1992 it had not cared if David Letterman was funnier, though many of those in the position to make that decision had little doubt that he was. What NBC did care about was, yes, those album sales—or ad sales, in this case. Jeff Zucker had never claimed that Jay Leno was funnier than Conan; nor had Jeff Gaspin. In a business of quantification, how was a comparison like that even relevant? Nobody counted laughs and sold them to advertisers.

But for all the top executives' efforts to walk away from the wretched experience and move on to the next item on the network agenda, something about Conan's departure hit NBC deep down where it lived—or at least where its self-image lived. Despite all its sorry, self-inflicted wounds of the past decade, NBC still seemed to stand for something distinctive in the television world, something a little hipper, cooler, more urban, and sophisticated than its rival networks. Could shows like *30 Rock* and *The Office* and even *SNL*, going on four decades old, exist anywhere but on NBC?

Conan, too, had belonged on that list—hip, urban, distinctive. Jeff Zucker and many others had always known that. Losing him was like losing another piece of NBC's heritage, its DNA, much like losing Letterman had been.

Gaspin could not help but wonder how things might have been different: Perhaps if he had gone to Conan first, before approaching Jay with the late-night changes; perhaps if he had just been able to get more time with Conan himself, get him into a real negotiating session. Or maybe if Conan had really been able to shine a flashlight under his chin and really look into the future—like, later in the year 2010? Gaspin wondered if that might have altered the outcome.

"If he knew there was no Fox . . . ," Gaspin mused. "If he knew he was going to end up on cable, do you think he would have done the same thing? The best you're going to do is TBS? Do you think he would have swallowed hard and would have come to the table and just asked for a few things?"

Such as? Hadn't NBC already offered him the big thing? Hadn't they kept him around once with a promise he would move up in five years?

"A guarantee," Gaspin suggested. "In three years, no question, you'll get rid of the guy—you'll shoot him; you'll put an arrow through his head."

But Gaspin already had the answer. "Who's going to believe me, right? Who's going to believe me after what we just did, right?"

Inevitably, the denouement involved dollars.

As NBC executives sorted through the impact and implications of the latest late-night tug-of-war, it was hard to find anyone who wasn't either muddied or nursing a few rope burns. Those, at least, could be salved and bandaged.

The real cost, one that could be assessed accurately only over time, was in the damage that may have been exacted on what had been, for a generation, television's most lucrative program. Soon after the pools of contract ink had dried, Jeff Gaspin offered a startling appraisal of where *The Tonight Show* stood financially.

To the charge from Conan's people that, if their cheaper version was allegedly losing money, Jay's *Tonight Show* surely must be, Gaspin had a forthright response: "Oh, we're going to lose money—but what *don't* we lose money on?"

The Tonight Show, which once generated profits of more than $150 million a year, no longer made money? That was Gaspin's honest admission in the first months after the Jay-Conan contretemps. By spring both he and Zucker were rescinding that analysis, noting that the television ad business had demonstrated a significant comeback, and upfront sales for NBC's late night had come in far more robust than expected.

But Gaspin had also raised longer-term questions, including a most ominous one. He suggested that within five years NBC might not necessarily even be programming a *Tonight Show*, or anything else for that matter, in what the networks labeled the late-night day part. "While we have this heritage in the day part, you know, we also all used to be in daytime," Gaspin said, recalling the days when networks filled the daytime hours with soap operas, fewer and fewer of which were surviving. "We all used to be in Saturday morning programming," he added, referring to the days when the networks made money on children's cartoons. "The broadcast business is changing."

It was not hard to find others who shared Gaspin's gloomy late-night forecast. Six months after the tempest over *The Tonight Show*, the ratings picture turned darker—and starker. Nobody was doing well; Leno's winning numbers were down by about a million viewers—more than 20 percent, and both he and Letterman had dropped to their worst audience levels ever. None of the late-night shows demonstrated significant growth or even real traction. The culprit, in most evaluations, was the digital video recorder, the increasingly ubiquitous machine that allows viewers to record all their favorite shows with ease. Now viewers could watch any show they had recorded at any time they liked—and many seemed especially to like playing them back in the late-night time period.

"I really think it's done," said one important late-night player. "I think late night is done. Everything we know it to be is over."

If the doomsaying sounded a bit like a demented prophet wearing a sign reading "The End Is Near," the speaker, having made a living off late-night for two decades, had apparently legitimate evidence to justify the sentiment.

Besides the DVR, whose impact was only likely to get worse as its penetration spread from under 40 percent of households to the more than 60 percent projected for just a few years down the road, the late-night shows were also seeing their relevance undercut by hyperavailability. "YouTube is like the icing on a horrible cake," the late-night hand-wringer said. "You always have a firm sense that if something great happens on one of these shows, you'll see it anyway." Recent examples included the actor Joaquin Phoenix's apparent freak-out on Letterman or Sarah Silverman's much-talked-about "I'm Fucking Matt Damon" music video on Kimmel's show. Everybody was talking about those moments, the late-night veteran said, "but they're on YouTube; why sit through the whole show to see them?"

Kimmel, for one, believed the time had come for the shows to address the threat posed by the easy availability of their best material online—an opinion he advanced even though his show generated its most buzz when its clips got passed around digitally. It especially distressed Kimmel because he was convinced his show had more impact online than anyone else's in late night. While the response to great clips was always huge, he noted, his ratings were still challenged. Kimmel thought it might be time for the late-night shows to get together and say, "We're not putting anything online anymore. You want to see it? You better fucking watch it."

To many executives at the networks, taking a stand against technology didn't seem a logical response, but threatened only to become one more way to turn late night into the equivalent of rest-home entertainment. Cutting young viewers off from their lifeline of clips of every kind, available at fingertips, would almost surely stir up some kind of organized protest and encourage them to write these network shows off as hopelessly mothball infested. Already NBC had begun exploring the notion that instead of selling late-night shows to advertisers on the basis of ratings for viewers between the ages of eighteen and forty-nine, it should consider raising the sales demo for late night to the group twenty-five to fifty-four, the same sales target used by—*gasp*—news shows, the hoariest genre in the medium.

A more reasonable response, said the longtime late-night figure, was a drastic change in how late-night shows got produced. "In a way, these shows are doomed and protected at the same time," the player said. "They're doomed for all these reasons; protected because what else can you put on television that's cheaper than this? But for sure the days of the $30 million salary for a host are gone forever. The days of the twelve-, thirteen-, fourteen-person writing staff are gone forever. Frankly, the days when there are house bands might come to a close."

The models for how to produce late-night shows for much less money were certainly out there. Jon Stewart and Stephen Colbert had smaller writing staffs and no house bands. Then there was *Live with Regis and Kelly,* ABC's morning entry. As the late-night participant put it, "They come out. They talk. They interview guests. There's your show. It costs a nickel."

But would a show like that ever seize the attention of the nation, the way Letterman had during his sex scandal? Or the way Conan had after he told the people of earth he was cutting the cord with NBC? No, said the late-night principal. "I think all the important and cultural relevance of these shows is done."

Maybe not yet. Another late-night leader of long significance, Lorne Michaels, refused to capitulate to the notion of inevitable extinction—or diminution. "They're wrong," Michaels said of the late-night eschatologists. "Of course these shows can still make money." Michaels could hardly believe anything less, having just thrust Jimmy Fallon upon the world. Lorne was convinced that Fallon had the rare talent to establish an audience, build it, and then emerge as their personal star, the way Letterman had, the way Conan had.

If nothing else, Michaels pointed out, the events of January 2010 had proved the continued relevance and impact of late night. They accomplished something for Conan that he had not quite been able to do for himself. "The big thing this did, at the end of the day, was make Conan O'Brien truly famous," Michaels said. "He wasn't famous before." It was the Hugh Grant comparison expressed a different way. But of course Jay

Leno had been able to ride his Hugh Grant moment to long-term triumph. Conan had ridden his right out of NBC. And that was unfortunate, as Michaels saw it. Justified, perhaps, but still unfortunate.

Lorne looked at the situation from the truly long view, the view of the hardened, occasionally scarred veteran of many network conflicts. "The fact that the network behaved badly?" Michaels said. "If you read the charter, that's what they do. Their thing is, they behave badly, and you can't go, 'Really? They did this?' Because they're the network. That's what they do."

Resigning in the face of network ingratitude, Lorne said, does not provide the anticipated satisfaction—an experience, he stressed, he knew well. In 1979 Michaels quit *Saturday Night Live* and NBC. He was unhappy with his treatment at that point, tired of battles with the network over things Lorne knew far better than they did would only improve the show. At the time, the executive in charge of NBC Entertainment was Irwin Segelstein, a small bear of a man, a generation older than Michaels, who was then not yet thirty-five. Lorne walked into Segelstein's office, sat down, and laid out all the reasons he had decided to resign. And Segelstein, who had a sardonic streak, listened patiently, not uttering a word until Michaels had finished. Then he launched into a story, a parable of sorts, one that touched on the religion of television.

"Let me just take you through what will happen when you leave," Segelstein began. "When you leave, the show will get worse. But not all of a sudden—gradually. And it will take the audience a while to figure that out. Maybe two, maybe three years. And when it gets to be, you know, awful, and the audience has abandoned it, then we will cancel it. And the show will be gone, but we will still be here, because we're the network and we are eternal. If you read your contract closely, it says that the show is to be ninety minutes in length. It is to cost X. That's the budget. Nowhere in that do we ever say that it has to be good. And if you are so robotic and driven that you feel the pressure to push yourself in that way to make it good, don't come to us and say you've been treated unfairly, because you're trying hard to make it good and we're getting in your way. Because at no point did we ask for it to be good. That you're neurotic is a bonus to us. Our job is to lie, cheat, and steal—and your job is to do the show."

Lorne's reaction had been a solitary word: "Whoa." The speech had left him mostly speechless because he realized that Segelstein was exactly right. Being in charge of *Saturday Night Live* or *The Tonight Show* or the *Nightly News*, Michaels concluded, was not an entitlement—it was a job. That got confused at times because the people involved in these shows put so much emotion and passion into them—and it was these very qualities that made the shows so good.

With that insight and all his own experience behind him, Lorne Michaels did his best to stand back and survey the television landscape after all the action on the late-night field from late 2004 to the middle of 2010. He saw the plans that had been laid, decisions that had been made, moves that had been played.

As he worked through it, breaking it all down, he believed he had a grasp of exactly what had transpired, and why. But then a piece wouldn't quite fit. Where did that piece come from? Did it make sense? For a time, Lorne thought he really had it, but then he realized he clearly didn't. Finally, he decided, it was probably time to shrug it off and just walk away.

"It's Chinatown," he said.

On September 24, 2010, just as the fall television season got under way, Jeff Zucker announced that he was stepping down; the new corporate owners at Comcast were inclined, after all, to install their own boss. No one should have been surprised, Zucker said; yet he knew that many inside NBC would be. Comcast offered no specific reason, and Zucker resigned himself to the fact that "ninety-nine times out of a hundred, when a company spends billions to buy another company, they want to put their own team in place." He certainly didn't believe that the late-night crisis of 2010 had played a hand. "That was just a risk that didn't work out," he concluded. Whatever the rationale, the departure removed Zucker from the only employer he had ever worked for, the only building he had ever worked in. "It's all I've ever known," Jeff said. "I met my wife here. My four kids were born while I was here. I endured colon cancer twice here." The pain of separation from an institution he had devoted his professional life to stirred "gut-wrenching" emotions in Jeff Zucker; it was something he suddenly had in common with a late-night host of his previous acquaintance. That, and Harvard.

ACKNOWLEDGEMENTS

This book is almost exclusively the product of firsthand reporting. I gained information from several other sources, especially in-depth interviews in *Rolling Stone* magazine. I also relied on some of my own reporting for *The New York Times*. But I was most fortunate to have the encouragement of some extraordinary editors there. I want especially to thank Bruce Headlam and Steve Reddicliffe.

At Viking, thanks to the president, Clare Ferraro, and the executive editor, Rick Kot, as well as Laura Tisdel, who rode herd on the copy. And of course I must once again thank my stalwart agent, Kathy Robbins, a supplier of great advice and confidence.

My fondest appreciation goes to Rich and Nikki Carter, Catherine and Dan O'Neill, Alexandra Carter and Greg Lembrich, Rich and Brittany Carter, John Carter, Bridget and Danny O'Neill, Tom and Regina Lembrich, Phil and Denise Andrews, Frank and Diane Guercio, Lori and Thom Peters, Aine and Paul McCambridge, Kathy and Eric Davidson, Leslie and Paul Marchese, Gerry Uehlinger, and Dr. Tom Ziering.

Thanks to Pat Berry, and a shout-out to the "cool kids" table on the 14th floor. I also benefited immeasurably from having an early reader, and always friend, Eric Mink.

From Fox, my great thanks to Kevin Reilly and Peter Rice. From ABC, Anne Sweeney. From TBS, Steve Koonin. From the E Channel, Ted Harbert.

I am grateful to two complete professionals from NBC, Allison Gollust and Rebecca Marks, as well as Cory Shields, Jeff DeRome, and Tracy St. Pierre.

Others I am indebted to at NBC include Marc Graboff, Rick Ludwin, Nick Bernstein, Alan Wurtzel, Ron Meyer, Michael Bass, and Michael Fiorile. Jeff Gaspin supplied his recollections with impressive frankness. Dick Ebersol has always related his experiences with color and candor—never more so than this time. Lorne Michaels, as he has often in the past, found remarkable ways to express the essence of what was really going on.

I want to express special appreciation to Jeff Zucker. He was, as he has always been, open, thoughtful, and giving with his time and his perspectives.

Thanks also to Gail Berman, Lloyd Braun, Alan Berger, Andrea Wong, Robert Morton, Jeff Garlin, Bob Thompson, Don Ohlmeyer, Marc Liepis, Brian Williams—and for great laughs and observations, Jerry Seinfeld. Others contributed reflections and comments and asked not to be identified. All of them have my deepest appreciation.

From *The Late, Late Show*, thanks to Craig Ferguson, Michael Naidus, and two of the best people I know, Peter and Alice Lassally. From *Late Night*, thanks to Jimmy Fallon and Mike Shoemaker. From *Late Night with David Letterman*, I greatly appreciate Tom Keaney's efforts on my behalf, as well as Rob Burnett's valuable contributions. Jon Stewart and Stephen Colbert share a common thread: their irrepressible agent, James Dixon. Big thanks to James and his clients, especially his third one, Jimmy Kimmel, whose extraordinary generosity of spirit has always extended to me.

Jay Leno has never been anything but warm and welcoming to me. I especially thank him for his thoughtfulness to me this year. I also appreciate the help and insights of Jay's wise and essential producer, Debbie Vickers.

From "Team Coco," thanks to Gavin Polone, Mike Sweeney, Drew Shane, and Andy Richter, as well as Ari Emanuel and especially the class act that is Rick Rosen. Throughout this effort, Conan's executive producer, Jeff Ross, was, as he has always been for me, the gold standard for generosity, dependability, and decency.

I have been privileged to chronicle much of Conan O'Brien's amazing ride through late night. This year, Conan displayed only more openness, honesty, and grace under pressure. He was generous beyond the call. Special thanks as well to Liza O'Brien.

Three people make everything in my life possible. My children, Caela Ellen Carter and Daniel Houston Carter, fill my days with the purest form of joy. Their mother, the love of my life, Beth Keating Carter, remains the wisest editor, most enthusiastic reader, and greatest partner anyone could ever have. No man has ever been more blessed.

INDEX

Frontispiece Photo Captions and Credits

TOP ROW: NBC Universal CEO Jeff Zucker with his two surviving late-night stars, Jimmy Fallon and Jay Leno (NBC Universal Photo Bank/Paul Morse); Conan O'Brien onstage at *Late Night* with his creative brain trust, executive producer Jeff Ross (left) and head writer Mike Sweeney (NBC Universal Photo Bank); David Letterman, for twenty-eight years a star of late night, at his post behind the desk at *Late Show* (JP Filo CBS/WORLDWIDE PANTS).

SECOND ROW: Jeff Gaspin, the new leader of NBC's Entertainment operation and the man with the plan to revamp late night (NBC Universal Photo Bank); Gavin Polone, manager to Conan O'Brien, agent provocateur to NBC (photo credit: Sarah Shatz); Jay getting advice from his longtime executive producer and closest adviser, Debbie Vickers, while a special guest shows some interest. It was the first visit ever for a sitting president to a late-night show (NBC Universal Photo Bank).

THIRD ROW: James Dixon (left), the busiest agent in late night, with one of his three stars, the multi-award-winning Jon Stewart (Stephen Colbert and Jimmy Kimmel are also his clients) (photo credit: James Dixon); Craig Ferguson, CBS's Scottish-born original in late night is joined by robot Geoff Peterson on *The Late Late Show with Craig Ferguson* on Monday, April 5, 2010, on the CBS Television Network (© 2010 CBS Broadcasting Inc. All Rights Reserved. Photo: Sonja Flemming/CBS); Marc Graboff, cochairman of NBC Entertainment and chief deal-maker at the network (NBC Universal Photo Bank).

BOTTOM ROW: Dick Ebersol (right), the chairman of NBC Universal Sports and Olympics, played many roles in the career of the NBC CEO Jeff Zucker, including mentor, close counselor, and longtime friend (Ben Hider/Getty Images Entertainment); Rick Rosen, one of the captains of Team Coco, agent, adviser, and friend to Conan O'Brien (Matthew Simmons/Getty Images Entertainment); Jimmy Kimmel channeling Jay Leno and "Headlines"—and generating headlines of his own (photo credit: Don Barris).